D0753444

Fiddle Tunes from
MISSISSIPPI

American Made Music Series

Advisory Board

David Evans, General Editor
Barry Jean Ancelet
Edward A. Berlin
Joyce J. Bolden
Rob Bowman
Susan C. Cook
Curtis Ellison
William Ferris
John Edward Hasse
Kip Lornell
Bill Malone
Eddie S. Meadows
Manuel H. Peña
Wayne D. Shirley
Robert Walser

Fiddle Tunes from
MISSISSIPPI

Commercial and Informal Recordings, 1920–2018

Harry Bolick and Tony Russell

with T. DeWayne Moore, *and* Joyce A. Cauthen and David Evans

University Press of Mississippi / Jackson

The University Press of Mississippi is the scholarly publishing agency of
the Mississippi Institutions of Higher Learning: Alcorn State University,
Delta State University, Jackson State University, Mississippi State University,
Mississippi University for Women, Mississippi Valley State University,
University of Mississippi, and University of Southern Mississippi.

www.upress.state.ms.us

The University Press of Mississippi is a member
of the Association of University Presses.

Any discriminatory or derogatory language or hate speech directed
toward people of color, people with disabilities, women, the
LGBTQ+ community, or any religious or ethnic group that have
been retained or appear in elided form is in no way an endorsement
of the use of such language outside a scholarly context.

Copyright © 2021 by Harry Bolick and Tony Russell

All rights reserved
Manufactured in the United States of America

First printing 2021
∞

Library of Congress Cataloging-in-Publication Data

Names: Bolick, Harry, author. | Russell, Tony, 1946- author. | Moore, T.
DeWayne, contributor. | Cauthen, Joyce H., 1944- contributor. | Evans,
David, 1944- contributor.
Title: Fiddle tunes from Mississippi: commercial and informal recordings,
1920-2018 / Harry Bolick and Tony Russell; with T. DeWayne Moore, Joyce
H. Cauthen, and David Evans.
Other titles: American made music series.
Description: Jackson : University Press of Mississippi, 2021. | Series:
American made music series | Includes bibliographical references and
index.
Identifiers: LCCN 2021023934 (print) | LCCN 2021023935 (ebook) | ISBN
978-1-4968-3579-6 (hardback) | ISBN 978-1-4968-3589-5 (trade paperback)
| ISBN
978-1-4968-3580-2 (epub) | ISBN 978-1-4968-3581-9 (epub) | ISBN
978-1-4968-3582-6
(pdf) | ISBN 978-1-4968-3583-3 (pdf)
Subjects: LCSH: Fiddle tunes—Mississippi—History and criticism. | Folk
music—Mississippi—History and criticism. | Fiddle tunes—Mississippi.
| Folk music—Mississippi. | Fiddle tunes—Mississippi—Discography. |
Folk music—Mississippi—Discography. | Fiddlers—Mississippi. | LCGFT:
Discographies. | Folk music. | Scores.
Classification: LCC ML3551.7.M6 B63 2021 (print) | LCC ML3551.7.M6
(ebook) | DDC 781.62/130762—dc23
LC record available at https://lccn.loc.gov/2021023934
LC ebook record available at https://lccn.loc.gov/2021023935

British Library Cataloging-in-Publication Data available

CONTENTS

◆ ◆ ◆

PREFACE

This book grew from my desire to complete the work begun in *Mississippi Fiddle Tunes and Songs from the 1930s*, which documents the 1930s WPA collections of Mississippi fiddle tunes. Those 320 tunes comprise a bit over half of the known old-time fiddle tunes from Mississippi. This book includes 270 tunes, covering the commercial recordings from the 1920s through the 1970s along with a few field or family recordings. Combined, these two books cover every unique Mississippi fiddle tune that I've been able to discover and include. The two books do not share any transcriptions of the same tunes from the same sources. While most of the musicians' families were delighted to be included in this book, two families declined. Perhaps one day those recordings and tunes will become public. If any more tunes or stories come to light, I will post them at mississippifiddle.com. I continue to hope that more of this rich tradition can be discovered.

I was born in the Delta, in Greenwood, Mississippi, in the 1950s, but I feel most connected to the music of Carroll County, where my mother was born and raised. It was while living in New York in the 1970s that I first became aware of and began to learn Mississippi fiddle music from the County records reissues of 78 rpm recordings, and from musician friends. In particular, I felt a strong pull toward Willie T. Narmour's fiddling. Much later, when I was doing my first tentative

research in the state, I came to realize that Narmour created or radically reshaped much of his recorded repertoire, as did Hoyt Ming, the Nations Brothers, and John Gatwood. As a fellow "tunesmith," I felt that I had found a mentor. Although I never heard him play, my great-uncle J. C. Moss was a fiddler. Additionally, I heard a story that my grandfather

J. C. "Shorty" Moss, fiddler. Photo courtesy of Elsie Berryhill.

in Carroll County, who was a fine dancer in his youth, also played fiddle.

In 2004 I recorded two tunes with my cousin and pianist Elsie Berryhill for my CD *Carroll County, Mississippi*. Through the years we have always played a bit when we visit. Her father, J. C. "Shorty" Moss, was a fiddler. Sadly, I never got to hear him play, but Elsie and I play some of the same tunes that he played: "Carroll County Blues," "When You and I Were Young, Maggie," "Down Yonder," and others. He is the only fiddler I know for certain that was in my family. I continue to wish I had heard him play.

I have spent decades learning and playing Mississippi fiddle tunes. Beyond preservation, I believe that new tunes need to be created to keep this "dialect" of southern fiddling alive. In the process of researching these two books, I have come across dozens of titles to tunes where the melodies are lost. They were mentioned but not recorded at fiddle contests, from unissued 78 rpm recordings, or mentioned elsewhere in print. These "orphan" titles have inspired me to compose new fiddle tunes to walk in the ghost of their memories. There is more information about this project, "The Completely Lost Mississippi Fiddle Tunes," at mississippifiddle.com.

Many, many people have helped and encouraged me along the long path of writing this book. First and foremost, I must thank my wife Pat Schories for cheerfully enduring the process with me, listening and proofreading. Master musician Ken Bloom has greatly enhanced this book by carefully reviewing and correcting my transcriptions. Pat Conte has helped decipher mysterious and nearly inaudible lyrics and offered astute advice. Joe Dejarnette digitized rare reel-to-reel tapes. My cousins Elsie and Walter Berryhill have housed me on my many research trips and helped track down families of the musicians. Sue Reano, Dee McCullough, Pat Sumrall, Frank Dillon, Joanna Barnes, Harold Clardy, Sue Duke, Jean Hopkins, Claudette Kennedy, Mike Collier, Tim Freeny, Virginia Gilmer, Georgia Snowden, James Fulcher, Shelby Sanders, Beth Alford, Don and Hazel Milner, Laura Oakes, Jerry O'Briant, Judy Reynolds, Tonie Prescott, and Bill Rogers all generously shared their time, memories, photographs, and in some cases recordings of their family members who were the musicians documented in this book. Much of the wealth of information in this book came from their hands. And so much of the joy of making this book came from meeting them; I gratefully thank each of them.

I am deeply in debt to my co-author, Tony Russell, for working with me on this book and for his pioneering 1970s detective work on Mississippi music as published in his magazine *Old Time Music*. For many years, those articles were my compass, pointing the way to the riches of this rich and unique body of music. T. DeWayne Moore joined this book later in its progress but has contributed mightily with his writing and research. On one of my last research trips for this book, I visited with Joyce and Jim Cauthen and was overjoyed to discover that they had documented and recorded a Mississippi fiddler who was previously unknown to me. Joyce graciously agreed to write about him for inclusion herein. David Evans graciously shared his field recordings of African American musicians Herb Quinn and Dink Brister and contributed essays about and photographs of them. I am humbled to be in such excellent company with this book.

—Harry Bolick

Fiddle Tunes from
MISSISSIPPI

December 28,1979, photo on steps of the governor's mansion by Gil Ford, used for 1980 *Mississippi Sawyers* LP cover.
Left to right: *Front row:* Mickey Davis, Alvis Massengale, Sylvester S. Moran, Bill Mitchell, Cartis Massengale.
Second row: W. D. Dickerson, Jack Moran, Glen Dickerson, Senator George Cecil McLeod Jr., Howard Smith,
Robert S. Alford. *Third row:* Lee Fulcher, Bryson Wilemon, Joe Cox.

INTRODUCTION

The late 1920s and early 1930s were the pivotal time for capturing Mississippi fiddle music when it was current and popular. To my knowledge there are no manuscripts or recordings of old-time fiddle music from the state from before the 1920s and only a few from after WW II, when southern musical tastes moved on. What we do know of this particular dialect of early southern fiddling comes from commercial 78 rpm recordings from 1927–36, 1936 WPA manuscripts, 1939 WPA field recordings, a 45 rpm recording, a precious few 33 rpm LP records, and a handful of field recordings from the 1970s and later. (See Appendix A for a complete listing.)

The musicians' biographies and photos are included to give context to the notated tunes. This music was created in another time and place, now far distant from our current life experiences. Most of the musicians were farmers or living in rural locations, with their lives rooted in the seasonal cycle of work. Music fit into their communities and their lives in ways that our modern society does not replicate. Most learned their tunes from family or neighbors or made them up. Thus each tune learned had a personal connection or connections. Sense of place, of family, of community is the current that runs through these tunes. I've been very blessed, in researching this book, to connect with the descendants of some of these fiddlers, which has enriched my life and my sense of connection to these tunes. By telling their stories and including their photographs, I am trying to share a small part of that sense of connection to the sources of this enduring music.

This appears to be a book of facts about fiddlers in Mississippi. To the best of my ability, that is true. However, I have collected these "facts" from the memories held by the fiddlers' children, grandchildren, or from the stories that a fiddler told to newspaper reporters or other writers. In some cases I am able to identify fictions or omissions in those stories. Many of the stories are well told, coming from accomplished storytellers, and often represent the fiddlers as they wanted to be seen. This is a book of stories about fiddlers, reinforced by photographs and transcriptions, but it is really a book about fiddling.

It is with joy that we are able to include some information and transcriptions of recordings from the little-known fiddlers John Anderson, Tom Dumas, John Gatwood, "Jabe" Dillon, Claude Kennedy, Senator George C. McLeod, Grover O'Briant, and Sylvester Moran. We were very fortunate to locate some of their descendants, who were so generous to share their stories, photos, and recordings. Many of these otherwise unheard recordings can be heard at mississippifiddle.com.

Although this old-time music dwindled in Mississippi to virtual extinction, the old tunes are being played and revived by musicians with roots in the state. John Anderson is included for his repertoire that reaches back a generation and for his unique perspective on learning music from Noxubee and Kemper counties in the 1970s. I had the great fortune and pleasure of meeting the late Jerry Prescott, who shared his music with me. Although he played bluegrass mandolin, his approach and a good proportion of his repertoire was old-time. I have included his compositions because they spring from Mississippi's soil, and to suggest how the music adapts and moves onward. For the same reasons, I am grateful to Mike Compton for allowing me to include his tune in this collection. Tim Avalon is another living fiddler and composer represented here. Through his playing, and even more so by his teaching, he is contributing greatly to the survival of this old-timey music in Mississippi.

Within the confines of the focus of this book, it seems obvious that music from African American fiddlers in Mississippi is underrepresented. We have a few tunes such as "Carroll County Blues" and "Brown Skin Gal" recorded by white musicians inspired by African American music. However we have included later field recordings of the African American musicians Dink Brister, Tom Dumas, Sid Hemphill, and Herb Quinn, and the 78 rpm recordings of the Mississippi Sheiks to give us a fuller sample of Mississippi fiddle music. The chapter "The Segregation of Sound: Unheard African American Fiddlers" discusses this topic.

Transcriptions of all six of the recordings recorded the 78 rpm era by Charlie McCoy and the Mississippi Mud Steppers, an offshoot of the Mississippi Sheiks, are included in this book. We have also included five tunes that were recorded by the Mississippi Sheiks. Because this book focuses on the Anglo-American tradition of fiddling, our criterion for including some, but not all, of the music recorded by the Sheiks has been to include tunes that are repetitive fiddle melodies that lend themselves to the old-time fiddlers' repertoire. The majority of the Sheiks' recorded works are songs with improvised fiddle parts. We did not undertake the far larger task of transcribing the solos in songs such as "Sitting on Top of the World," which would be a worthy project for some other author.

In the lyrics and some of the titles of the music in this book, there is content reflecting misogyny, racism, and minstrelsy's romanticized view of slavery. While modern practice among fiddlers tends to alter titles or lyrics or simply not play those tunes, they are included here. I think we must acknowledge our history in hopes of not repeating it. Perhaps because this is primarily a book of melodies rather than song lyrics, such tunes form only a small part of this collection.

Although Cajun fiddle tunes are rarely documented in Mississippi, we are able to include a few tunes from John Anderson and Sylvester Moran. I suspect that collectors of Cajun music stayed on the Louisiana side of the border and overlooked Mississippians playing Cajun tunes.

Just as my father was able to sample tamales sold by Mexican immigrants on the streets of Jackson in the late 1930s, we can taste traces of Mexico in some of the tunes in this book. Alvis Massengale credited his tune "Sebastapol" to his grandfather learning it from "some Mexican." Juventino Rosas's 1888 waltz "Sobre las Olas," known in the states as "Over the Waves," was very popular in Mississippi and is included in several versions, including Willie Narmour's "Winona Echoes." The Leake County String Band played a version of "El Rancho Grande." Milner and Curtis's "Evening Shade Waltz" and many of Narmour and Smith's waltzes have a Southwest flavor. A handful of their other tunes resemble Mexican polkas.

It's interesting to note that twice as many tunes in this collection are in standard tuning and in the keys of C or G as in the fiddle keys of D and A. However, when combined with the tunes in *Mississippi Fiddle Tunes and Songs from the 1930s*, where few tunes are in C and many are in alternate tunings, it's hard to draw much of a general conclusion about preferences in these matters for fiddlers in the state.

In 1923 producer Ralph Peer with OKeh records used a "portable" recording studio to record Fiddlin' John Carson in Atlanta, Georgia. The surprising sales of Fiddlin' John Carson's "Little Old Log Cabin in the Lane" put southern folk music with fiddles front and center as a likely new source of revenue. Mississippi artists recorded in Atlanta; Chicago; New York; Memphis, Tennessee; New Orleans and Shreveport, Louisiana; Jackson and Hattiesburg, Mississippi; and San Antonio, Texas, producing a little over 150 recordings of Mississippi string band music. Initially intent on simply locating southern musicians and selling the recordings, producers like Ralph Peer realized that there was more money to be recorded recording "original" folk music, i.e., copyrightable compositions. Perhaps this was a significant factor in the selection of the fiddle tunes commercially recorded by Mississippi string bands or perhaps it was simply their attempt to avoid duplicating previously recorded titles. Certainly, few of the most familiar southern tunes were recorded in the state. Many of the recorded tunes are unique to Mississippi. The chapter "Doc Bailey: Talent Scout, Winona" gives a very localized account of how some of the Mississippi string bands came to be recorded.

It is difficult to describe a Mississippi fiddling style. Each band had its own strong individual musical personality distinct from the others. They varied from the polished pop styling of the Leake County Revelers, to the hard-charging Carter Brothers and Son, to the quirky melodies of Narmour and Smith, to the ragtime and blues flavors of the Mississippi Sheiks and the Mississippi Mud Steppers. The truly distinctive thing about Mississippi string band music is the melodies themselves. A very large percentage of the tunes appear to have originated with these musicians or their musical neighbors, or are, at least, unique to the state.

Even though each of the recorded Mississippi fiddlers seems to stand alone with his distinct musical identity, they did live in communities. In some cases, I've been able to draw connections between some of the fiddlers and observe that they would have been able to hear, and perhaps be influenced by, each other. The chapter "Communities of Fiddlers in Mississippi" utilizes contemporary newspaper accounts of fiddle contests to show that the recorded fiddlers were only the most prominent part of a larger body of fiddling in the state.

With fifty-three of the 270 tunes in this collection, waltzes seem to be a larger percentage of the Mississippi repertoire than in other states. But much of that perception comes from four bands: the Leake County Revelers (who were known as the "Waltz Kings"), the Collier Trio, the Mississippi Mud Steppers, and Narmour and Smith. In Narmour's case, this reflects the taste of dancers in his area for waltzes and two-steps, not square dances. Perhaps inspired by the Leake County Revelers' recordings, we hear harmony on a second fiddle or mandolin in recordings by the Freeny bands, the Collier Trio, the Leake County String Band, and slightly farther south in John Gatwood's "Crawford March."

Mississippi fiddle tunes are dance music. Many of the tunes are of irregular lengths but are strongly rhythmic, propulsive, and inviting for dancers. Throughout the South, the basic form for dance tunes is two melodic phrases, each of eight measures, repeated twice and alternated with each other. This form holds true in Mississippi for the most common tunes known throughout the South and for a handful of the local tunes. However, a large percentage of the tunes from the state are of irregular but consistently repeated lengths. Dancing to irregular musical phrases evidently did not trouble local dancers and callers.

A knowledgeable contemporary fiddler will recognize familiar short melodic phrases within these otherwise unfamiliar tunes. Consider these phrases as "words" being used in new "sentences" to form new thoughts relevant to each player's experiences. To stretch the analogy even further, consider each tune part of a long conversation with the story of fiddling in Mississippi. This volume presents what they have to say and share with the world.

What possible contemporary meaning can these fiddle tunes have? They often come to us without lyrics or with mysterious titles—that is to say, without explanation. When I first heard many of these tunes nearly forty years ago, they were new and exotic. Time and repetition have given me deep and abiding affection for the character and the quirks of these tunes, along with a feeling for the people that were their source. In my life, additional meaning has come from the many friends and relationships I have been fortunate enough to make through the shared joy in researching, playing, and freeing these tunes to continue to live and breathe again. Herein I share them to a wider audience in hopes that they find a place in your life as well.

—Harry Bolick
Hopewell Junction, New York
2019

The roots of my contribution to this book lie in a research trip I took in Mississippi in October 1975 in the company of the folklorist and photographer Carl Fleischhauer. The interviews I conducted and the data I gathered formed the basis of a special Mississippi issue of my magazine *Old Time Music* (20, Spring 1976), for which I wrote articles, accompanied by Carl's wonderful photographs, about Dr. A. M. Bailey, the Carter Brothers and Son, the Collier Trio, the Leake County Revelers, Hoyt and Rozelle Ming, and the Mississippi 'Possum Hunters, as well as shorter pieces on Mumford Bean, the Meridian Hustlers, and the Ray Brothers. I had earlier published articles on Freeny's Barn Dance Band and the Freeny Harmonizers (*OTM* 8, Spring 1973) and the Nations Brothers (*OTM* 10, Autumn 1973), both based on correspondence with surviving members of those bands.

I have extensively revised and updated those *OTM* articles, drawing on four decades of my own research into old-time music in general, and of books and articles published by other scholars. I have also added material, not available to me in the 1970s, from public records and online newspaper archives.

All the musicians I met or corresponded with are dead, and a small, sad part of my revision was converting phrases like "Hoyt Ming says" or "Carlton Freeny recalls" to the past tense. But I remember these men and women very clearly, and how they greeted their visitors, one from far away and speaking in an unfamiliar accent, with hospitality and friendship that were unstinting and unforgettable.

—Tony Russell
London, England
2019

DOC BAILEY (1893–1993)

Talent Scout, Winona

Once it got on to records, old-time music may or may not have been art; it was certainly business. And when the romantic stories of the early days are edged aside, we can see a complex business, carried out with all the thrust and enterprise that American businessmen thought of themselves as possessing in the 1920s. It was rarely a haphazard affair: finding musicians, preparing them for making records, getting them to recording centers, selecting their material, and so forth. Record companies, being based in the North and run by northerners, organized it the sensible way. The word went out to all their dealers: every record store owner could be his own talent scout. After all, it was the dealer who knew his home market and was most aware of locally popular musicians who might sell on record. He could find them, groom them, publicize them, and finally sell them. Altogether, it was a fine chance to improve business, make some useful acquaintances, and even gain a degree of standing in one's community. And if the dealer happened to like his neighborhood music, too, then there was that satisfaction in the business as well.

In the 1920s Winona, like most towns in Mississippi, was discovering the boons of electricity. Retailers of electrical goods were few, but it was

becoming plain that that was a good business for an enterprising man.

At that time Dr. Andrew M. Bailey (1893–1993), or "Doc" Bailey, as most people knew him, was a veterinarian with an office behind the Kelly drugstore in the middle of Winona, a block or two over from the courthouse. He became interested in electrical merchandise and expanded his premises to take in a store area, where he sold radios, refrigerators, and Delco lighting systems. He gained the Victor franchise for the region and began to sell Victrolas. When records of Southern music began to be put on the market, he added that line, too.[1] "I reckon I had two thousand records. I took all the releases of three or four companies—I mean advance releases."

In fact, Doc Bailey estimates that he carried just about every record of old-time music that was issued. He placed a regular order for anything of that kind, two weeks before every release day. He came to know the local people's preferences so well that they let him do their choosing:

"[They'd] come in here and they'd say, 'Doc, give us about ten of your best records.' And I'd hand them to 'em, and I'd pick 'em out, and I knew about what they wanted because I knew the people, you see."

He carried blues records along with the country ones, and sold to many Black customers; in fact, he reckoned that Black and white records sold about equally well on his premises. The most records he ever sold in one day was seventy-five. At that time, all the lines were retailing at seventy-five cents each.

As a successful dealer, Doc Bailey was a likely source of recommendations for new recording artists. He had been organizing fiddling contests in the Winona courthouse, and he put up posters for the February 3, 1928, contest, mentioning the possibility of recording opportunities. As the Winona paper subsequently reported: "Nine fiddlers from Montgomery, Carroll and Coahoma counties participated. Messrs. Stephenson [*sic*, Stephens] and Rockwell, of New York City[,] assisted by Mrs. N. V. Hutchinson, of Winona, were the judges. The winner of the first prize was W. T. Normour [*sic*], of Carroll County. . . . The winners in the contest were awarded cash prizes, and in addition, a trip to Memphis with all expenses paid, for the purpose of making records for the Okeh Record Company."[2]

◆ ◆ ◆

About two years later, Victor agents came down to visit their Winona franchise-holder. They'd already been to Vicksburg, where an acquaintance of Bailey's had recommended him as a man knowledgeable about country music. They enquired about local players, whom they wanted Bailey to bring up to Memphis, where they would be holding a session in May 1930, at Ellis Auditorium. It sounded to Doc like a time-consuming business:

I said, "I ain't gonna let nobody keep me a sitting there five minutes still, waiting for somebody else to do a lot of recording and messing around up there, interviewing and fooling around . . . That's not for me." They said, "If you give us that talent, well, you sell our machines, you sell our records, we should have some consideration." They said, "If you give us some of that talent, we'll shut the machine down the minute you get there, I don't care who's on it."

So . . . they had V. O. Stamps recording. They shut it off just like they'd cut a mule's tail off. Said,

"We've got to take care of this man right here." I took six or seven men up there at that time.

Among that party were the Mississippi 'Possum Hunters and the Ray Brothers. Ralph Peer's notes on the session are explicit that Bailey brought both acts to Victor. Bailey had heard about the Rays and went down to visit them after his preliminary talk with the Victor agents. At first taciturn and even suspicious, the brothers warmed to Doc's appreciation of their music and his offer of a chance at recording. One of the tunes they recorded at this first session, the "Jake Leg Wobble," was given its name by Doc.

These were not the only recordings Doc set up that year. A location recording team from Vocalion Records was in Memphis in February, and the astute talent scout was able to send them the Carroll County fiddler Gene Clardy, with guitarist Stan Clements, the Attala County band led by fiddlers Luke Milner and Luke Curtis, and the Central Mississippi Quartet.[3]

Doc Bailey was a hard man to keep still, and when there was less call for his services as a talent scout, he engaged in other activities connected with music. He booked Jimmie Rodgers into the Winona Theatre, with a cast of hopefuls to support him. Rodgers spent a whole week in town. But a more daredevil impulse involved Doc in a venture with a good deal of risk: he opened an "independent" radio station: "To be frank with you . . . I had a broadcasting station. And the people didn't know it! There wasn't ten people did know it . . . I took that Smith radio course, correspondence radio course. They sent me a block of cards—'radiotrician,' they said."

The station was in the basement beneath his store.

"We'd play these records down there, and my announcer—he had a lot of gab—he'd say, 'You can find these records at all music stores.' But hell, there wasn't but one music store here, and I had it."

Doc's announcer came on the air from noon till 1:00 p.m., the country lunch hour. "I had radios scattered all over the country," Bailey explained. "These battery radios, you know." The programs were confined to talk and records; no live broadcasts

Tony Russell

were possible, of course, because they would have spread the secret.

Finally, after about a year of operation, Doc had a phone call from a friend down at Kosciusko. He had been running a similar "underground" station there, KOS, which had been picked up by federal commissioners in New Orleans, listening in for just such infringements of the broadcasting regulations. They gave the Kosciusko operator the choice of dismantling his setup or going to Washington to take an official station operator's examination. If he just kept going, he would be heavily fined. It was only a matter of time before the commissioners caught up with the Winona signal, so Doc packed his broadcasting bags. His cover would have been blown in time anyway, because the local mayor, one of the few privy to the secret, had let it slip to a lady friend he used to visit, and after that the confidential character of the operation was doomed.

The Depression provided few opportunities for talent-spotting anywhere, and little enough business even for established record dealers. Bailey hung on until 1936 and then quit. Veterinary work was always plentiful.

Looking back on his wheeling and dealing for the record companies, Doc Bailey recalled putting twenty-one men on record. Narmour and Smith, the Ray Brothers, the Mississippi 'Possum Hunters, Clardy and Clements, the Milner-Curtis group, and the Central Mississippi Quartet account for seventeen of these (eighteen with the quartet's pianist), but no other names were remembered. He vaguely recalled the name Long, which might refer to George Long and His Singers, a group led by a prosperous cattle dealer in Tupelo, which recorded for Victor in Memphis in 1927. He also placed one Black musician, a guitar player from a plantation outside Winona, but could not identify him. (John Hurt, of Avalon in Carroll County, was recorded by OKeh in 1928, reportedly on the recommendation of Shell Smith. It may be Hurt of whom Doc was thinking, but arguably not.)

The value of Doc Bailey's recollections lies in their account of how rural music was transported from field and farm, taken to the city, and put on record, and thus spread over the country in a huge process of musical cross-pollination, which in time caused many of the changes that have shaped modern country music. There was probably a Doc Bailey in towns in every Southern state, forming a network like a news service's "stringer," keeping the record companies' head offices continuously in touch with taste, topicality, and talent. Had it not been for these field scouts, much of what was saved for later generations on 78 rpm discs would simply have died with its practitioners. We owe a great deal to those uncredited behind-the-scenes people.

—Tony Russell

NOTES

1. "An Exclusive Music Store to Be Opened in Winona on December First by the Kelly Drug Company.—. . . This will be an exclusive Victrola and Radio Store. All kinds of records Victrolas and R C A Radios will be sold." *Winona Times*, Winona, MS, November 30, 1928.

2. "Fiddlers Contest Held at Winona. W. T. Narmour, of Carroll County, Carried Off the First Honors." *Winona Times*, Winona, MS, February 10, 1928. It is likely that the record store owner and talent scout Ralph Lembo of Itta Bena also played a part in connecting OKeh's Bob Stephens and Tommy Rockwell with Narmour. See the article on Narmour and Smith.

3. "Winona Citizen Organizes Four Who Broadcast.— Many citizens of Winona heard the Central Mississippi quartett [sic] broadcast last Sunday over W. J. D. X. of Jackson, Mississippi. This quartett was originated by Dr. A. M. Bailey of this city. He carried them to Memphis several weeks ago and had 14 Victor records recorded by them." *Winona Times*, Winona, MS, March 28, 1930.

COMMUNITIES OF FIDDLERS
IN MISSISSIPPI

With the recorded fiddlers and string bands from the 1920s and '30s it's difficult to point out audible influences. There are only a few tunes, like the Leake County Revelers' "Saturday Night Breakdown," where we have multiple recordings from more than one fiddler to compare. Stylistically, each seems distinct and separate. However, we can show that some groups of fiddlers attended the same fiddle contests and events and knew or knew of each other. Though they were strongly individual musical personalities, they did not learn and play in a vacuum. There were many fiddlers. Many fiddle contests were advertised in newspapers within the state, particularly between 1900 and 1940, but only a few contained any information about the fiddlers and the tunes they played. The descriptions that follow will suggest something about the quantity of the fiddlers and the interest in the music to supplement the recorded tunes transcribed in the rest of this book. Fiddlers' names in *italic* appear in other chapters in this book.

The Kosciusko fiddling contest

"Such pleasures as checker-playing and domino games are still part of the social life. Each fall an Old Fiddler's Contest is held in the courtroom of the courthouse before judges and a large audience. While prizes are offered to the best players on various instruments, the fiddle receives the most attention. There are several prizes for performances on this instrument, the contestants being divided according to age. 'Yankee Doodle,' 'Turkey in the Straw,' and 'Leather Breeches' are favorite tunes. The winners of the contest usually receive small amounts of cash and runners-up receive such commodities as flour, coffee and sugar. The giving of the latter is a custom dating from a time when such everyday articles were luxuries. Music of a more modern and standardized type is taught in the public schools."[1]

A local barber, Andy Hemphill,[2] organized the first contest in Kosciusko, held on November 18, 1914, and "over 200 contestants were present, including fiddlers, novelty instruments, guitar players, banjoers, clog dancers, hog callers, and those accompanying the contestants."[3] In 1916 there were at least two contests, one at the Kosciusko High School on February 25[4] and one at the Court House on November 6.[5] With the October 17, 1917, event, the contest became an annual event continuing until 1947, sometimes having up to 300 contestants.[6] *Grover O'Briant*, who attended it as a child in

A GREAT DAY
IN GRENADA!

For the Fifteenth Regiment Monumental Fund.

On the occasion of the ANNUAL REUNION OF W. R. BARKSDALE CAMP, NO. 189, UNITED CONFEDERATE VETERANS, and the Annual Reunion of the survivors of the Fifteenth Regiment of Mississippi Volunteers, the Dixie Chapter. No. 53, U. D. C. of Grenada, will present

A Grand Old-Time Fiddlers' Contest
(OPEN TO THE WORLD)

Grenada, Thursday, August 2, 1900,

for the purpose of raising funds for the erection of a Monument in Grenada to the memory of the heroic members of the gallant Fifteenth Mississippi Regiment of Volunteers.

Preceding the Grand Fiddlers' Contest there will be a speech by Hon. W. S. Hill, of Winona. who will be followed in a short talk to the "old guard" by Hon. J. C. Longstreet.

Col. Rounsaville's band of horse traders will be present and a good prize will be given to the best horse swapper.

The Old-Time Fiddlers' Contest will be a rare event. The following tunes will be played, and each will bring back to memory the good old times of good old days:

1.—Gray Eagle.	14.—Chicken in de Bread Tray.
2.—Forked Deer.	15.—Mollie Put de Kittle on.
3.—Soap Suds Over de Fence.	16.—Arkansaw Traveler.
4.—Leather Breeches.	17.—Natchez Under de Hill.
5.—Devil's Dream.	18.—Cotton Eyed Joe.
6.—Roundin' up de Corn.	19.—Old Mollie Hare.
7.—Run, Nigger, Run.	20.—'Possum up de Gum Stump.
8.—Old Sallie Goodin.	21.—Buffalo Gals.
9.—Eighth of January.	22.—Fishers Hornpipe.
10.—Mississippi Sawyer.	23.—Billie in de Low Groun'.
11.—Old Hen Cackle.	24.—Give de Fiddler a Dram.
12.—Black Eyed Susie.	25.—Puncheon Floor.
13.—Sugar in de Goad.	26.—The Girl I Left Behind Me.

THE PRIZES.

1.—For the best fiddler, suit of clothes.
2.—For the second best fiddler, handsome pair of shoes.
3.—For the best fiddler on "Arkansaw Traveler," watch and chain.
4.—For the best left handed fiddler, left handed pocket knife.
5.—For the tallest fiddler, short linen duster.
6.—For the leanest fiddler, side of bacon and box of oatmeal.
7.—For the fattest fiddler, half dozen fans and 100 lbs. of ice.
8.—For the ugliest fiddler, five pounds of candy.
9.—For the handsomest fiddler, mirror.
10.—For the worst fiddler, hammock and new fiddle bow.
11.—For the youngest fiddler, razor.
12.—For the oldest fiddler, rocking chair and a year's subscription to the Grenada Sentinel.
13.—For the best duet, saddle bags and umbrella.
14.—For the laziest fiddler, his choice between an ax or hoe.
15.—For the best horse swapper, copy of New Testament and riding whip.

Banjo and guitar accompaniments will be allowed. Each contestant will be required to play "Arkansaw Traveler." Every contestant will be required to register his name with Mr. J. S. King, and secure badge from him.

SENTINEL PRINT, Grenada, Miss.

Ball Game in Evening
Old time dance at night *Howdy.*
K

A BIG DAY IN GRENADA.

An Old-Time Fiddlers' Contest Open to the World.

On Thursday. August 2, 1900, there will be held in Grenada a grand Old-Time Fiddlers' Contest under the auspices of Dixie Chapter, Daughters of the Confederacy, that day being fixed upon in conjunction with the annual reunion of the survivors of the 15 Mississippi Regiment of Volunteers, and W. R. Barksdale Camp, U. C. V. The proceeds are to be added to a fund for the erection in Grenada of a monument in memory of the above named regiment, one of the most gallant in the Confederate service.

It will be a grand reunion of the boys who wore the gray. Everything will be without cost to every veteran and his family. A dinner will be served to all. The fiddlers' contest will be open to all comers. Send to J. S. King, Grenada, for rules governing the contest.

Hon. W. S. Hill of Winona. will deliver an address as will also Hon. J. C. Longstreet, of Grenada.

Reduced rates will be secured if possible. We want everybody who can to come. We can assure you a pleasant day and they will assist in a worthy cause.

MRS. J. W. BUCHANAN,
President of Dixie Chapter.

Grenada Star Herald, July 20, 1900.

Poster courtesy of Archives and Special Collections, University of Mississippi (folder 26, Small Manuscripts Collection: Broadsheets and Broadsides).

The Burrell family string band, Radio Station WHEF in Kosciusko, Attala County, about 1933. Photo courtesy of Cecil Abels.

1920, attempted to revive the contest in the 1970s, succeeded in doing so in 1984, and it continued at least into the 1990s. In 1984 two of the judges were fiddlers: Bill Mitchell, and Frank Childrey, who was the director of the Center for the Study of Southern Culture at the University of Mississippi. Due to deaths and changing musical tastes, the last contest had only three contestants: Grover O'Briant, Homer Grice, and Buster Reynolds. The judges were not musicians. One was Grover's son, Jerry O'Briant.[7] But this contest in its early incarnation seems to have been the most influential and popular fiddle contest in Mississippi.

In 1916 "The Court House was crowded to its utmost capacity with eager listeners, while many were turned away for lack of even standing room."[8] In 1917 "a telephone was installed under the stage and people in 28 towns were able to enjoy the music."[9] The 1917 contest was promoted in the newspaper with enthusiasm. "New features and new tunes will be mixed with old favorites this year. There will be a celebrated swamp fiddler from south Mississippi, accustomed to fiddle and fight mosquitoes at the same time. A noted frog-eating fiddler from New Orleans is coming, who uses his bow like a fiddler-crab crawling sideways over the sand. An old Attala man is coming all the way from Texas to take part; he got his technique from

Pearl Burdine and "Juanita," October 1917. Photo courtesy of Elizabeth Shown Mills. Burdine was Hoyt Ming's cousin and the source for "Indian War Whoop." He won the Kosciusko contest several times.

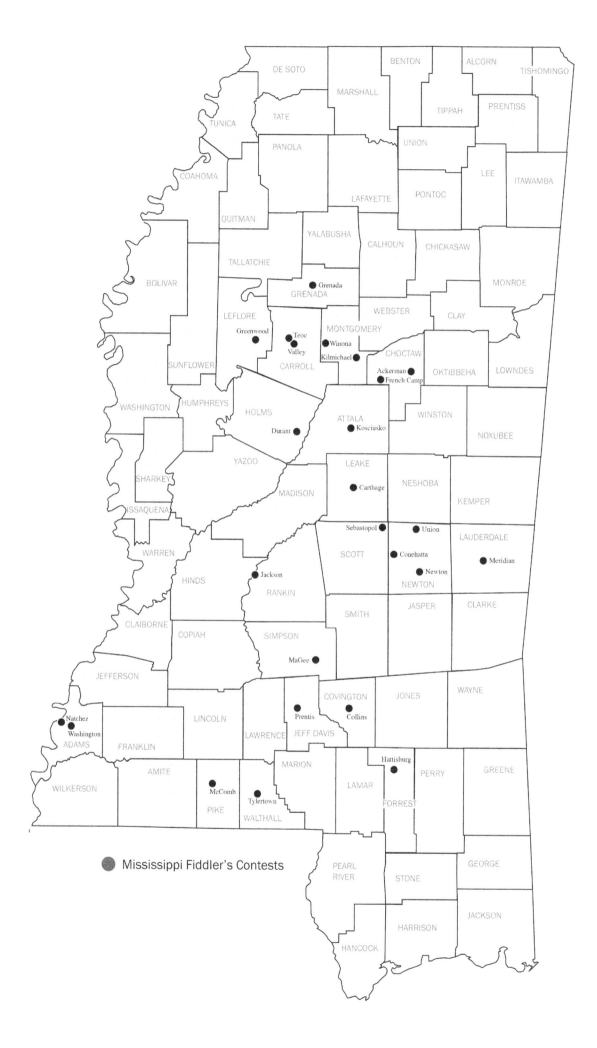

Mississippi Fiddler's Contests

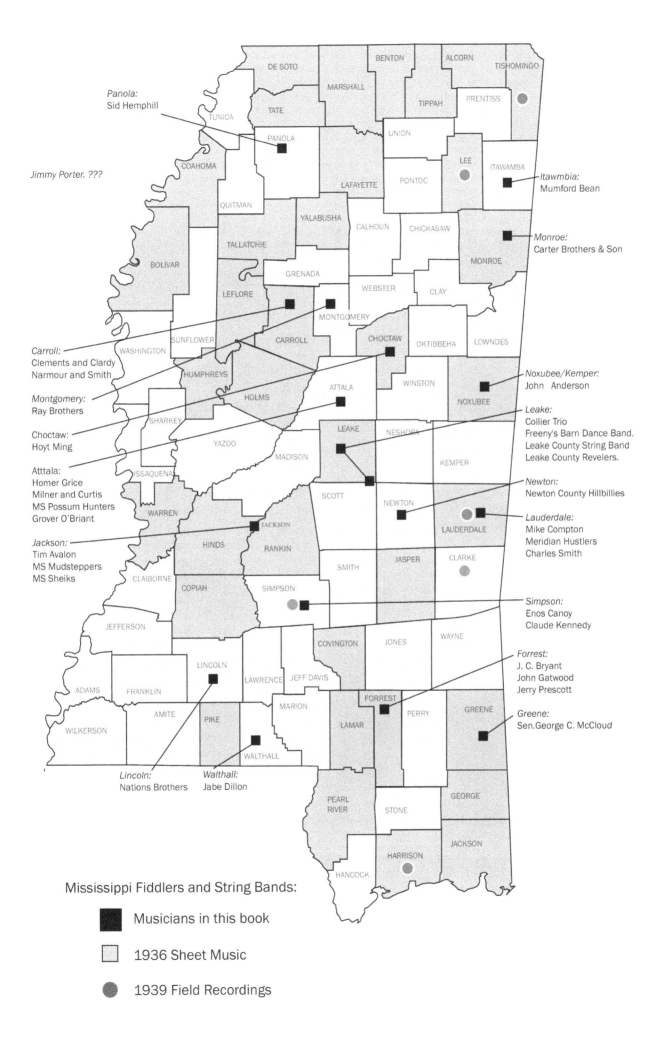

Panola:
Sid Hemphill

Jimmy Porter. ???

Itawmbia:
Mumford Bean

Monroe:
Carter Brothers & Son

Carroll:
Clements and Clardy
Narmour and Smith

Noxubee/Kemper:
John Anderson

Montgomery:
Ray Brothers

Leake:
Collier Trio
Freeny's Barn Dance Band.
Leake County String Band
Leake County Revelers.

Choctaw:
Hoyt Ming

Newton:
Newton County Hillbillies

Atttala:
Homer Grice
Milner and Curtis
MS Possum Hunters
Grover O'Briant

Lauderdale:
Mike Compton
Meridian Hustlers
Charles Smith

Jackson:
Tim Avalon
MS Mudsteppers
MS Sheiks

Simpson:
Enos Canoy
Claude Kennedy

Forrest:
J. C. Bryant
John Gatwood
Jerry Prescott

Greene:
Sen.George C. McCloud

Lincoln:
Nations Brothers

Walthall:
Jabe Dillon

Mississippi Fiddlers and String Bands:

■ Musicians in this book

　 1936 Sheet Music

● 1939 Field Recordings

watching a tarantula scratch its head with its hind heel. A Choctaw County fiddler is coming who can work his ears back and forth in perfect time to his bow. Then there is the noted artist from on the forks of Zilpha Creek who has seven sets of rattlesnake rattles in his fiddle and on his bow; he makes sweet music that will cause your hair to rise up like a wildcat's."[10]

Fiddlers that attended the 1916, 1917, and 1919 contests were listed as: A. Albright, Mark D. Allen, Oliver Allen, E. O. Allen, Gus Armstrong, L. Beckham, J. Bell, J. R. Bell, Theodore Bilbo, Elmer Blaine, J. M. Brooks, Ed Burt, G. Burden, Pearl Burden, J. A. Burns, John Burt, J. A. Byars, William Campbell, Emmett L. Conner, William Culpeper, Jack L. Cummings, Marvin Cummins, *Luther H. Curtis*, W. D. Curtis, James Frederick, L. G. Fulton, Ras Gamble, Uncle Jack Gaston, Jack Greer, John C. Gregory, J. C. Goyne, Charley Guyton, Patrick Harrison, N. C. Henderson, J. A. Hodges, J. R. Hodges, Bill Holloway, Joncy Jennings, Selma Jennings, W. J. Jennings, the Jennings boys, Will Johnson, Ed Johnson, Walter A. Lindsey, Peter Lowery, Emmett Mangrum, John Mangrum, Mangrum, W. M. Mathis, Charley Maxwell, T. J. Mayo Sr. and Jr., J. McMann, L. L. Megs, Bob Milner, J. W. Milner, *Luther B. Milner*, Fred Milner, Bud Moore, Ed Noel, Jim B. Owens, William Pickle, Bill Poole, Uncle Frank Poole, Calvin Pope, Alton Ratliff, Arthur Ray, J. A. Ray, Phillip A. Reel, William Reel, H. H. Rogers, J. R. Rogers, Wren Rogers, D. W. Tims, Thomas U. Sisson, John Shipp, J. C. Smith, O. L. Smith, Archie Stephens, Percy Stephens, Captain J. Pick Stephens, Shelly Stonestreet, Turp Sweatt, J. E. Sweatt, W. E. Sweatt, Leland Terry, James K. Vardaman, Mr. Walters, Joe Weeks, and John Sharp Williams.

Newspaper accounts announced: "Masters of the fiddle will render such classics of carnal music as . . ."[11] "Arkansas Traveler," "Bacon and Greens," "Billie In the Low Ground," "Black Eyed Susan," "Bonnie Blue Flag," "Coon Dog," "Cotton Eyed Joe," "Dixie," "Greenbacks, Ham and Gravy," "Hop Light Ladies, Your Cake's All Dough," "Home Sweet Home," "I Love Sugar in My Coffee Oh," "Indian War Whoop," "Mississippi Sawyer," "Nellie Gray," "Peckerwood on the Post-Oak Tree," "The Pirroters," Raise Big Taters in Sandy Land," "Rocky Road to Alabama," "Rooster Crowing on Sourwood Mountain," "Rozum the Bow," "Run Nigger Run," "Old Dan Tucker," "Sold My Horse in Tennessee," "Soldier's Joy," "Sopping Up Sorghum," "Shortnin' Bread," "Shucking Out Nubbins," "Tallahassee or Evening Star Waltz," "Taters in the Sandy Land," "Then You'll Remember Me," "Walls of Jericho," "Weevilly Wheat," and "Whoa Mule I Can't Git the Bridle On."

In the 1932 contest more fiddlers appear: T. B. Adams, J. E. Armstrong, Miss Mattie Armstrong, Elton Blailock, *Collier Brothers*, T. B. Collins, E. L. Conner, Hallies Ellis, J. H. Ellis, *Leo Ellis, Lonnie Ellis, Homer Grice*, J. R. Grice, E. R. Hedgwood, R. S. Hedgwood, A. J. Hemphill, J. E. Johnson, J. H. Kimbrough, W. R. Kimbrough, J. J. McKay, R. C. Mayo, Miss Ethel Milner, A. D. Montgomery, C. H. O'Cain, G. W. O'Cain, W. E. Ray, Earl Reynolds, J. D. Roberts and W. J. White.[12]

In 1991 the fiddlers were Jason Daniel Guthrie, Bernie Linton, *George Cecil McLeod*, Amanda Smith, Janell Smith, Teresa Taylor, and Lamar Wells. The string bands were Bluegrass Men, Magnolia Bluegrass, and the Pearl Ramblers. The mandolinists were Bernie Linton and Pug Kea. The banjoists were Ricky Windham and Darrell Lloyd.

The nearby town of Durant hosted fiddle contests in 1917 and in 1983.[13] In 1917 Pearl Burdine (sometimes spelled Burden) played "Mississippi Sawyer" and "Indian War Whoop" for an audience of three hundred.[14] His "Indian War Whoop" won the special feature prize for him at the contest in Kosciusko in 1916. Burdine influenced Hoyt Ming and his version of that tune.

In 1971 fiddlers Billy Cook, Homer Grice, Earl Reynolds, Harlan Reynolds, and Ralph Townsend performed at the annual Natchez Trace Festival in Kosciusko.[15]

In 1986 fiddlers Billy Cook, *Homer Grice, Grover O'Briant*, James Ward, and Bill Womble played for a Fourth of July celebration at the lodge at Liberty Chapel in Kosciusko.[16]

Greenwood, Winona, Kilmichael, French Camp, and Ackerman

Fiddle contests in or near Greenwood occurred in at least March 31, 1927,[17] April 23, 1934,[18] May 5, 1934,[19] and October 21, 1937.[20] The fiddlers at the May 5, 1934, contest were: *A. E. Clardy*, L. L. Clark, W. E. Duke, Mr. F. Ezell, Maizie Harper, O. D. Jordan, Ed Kittrell, Robert Lewis, *W. T. Narmour*, *Charles T. Smith*, M. E. Tindall, Chief Two House, and Walter White.

Tunes played were "Ain't No Flies on Aunty," "Billy in the Low Ground," "Coming Round the Mountain," "Don't Go to the Ball Tonight," "Frankie and Johnnie," "Got to See Mama," "Hen Cackles," "Home Brew Rag," "I Spy the Spider," "Irish Washerwoman," "Leather Breeches," "Midnight Waltz," "Peek a-boo Waltz," "The Second Fair," "Schottische," "Smoky Moke," "Sweet Bunch of Daisies," "Valley School Blues," "Wed Night Waltz," "Whistling Coon," "Wild Irish Rose," and "The Wreck of the Old 97."

Winona had fiddle contests on February 10, 1928,[21] and November 20, 1931.[22] Vaiden had one on May 27, 1916,[23] and Kilmichael had a contest on June 18, 1962, that was organized by *Homer Grice*.[24]

A fiddle contest in Ackerman, on July 10, 1919, had the string bands of the *Ray Brothers* and the *Ming* band. The fiddlers were Alvin Dodd, Mrs. Gladney, Nealy Henderson, *Mr. Ming*, *Bill Ray*, and D. Medders Ruff. Guitar: Mr. Scott, Jarvis Daves, and *Vardaman Ray*. The banjo players were Joa Biggers, Jarvis Daves, and *Vardaman Ray*. The harmonica players were Webb Ray, Direl Simpson, and Edwin Tennyson. The quartets were the Blackwood Brothers and the *Ray Brothers*.

The whistlers were Edwin Tenyson, Sam C. Ray, and Floyd Medders.[25]

James Hill, a music teacher from the French Camp academy a few miles west of Ackerman, organized a festival in 1975 and 1977 to raise funds for his music classes. Fiddlers who attended were Billy Cook, *Grover O'Briant*, Elizabeth Cocroft, *Hoyt Ming*, *Charles Smith*, and *Homer Grice*.[26]

In Bruce, Mississippi, about ten miles north east of Winona, there was a 1929 fiddle contest with fiddlers H. N. Dykes, Morris Dykes, Dennis Granberry, John Maxey, Ruth Maxey, and More Meeks.[27]

The fiddlers from this area with chapters in this book are: *Eugene Clardy*, *Tom Dumas*, *Homer Grice*, *Hoyt Ming*, the *Mississippi Possum Hunters*, *Milner and Curtis*, *W. T. Narmour*, *Grover O'Briant*, and the *Ray Brothers*. Fiddlers from this area with tunes transcribed in *Mississippi Fiddle Tunes and Songs from the 1930s* are F. Ezell (104) and Ed Kittrell (127, 128).

Jackson to Leake, Newton, and Scott Counties

The Mississippi State Fair in Jackson was founded in 1858 and has regularly had fiddle contests as a small part of the much larger event. The *Leake County String Band* and its members individually, Mickey Davis, *Alvis Massengale*, *Senator George C. McLeod*, the Newton County String Band, and *Hoyt Ming* often entered in the 1970s through the 1990s.[28] Charles T. Smith of Starkville won first place in 1986 and 1988 and second place in 1990. In 1938 there were six old-time bands entered from the Jackson area: the Alonzo McKay band, the Ras Pace band, the Spur Ramblers, the Texas Rangers, and two unnamed bands from Carthage.[29]

The Daughters of Veterans and the United Daughters of the Confederacy sponsored a 1916 fiddle contest that was held at the Majestic Theatre in Jackson. The fiddlers mentioned were William Collins, Tom Dickerson, M. L. Lott, Charles Reed, and William Willins.

The Men's Bible class and the Athletic Club of Griffith Memorial Church sponsored a fiddle contest July 26, 1929, in Jackson. The contest categories were for fiddle, wind instruments (limited to the French harp [harmonica], saxophone, cornet, and trumpet), and vocal quartets and quintets. They described their previous contest as being attended by twelve to fifteen hundred people.[30]

Carthage, Newton, Union, Sebastapol, and Meridian

The Neshoba County Fair, which began in 1889, has occasionally had fiddle events, a minstrel show in 1906,[31] a fiddle contest in 1930,[32] and in 1975 and 1976 the *Leake County String Band*.[33]

Claud Pickle, a fiddler from Carthage, appeared at the Kosciusko contest several times before 1925, when he was noted in his final appearance anywhere:

> Claud Pickle is dead and Lonnie Pickle, his cousin, is suffering knife wounds and faces charge of murder as the result of a fight over who should pay the fiddler.
>
> The two men attended a dance at Dossville, 12 miles north of here Monday Night. When the fiddler played 'Home Sweet Home', and started to put his fiddle away, Claud who hade been dancing with a young woman with whom both men were acquainted offered him 50 cents to play for one more dance. Lonnie offered the fiddler $1 not to play and held out a bill. Claud knocked it out of his hand, according to bystanders. Both men drew knives and they fought on the dance floor, for several minutes before Claud fell, mortally wounded. Lonnie was not seriously hurt.
>
> Claud died Tuesday.[34]

William Claud Pickle (1897–1925) is buried in the County Line Cemetery, Leake County, Mississippi.[35]

The 1910 Meridian *Evening Star* billed an event as a fiddle contest and described the planned concert, which was to be a benefit for the Walthall Camp of Confederate Veterans.[36] The fiddlers mentioned were W. Bridges, W. W. Daws, Miss. Hoyt Dunn, S. J. Girardean, N. E. Katz, J. D. Miller, R. S. Neville, S. S. Neville, and D. W. Thompson. C. A. Hancock played a banjo solo. The guitarists were Chester Thompson and D. W. Thompson.

Some of the tunes they played were "Dixie," "Hawthorn Waltz," "It Makes No Difference Where I Go, I Can't Get Around for the Calico," "Just Before the Battle, Mother," "Liza Jane," "Whistling Rufus," and the "Wild West Waltz."

The winners in the 1957 Conehatta fiddlers contest were *Alvis Massengale*, Dolphis Jordon, and Julian Colpra.[37]

The fiddlers from this area with chapters in this book are *Collier Trio*, *Freeny Barn Dance Band*, *Leake County Revelers*, *Leake County String Band*, and the *Newton County Hill Billies*.

McComb, Tylertown

McComb's Jubilee Day Celebration included a fiddle contest; the fiddlers were Alex Bass, A. M. Brister, G. W. Brister, Robert B. Johnson of Tylertown (who won first prize), Obed W. Magee of Tylertown (who was described as the three-time fiddlin' champion of Walthall County and was a friend of Jabe Dillon's), Cage Wroten, and L. A. Wroten.[38] African American string band musicians from the Tylertown area of Walthall County were Herb Quinn, Dink Brister, Babe Stovall, and Roosevelt Holts. David Evans's field recordings from 1966 and 1970 sample their repertoire, which consisted of a mixture of blues and old-time fiddle tunes.

The fiddlers and mandolinists from this area with a chapter in this book are *Dink Brister*, *Jabe Dillon*, and *Herb Quinn*.

Magee, Prentis

Prentis, in Jeff Davis County, was the stomping ground of fiddler Van Baker, who was much appreciated by the local newspaper. The columnist, writing a few times under the byline of G. L. Martin, seems to have begun writing about events in Jeff Davis County as early as 1932 and then began writing the "Jeff Davis Folks" column in late 1934 and continued the column until August 1948. Descriptions of music, dance, songs, and practical jokes abound in full-bodied prose. The stories seem grounded in the local folklore but are richly embroidered. Excerpts detailing the exploits of the fiddler Van Baker are included here as much for their folktale quality as for the descriptions of county fiddling events.

When the big old-fashioned square dance is staged at the new county log hut here on Tuesday night, following a program of speeches dedicating the hut, lauding the president and commemorating his fifty-second birthday, folks are going to hear old Van Baker and his orchestra, the foxiest old boy in this country, they say, with a fiddle and the bow, scream out in a high crescendo, "Don't you Hear Them Wolves A-Howling," and then Will Langston, bearing down on the "counter," Henry Baker doing the high notes and Boss Loftin, with his mandolin and a half a dozen banjos and guitars throbbing like a lot of Greek gods in pain, all joining in with the opening "grand waltz." Van is an old-time fiddler; draws a full bow, keeps her well waxed and the strings a-whining for more, and now and then, just to shove in a little punch, throws back his massive head far back and yells out in company with the throbbing music, "Don't You Hear Then Bones A-Snapping," with everybody getting in a weaving way and Will Langston, who pats the floor with a full boot, joining in on the second stanza.[39]

Van Baker, who has held more offices in Jeff Davis county than any other man, and who is perhaps as well posted on official routine as any fellow in three states, and along with Mack Davis has courted more widows, both grass and sod, than any other fellow in this section, is about the smoothest fiddler since the days of old Bob Taylor. When Van draws his bow across the bosom of that old fiddle, throws his head and wades into "Old Hen, She Cackled" or "Billie in the Low Ground," with now and then some classic stuff to give it finish, the feet of every old boy and old girl at these old-fashioned square dances quiver with excitement and away go walking sticks and shin plasters. Then after about three hours of straight fiddling and dancing, you'll hear old Van's fiddle screaming out, "Give That Fiddler a Dram." That means the show is over.[40]

Van Baker and Lon Burrow, who court widows, both grass and sod, over half a dozen counties, fair-to-middling courting, with Van playing the fiddle and Lon blowing the harmonica, got into a nice little scrape the other night at a big square dance over there on Boule River. These boys had on these big long dusters. The feller down there had so

many knotholes in his floor, he had them to hold the dance in a big smoke house, dirt floor, with barrels of molasses scattered about, light mighty bad. When Van and Lon got into a weaving way in there and dust so thick you could bite it, one of them tail flaps got hung on a corncob the feller had in the molasses bunghole and before they knew it out came about 50 gallons of the stuff and the whole place was knee deep in molasses before they knew it. It all may blow over.[41]

Other Van Baker tunes mentioned were "Bonaparte's Retreat," "Lost Babes," and "Sally Am the Gal for Me." Sadly we have no recordings of his playing.

"Van Baker's neighbor, Charles Mikell, who plays the fiddle and dances all at the same time, leader of the old-fashioned square dance, is said to have joined a traveling minstrel show of some kind and wandered off into Louisiana for a few weeks. He came back it is stated, with a lot of new tunes and one of these big brass horns that wins around the neck like a rope."[42]

The fiddlers at the 1925 Hazelhurst contest were Buck Ashley, Burnice Ashley, Mrs. Beasley, T. L. Hoo Jr., T. L. Hood Sr., W. F. Hood, C. A. Hughes, A. M. Knight, Harvey Knight, J. D. Knight, Ollie Knight, Robert Knight, E. L. Massey, Hugh Martin, Miss Mittie Martin, E. V. Sheeley, T. C. Tillman, and John Wootmen.

Some of the tunes played were "Arkansas Traveler," Capt. Jack," "Old Hen Cackled," "Shoo Fly," and "Turkey in the Straw."[43]

The fiddlers from this area with chapters in this book are *Enos Canoy* with the Wildcats and *Claude Kennedy* with the Six Towns Band.

Hattiesburg

John Calvin Bryant (1869–1950) of Hattiesburg, along with another fiddler, M. L. Mathews, organized and managed the Forrest County Fiddlers Association, which met at the Forrest County courthouse in the courtroom beginning in 1944 and continuing until about 1950. While recordings of his playing have not yet been found, he was most likely recorded at the December, 1944 association meeting when County Judge William Harrison recorded several selections on his "Sound Scriber," a disc recorder for dictation that had just become available.[44] On January 3, 1948, the association was recorded once again by Sgt. W. E. Ward of the US Army recruiting service.[45]

Bryant worked in the lumber business and had three sons and five daughters with Martha Hamilton Bryant. His brother, S. E. Bryant, played guitar.[46]

In addition to fiddling, Bryant built three violins, one at age sixty, the second at sixty-five, and the last at age seventy. The second one was described, "The face—Roman-striped in its composition of many woods—is composed of tiny pieces of cherry, chestnut, sassafras, mulberry, sumac, grapevine, rattan vine, cross-vine, yellow jessamine, holly, pine and mahogany. The back is of poplar, with cedar sides."[47]

Bryant was known to play the tunes "Alabama Girl," "The Eighth of January," "Heel and Toe Polka," "Old Pot Pie" (a tune that he played on his wedding day in 1890 and his anniversaries),[48] "Possum in the Gum Stump," "Sweetheart Waltz," and "The Tom Creel Tune."[49]

John Gatwood, who lived in Petal, only a short distance from Hattiesburg, attended the association meetings on several occasions. For at least the November 1945 meeting, his bandmate, F. M. Smith, "accompanied the violinists on the guitar."[50]

Bryant grew up with and played music with the blind fiddler Charlie Edmundson (1867–1944)[51] of Eatonville.[52] As late as August 1944, Edmundson was attending the association meetings. Some of Edmundson's tunes were transcribed in 1936.[53] E. A. Ladner was another Forrest County Association fiddler documented in 1936.[54]

Other Forrest County Fiddlers Association musicians: (fiddlers) Tom Baker, R. T. Berry, E. Blackwell, Green Brackin, W. T. Breland, S. E. Bryant, J. C. Bryant Jr., J. A. Columbus, Ray Deerman, Ervin Ford, Fate Guy, W. H. Green, J. B. Horn, Melton Ingram, T. W. Kelly, R. C. Lott, M. L. Mathews, S. Maxwell, L. A. McMurray, L. C. McSwain, Scott Estus, Vaster McLemore, J. S. Morris, Jim Owen, Pat Patterson, Pete and Plummer Saucier, Amos Smith, Frank Smith, A. S. Raney (or Rayner), G. N. Rainer, A. B. Rutlin, Mack Sanford, Bob Simms, Van Slade, Grover Speed, Clarence Triggs, Ray Walters, John Whitehead, Arnise Youngblood; (guitarists) T. M. Gibson, Leo Lee, F. T. Lewis, Carnell Saucier, F. M. Smith, I. T. Sanford, and Tom L. Thompson.

Other tunes played at association meetings were "Arkansas Traveler," "Black-Eyed Susan," "Carroll County Blues," "Creole Belle, "Evening Star Waltz,"[55] "Georgia Camp Meeting," "Get Along Home, Cindy," "Green Valley Waltz," "Jennie's Got a Red Dress," "Johnson's Old Gray Mule," "Make Me a Pallet Down on the Floor," "Old Joe Clark," "The Old Santonio Road [San Antonio Rose?]," "Prettiest Girl in the County," "Sherman's March" or "Black Snake Driving a Wagon," "Smith Brothers Special," "Ragtime Annie," "The Railroad Man," and "The World Keeps On Turning."

In the 1970s and later, *George C. McLeod, Jerry Prescott, Lee Fulcher*, and others played some old-time tunes along with bluegrass and appeared at local bluegrass festivals in Wiggins, Mississippi.

The fiddlers from this area with chapters in this book are *John Gatwood, Jerry Prescott*, and *George C. McLeod*.

Currently in Mississippi

The Mississippi Old Time Music Society, founded in 1996 by Alvin Hudson, Sandra Melscheimer, and Ted Holman, is the hub for old-time music in Mississippi. Along with *Tim Avalon*, Alvin and Sandra performed together in the string band Old Hat.

The society organizes two open jam sessions a month and other less formal social and musical get-togethers. Once a month, *Tim Avalon* teaches a workshop on old-time tunes. From these activities a handful of new local bands have formed. Several members of the group have been awarded study grants from the Mississippi Arts Commission. Once a year, a nationally known teacher will be brought in to teach a two-day workshop. The ongoing active membership floats between twenty to over fifty.

The organization has sponsored and co-sponsored festivals, singing workshops, and music workshops in the state and has collaborated with the Mississippi Dulcimer Society, Mississippi Arts Commission, Old Court House Museum, Mississippi Agriculture Museum, Jefferson College, Clinton Welcome Center, and the Mississippi Welcome Center on music events.

The music also lives on at the annual Great Big Yam Potatoes Gathering, a free two-day festival founded in May 2008, by organizer Robert Gray. It takes place outside of Natchez on the grounds of the historic Jefferson College in Washington, Mississippi. Attended by local musicians and some from neighboring states; it is a small but very friendly and welcoming old-time-only festival. For photos, videos, and the gorgeous color posters designed and illustrated by Dave Morgan, see Great Big Yam Potatoes on Facebook. Morgan's 2014 poster features Willie T. Narmour. A small version may be seen in the Narmour and Smith chapter in this book.

Fiddler *Tim Avalon* has a chapter in this book. Jack Magee, one of the best-known local fiddlers, has his CD listed in Appendix A.

—Harry Bolick, 2019

NOTES

1. *Mississippi: The WPA Guide to the Magnolia State* (Jackson: University Press of Mississippi, 1988; first published 1938, Viking Press), 495.

2. Barbara Shoemake, "Fiddling Convention Revived," *Star-Herald*, Kosciusko, MS, March. 29, 1984.

3. "Kosciusko," *Jackson State Tribune*, Jackson, MS, November 24,1914, 6.

4. "Old Fiddlers Contest!" *Star Herald*, Kosciusko, MS, February 18, 1916, 2.

5. "Fiddlers' Contest a Great Success," *Star Herald*, Kosciusko, MS, November 10, 1916, 1.

6. "Gum Prize Starts Fiddling Career," *Star Herald*, Kosciusko, MS, March 19, 1987, 2.

7. Interview with Grover's son, Jerry O'Briant, Kilmichael, MS, February 6, 2019.

8. "Fiddlers' Contest a Great Success," *Star Herald*, Kosciusko, MS, November 10, 1916, 1.

9. "Fiddlers' Contest a Perfect Success, Thirty-six Take Part in Meeting at Kosciusko—Old-Time Favorites Played," *Jackson Daily News*, Jackson, MS, October 17, 1917, 1.

10. "The Fiddlers' Contest," *Star Herald*, Kosciusko, MS, October 5, 1917, 5.

11. "The Fiddlers' Contest," *Star Herald*, Kosciusko, MS, October 5, 1917, 5.

12. "Old Fiddlers in Attala Compete," *Clarion-Ledger*, Jackson, MS, October 16, 1932, 12.

13. "Folks Sought to Fiddle in Durant," *Star Herald*, Kosciusko, MS, April 28, 1983, 13.

14. "Fiddlers Contest Held," *Jackson Daily News*, Jackson, MS, April 28, 1917, 5.

15. Ethel Stewart, "Bee Hive to Buzz at Saturday Festival," *Clarion-Ledger*, Jackson, MS, June 10, 1971, 4.

16. "Many families Entertain July 4 Holiday Visitors," *Star Herald*, Kosciusko, MS, July 10, 1986, B1.

17. "Old Fashioned Fiddlers Contest Here At Local Theatre Friday," *Greenwood Commonwealth*, Greenwood, MS, March 31, 1927, 1.

18. "Old Fiddlers Contest Will Feature Festival," *Greenwood Commonwealth*, Greeenwood, MS, April 23, 1934, 1.

19. "Fiddlers Contest Pleasing to Crowd," *Greenwood Commonwealth*, Greenwood, MS, May 5, 1934, 8.

20. "The Valley Boys HI Y," ad, *Greenwood Commonwealth*, Greenwood, MS, October 21, 1937, 3.

21. "Fiddlers Contest Held at Winona," *Winona Times*, Winona, MS, February 10, 1928, 1.

22. "Fiddlers Contest Was a Big Success," *Winona Times*, Winona, MS, November 20, 1931, 8.

23. "Citizens of Vaiden Making Prep for Trade Day and OT Fiddle Contest," *Winona Times*, Winona, MS, May 12, 1916, 4.

24. "Winners Listed in Kilmichael Fiddlers Contest," *Webster Progress*, Eupora, MS, June 21, 1962, 1.

25. "Union School Fiddling Contest Winners Named," *Choctaw Plaindealer*, Ackerman, MS, November 3, 1933, 1.

26. Tony Russell, "Festival at French Camp," *Old Time Music* 20 (Spring 1976), UK.

27. "Bruce T.A. Is Host at Gala Affair," *Morning Call*, Laurel, MS, November 30, 1929, 2.

28. "Fiddlers, Git-Pickers Raise Coliseum Roof," unidentified in photo, *Clarion-Ledger*, Jackson, MS, October 28, 1974, 22.

29. "Fiddlers Stage Finals Tonight for Big Prizes," *Clarion-Ledger*, Jackson, MS, October 1, 1938, 10.

30. "Old Fiddlers to Vie on July 26," *Clarion-Ledger*, Jackson, MS, July 13, 1929.

31. "Neshoba County Fair. It Promises to be More Interesting This Year Than Usual," *Newton Record*, Newton, MS, August 9, 1906, 5.

32. "39th Annual Session Neshoba County Fair," *Union Appeal*, Union, MS, July 24, 1930, 3.

33. "1976 Neshoba County Fair Program," ad, *Union Appeal*, Union, MS, July 29, 1976, 10; and "87th Neshoba County Fair," ad, *Union Appeal*, Union, MS, July 17, 1975, 13.

34. "Paying Fiddler Causes Killing," *Winona Times*, Winona, MS, December 18, 1925, 1.

35. William Claude Pickle grave, www.findagrave.com/memorial/35182190/william-claude-pickle.

36. "Old Fiddlers Ready for Contest," *Meridian Evening Star*, Meridian, MS, March 27, 1910, 2.

37. "Winners Announced in Fiddlers Contest," *Scott County Times*, Forest, MS, January 17, /1957, 2.

38. "Jubilee Day Celebration Attracts Thousands Here; Many Enter Competitions," *Enterprise Journal*, McComb, MS, April 29, 1932, 1.

39. "Jeff Davis Will Revive Old Dance Tunes Tonight," *Clarion-Ledger*, Jackson, MS, January 30, 1934, 3.

40. "Jeff Davis Folks," *Clarion-Ledger*, Jackson, MS, May 6, 1940, 10.

41. "Jeff Davis Folks," *Clarion-Ledger*, Jackson, MS, October 27, 1940, 10.

42. "Jeff Davis Folks," *Clarion-Ledger*, Jackson, MS, March 4, 1937, 7.

43. "Fiddlers Contest Gets Much Praise," *Clarion-Ledger*, Jackson, MS, March 1, 1925, 12.

44. Mary Lee Nelson, "Fiddlers Give with Gleeful Vim," *Hattiesburg American*, Hattiesburg, MS, December 4, 1944, 9.

45. "Recordings Made at Fiddler's Meeting," *Hattiesburg American*, Hattiesburg, MS, January 5, 1948, 10.

46. "Funeral Services Held for J. C. Bryant," *Hattiesburg American*, Hattiesburg, MS, December 12, 1950, 6.

47. "Violin Prescribed as Cure-All for Ailments," *Hattiesburg American*, Hattiesburg, MS, December 11, 1945, 1, 11.

48. "J. C. Bryants Wed 55 Years Ago Today," *Hattiesburg American*, Hattiesburg, MS, January 16, 1945, 9.

49. "Fiddlers Give with Old Favorites," *Hattiesburg American*, Hattiesburg, MS, February 5, 1945, 5.

50. "Fiddlers Play Next Dec. 1," *Hattiesburg American*, Hattiesburg, MS, November 5, 1945, 7.

51. "Fiddlers' Association Meets Saturday," *Hattiesburg American*, Hattiesburg, MS, January 4, 1945, 4.

52. Chris Goertzen, "Bill Rogers, Contemporary Traditional Mississippi Fiddler," *American Music* (Winter 2015). University of Illinois. Bill Rogers's wife's grandfather, fiddler Hugh Cole, learned some fiddle from Edmundson.

53. Bolick and Austin, Mississippi Fiddle Tunes and Songs from the 1930s, 94–102.

54. Bolick and Austin, Mississippi Fiddle Tunes and Songs from the 1930s, 129, 130.

55. Bolick and Austin, Mississippi Fiddle Tunes and Songs from the 1930s, 96.

THE SEGREGATION OF SOUND

Unheard African American Fiddlers

African American have always made up a significant proportion of Mississippi's population. Indeed, the state had some the largest concentrations of the enslaved in the antebellum period. More African Americans held public office in Mississippi after the Civil War than any other state in the Union. Emanuel Handy, for example, was a formerly enslaved member of the House of Representatives from Copiah County. According to one state newspaper, he was "the best scraper of cat gut in the state."[1] African Americans helped destroy slavery and subsequently worked to build a new order on the ruins of the old. Lawmakers crafted constitutional amendments that permanently abolished slavery, established birthright citizenship, defined civil rights, and made the right to vote a matter of national concern. Reconstruction governments in the South created their first systems of public education, and the formerly slaved negotiated employment contracts with their former owners.

The hopeful and important period of Reconstruction reminds us that for much of the state's history they were invisible, not able to own property, to vote, to hold public office, to be counted as citizens. From the hundreds of white fiddle contests advertised and reviewed in newspapers in Mississippi in the period of years that this book covers, I could only find one that mentioned a contest for African American fiddlers. Newspapers, recording companies, and scholars simply did not take notice of African American fiddlers.

The record of African American musicians playing this old-time music, which is thought of as "white," is poorly documented. And yet, we do know that some, quite likely many, African Americans played the same music as other Mississippians. At this late date, we cannot overcome the cultural blindness that simply did not see African American fiddlers in their time, but we include what we could find. They are part of this story of Mississippi fiddling.

Allen Alsop, Theodore Harris, Prince McCoy, and Frank Wharton are four such fiddlers included in this chapter. For Alsop we have the transcriptions reproduced in our previous book,[2] but sadly, for Harris, McCoy, and Wharton we have no actual documented music.

Elsewhere in this book we are able write about and transcribe the music of other African American musicians: Dink Brister, Tom Dumas, Sid Hemphill, Charlie McCoy, the Mississippi Sheiks, Bob Pratcher, and Herb Quinn.

Advertisement from the *Simpson County News*, June 29, 1937. Note the last line: "Colored Fiddlers Contest $1. (Bring fiddle)." This is sole mention of a contest or gathering for "Colored" fiddlers from a newspaper search that returned hundreds for "fiddlers."

Allen Alsop

Alsop was a dance fiddler for the Teoc, Carroll County community for over fifty years. The census dates for his birth range from 1861 to 1870 and have a variety of spellings for his last name: Alsop, Alsopp, and Alsup. His parents were listed as Jack Alsup and Emmaline Topp. In 1900 he was married to Francis Alsop. In 1910 and 1920, the census lists him as married to Josephine Alsop. According to an entry at Ancestry.com they had at least seven sons and four daughters. In the 1940 census he was listed as widowed and as a farm laborer. There is a Social Security record listing his date of death in Detroit, Michigan, as May 15, 1972, at age 104.

Mississippi Fiddle Tunes and Songs from the 1930s contains fourteen transcriptions of his tunes.

Theodore Harris

In a brief filmed interview with Belton Sutherland that is viewable only in the archives, Alan Lomax films folks singing and plowing behind a mule, which reminds Sutherland of the farming communities around Camden in the 1930s. One of his playing partners at that time was fiddler Theodore Harris, who, in his opinion, was "the only man that could play 'John Henry.' See, I used to play with [him]. So help me, he could play it too. Yeah, he could really play it. There wasn't no maybe about it. He's the best fiddle player that ever went through here." Sutherland freely declared that in the 1930s, when folks lived more spread out on all the farms in Madison County, "We had this country sewed up back then."[3]

Harris was indeed a popular local musician. He sometimes attracted so many people to his gigs in Canton that it required blocking off the streets, and not a single musician from Madison County offered anything less than glowing praise in interviews. In his interview with Pete Welding in Chicago in December 1965, Canton harmonicist John Lee Henley talks about the music of Theodore Harris. The artist's name, however, is misunderstood and recorded as "Fado Harris."[4] In one interview published in *Living Blues*, Madison County native K. C. Douglas discussed a fiddler from Canton who Tom Mazzolini later heard as "Fadel Harrison."[5] He had, in fact, referred to Theodore Harris, an assertion that he corroborates in another interview from 1972. On his first visit to America, sixteen-year-old blues enthusiast Axel Küstner conducted an interview at the Berkeley, California, home of K. C. Douglas, who had indeed known the elder fiddler. While he certainly knew many blues singers under contract as recording artists, he knew of some musicians who were:

just as good as some o' those fellers, but still they had not recorded no records. Well, he wasn't ... he wasn't considered as being known. Because it was there, the guy at my home, name, ah . . . Theodore Haze [sic]; he was a fiddler and brother, that man could play a fiddle. I mean he could play it. He was so good; he get on his fiddle and a guitar. And they would allow him [to] play on the streets, because them peoples stopped them cars out there on the streets. And that man could play. And it's too bad that no record company [n]ever got him and recorded. He played the blues on the fiddle, just like he can on his guitar. He was, we followed him out, in my teen years, almost grown, when they had him the different places on Saturday nights for dances, we used to walk four an' five an' eight, nine miles . . . see Theodore Haze [sic] play that fiddle. That man could play it brother, I mean he could play it. See, I knew a lot of musicians, I mean, that [were] good. But they wasn't record artists.[6]

Prince Albert McCoy
(March 19, 1882–February 4, 1968)

Prince Albert McCoy is perhaps the best example of an African American musician and fiddler whose diverse and multifaceted repertoire refutes the stereotypes that undergird his seminal role in the early history of the Delta blues. It is also fitting that he grew up in the cultural cauldron that existed in turn-of-the-twentieth-century Greenville, Mississippi, the Queen City of the Delta. In the 1890s, the state of Mississippi disfranchised African Americans in the new state constitution, and the Supreme Court's 1896 *Plessy v. Ferguson* decision codified racial segregation into the law. These legal developments established the social context that gave rise to segregated business districts, specifically the white business districts on Main and Washington Streets and the segregated business district on Nelson Street, the thriving nineteenth-century heart of Black Greenville.

African American preachers and the formerly enslaved believed that the pulpit, the press, and the public school were the most important forums used to influence public sentiment, mold society, and shape the future of the American people.[7] Rev.

Adam Jackson asserted that the destiny of African Americans in Greenville hinged upon the united efforts of the Black institutions that emerged in the New Town neighborhood along Nelson Street. In 1905 that destiny did not include any saloons or brothels. "To open a saloon on Nelson Street," Jackson argued,

> right in the heart of half a dozen churches and right in the doors of two colored public school houses, where all the colored children of the city are being taught, would be equivalent to opening the door of a cage in which a lion was confined, turning him loose upon a community, for, with all these restraining agencies and restrictive measures brought to bear upon our youths, still the county and state prisons and government farms are continuously being filled with our young men while we make no general attack upon saloons.[8]

"On behalf of humanity and the general good of all," Jackson called on everyone to make sure that "no saloon will be allowed to be opened . . . on Nelson Street."[9] In fact, the earliest conception of Black Main Street in Greenville was "clean and respectable and a safe and convenient harbor for women."[10] Due to racial segregation, the Black business districts in Mississippi soon suffered from an unsavory reputation that stood in stark contrast to the respectable businesses of segregated, white Main Street. Rev. Jackson and his allies objected to the opening of saloons but, due to racial segregation in Greenville and the disfranchisement of most Black citizens, African Americans had no power to stop the opening of such establishments in the heart of the Black community. By permitting taverns and watering holes to set up shop so close to the doors of many schoolhouses and churches, the city rendered futile the efforts to guide African American youths away from the various forms of vice that increasingly became associated with Black Main Street.

The saloons and clubs on Nelson Street rose in conjunction with the opening of brothels on Blanton Street, and the conspicuous presence of prostitutes, many of whom serviced an exclusive white clientele.[11] The brothels on Blanton Street (changed to North Street after 1910 at the request of the Blanton family)[12] conducted a brisk business in the notorious red-light district of Greenville, where all prostitutes had to get a health certificate each week.[13] The bawdy houses were supplied with alcohol from surrounding saloons, and on some nights each of the brothels might entertain more than one hundred randy clients. "On Sundays," one local complained, "these places fairly run over with the men and boys of our town, drinking and carousing." Though absent from the thorough-fares leading to the depots and steamboat landings, "where decent people are compelled to pass at all hours," the "houses of prostitution" served as much more than a place where men could quench their sexual appetites.[14]

The red-light district also allowed its white patrons to propagate lies about Black women's inherent sexual inclinations and indiscriminate tastes. The hedonistic stereotype of the "Jezebel," a sexually insatiable temptress, had its roots in the antebellum South, when slave owners auctioned off and bred Black women, who had no control over their own bodies, to maximize profits. "Emancipation did not end the social and political usefulness of this stereotype," argues historian Melissa Harris-Perry, who succinctly points out that "access to Black women's bodies was an assumption supported both by their history as legal property and by the myth of their sexual promiscuity."[15] The sexual temptress, indeed, was not the only negative stereotype attached to Black women, but it served as a powerful promotional device for Greenville's brothels—savage, wild animals of lust, ready to go anyplace, anytime, with anyone.[16] The hardening of racial stereotypes at the end of the nineteenth century projected clear messages about Black women to white men—telling them, since they are all prostitutes, "it is all right to solicit Black women and girls for sex." It also sent unambiguous messages to Black women—saying, "this is how it is," white men can rape you; "this is who you are," a whore; "this is what you're for," satiating the sexual desires of white men.[17]

Historian Danielle McGuire has recently examined sexualized violence and the defense of Black womanhood in the South and found it served as a catalyst in the Black freedom struggle. The unpunished rape of Black women—in many ways similar to lynching—functioned as both a psychological and physical tool of intimidation, which buttressed male domination as well as white supremacy. And yet, sexualized violence has yet to be included in the history of the Black freedom struggle. McGuire's recent study "At the Dark End of the Street" argues that white males used sex as a weapon of terror not only to undermine the Black freedom struggle but also to maintain both white privilege and the power to control access to Black and white women's bodies.[18]

The old-red light district along Blanton Street ran into Nelson Street, the Black business section where African Americans "made their way until segregation ended," or what Wilmoth Carter called "Negro Main Street." The same reasons that gave rise to the segregation of sound gave rise to what some locals once referred to as "the Black Wall Street of Greenville, Mississippi."[19] Not only did racial segregation dictate the nature of life in Greenville, Mississippi; it briefly impelled the rise of some of the richest Black men in the country. In Greenville, the Black bourgeois held dances at the Knights of Pythias Hall, located on Nelson and Cately Street, as well as Casa Calvo, a two-story venue located on the corner of Redbud and Nelson. George Neil operated the Royal Palm Theatre on Nelson, which catered to "the colored people of the better class."[20] In addition to a "picture show," the Royal Palm Theatre sponsored dances, and the city turned into a regular stop for many travelling minstrels show. The Silas Green Minstrel Show was a local favorite, but there were several other popular shows, such as Sugar Foot Green Minstrels, Rabbit Foot Minstrels, Huntington Minstrels, Alabama Minstrels, and the minstrel show of A.G. Allen.[21] As early as 1875, minstrel entertainers held benefit concerts in Greenville for the instrument purchases of the brass band, who had "spent their money and time for our benefit in perfecting themselves in music, and will soon make up a band that will be a pride to the town."[22]

Greenville offered plenty of work for several local and popular Black musicians in the early twentieth century. Ed Gray was one of the most consistent among the local musicians who had a band.[23] He continued to perform in later years as part of Wynchester Davis's orchestra.[24] A "little low fellow" named George "Rabbit" McMillan was the leader of a local band that performed for dances in the white and Black community.[25] "Rabbit," as local drummer John Johnson recalled, "could play a violin and mandolin, banjo, guitar, [and] trombone; he was a whole band."[26] Despite the proficient musical ability of McMillan, his past is more obscure than most. We found a serious dearth of information on McMillan.

We now know quite a bit about Prince Albert McCoy, who led a popular seven-piece orchestra in Greenville during the 1920s, and also played the violin at classical music recitals in Vicksburg. He would be heard performing such songs as "Brown Skin," "Walkin' the Dog," and "Way Down in Arkansas" with his band in the Queen City, but he has recently been ascribed a new significance in the early annals of blues history.[27] In the 1941 autobiographical account of his "enlightenment'" at Cleveland, W. C. Handy tells the story of a ragged local string band getting showered with money after his professional orchestra failed to excite the crowd. After fifteen years of research on Handy, music historian Elliot Hurwitt located four early manuscripts of *Father of the Blues*, in which Handy identified the leader of the trio as Prince McCoy.[28] The book went to press, however, without the name of McCoy, who never received public recognition for his role in inspiring Handy. In an early manuscript of his book *Father of the Blues*, Handy admitted:

> My own enlightenment came in Cleveland, Mississippi. I was conducting the orchestra in a dance program when someone sent up an odd request. Would we play some of "our native music" . . . later a second request came up. Would we object if a local colored band played a few dances? . . . We eased out gracefully as the newcomers entered. They were led by a long-legged chocolate boy called *Prince McCoy*, and their band consisted of just three pieces, a battered guitar, a mandolin and a bass. The musicians themselves were a sorry lot . . . They struck up one of those over-and-over strains . . . the kind of stuff that has long been associated with cane rows and levee camps . . . A rain of silver dollars began to fall around the outlandish, stomping feet. The dancers went wild . . . These boys had the stuff the people wanted . . . Folks would pay money for it . . . That night a composer was born, an American composer. Those country black boys at Cleveland had taught me something . . . My inspiration came from the sight of that silver money.[29]

Even though Hurwitt is skeptical of the assertion that McCoy led the string band that evening in Cleveland, arguing that he was not a "poor, illiterate musician" but rather the leader of a respectable brass band, a closer examination of McCoy's life and music career leaves little doubt that he was the bandleader of the three-piece. Born March 19, 1882, McCoy had moved to Greenville with his widowed mother Lettie Henderson and started working as a porter by 1900.[30] Considering that his mother married sharecropper Richard Harris and moved to Beat 5 of Bolivar County sometime after the turn of the twentieth century, it stands to reason that McCoy may have come with them, if only for a little while.[31] His job as a railroad porter was pretty good compared to sharecropping, and it put McCoy right in the heart of the Delta music scene at that time. After all, a picture of the Delta during the time that Handy spent there "would be incomplete without the footloose bards and the blind singers that were forever coming and going . . . Some came sauntering down the railroad tracks, others dropped from freight cars, while still others caught a ride on the big road and entered town on the top of cotton bales. A favorite hangout for them was the railroad station. There, surrounded by crowds of country folks, they would pour out their hearts in songs while the audience ate fish and bread, chewed sugar cane, dipped snuff while waiting for trains to carry them down the lines."[32]

Considering he worked for the railroad, his work did not demand his continued residence in Greenville.[33] McCoy was, therefore, free to become the leader of the three-piece string band, featuring mandolin, guitar, and bass viol, which showed up in the Bolivar County seat and schooled the classically trained musician and then rookie songwriter from Florence, Alabama.

Hurwitt bases his argument on the misconception that African American musicians, who performed highbrow orchestral music, simply would not perform "native" string band music. He also fails to consider that McCoy received little to no publicity as an orchestra leader until the mid-1910s. The earliest reference to McCoy in the newspaper was the *Vicksburg Herald* in 1909; the article referred to his group as "Prince's band," and it tells us that the band was renowned for its performances in the Delta.

McCoy started his music career in a string band. After cultivating his talents and receiving some inspiration while watching the performances of Handy's orchestra in Cleveland, McCoy eventually left the string band world behind to start his own, larger brass band in Greenville. Several respected and versatile Black musicians, such as "Rabbit" McMillan and "Uncle" Bob Johnson, a blind musician who busked on Nelson Street, had learned to play most "any kind of musical instrument commonly known" while living in the Delta. Johnson was especially good on the piano and guitar, but he could play the saxophone and some wind instruments.[34] Leon "Pee Wee" Whitaker, who was much younger yet lived in the same town as McCoy, learned how to read music and play the guitar, string bass, mandolin, clarinet, and trombone during his time at Alcorn State University (then Alcorn State College) outside Lorman, Mississippi. He played the string bass in Tulius Washington's band while in Greenville, but he later became known as a trombone player.[35] Similar to Whitaker and other versatile musicians based in Greenville, McCoy may have even joined a traveling minstrel show, and later returned to Greenville to find musicians and put together an orchestra. At some point he became a bandleader, leading an orchestra that played dances, civic functions, and even the Alabama–Ole Miss football game in 1910.

McCoy does not start showing up in the newspaper as performing with his orchestra until the mid-1910s. On August 10, 1916, Prince McCoy and his "band of musicians rendered much assistance to the success" of the meeting of the Working Men's Democratic Club, of Greenville.[36] His World War I registration card from September 11, 1918, lists his occupation as a professional "musician" in "Princes Orchestra."[37] Prince's Orchestra, composed of seven pieces, performed a benefit concert for the Red Cross at the Kandy Kitchen in June 1918.

Prince's Orchestra managed to raise over twelve dollars at the Kandy Kitchen. After taking up the collection in a little prepared box for the occasion, he promptly turned the contents over to the Red Cross.[38]

The historiographical consensus holds that the Black community on the home front was ambivalent in its attitudes during World War I. The absurdity of a nation fighting for democracy abroad while not practicing it at home or in the military was not lost on America's Black communities. Their leaders, however, believed that full Black participation in America's wars was a prerequisite for full citizenship. This created a tension between Black leaders and their followers, which they tried to resolve through criticizing racism and tyranny at home and in the military while encouraging Blacks to fight against it abroad. While this strategy served as the ideological foundation of the prominent Double V program of World War II, it was no doubt also practiced, albeit covertly, during World War I, which led to the federal government branding the Black press as a subversive element of the radical Left, certainly making it a target of investigation and suppression. Some historians contend that the early underground campaigns failed to reconcile the rift between the Black community and its leaders, and did not radicalize African Americans to ramp up the civil rights movement. In his words, "It substituted militant rhetoric for its lack of innovative direction."[39]

McCoy acquired quite a popular reputation in the region and managed to sustain it until the

Prince McCoy is the tallest in the photo and is wearing glasses. Photo courtesy Wake Forest School of Medicine Coy C. Carpenter Library/ Dorothy Carpenter Archives publications collection, Winston-Salem, North Carolina *Baptist Hospital News*, January 1951.

Great Flood of 1927, at which time he, along with tens of thousands of other African Americans, fled the inundated Queen City. Unlike most folks who migrated to Chicago and Detroit, McCoy moved to North Carolina, where he married Carry Young of Chester County, South Carolina, and continued working as a musician in Winston-Salem.[40]

McCoy and his wife first show up in the city directory in 1934, where he listed his occupation as a musician, living on East Eighth Street. In 2017 blues researcher Jim O'Neal located an advertisement in Boston, Massachusetts, that linked Prince McCoy to the musicians who traveled with Maxey's Medicine Show. O'Neal claims that he started playing with an eight-piece orchestra that traveled with Maxey's Medicine Show in the late 1920s. "This was a big show on the scale of the larger minstrel shows with a fleet of vehicles carrying people around," O'Neal said. "It was a free show, and Maxey would make his money trying to sell tonics to the crowd." Haywood Bates Maxey, of Owensboro, Kentucky, founded Maxey's Medicine Show. His father, Augustus G. Maxey, had made a name for himself as a maker of medicine in the late nineteenth century. Maxey's Medicines were advertised in Owensboro as early as 1888 in the local newspaper, and A. G. Maxey is listed in the 1890s as a preparer of medicine in the city directory. Though his father did invent and patent a portable scaffold in 1904, the patent medicine

business seems to have been only one of the many elaborate confidence schemes perpetrated by the Maxey family over the years.[41] Haywood Maxey was the manager of amateur athletic contests at the Wonderland Theatre.[42] In the winter of 1909, Haywood and his father were indicted for setting up a game of chance by the operation of a wheel of fortune at the county fair.[43] Haywood Maxey worked as a traveling salesman in the 1910s, but he returned home to Owensboro by 1920, where one census enumerator found him and his brother working as painters. At some point, the Maxey brothers took to the road and began spending their winters on Miami Beach.

Around 1943 McCoy put down his music as a professional pursuit and took a job as a janitor for the Bowman Gray School of Medicine, a position he held for several years. In 2017, we allowed Jim O'Neal, an investigator with the Mississippi Blues Trail, to use our research while writing the text for the marker of McCoy. Looking for information on McCoy, O'Neal contacted the *Winston-Salem Journal*, hoping readers might provide some information on McCoy or unearth a photograph. A librarian at Wake Forest Baptist Medical Center's Coy C. Carpenter Library flipped through stacks of company newsletters in search of McCoy and came across a photo from the January 1951 edition of *Baptist Hospital News*.

Black men and women crowded the frame of a hospital Christmas party. Two women stand in front of a punch bowl, holiday trimmings at its base. A bald, bespectacled man towers over the crowd, a violin case tucked under his left arm, indicating he had been part of the party's music program. He is, indeed, long-legged. The caption for the photo identifies him as someone who "proved his ability as a violinist for the occasion." It was McCoy.

In October 2017, the state of Mississippi erected a Blues Trail marker for McCoy in downtown Greenville, Mississippi—on the same day the photograph and the story ran in the *Journal*. The photograph stirred the memories of a local African American woman named Alma Peay. She was only a little girl of perhaps five years old when she lived next to Prince McCoy in a duplex between Patterson Avenue and Chestnut Street in the 1950s. Her memories of him, therefore, were admittedly somewhat hazy, but when she saw the picture of that tall, bespectacled man that ran in the *Winston-Salem Journal*, it brought some clarity to her memories. She remembered him as being quiet and kind. More importantly, Peay exclaimed, "I remember him playing fiddle!" She recalled that the tall, soft-spoken man used to play his violin on the front porch of the duplex that the McCoys lived in, next to Peay and her mother and grandparents. The McCoys and the Peays attended First Baptist Church, then on the corner of Sixth and Chestnut streets. In December 2017, Peay viewed a film that someone in the church made to commemorate the groundbreaking of its new home on Highland Avenue. The remarkable footage was shot on January 26, 1947, and it shows streams of churchgoers in long coats and hats, dressed in their Sunday finest on a cold and misty winter day. The sharp-eyed Peay spotted McCoy, playing in a small orchestra outside the site of the new church, a violin propped against his chin. Unfortunately, there is no sound to the footage. As she watched people file out of the church and onto the sidewalk, she pointed to the ones that she knew. When the camera panned to McCoy, Peay identified the young clarinet player in front of him as Christine Hedgley, the daughter of the church's pastor at the time, Rev. David Hedgley. She is now Christine Hedgley Johnson, who lives in

Prince McCoy's gravesite. Photo by T. DeWayne Moore.

Santa Fe, New Mexico, after a long career with the US Public Health Commissioned Corps. In the film, she was about eleven years old and was a student at 14th Street Elementary School.

"In the Black community at that time, if you played an instrument in the school band, you automatically played in the church band," Johnson explained last month. She knew McCoy as a reserved man who played jazz gigs with local Black musicians, including Harry Wheeler, a legendary band director at the old Atkins High School. "Most of his music was outside the church. White people paid for him and his band to play gigs, their graduations and receptions and stuff like that," Johnson stated. "He did a lot of music for the doctors when they had receptions and Christmas parties."

Late in life, he moved to Blair's Rest Home on East Fourth Street in Winston-Salem, and died on February 4, 1968, at the age of eighty-five. He and Carry, who died in 1962 at the age of sixty-two, had no children, and no relatives have been found. McCoy is buried at Evergreen Cemetery off New Walkertown Road in Winston-Salem, his simple, nondescript grave marker engraved with the words: Prince McCoy, 1882–1968.

Frank Wharton (1823–1893)

Fiddler Frank Wharton, "An old and well-known colored fiddler of this city"[44] who died in September

1893, may be the last African American buried in the Jackson city cemetery before the white racial attitudes pressured the mayor into purchasing lots for the establishment of a completely segregated cemetery, which became the Mt. Carmel Cemetery, now on the list of the National Historic Register of Places. For many years before the war, Wharton was a servant for the family of Judge Wharton. Frank Wharton, age seventy, died of hemorrhage, and was buried in the city cemetery on September 24, 1893.[45]

—T. DeWayne Moore

NOTES

1. *Hinds County Gazette*, January 14, 1874.

2. Bolick and Austin, Mississippi Fiddle Tunes and Songs from the 1930s, 42–56.

3. Association for Cultural Equity, Alan Lomax Collection–DVD 199, The Blues Archive at the University of Mississippi.

4. Lawrence Cohn, ed., *Nothing But the Blues: The Music and the Musicians* (New York: Abbeville Press, 1993), 82.

5. Tom Mazzolini, "Living Blues Interview: K.C. Douglas," *Living Blues* 15 (Winter 1973–74): 15.

6. K.C. Douglas, interview by Axel Kustner, Berkeley, California, August 15, 1972.

7. "Adam Jackson," 1910 US Census, Beat 5, Washington, Mississippi; Roll: T624_763; Page: 8A; Enumeration District:0129; FHL microfilm: 1374776.

8. Rev. Adam Jackson, "Don't Want Saloon: Appeal to Not Establish One at New Town," *Greenville Times*, May 10, 1902, 1.

9. Rev. Adam Jackson, "Don't Want Saloon: Appeal to Not Establish One at New Town," *Greenville Times*, May 10, 1902, 1.

10. Wilmoth A. Carter, "Negro Main Street as a Symbol of Discrimination," *Phylon* (Fall 1960): 237.

11. Levye Chapple Sr. et al., *History of Blacks in Greenville, Mississippi, 1868–1975* (Greenville, MS: Greenville Travel Club, 1975), 2.

12. Ben Wasson, "Crescent City Remembered," *Delta Democrat Times* (Greenville, MS), May 29, 1977, 13.

13. Salvadore Signa, interview by Roberta Miller, December 1, 1976, Washington County Library System Oral History Project: Greenville and Vicinity.

14. *Greenville Times*, July 22, 1905, 1.

15. Karn Williams, review of *Sister Citizen: Shame, Stereotypes, and Black Women in America*, by Melissa V. Harris-Perry, *African American Red Star* (Washington, DC), September 24, 2011, C8.

16. Patricia Hill Collins, *Black Feminist Thought: Knowledge, Consciousness, and the Politics of Empowerment* (Boston: Unwin Hyman, 1991), 21–30.

17. Jessica Spector, *Prostitution and Pornography: Philosophical Debate about the Sex Industry* (Stanford, CA: Stanford University Press, 2006), 20.

18. Danielle L. McGuire, "At The Dark End of the Street: Sexualized Violence, Community Mobilization, and the African-American Freedom Struggle," diss., Rutgers University, 2007.

19. Dr. L. Jordan Jackson, *Triggering the Memories* (Bloomington, IN: Xlibris, 2012), 52; Wilmoth A. Carter, "Negro Main Street as a Symbol of Discrimination," *Phylon* (Fall 1960): 237.

20. "Royal Palm to Open," *Delta Democrat Times* (Greenville, MS), April 9, 1915, 8.

21. John W. Johnson, interview with Roberta Miller, April 28, 1977, Mississippi Department of Archives and History and Washington County Library System Oral History Project: Greenville and Vicinity, 101–6.

22. *Greenville Times*, September 4, 1875, 3.

23. From 1920 to 1940, the census lists the occupation of Ed Gray as a "musician" working on his own account. At the age of sixty, he added "amusement" as his business; see 1940 US Census, Greenville, Washington, Mississippi; Roll: T627_2075; Page: 1A; Enumeration District: 76–17A.

24. Winchester Davis, interview with Daisy Greene, January 1977, MDAH and Washington County Library System Oral History Project: Greenville and Vicinity.

25. One census enumerator listed George McMillan as a musician in 1920; see, 1920 US Census, Greenville, Washington, Mississippi; Roll: T625_899; Page: 28B; Enumeration District: 149; Image: 228.

26. John W. Johnson, interview with Roberta Miller, April 28, 1977, MDAH and Washington County Library System Oral History Project: Greenville and Vicinity, 101–6.

27. Brodie Crump, "Mostly Old Stuff," *Delta Democrat Times* (Greenville, MS), May 2, 1951, 6.

28. Stephen A. King, *I'm Feeling the Blues Right Now: Blues Tourism and the Mississippi Delta* (Jackson: University Press of Mississippi, 2011), 84–85.

29. Some of the wording was changed in the 1941 publication, most notably the omission of McCoy's name.

30. Prince McCoy lived with his mother Lettie Henderson; see 1900 US Census, Greenville, Washington, Mississippi; Roll: 832; Page: 13A; Enumeration District:0081; FHL microfilm: 1240832.

31. According to census taker Arnold Pye, who enumerated seventy-six-year-old Richard and forty-three-year-old Lottie Harris, as well as his six-year-old granddaughter Norlee Cosey, on a farm in Beat 5 on April 20, 1910, the couple had been married for five years; see 1910 US Census Place: Beat 5, Bolivar, Mississippi; Roll: T624_733; Page: 3B; Enumeration District: 0022; FHL microfilm: 1374746.

32. Handy, *The Father of the Blues* (New York: Da Capo Press, 1941), 87.

33. Before World War I, African American railroad workers in the South constituted a large majority of menial positions in the industry. Despite the fact that promotions on the railways centered almost exclusively upon seniority, Blacks were largely ineligible for promotions and often received lower pay than white men who did the same work. Black railroad workers, therefore, soon became the pawns in the chess game between big business and organized labor. Railroads hired more Blacks to fight unions and depress wages, while unions retaliated by limiting their recruitment or driving those already employed from the railroads. "The Negro in the Railway Unions," *Phylon* 5, no. 2 (2nd Qtr. 1944): 159–64.

34. "Uncle Bob Totally Blind," *Delta Democrat Times* (Greenville, MS), November 13, 1937, 1.

35. Lynn Abbot and Doug Seroff, *Ragged but Right: Black Traveling Shows, "Coon Songs," and the Dark Pathway to Blues and Jazz* (Jackson: University Press of Mississippi, 2009), 281–82.

36. *Weekly Democrat* (Greenville, MS), August 10, 1916, 5.

37. "Prince McCoy," US World War I Draft Registration Cards, 1917–1918, Ancestry.com, 2005.

38. "Patriotic Musicians Red Cross Helpers," *Delta Democrat Times*, June 6, 1918, 1.

39. Lee Finkle, *Forum for Protest: The Black Press during World War II* (Vancouver, BC: Fairleigh Dickinson University Press, 1975).

40. Prince McCoy married Carry Young on November 22, 1927, in Forsyth County, North Carolina; see North Carolina, Marriage Records, 1741–2011, Ancestry.com, 2015; Prince and Carry McCoy lived at 205 East 8th Street in 1934: see U.S. City Directories, 1822–1995, Ancestry.com, 2011.

41. "To Extend Patent," *Messenger Inquirer* (Owensboro, KY), June 26, 1904.

42. *Messenger Inquirer* (Owensboro, KY), May 30, 1909.

43. *Messenger Inquirer* (Owensboro, KY), December 17, 1909.

44. *Clarion-Ledger*, Jackson, MS, September 28, 1893, 8.

45. *Clarion-Ledger*, Jackson, MS, October 21, 1893, 3.

ABOUT THE MUSIC

Actual recordings for most of the transcriptions in this book can and should be heard before attempting to learn one of these tunes from notation. There is much that notation is poor at conveying. Subtle shadings of pitch and timing easily apprehended by ear can be quite dense on the written page. Please see Appendix A to locate sources for these tunes. Recordings of tunes from Tim Avalon, Enos Canoy, "Jabe" Dillon, Jerry Prescott, and Claude Kennedy, supplied by the fiddlers or their families, are posted for free download at harrybolick.com/mississippi-music/field-recordings.

Footnotes for each tune contain comments about the performer or performance notated, bits of information about the recording, and a short list of comparable recordings. The list is included to give a sense of history and place to the tune, but more importantly, to reference common melodic phrases. It is useful to know, for example, the B part of a "new" tune is identical or similar to an already learned tune. If the phrase is identical, less work is needed to absorb the new tune. If the phrase is only similar, attention will need to be paid to its differences so that confusion can be avoided.

If you are intrigued by tune comparisons, Andy Kuntz's detailed articles on tune history in *Fiddler* magazine and his website, the Traditional Tune Archive; Samuel Bayard's books; and Gus Meade's encyclopedic work *Country Music Sources* should all be of interest. These are listed in Appendix A.

Unless the footnotes indicate an alternate tuning, all fiddles and mandolins were tuned (low to high) GDAE. See Appendix B for an index of tunes listed by tuning, key, and meter.

Unlike our previous book *Mississippi Fiddle Tunes and Songs from the 1930s*, most of the transcriptions included here are band recordings with at least a guitarist. For accompanied tunes I have indicated the chords as played on the recording. In most cases the guitarist would play the tonic note of the chord on the downbeat and strum the chord on the upbeat. For some tunes, the guitarist would alternate playing the tonic with the fifth note of the scale on the downbeat. This is standard practice throughout the South. However, for tunes that that have an uneven number of beats, this approach can create problems. Unless the guitar part is written out, I suggest beginning to play a guitar accompaniment without an alternating bass note on the downbeat. Shell Smith of the Narmour and Smith recordings is the master for this approach. This approach sounds primitive but frees the fiddler to syncopate heavily.

Other guitarists play a string of bass runs, mixed with the occasional chord strum. If I have not written out the guitar part, then the bass runs suggest the chord changes indicated. Jimmie Carter of Carter Brothers and Son had an extreme case of guitar "runs" almost doubling the fiddle melody and not defining the chords. In some tunes, there are no chord changes; the tonic chord is played throughout. "Jabe" Dillon's virtuoso compositions are all in one chord.

Slurs, indicated where the lead instrument is a mandolin, should be played as "hammer-ons." On fiddle they indicate that the slurred notes are played with one bow stroke.

Determining the original keys that the fiddlers used to finger these tunes is difficult. The fiddle could have been tuned high or low, the recording speed or playback speed may not have been standard, and in some cases I have needed to work from a copy of a copy. Some of the recordings are of quite low fidelity and obscure the ability to hear bowing and string crossings, which could confirm the key. Moreover, in the revival era some tunes such as "Sullivan's Hollow" are usually played in keys that careful listening suggests are not what the source played. In some cases, listening to the guitar is helpful in determining the key; however, with the common practice of fingering in the keys of C and G and using a capo to pitch the guitar to D and A, it is of limited help. Where I have been uncertain as to the key, I have placed the tune in the more common keys of C, D, G, and A. When a fiddle is tuned low but the strings are in the relationship of AEAE or GDGD, I have written the tune in the key of A.

In counting fiddle tunes, my practice is to have my foot tap the floor twice per measure. In effect, I think in 2/4. Most of the time my foot would fall off if I attempted to tap four beats to a measure. However I have transcribed most of the tunes in 4/4 to make them more inviting to read.

Many fiddlers anticipate a downbeat by starting a note somewhere in beat 4 of the preceding measure. When this is quite exaggerated, I have written the note in the preceding measure. In most cases I have indicated this common stylistic habit with grace notes within the measure, leaving it to the reader to interpret after referring to the original recording.

Where a fiddler varies a phrase in some limited fashion, I have indicated "alt" measures at the end

of the notation. When the variations are more extensive, I have written out the entire passage. In the case of several of "Jabe" Dillon's tunes for example, I transcribed every note on the recording.

While I have listened and transcribed each tune to the best of my ability, I must gratefully acknowledge that Ken Bloom reviewed every tune, correcting errors and greatly enhancing the quality of the transcriptions. Any remaining errors in transcription are mine.

—Harry Bolick

THE MUSICIANS
AND THE MUSIC

Photo courtesy of John Anderson, 2018.

JOHN ANDERSON

John Anderson (1955–) took up banjo at age nine, starting out in the Scruggs style, but upon hearing local banjo players, became fascinated with the older styles. On Saturdays, from age eleven through fifteen, Anderson accompanied and later drove his father on his rounds as he visited small country stores to collect for newspaper subscriptions. These stores would carry most if not all of the commodities that one would need, all in around four hundred square feet. There would be a gas pump and a porch out front, where musicians gathered, seldom more than two at a time. They would be mostly banjo or guitarists in their seventies or older, playing for their own amusement. Invariably they played solo, whether playing an old tune or something they recently learned from the radio. As John was quite young, and the old musicians tended to be close-mouthed, he only knew most of them by the name of "Mr." The musicians lived in the nearby towns of Brooksville, Gholson, Lauderdale, Louisville, Macon, Noxapater, and Shuqualak.

After his father's paper collections ended, and until he left for college at eighteen, John continued to visit the country stores and other music venues such as barbeques and fish fries, to hear and learn the local old-time music and banjo styles. At one nearly identical country store for African Americans, right across the street from a "white" country store near his grandmother's house, older musicians would play together, usually guitar and occasionally banjo. In both Black and white communities, fiddlers at that time were rare. In earlier generations, they had been abundant. The musicians, Black and white, did not play together and would have been unwelcome in each other's stores. However, Anderson was easily able to hear and learn from the African American musicians just across the street. He described the music of the oldest musicians, two of whom played banjo, as being very similar, many of the same tunes, the same instruments, both playing in the old-time genre but with the African Americans playing a less melodic style with more complex rhythms.

John's great grandfather, Cyrus Gee Thompson, was a well-known Noxubee fiddler who also played guitar and banjo. Cyrus Gee's father, Cyrus Y. Thompson, reportedly also played fiddle. John's great-uncle Frank Thompson played banjo, mandolin, and guitar and was the initial inspiration for John's banjo style. In John's travels within Mississippi and Louisiana, he found that Frank's banjo style seemed to be confined to Noxubee County. Many of Frank's tunes have the banjo tuned in the key of F. John suspected the reason that Frank played in F was because his guitar and mandolin-playing brothers found it difficult to play in that key. In this way, he was able to play solo.

In addition to common clawhammer and two- and three-finger up-picking styles, Anderson plays in a complex banjo style, which combines clawhammer with two-finger up-picking, which he learned by listening closely to these local musicians. This was a common solo style in Noxubee County region, but he has never encountered it elsewhere. His one banjo "lesson" came from his uncle Frank. John had just gotten his first, inexpensive banjo from a store in Columbus and was sitting on the back porch playing it in the Scruggs style. Uncle Frank stood nearby and watched for a long time. Then he took the banjo, retuned it and played "Sally Ann." He handed it back and said, "Play it like that." John would have to just listen and either "get it" or not.

John has been described as "never playing a tune the same way once." Like most of the older musicians from whom he learned, he will play the basic melody on the first pass, but subsequent iterations of the tune will contain subtle melodic variation and may add or subtract beats, which can make his playing difficult to accompany, but adds interest to his solo playing.

When he was learning, tape recorders were not cheap and would probably not have been allowed by the older musicians, so he has no recordings of his sources. He recalls that there were no definitive regional versions of the common tunes. Each player had his own version. However, when the tune was recent, for example, learned from the radio, it would vary little from the radio version. Waltzes were common in the local repertoire even on banjo. The local tunes were originally dance tunes but, due to the overwhelming Baptist influence, dancing and music for dancing was rare among the old musicians, although popular with the younger generations.

Common tunes in both Black and white repertoires were "Cindy," "John Henry," "Noxapater Stomp," "Fatback and Dumplings," "Possum on a Stump"; minstrel show tunes like "Jawbone," and a few "Creole" or Cajun tunes such as "J'ai Passé," "Port Arthur Blues," and "Jolie Blon." In this area, only "Sullivan's Hollow" and "Charleston #1" seem to have been learned from the classic Mississippi string band 78 rpm recordings.

The most common banjo tuning when John was listening and learning from the local banjo players was C tuning (G-CGBD–from the fifth string to the first string). Other tunings used in the area were F (F=CFCD), G (G=DGBD), G (G=GDGD), "G modal or sawmill" (G=DGCD), D (F#=BEAD), D (F#=DF#AD), and Dm (F=DFAD).

Fish fries and the country store porches constituted the main places for old-time music. Anderson was unaware of any fiddle contests in the vicinity. He recalls one banjo contest, at a junior college in Scooba, Mississippi, where a child playing Scruggs style won first place. John placed second. Acknowledging that Anderson played old-time, one of the judges asked him, "What do you want to do that for?"

There were also many ballad singers in the area. Anderson's great-aunt, Lilly Morgan, occasionally sang the classic words for the Child ballad "Little Margaret" under the title of "Little Maggie" and used a different melody. She sang other ballads, including "Barbara Allen."

John was born August 26, 1955, in San Antonio, Texas. His father was in the Air Force and moves followed: first the Philippines, then to Virginia, and then to Macon, Mississippi, around the time John was six. John went to Mississippi State University on an Air Force scholarship, studying electrical engineering. In 1977 he married Lora Resh and was commissioned a second lieutenant in the Air Force. He was assigned to San Antonio, Texas; Dayton, Ohio; Melbourne, Florida; and lastly in Albuquerque, New Mexico, where he retired from the Air Force and remains, working as an optical engineer and program manager.

Throughout the moves and years John continued to play music for himself. He never pursued gigs or joined a band. Banjo is his primary instrument but he also plays guitar, fiddle, mandolin, and dulcimer.

Anderson's early repertoire from Noxubee and Kemper counties:

Ash Tree
Caledonia (Bonaparte Crossing the Rhine)
Cindy
Fatback and Dumplings (three parts)

Grub Springs

J'ai Passé

Tombigbee Waltz

John Henry

Lake Pontchartrain Waltz

Little Margaret (Little Maggie)

Loch Lomond

Magnolia Waltz (unlike the Leake County Revelers
  version)

Macdonald's Reel (Leather Britches)

Mole in the Ground

Nancy Roland

Parting Waltz

Natchez Under the Hill

Noxapater Stomp

Possum on a Rail

Possum on a Stump

Ragged Old Bill

Sally Ann

Sally in the Garden

Spanish Fandango

Sullivan's Hollow

—Harry Bolick

This chapter is based on June 30, 2015, August 14, 2016, and December 27, 2017, phone interviews with John Anderson by the author, and October 23, 2016, Albuquerque, New Mexico, interview with author.

Recordings

Examples of John Anderson's playing can be seen and heard at mississippifiddle.com. Video examples from the SW Picker's Festival 2015 that can be seen at youtube.com: "Fatback and Dumplings," "Grand Texas," "Tombigbee Waltz," "Grub Springs," and "Possum Up a Gum Stump."

Fatback and Dumplings

Harry Bolick

Author's note: To aid my transcriptions, John played these tunes for me on fiddle instead of his usual banjo versions, which are more fluid and varied. See mississippifiddle.com for links to youtube.com video of his impressive banjo playing.

Comparable versions:
"Texas Gals," The Hill Billies, 10/22/1926, New York, Columbia 15435-D

Grub Springs

Harry Bolick

Author's note: John played this at the 41st annual SW Picker's Fiddle Contest, August 30, 2015, Santa Fe, New Mexico, in cross-key tuned down one step to G. I've notated it in A modal to match his fingering. A and B parts are labeled on first pass, subsequent passes of the melody show Anderson's flair for exploring the tune.

John said, "it's the same tune recorded by John Hatcher, but a little different version. It's the way everyone played it in the Gholson/Louisville/DeKalb area, in or near Kemper County, so I just called it the Kemper County version. I don't know what other versions there are, other than Hatcher's, which always sounded a bit crude to me."

Comparable versions:

Bolick and Austin, *Mississippi Fiddle Tunes and Songs from the 1930s*: John Hatcher, "Grub Springs," 294; and W. E. Claunch, "Grub Springs," 262 (an unrelated melody of same name)

Magnolia Waltz

Author's note: Anderson plays this tune in the key of G on the fiddle and in F on the banjo.

Comparable versions: None known

Harry Bolick

Nancy Rowland

Author's note: Anderson plays this tune on the banjo in the key of F.

Some variations (1, 2, 3) are noted here in the third and fourth lines. He also plays the first part of the tune up an octave with similar variations. Each pass through the tune has the standard eight-measure structure, with no added or subtracted beats. This version has little in common with the Carter Brothers' version.

Comparable versions:

In this book: "Nancy Rowland," Carter Brothers & Son, 11/22/1928, Memphis, TN, Vocalion 5349

"Nancy Rowland," Fiddlin' John Carson, 11/08/1923, New York, OKeh 40238

"Nancy Rowlin'," Gid Tanner & His Skillet Lickers, 10/22/1928, Atlanta, GA, Columbia 15382-D

Noxapater Stomp

alt for m7-8, with added m

Author's note: Played as noted the first time through, subsequent times use the three measure alt for M7–8. This is John's title for the tune; his sources did not call the tune "Noxapater Stomp," but John thinks it was from the Noxapater area, near Louis-ville, in Winston County.

Comparable versions:
The C part is very similar to the song, "Poor Howard Is Dead and Gone."
"Poor Howard," Leadbelly, *Negro Sinful Songs, sung by Leadbelly*, 1939, New York, Musicraft 225

Parting Waltz

Comparable versions: None known

John Anderson   [47]

Possum Up a Gum Stump

Author's note: Anderson plays this in standard tuning, tuned down a step.

Comparable versions:

"Village Hornpipe," White's Unique Collection (1896); No. 108

"Old Debuque," R. P. Christenson (from Bob Walters), *Old Time Fiddler's Repertory* vol. 1 (Columbia: University of Missouri, 2010), 65

"Duck River," John Salyer, Magoffin County, KY, 02/16/1941, Digital Library of Appalachia, https://dla.acaweb.org/

Tombigbee Waltz

Author's note: This is transcribed from Anderson's fiddle version.

Anderson said, "'Tombigbee Waltz' was a common tune but never under that title. The old musicians called it 'Miss Mary's Waltz,' 'Black River,' 'Coffeeville,' and a few others."

Comparable but loosely related versions:

"Gum Tree Canoe," George Reed, music and lyrics, 1847

"Gum Tree Canoe," Frank Crumit, 12/02/1929, New York, Victor 24091

Wolves a Howling

Author's note: Anderson plays this tuned GDGD in the key of G, but it is shown here in AEAE.

Comparable versions:
A part is similar to "Sourwood Mountain":
"Sourwood Mountain," Fiddlin' Powers & His Family, 08/18/1924, Camden, NJ, Victor 19448
"Sourwood Mountain," Gid Tanner & Riley Puckett, 09/10/1924, New York, Columbia 245-D

(Unrelated except by title to:)
Thede, Marion, *The Fiddle Book* (New York: Oak Publication, 1970), 133
Bolick and Austin, *Mississippi Fiddle Tunes and Songs from the 1930s*: John A. Brown, "Wolves a Howling," 235; W. E. Claunch,
    "Wolves a Howling," 279
"Wolves Howling," Stripling Brothers, 08/19/1929, Chicago, Vocalion 5412

Lyrics:

Can't you hear them wolves a howling
All round my poor little darling.
Two on the hillside, three in the hollar
They're gonna get you, bet you a dollar.
Sheep and hogs walking though the pasture
Sheep said hogs "walk a little faster."
Shut your mouth, stop your growling
Can't you hear them wolves a howling.

TIM AVALON

Tim Avalon, born December 7, 1955, is a full-time musician who was born and remains in Jackson, Mississippi. Music has been his sole profession.

Tim started to play the popular music of the day, on guitar, at about age thirteen. Around 1971, after hearing the album *Will the Circle Be Unbroken*, he began to play bluegrass on the banjo. Around 1980, at age twenty-five, he started to learn fiddle, mostly on standard tunes like "Boil Them Cabbage Down," "Faded Love," and "Soldier's Joy." About this time he began doing recording sessions as a sideman in a wide variety of genres and instruments, in his words on "pretty much anything with strings." He plays fiddle, electric and acoustic guitars, bass, mandolin, pedal steel, Dobro, and banjo. He learned bluegrass and old-time in his spare time. Some of the other genres he plays include a variety of rock styles, reggae, R&B, Irish, jazz standards, bluegrass, country, and singer-songwriter. Finding himself in situations where reading music notation was necessary, he took a couple semesters of classical violin in order to learn to read, hold the instrument correctly, and to play in tune. He also pointed out that "books are cheaper than records" when learning tunes.

For about ten years starting in 1980, Tim played in a mandolin and guitar duo, The Dawg Band, with Wayne Smith. When that band dissolved, Tim began

Tim Avalon, 2018. Photo by Mary Fitzgerald

to play fiddle on some old-timey music gigs with clawhammer banjoist Alvin Hudson. That pairing soon evolved into the string band Old Hat, adding Sandra Melsheimer on fiddle, Doug Webb on guitar, and Rhonda Turner on guitar. The band played for

The Old Hat String Band, 2003: Alvin Hudson, Sandra Melscheimer, Tim Avalon, and Rhonda Turner. Photo by Robert Gray.

weddings, family events, schools, concerts, and small local festivals such as the Catfish Festival, the Muscadine Festival, Port Gibson's festival, and Vicksburg's festival. They were listed in the Mississippi Arts Council's Artist Roster.

At one point, Old Hat was invited to the Sebastopol Opry, a once-a-month Thursday community concert in Sebastopol, Mississippi. Charles Gilmer arrived with Will Gilmer's fiddle, and Tim played it for the set. (Will Gilmer recorded with the Leake County Revelers in the 1930s.) Subsequently, Old Hat was invited to play for the Gilmer family reunion. Tim was able to borrow the Gilmer fiddle again to play some tunes on his *Rural* CD in 2005. (See mississippifiddle.com to download the tracks from the CD.) Old Hat also played for an event

for retired Mississippi senators with Senator and fiddler George C. McLeod in attendance. Then in his eighties, Senator McLeod played some of his tunes for them. Old Hat dissolved upon Alvin's death in 2006.

Alvin and Sandra Melsheimer started the Mississippi Old Time Music Society in 1996. The organization continues to organize Mississippi old-time music workshops, often with Tim teaching.

Tim's next local old-timey band, Hired Man's Horse, began around 2006, and included Tim, Susan Farley, Johnny Rawls, and Jamie Weems. The band lasted for about ten years playing the few gigs available. Current interest in performance of old-time fiddle music in Mississippi appears to be at a low-water mark.

In addition to his 2005 CD *Rural*, Tim was a member of Bounds Street, a traditional Irish band that issued two CDs, *Diaspora* and *Mary Morning Dew*. Old Hat had an informal home-produced demo, *Hats Off*.

Tim has appeared as a sideman on recordings since 1980, in his words "tons of 'em." Tim has been teaching since 1983. He self-published a tune book *Mississippi Echoes* in 2011.

—Harry Bolick

This chapter is based on a telephone interview by the author May 23, 2018.

Recordings

Rural, self-released CD, circa 2005

Big Eyed Rabbit

Author's note: Composed 06/09/2001.

Comparable versions: None known

Harry Bolick

Bill Tyler

Author's note: Composed 1/17/2017.

Comparable versions: None known

Billy Cochran

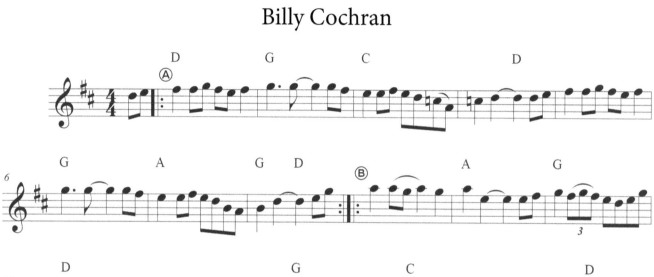

Author's note: Composed 2/25/2011.

Comparable versions: None known

Harry Bolick

Captain Waldo's Old Hat

Author' note: Composed 6/25/2001. After learning this fine tune from Tim, I felt compelled to learn about any others he had composed.

Comparable versions: None known

Lazy Cat

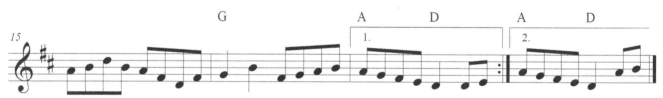

Author's note: Composed 03/17/2013.

Comparable versions: None known

Harry Bolick

Morning Crow

Author's note: Composed 12/27/2014.

Comparable versions: None known

My Honey by the Fire

Author's note: Composed 12/23/2011.

Comparable versions: None known

Harry Bolick

Pink Lady's Slipper

Author's note: Composed 12/25/2011.

Comparable versions: None known

MUMFORD BEAN AND HIS ITAWAMBIANS

Charles Mumford Bean (1913–1992) was born in Fulton, the largest town of Itawamba County in northeastern Mississippi. He learned banjo and fiddle from his father George, and about 1924 formed a string band with his distant cousins Clarence Relder Priddy (1917–1997) on mandolin and Morine Little (1910–2000) on guitar. Bean won the tri-county (Itawamba–Monroe–Lee) fiddlers' contest in 1925. The trio played over WELO, Tupelo on Saturday-night jamborees, and at dances, political rallies, and other functions. In February 1928 they made their only recordings, for OKeh at a location session in Memphis. Both issued tunes were waltzes, "Slow Time Waltz" and "Flow Rain Waltz," the latter a mistitling of "Florine Waltz" (also recorded in 1928, as "Floraine Waltz," by the Northlanders, a group from Birmingham, Alabama). "Downfall of Paris" and "A New Coon in Town" remained unissued.

Mumford Bean, 1970. Photo from collection of Tony Russell.

Band photo circa 1930. Photo from *Old Time Music* 20 (Spring 1976).

Within months of the recording session, George Bean, who managed the band, died, and the group broke up. In later years, Bean played occasionally with visiting bands, and after World War II formed a dance band of his own, which lasted a couple of years. In 1950 he moved to South Bend, Indiana, where the researcher Donald Lee Nelson contacted him in the early seventies and secured the first published information on this band.[1]

—Tony Russell

NOTES

1. Donald Lee Nelson, "OKeh 45303." *JEMF Quarterly* VIII:4, no. 28 (Winter 1972): 194–95.

Flow Rain Waltz

Author's note: This transcription is from OKeh 45303, recorded Memphis in 02/17/1928.

Comparable versions:
In this book: "Bouquets of June Waltz," W. T. Narmour & S. W. Smith, 06/07/1930, San Antonio, TX, OKeh 45480

Slow Time Waltz

Author's note: This transcription is from OKeh 45303, recorded Memphis in 02/17/1928. The first time through the high octave is played twice, followed by the low octave version, then the low octave plucked. After that the tune is played once through for each of the high, low, and plucked versions but in no particular order.

Comparable versions:
"Old Shoes and Leggins," Gavin Greig, *Folk-Song of the Northeast of Scotland*, vol. II, Peterhead, Scotland, 1909–14, #149
"Floraine Waltz," The Northlanders, 1928, Vocalion 5274
"There Was an Old Tramp," Henry Whitter, 08/1926 New York, Broadway 8024
"Old Shoes and Leggins," Uncle Eck Dunford, 10/31/1928, Bristol, TN, Victor V40060

DINK BRISTER

I visited and recorded Dink Brister (August 25, 1914–August 2, 1991) on August 14, 1966. Marina Bokelman and I were led to him by Babe Stovall and O. D. Jones, two of his fellow African American blues and string band musicians from around Tylertown, Mississippi (Walthall County). All three men had been part of a post–World War II diaspora of musicians and others from the Tylertown area across the state line to Louisiana and such communities as Franklinton, Clifton, Covington, Bogalusa, Angie, and New Orleans. The reasons for this diaspora were the better racial climate in Louisiana and the lure of jobs in mills, factories, and other industrial settings. For musicians there was also the lure of the money that these jobs provided to people who might become their patrons. Brister, Stovall, and Jones had made it as far as New Orleans, where their lives took different directions. Stovall remained as a singer and guitarist and was living in the French Quarter playing music for hippies, tourists, and denizens of the local Dream Castle Bar. Jones became a dockworker and was making a steady salary of about $35 per day. Brister tied steel and made $37 a day. Jones and Brister debated with Stovall about whether it was better to make $35 in an hour or two irregularly as a musician or make it steadily per day in an industrial job. Brister obviously preferred the steady salary. He lived in a

Dink Brister, 1966. Photo courtesy of David Evans.

spotless four-room garage apartment with his sister and seemed to be doing well for himself.

Marina and I were interested in Dink Brister mainly as a blues musician to play mandolin accompaniment to guitarists Stovall and Jones. In earlier years in Mississippi, the three musicians and others had played in string bands, which in their full instrumentation consisted of violin, mandolin, guitar, and bass viol. These bands played for both white and Black audiences. I recorded the three men in various combinations and gathered some bare biographical facts about Brister and Jones. (I had already worked more extensively with Stovall.) Marina took photographs and gathered some genealogical and residence information.

Dink Brister stated that he was born on August 25, 1914, east of Tylertown. He is difficult to locate in US Census records before 1940. Probably "Dink" was a nickname that he took as his real name when he became an adult. There are several Brister families in the area with sons around his age who could be him. In any case, in 1940 he is clearly listed as Dink Brister, age twenty-four (*sic*), in Marion, Mississippi, a community on the Darbun-Kokomo Road east of Tylertown. He had a wife, Cestie, age twenty-two, and four children between the ages of one and five. They had lived in the same residence in 1935. Dink was described as a farmer and renter, "working on own account." He had only a second-grade education, while Cestie had reached the fifth grade. Dink worked fifty hours per week every week of the year, while Cestie was listed as an unpaid family worker at thirty hours per week every week of the year. Both had zero income, which indicates that their rental arrangement was actually share-cropping on credit. Dink, however, reported that he had income from other sources, which probably meant playing music.

Dink Brister was part of a network of inter-marrying families containing musicians. He and his brother Tom Brister were first cousins of local guitar bluesman Frank "Nig" Butler. Butler's sister Mandy had married Fredro Stovall, an older brother of Babe and his musician brother Tom Stovall. The Stovalls' half-brother was guitarist Myrt Holmes, who was married to Dink's first cousin Heddie Brister. Heddie's uncle was Herb Quinn, the man who taught Dink to play the mandolin. Dink and Tom Brister's cousin Spellman "Babe" Brister played in a string band with guitarist O. D. Jones and other local musicians. Babe Brister had taught Jones his first guitar chord and married O. D.'s older sister. O. D.'s father also used to play guitar and mandolin. They were all "raised together" out in the country

east of Tylertown and used to play music with one another. They would swap instruments, but Dink stayed with the mandolin, the only instrument he ever learned to play. Other musicians who sometimes played with them were Roosevelt Holts and Roosevelt's cousin Isaac Youngblood. The famous Mississippi bluesman Tommy Johnson had married Youngblood's cousin Rosa around 1929 and lived off and on around Tylertown for several years. Dink said that he knew Johnson but never played music with him.

Dink Brister did not own a mandolin when we visited him and was somewhat rusty in his playing. He would play complementary mandolin lines and chords in accompaniment to guitar blues by Jones and Stovall in the keys of C, G, D, and E, sounding the best in C. The other tunes he played were mostly in C and were the type of ragtime and dance songs that appealed to both white and Black audiences, such as "Candy Man," "Stop Time," "Tennessee Waltz," "Red River Valley," "After the Ball," and "Sweet Bunch of Daisies." Brister only sang on two blues selections on the day I recorded him and probably always was mainly an instrumentalist.

Dink Brister belonged to the last generation of Black rural musicians to be attracted to string band music and to play for local white audiences in the 1930s and 1940s. Toward the end of this period, southern music, both Black and white, was becoming electrified and moving away from the string band sound. Many white singers and musicians were emerging to play the new sounds, and southern white rural audiences became less interested in hearing and dancing to the music of Black string bands. This loss of white musical patronage may have been another contributing factor to the diaspora of Black musicians from the area. Dink Brister, in fact, had a son who had moved all the way to Brooklyn, New York, where he played in an electric blues band. Dink's brother Tom was still performing music in 1966 but had become a Christian and was playing guitar for the Sanctified church in Kokomo, a little settlement east of Tylertown. Dink Brister died in New Orleans on August 2, 1991.

—David Evans

After the Ball

Author's note: Transcribed from a 1966 David Evans field recording of Dink Brister on mandolin with Babe Stovall on guitar. Both instruments played the melody.

Comparable versions:
In this book: "After the Ball," The Collier Trio, 11/28/1930, New Orleans, Brunswick 507
"After the Ball," Tom Darby & Jimmie Tarlton, 04/12/1928, Atlanta, Columbia 15254-D
"After the Ball," Crockett's Kentucky Mountaineers, 11/25/1929, New York, Brunswick 394
"After the Ball," Fiddling John Carson, 12/09/1930, Atlanta, OKeh 45569

David Evans

Stop-Time

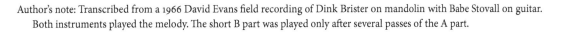

Author's note: Transcribed from a 1966 David Evans field recording of Dink Brister on mandolin with Babe Stovall on guitar. Both instruments played the melody. The short B part was played only after several passes of the A part.

Comparable versions: None known

ENOS CANOY AND THE CANOY WILDCATS

The Canoy Wildcats were a Simpson County family string band led by Enos Washington Canoy (August 3, 1909–August 5, 1970) with his children Durwood and Herbert, his cousin Tim, and Tim's children "Mellie" Jean and Sadie. Other musicians that participated in the band from time to time were guitarists James Ferrel Amason, Billy Ray Reynolds, Curtis Mangum, and a Mr. Weathersby. The band was active in the 1940s and 1950s, playing as far away as Jackson for a Mason's Lodge dance and a weekly radio show on WSJC. Sometime in the late 1940s, they were the first band to appear on Magee radio station WSKC, where they had a radio show every Saturday. They played for local square dances with a caller. Often dancers would jitterbug to old-time fiddle tunes. The band would travel a little bit for appearances but came home every night. In 1959 Canoy provided

Left to right: Tim Canoy, Enos Canoy, Durwood Canoy, Jean Hopkins Canoy, Sadie Canoy Thornton, Herbert Canoy, ca. 1939. Photo courtesy Mississippi Department of Archives and History.

Canoy Wildcats. Left to right: W. A. Green, guitar; Mr. Weathersby, guitar; Enos Canoy, fiddle; Curtis Mangum, guitar; Deward Canoy, bass; Herbert Canoy, pedal steel, ca. 1939. Photo courtesy Mississippi Department of Archives and History.

and operated the public address system for events in the county elections and ran an advertisement for his services.[1]

Enos had recorded in 1939 for the Federal Music Project with Tim and his wife Lola.[2] Not wanting to play for rowdy crowds in less than wholesome venues, Lola had mostly quit playing music before the Wildcats formed. A skilled musician and singer, she played piano, guitar, a little mandolin, and harmonica. Her daughter, Jean, remembers playing with Lola accompanying on piano, for a Hattiesburg radio appearance in the mid-1950s, filling in for Jean's husband who was not able to show up for the appearance.

Enos's unique version of "Arkansas Traveler," which was his radio theme song, is included here. He was also very fond of "Down Yonder," playing it at least once at every performance. Another favorite

was the "Orange Blossom Special." One can only wonder how he might have reshaped those well-known tunes. The band played reels, waltzes, pop and country songs, and whatever the local audiences wanted to hear. Enos played fairly standard versions of the "Tennessee Waltz," "The Waltz You Saved for Me" and "When You and I Were Young, Maggie." Jean taught herself guitar and played with a distant relative, neighbor, and fiddler Robert Runnels, before being drafted into the Wildcats by Enos, who lived next door. Lola was dubious about Jean joining the band but her father, Tim, insisted. Jean would sing some of the waltzes, such as "Waltz Across Texas" and the "Kentucky Waltz." Her singing on "My Bucket's Got a Hole in It," was a real crowd-pleaser. Enos would play some kind of fiddle lines between the verses when they functioned as a country band. After she moved away, Enos would

Enos Canoy, mandolin; Jimmy Tugwell, bass; Lola
Canoy, piano, ca. 1939. Photo courtesy Mississippi
Department of Archives and History.

Back row, left to right: Tim, Lola, Onie, Enos Canoy; front row: Joanna and Travis, ca. 1940s Photo from *All Shook Up*,
published by Mississippi Department of Archives and History, 1995. Used with permission of the Canoy family.

Harry Bolick

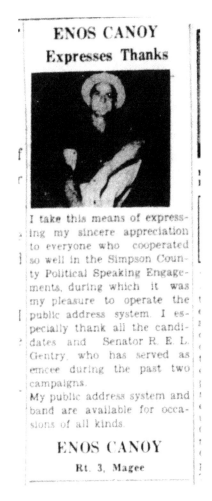

ENOS CANOY
Expresses Thanks

I take this means of express-ing my sincere appreciation to everyone who cooperated so well in the Simpson Coun-ty Political Speaking Engage-ments, during which it was my pleasure to operate the public address system. I es-pecially thank all the candi-dates and Senator R. E. L. Gentry, who has served as emcee during the past two campaigns.

My public address system and band are available for occa-sions of all kinds.

ENOS CANOY
Rt. 3, Magee

Ad, *Simpson County News*, August 20, 1959.

come and pick Jean up for appearances until she quit in 1953. In addition to mandolin, Tim Canoy was known to play spoons and to yodel with the band. The band apparently functioned without a "front man" on stage. Enos would occasionally introduce a tune or tell a story but did not speak much at a performance. His son, Herbert, was also quiet but in spite of his cerebral palsy, quite competently played steel guitar. Although one can imagine Black influences in Enos's fiddling, Jean did not recall any African American musicians in the area. The Canoy families did not have any records at home, but did listen to the radio, learning some of the contemporary songs in that way.

—Harry Bolick

This chapter is based on interviews:
Mellie Jean Canoy Hopkins at her home in Star, MS, May 15, 2017.
James Ferrel Amason, at his home in Braxton, MS, May 12, 2017.

Recordings

1939: Ten tunes recorded by Herbert Halpert for the Federal Music Project. Recorded discs are now located at the Library of Congress, Washington, DC.

Two home-recorded 78 rpm discs from 1947 or 1948 in the collection of James Ferrel Amason, which can be heard at mississippifiddle.com.

Disc 1

April 3, 1949—Jesse Amason's home between Mey-ers and MaGee, MS:
Johnny Martin, fiddle, Enos Canoy, mandolin, Herbert Canoy, steel guitar, James Ferrel Amason, electric guitar
    1. John Henry

April 4, 1949: same musicians
    2. True Life Blues
    3. Carroll County Blues
    4. My Rose of Old Kentucky

Disc 2

1947–48, Community Center at MaGee:
Enos Canoy, fiddle, Johnny Martin, mandolin, Herbert Canoy, steel guitar, James Ferrel Amason, electric guitar, and possibly Bob Martin, bass
    1. Boogie
    2. Arkansas Traveler
    3. Bye Little Bonnie Blue Eyes: Johnny Martin, fiddle, Enos Canoy, mandolin, Jessie Amason, vocal
    4. Arkansas Traveler, 2nd take

NOTES

1. *Simpson County News*, Mendenhall, MS, 08/29/1959, 12.
2. Bolick and Austin, Mississippi Fiddle Tunes and Songs from the 1930s, 236–47.

Arkansas Traveler

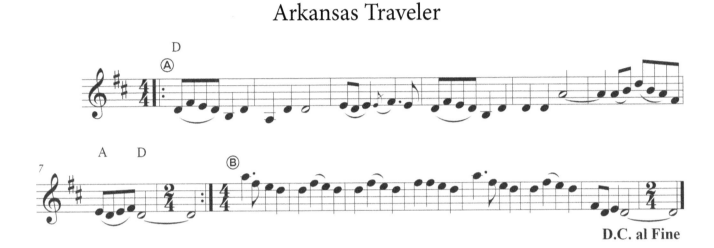

D.C. al Fine

Author's note: This 1947 or '48 home recording of the Canoy Wildcats is posted at mississippifiddle.com with permission of the family. This tune was their radio theme song.

Comparable versions:
Only the first half of the first part of this version is comparable to the sources below.
"The Arkansas Traveler," *The Arkansas Traveller's Songster* (New York: Dick & Fitzgerald, 1864), 5–9.
Bolick and Austin, *Mississippi Fiddle Tunes and Songs from the 1930s*: All with the title of "The Arkansas Traveler": W. E. Claunch, 251; John Hatcher, 284; Stephen B. Tucker, 344
In this book:
"Arkansas Traveler," Sid Hemphill
"Arkansas Traveler," Henry C. Gilliland and A. C. "Eck" Robertson, 06/30/1922, New York, Victor 18956
"Arkansas Traveler," Fiddlin' John Carson & His Virginia Reelers, 03/1924, Atlanta, OKeh 40108
"Arkansas Traveler," Kessinger Brothers, 02/11/1928, Ashland, KY, Brunswick 247

THE CARTER BROTHERS AND SON

One of the wildest fiddle bands of all time consisted of George Washington Carter (1869–1948), Andrew Jackson Carter (1877–1956), and George's son James Auguston "Jimmie" Carter (1900–1979), from Quincy, Monroe County. Here is their story, mostly in the words of Jimmie Carter himself.

Talk about old-time dances. "We'd go through the wintertime," says Jimmie Carter, "from the time folks gathered in the corn, from then till along, I'd say, February, March, something like that. We'd go from in the early fall to early spring.

"Here's the way they'd do it. They'd have one at this man's house tonight. Well, all they did, back then,

Left to right: Jimmie, Ruby, George, Anna, Mary (with baby Early Mae), Mamie, Frank, Alva, and David Carter. Quincy, Monroe County, ca. 1913. Photo courtesy Carl Fleischhauer.

Jimmy Carter, 1975. Photo courtesy Carl Fleischhauer.

Andrew and Ila Carter. Photo courtesy Carl Fleischhauer.

was farm a little and bootleg a little, you know, make whiskey. But this feller here tonight, they'd have one at his house—well, he'd sell all he could, you know. Well, they'd have one over at the other feller's next night, and he'd do the same, you know, and they'd just protract it like that. And that's the way they were."

"Oh, they had a good time, you know. Never had no fightin'. Oh, if they got into a fight anywhere, they always had a crib or something where they'd go carry him out there and lock him up. And they don't do like they do now, you know—they shoot and cut and do everything else now. They didn't do that then. If it got a little too much, tryin' to raise a racket, like I say, they carried him to the crib and locked him up."

Jimmie Carter started out on the guitar when he was seven, taught by his father. "I beat a hole in about four or five, my comin' up, down there, you know, pickin' like that." Within a year he was accompanying his dad at breakdown parties—just the two of them, no other musicians.

"Boy, I tell you, they generally set us—we didn't have electricity like they got now—set us over in the

corner of a great big old building. And a big, heavy feller—we used to have a guy, name was Ernest Boyd, weighed about two-fifty or three hundred—boy, he'd get out there and jump up and down, and man, the dust would just fall. Me and him [George] would sit over in the corner, and when it was cold weather, boy, just freeze to death nearly. And that dust would get that thick on my head and on that little old guitar, you know. And me and him, we'd sit there in that corner and play, God, all night. It wouldn't be but sometimes we'd quit at midnight—and then sometimes we'd play all night long. Just only how they felt and, I guess, how much liquor that feller had sold at midnight. He'd say, 'Let's run it all on.' Doin' business, carryin' it on all night.

"I tell you what he [George] could do. You give him enough to feelin' pretty good, he'd sit down over there in that corner, hang that head over that fiddle, he'd play two hours at a time and never stop. See, they used to run these old what they call square set, they used to run them sometimes thirty minutes, an hour, before they got through, you know. Well, he'd be settin' there with his head over, playin' right on, and turn right around, start another and run that

Tony Russell

un on out—play two hours. And boy, you talkin' about somethin'.

"Back then, they had—I call them just old cheap two-bit instruments—guitar—and strings that far from the fingerboard, there's been gashes on every one of them fingers right there, from them strings—plumb to the bone nearly. And sit right there and play that thing with him, say, two hours at a time. And it wasn't just slow knockin'—boy, you had to git it! Sometimes when they'd get out, you know, get that set out, I'd punch him so he'd quit, you know, so we'd take a little break. That was somethin', I'm tellin' you."

George and Jimmie entered the local fiddlers' contests held in the old Aberdeen Opera House until it burned down. Around thirty-two fiddlers from the area would compete. George often won a prize, and on at least one occasion got the gold medal, for "Leather Britches." Among the fiddlers they were up against were Isom Hadaway, Horace Justice of Hadley, and "a little humpbacked feller" called Walker, who had a small band.

Andrew Carter, unlike his brother, was not a breakdown fiddler. He played waltzes and songs, often with one of his daughters on piano. At one time Jimmie played guitar with him, not for hoedowns but for waltzes and round dances. Andrew's favorite tunes were pieces like "In the Good Old Summertime."

Early in 1928 the OKeh people contacted George Carter to make records.

"My daddy was livin' back this side of Hadley, up there. And all I can remember, they come out there. Somebody, you know, told 'em and they come out there. And my daddy told me, said, 'They want us to go and play for 'em, make some records.' I said, 'Where?' He said, 'Well, we'll go to Memphis.' I said, 'How we goin'?' Says, 'They're comin' after us.' And then he got a hold of my uncle, you know, and got him to go with us. I was drivin' a truck for that Amory Gas and Oil Company. I was workin' drillin' wells, you know. I went right off a truck and a feller picked us up, carried us up there. We played and stayed there that night, come back next morning.

"I never thought no more about it then, till I guess it was maybe a month later, they come back, said they wanted us to go back. So we went back

then and made two more records. And they did the same thing, they brought us back. [This second session was actually for a different label, Vocalion, and nine months after the first. TR]

"Course, they wanted my daddy. Says, 'We want him to go with us over across the water'—where they come from, you see. Might have been from London or some place over there—anyhow, over there. My daddy was willing but my uncle said, 'No, that's too far away from home.' And I guess, if me and my daddy had went, we'd probably have been better off. Course, can't never tell what'll be.

"They paid us for that, and then a few weeks later they sent a whole box of those records. They sold 'em—I don't know who bought 'em, but a lot of folks bought 'em. And them records went everywhere, I reckon. According to what I can find out. Course, if I'd a thought it'd ever been anything to it, you know, I'd have taken more interest in it. Didn't think there was anything to it or they were worth anything.

"My uncle was supposed to be what they call a scientific fiddler, you know—he played the violin, he wasn't no fiddler. And he could sing. 'Bout the first feller I ever saw could just sit up there and play the fiddle and sing all the same time. But we carried him on account of my daddy thought that he could do the singing, you know, and help him out with the fiddling, and he [George] could do the fiddling. But the lil' old microphone wouldn't take his voice at all. And well, he [the man from the record company] asks my daddy, 'Can you sing?' 'Oh,' he said, 'I can do that old timey stuff, you know, like old "Liza Jane" and old stuff like that.' He says, 'Oh, I can sing a little few words, holler a little.' 'Well,' they said, 'you go ahead then and you sing and just holler 'n' hoot and do anything you want to.' Well, my daddy did that, you know, and course that suited them all right.... Well, when you heard them, you couldn't tell hardly that my uncle was even on the record. Didn't have to have him at all. But on account of his being my daddy's brother we carried him with us."

◆ ◆ ◆

After the sessions the Carters had a call from Birmingham, Alabama, to come over and play. A man

named Taylor, whose father was in real estate there but who had been born and raised in the Carters' locality, asked them to play for a land sale. They went over there four times, expenses paid and taking home $25.

In later years Jimmie learned fiddle. He played differently from his father—waltzes and some blues, not breakdowns. He never sang much, but he could do a few Jimmie Rodgers–type numbers with guitar. After he married he would play fiddle at parties with his wife Johnnie backing him up on guitar. Later, they organized a family band with their children and played political rallies held by Sen. Abernethy from Okolona. At the time of the interview, their son Joe was playing in a band with country singer Carmol Taylor.

After working as a roughneck, drilling wells in Mississippi, Alabama, and Arkansas—a life that was briefly interrupted by a period of sharecropping in the Delta during the 1930s—Jimmie Carter settled in the Aberdeen area in the late 1950s.

—Tony Russell

Cotton Eyed Joe

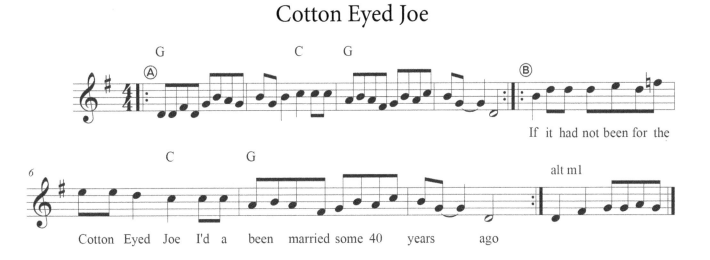

If it had not been for the

Cotton Eyed Joe I'd a been married some 40 years ago

Author's note: This transcription is from Vocalion 5349, recorded Memphis, TN, 11/22/1928. The fiddles are tuned GDAD. On guitar, Jimmie Carter is playing a simple version of the melody, not chords, but does walk into a low C note where I have indicated a C chord.

Comparable versions:
Bolick and Austin, *Mississippi Fiddle Tunes and Songs from the 1930s*, 2015: Allen Alsop, 44; Rev. J. E. Williams, 207
In this book:
"Cotton-Eyed Joe," Tom Dumas
"Cotton-Eyed Joe," Dykes' Magic Trio, 07/1927, New York, Brunswick 120
"Cotton-Eyed Joe," Pope's Arkansas Mountaineers, 07/1928, Memphis, TN, Victor 21469
"Cotton-Eyed Joe," Gid Tanner & His Skillet Lickers, 10/1928, Atlanta, Columbia 15283-D

Give Me a Chaw Tobacco

Bear Creek's up and the Bear Creek's muddy Bear Creek gals all raise much study

Author's note: This transcription is from Vocalion 5295, recorded Memphis, TN, on 11/22/1928. On guitar, Jimmie Carter is playing a simple low octave version of the melody, not chords.

Comparable versions: None known

Lyrics:

Bear Creek's up and the Bear Creek's muddy
Bear Creek gals all raise much study

Had a little dog and his name was Rover
When he died, he died all over

Dance hall gals oh how I love ya
Same ole gals give me chaw tobacca

Comparable versions:
"Roaring River," J. B. Farrell, music 1848
W. E. Claunch, 05/10/1939, Guntown, MS, AFS 2972B1 (A parts related)
Bolick and Austin, *Mississippi Fiddle Tunes and Songs from the 1930s*: W. E. Claunch, "Bear Creek's Up," 252

Give the Fiddler a Dram

wheee weeo

Lets give a party, give the fiddler a dram

Author's note: This transcription is from OKeh 45289, recorded Memphis, TN, 02/24/1928. The Fiddles are tuned AEAE. On guitar, Jimmie Carter is playing a simplified low version of the melody, not chords as backup. A serviceable chord alternative is indicated.

Comparable versions:

Bolick and Austin, *Mississippi Fiddle Tunes and Songs from the 1930s*: John A. Brown, "Give the Fiddler a Dram," 231 (B parts related); W. E. Claunch, "Give the Fiddler a Dram," 259 (A parts related); Stephen B. Tucker, "Calico," 347 (B parts related).

Jenny on the Railroad

Author's note: This transcription is from Vocalion 5297, recorded Memphis, TN, 11/22/1928. The fiddles are tuned AEAE. On the recording alt M1 is only played on the first pass of the tune and the other parts are a bit jumbled. This transcription is based on the later passes through the tune. M24–26 are usually played as in M11–12 but beats are added and subtracted throughout the performance, which is very loose, aggressive, and energetic. On guitar, Jimmie Carter is playing a simplified low version of the melody, not chords as backup. A serviceable chord alternative is indicated.

Comparable versions:

"Colonel Crockett," George Knauff, *Virginia Reels*, Vol. 3 (Baltimore: George Willig Jr., 1839)

"Jack Smith's Favorite Reel," M. M. Cole, *One Thousand Fiddle Tunes* (Chicago: M. M. Cole, 1940 [reprinted from *Ryan's Mammoth Collection* (1883)]), 40

In this book:

"(Paddy On the Turnpike)," Claude Kennedy

"The Gal on the Log," Cap. Moses J. Bonner, 03/17/1925, Houston, TX, Victor 19699 (A and B parts only)

Leather Breeches

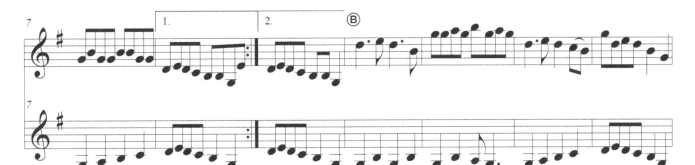

Author's note: This transcription is from Vocalion 5295, recorded Memphis, TN, 11/22/1928. This transcription is from the first pass of the tune, where the sound is the clearest.

Comparable versions:

"Lord McDonald's Reel," Niel & Nathaniel Gow, *Third Collection of Niel Gow's Reels* (ca. 1792), 9

"Leather Breeches," M. M. Cole, *One Thousand Fiddle Tunes* (Chicago: M.M. Cole, 1940 [reprinted from *Ryan's Mammoth Collection* (1883)]), 22

Bolick and Austin, *Mississippi Fiddle Tunes and Songs from the 1930s*: Mr. J. H. Wheeler, "Leather Breeches," 202; John Hatcher, "Leather Britches," 295; Hardy C. Sharp, "Leather Britches," 338; Stephen B. Tucker, "Leather Britches," 359

In this book:

"Leather Breeches," Sid Hemphill

"Leather Breeches," Leake County Revelers, 04/13/1927, New Orleans, Columbia 15149-D

Liza Jane

Author's note: This transcription is from OKeh 45202, recorded Memphis, TN, 02/24/1928. The fiddles are tuned AEAE. On guitar, Jimmie Carter is playing a simplified low version of the melody, not chords as backup. A serviceable chord alternative is indicated.

Comparable versions:

(If played with the pickup notes as the first downbeat, this tune resembles the high part of "Old Dan Tucker.")
"Old Dan Tucker," Dan Emmett, *Aldophous Morning Glory Songster* (1843), 14
Bolick and Austin, *Mississippi Fiddle Tunes and Songs from the 1930s*: Thaddeus C. Willingham, "Old Dan Tucker," 388
"Old Dan Tucker," Uncle Dave Macon, 04/13/1925, New York, Vocalion 15033
"Old Dan Tucker," Fiddlin' John Carson, 12/18/1924, New York, OKeh 4026

Lyrics:

I asked that gal to be my wife and reckon what she said
Don't get away with your foolish soap getta your devilish head

La-da-da-da
Somebody stole my old coon dog and I wish they'd bring him back
Run the old sow over the fence and the little ones through the crack

If I had a scolding wife take her sure as you're born
Take her down to New Orleans and trade her off for corn

Miss Brown

Never   get it up,   never get it   down,   never get it up for old Miss Brown

Author's note: This transcription is from Vocalion 5297, recorded Memphis, TN, 11/22/1928. The fiddles are tuned GDAD. On
   guitar, Jimmie Carter is playing a simplified low version of the melody, not chords as backup. A serviceable chord alternative
   is indicated.

Comparable versions:
"Cousin Sally Brown," Sweet Brothers & Ernest Stoneman, 07/10/1928, Richmond, IN, Gennett 6687 (Loosely related)

Nancy Rowland

I got a dog and his name is Rover, when he died he died all over.

Ya - da - da - yadda. Howdy ya da Howdy

Author's note: This transcription is from Vocalion 5349, recorded Memphis, TN, 11/22/1928. Jimmie Carter on guitar is playing a simplified low version of the melody, not chords as backup. A serviceable chord alternative is indicated.

Comparable versions:
In this book:
"Nancy Rowland," John Anderson
"Nancy Rowland," Fiddlin' John Carson, 11/08/1923, New York, OKeh 40238
"Nancy Rowlin," Gid Tanner & His Skillet Lickers, 10/22/1928, Atlanta, Columbia 15382-D

Lyrics:

Had a little dog and his name was Rover,
When he died he died all over.

Married me a wife and she was a Quaker
She wouldn't work and I wouldn't make her
Ya-da-da-yadda....

Old Joe Bone

Author's note: This transcription is from OKeh 45289, recorded Memphis, TN, 02/24/1928. The fiddles are tuned AEAE. Jimmie
Carter, on guitar, is playing a simplified low version of the melody, not chords as backup. A serviceable chord alternative is
indicated.

Comparable versions:
"Walk Jawbone," S. S. Steele, *Minstrel Songs Old and New: A Collection of World-Wide Famous Minstrel and Plantation Songs*
(Boston: Oliver Ditson Co., 1882)
"Jawbone," Pope's Arkansas Mountaineers, 02/06/1928, Memphis, TN, Victor 21577

Lyrics:

My wife died in Tennessee, they gave that jawbone back to me
Laid that jawbone on that fence, and ain't been back for to see it since
Walk Jawbone, Jenny come along, and in steps Sally with the red boots on

Walk jawbone, talk jawbone, jawbone eat with a knife and a fork
Laid that jawbone on that fence, and ain't been back for to see it since
Walk jawbone, Jenny come along, and in steps Sally with the red dress on

Yadda da yadda . . .
And in steps Sally with the blue dress on

Saddle Up the Grey

Sa-ddle up the grey, better get a-way   ain't gonna get no dinner here today

Author's note: This transcription is from OKeh 45202, recorded Memphis, TN, 02/24/1928. The fiddles are tuned GDAD. Jimmie
Carter, on guitar, is playing a simplified low version of the melody, not chords as backup. A serviceable chord alternative is
indicated.

Comparable versions:
Bolick and Austin, *Mississippi Fiddle Tunes and Songs from the 1930s*: John A. Brown, "Not A-Gonna Have No Supper Here
Tonight," 232

Lyrics:

Saddle up the grey, better get away
Ain't gonna be no dinner here today
Yadda yadda da day

Haul out the jug and put out the light
Ain't gonna be no dinner here tonight

Roll around the jug and put out the light,
There ain't a-gonna be no supper here tonight

Saddle up the grey, and you better get away,
There ain't a-gonna be no dinner here today

Leadin' of a goat and a-ridin' of a sheep,
I ain't a-gonna get back till the middle of the week

Roll around the jug and put out the light,
Ain't gonna get no supper here tonight.

Tony Russell

AUGUSTUS EUGENE CLARDY

On February 18, 1930, the blue-eyed, forty-four-year-old Augustus Eugene Clardy (pronounced Clair-Dee) (1886–1935) made his way to Memphis to record his only session for Vocalion Records. Along with his guitar accompanist, twenty-three-year-old Stan Clements from Alabama, the champion fiddle player from Carroll County, Mississippi, cut four sides in "tantalizing brevity"[1] that constitute his recorded legacy. Judging from the recordings, Clardy was a "by the book" player, not inclined to creating new music or reshaping standard tunes. During the 1970s, Tony Russell interviewed older musicians in central Mississippi who often spoke of Clardy. Several of his informants believed that Clardy was the elder statesman who "taught Willie Narmour" how to play fiddle, and many others suggested that he was the original creator of the "Carroll County Blues." By examining heretofore unseen newspaper accounts of Clardy's activities, surveying government documents, and drawing from the prior literature, this article clarifies the assertions of older Central Mississippi musicians about Clardy's musical talents and traces his mid-1930s murder at the hands of a knife-wielding teenager at Leflore Station.

Augustus Eugene Clardy was the grandson of John Clardy, who served in the 35th Mississippi Infantry during the Civil War, and the son of James Clardy, of Grenada County, Mississippi, and Van Clardy, of Starkville. He was born on May 11, 1886, according to his World War I registration card.[2] The first census to note his existence in 1900, however, stated that he was born February 1888. His sharecropping parents raised him in rural Beat 5 of Grenada County, where the young fiddler probably developed the first tunes in his repertoire. Clardy had received some violin training at some point in his life, at least learning to read music, and he may have been the source for some of the more standard tunes in Carroll County, such as "Fishers Hornpipe," "Rustic Dance," and "Sailors Hornpipe." It's unlikely that he taught Narmour how to play the fiddle. However, upon hearing Clardy play, it's quite possible that Narmour acquired the ambition to play, and to compose tunes using the upper reaches of the fiddle's fingerboard, from seeing Clardy play. Judging by Narmour's less-than-precise pitch in third position, it's unlikely he ever took lessons. In the case of Narmour, "taught" might best be interpreted as "inspired by."

The claims of older musicians that Willie Narmour learned from Clardy may be "unlikely rumors," but their assertions that Clardy composed "Carroll County Blues" are not as unlikely as once thought. The naming of songs was a regional tradition in Mississippi. Sometimes different names

Unknown, guitar; Seifus Clements, fiddle; Eugene Clardy, mandolin, ca. 1910. Photo courtesy Harold Clardy.

were imposed on the same tune. "Charleston No. 3," for example, was also known as "Sailor's Hornpipe." Choctaw County fiddler Hoyt Ming explained:

Now in one section of the country, say a fiddler's playing a tune he learned from someone, that's going by that name. Well, you might go into another area, way off a distance, or some other state, and they play the same tune by a different name, you see. And there's sometimes a fiddler would learn to play a certain piece—well, especially back in the blues days—and he'd heard somebody play that all right, but he didn't know what he called it, didn't know the tune. Well, he'd just name it some kind of blues. Maybe now like Narmour and Smith—the blues that they put out, "Carroll County Blues," and, let me see, there's several other of these—in other words, because they

named it from Carroll County where they lived. It went really under a different name in that area, and probably they didn't know the name of it but knew the tune, or maybe did know the name but it wasn't nationally known, and they just named it "Carroll County Blues." People wouldn't know the difference.[3]

"The Carroll County Blues" may have come into existence under another name elsewhere, perhaps in Grenada County—the place in which James Clardy raised his musical family, perhaps in Carroll County. In 1910 one "Jene Clardy" married Isabelle Woodward in Alabama and then lived in Beat 2 of Carroll County with their infant daughter, Hazel. A more likely cauldron of acculturation was the city of Memphis, where Gene and Isabelle Clardy lived sometime after September 12, 1918. When the

T. DeWayne Moore

blue-eyed, dark-haired Clardy registered for service in World War I, he lived in Carrollton, Mississippi, working on the farm of J. H. Flanigan.

The titles recorded with Clements do not suggest that Clardy had much of an influence on Narmour, nor do they contain any trace of Narmour's blues phrasing. Yet, Tony Russell noted a "certain tonal similarity" between the song and Clardy's records. "Carroll County Blues" also shares a "short melodic fragment" with Clardy's recording of "Black Mustache." In Memphis, Clardy may have played on the street or worked as a professional musician. He may have heard some of the nascent popular blues tunes of such figures as Frank Stokes, Dan Sane, Furry Lewis, and Will Shade. In truth, we don't know much about his time in Memphis, but the death certificate of Gene Clardy's first wife, Isabelle, reveals she died at age thirty-seven from pneumonia on May 19, 1926, in Memphis. Sometime after the death of his wife he moved back to the hills outside the mid-Delta.

Though we don't know when he made the decision to come back, it was probably before his February 1930 recording session. He may have met Stan Clements in Memphis. In any case, Clardy recorded four tunes with Clements for Vocalion in February: "Sleeping Time Waltz," "Black Mustache" (also recorded four years later by the Nations Brothers), "Harvest Home Waltz," and "Moonlight Clog." He

never made it into another studio; Stan Clements did make two solo recordings in 1931 and recorded again after 1942.

Clardy remarried and moved to the town of Teoc, not far from both John Hurt and Willie Narmour. The 1930 census listed Eugene and new wife Maud Clardy as renting a home on Teoc Road and living with eight children.[4] He had a hard row to hoe with so many mouths to feed at the start of the Great Depression, but at least he could provide for his family by farming and hunting.

Clardy was one of the local champions of the fiddle. At the first annual fiddlers' contest in Winona at the Friendship Consolidated School, the audience enjoyed splendid weather in November 1931. Not requiring any kindling for fires or fuel for the heaters, the school auditorium was at capacity by sundown to view the entertainment, which included buck dancers, guitar players, and the "sidesplitting comedy furnished by 'Jake' the Negro comedian."[5] Since "all of the fiddlers played equally well" except for Gene Clardy and Sam Jones, who "led by a great bound and were called back to the stage after the judging was over," it took the judges a great deal of time to select the winners. Clardy won first prize of three dollars; Jones won a dollar fifty, and L. J. Ellis (possibly Lonnie Ellis of the Mississippi Possum Hunters) won a dollar.[6]

Clardy surely enjoyed getting compensated for his talents, and he taught his children to respect their musical talents, too. It's likely that he also appreciated a good-natured competition as well as the bragging that went with the prize. In the May 1, 1934, edition of *The Winona Times* "Festival Flashes" section, Willie Narmour announced to all the other fiddlers that he planned to enter the Old Fiddler's Contest at the Williams Landing Exhibit the next weekend and play "The Whistling Coon" and "Midnight Waltz."[7] He was a man of his word, and perhaps it was his presence that attracted some of the most talented musicians to enter the challenge.

Gene Clardy was met with great enthusiasm and applause along with the rest of the contestants who stepped onto the stage at the Williams Landing Exhibit. The star-studded lineup included W. T. Narmour, W. E. Duke, and Clardy, who placed second with the tune "Home Brew Rag."[8] He also played "The Second Fair," which could be almost any sort of tune. Narmour played the songs he announced with W. E. Duke backing him up on guitar before the latter switched over to the fiddle and played "Valley School Blues" and "Wednesday Night Waltz." Neither Duke nor Narmour placed that evening. The thirteen-year-old Ed Kittrell won first prize playing with Duke on "Wild Irish Rose" and "Wreck of the Old 97."

It may have been the last fiddlers' contest in which the champions of Carroll County faced off against each other. Narmour and Smith signed with Victor Records in July and traveled to Atlanta to record sixteen tracks—all covers of their prior offerings—for session supervisor Eli E. Oberstein. Though Narmour continued to perform locally, sometimes with his other playing partner W. E. Duke, Shell Smith retired from performing music to raise his children and support his family. Gene Clardy, on the other hand, performed picnics and parties until his last days and would occasionally play on the street corner in Carrollton.

The available oral accounts about his death center on his alleged refusal to continue performing at a rural dance one evening in the mid-1930s. He "was killed . . . by a dancer at a dance after refusing to continue playing." Several interviews with local informants and varying details, reports that "one of his audience asked him to go on playing after he'd finished for the night, and, when Clardy refused, killed him." Both stories are drawn from oral tradition, and each one of them depicts his end as the irrational result of one man's attempt to keep the party going.[9]

The significant coverage of the murder in the *Greenwood Commonwealth* reveals another side to the story. On the evening of July 6, 1935, A. E. Clardy and Russell Clardy agreed to play a dance at Leflore Station, which sits about halfway between Grenada and Greenwood. Russell's son Harold places the dance at a house near the Clardy home, perhaps the Bailey home. The Baileys were close neighbors to the Clardys, living "right across the road, in an area known as 'the flats.'"[10] The actual events that transpired that evening remain the subject of

debate, depending on whose testimony is believed. Around midnight, the Clardys probably learned that they would not receive due compensation for providing the evening's entertainment, which led them to discontinue the performance. The teenaged host for the evening, Dalton Bailey, claimed that three members of the Clardy family backed him into a corner and demanded satisfaction. Gene's son, Russell Clardy, admitted that he started to fight with two Bailey brothers "over paying the orchestra playing for the dance." Gene Clardy, at this point, may have attempted to act as peacemaker between the two parties. Perhaps feeling that he was outnumbered and in great peril, Dalton Bailey backed up into a corner and decided to "cut his way out with a knife."[11] He wounded Russell Clardy in the melee, but he buried the blade into the chest of the elder Gene Clardy, who "died before medical aid could reach him."[12]

In a family version of the story, Harold Clardy suggested that the fight might have been "over a woman." Harold's two aunts, Elma and Thelma, were at the dance. They had just gotten old enough to go to a dance and it was their first one. Russell was about seventeen and had been cornered into a back room where they had "cut him across the stomach." Then "somebody come up and told his daddy, Gene, that 'they cut your son up back there.' When Gene went back there, they killed him."[13]

It was a solemn affair at the funeral for the legendary fiddler at Pisgah Church near Valley, Carroll County. Augustus Eugene Clardy was survived by his wife, Maud, and his daughter Louise Itrich, of New Salem, North Dakota; Hoyt Clardy, Louise Clardy, Mamie Clardy and Edit Clardy, all of Holcomb; a stepdaughter Ida McCaskin, and one sister, Eula Woodward. Rev. L. D. Sellers officiated the funeral and gave the eulogy for the master fiddler who left us a legacy of those precious few recordings. The subsequent trial of Dalton Bailey, in contrast, was quite a boisterous affair, with forty witnesses in attendance at the dance summoned to give testimony. About half of the group supported Bailey's claims of self-defense, but the other half told a story that supported Clardy's relatives, who testified that he acted as a peacemaker to prevent the fight.[14] "Major conflicts in the testimony," according to the *Greenwood Commonwealth*, "caused the judge to state in his opinion that the jury would have been warranted in convicting Bailey of murder or manslaughter, or acquitting him of the charge altogether."[15] The judge sentenced Dalton Bailey to ten years in the state penitentiary for manslaughter, and the conviction held up on appeal.[16] The murderer of Gene Clardy, however, did not serve even a quarter of his sentence. Governor Hugh White granted him a suspension on October 28, 1937.[17] Bailey got out of prison and reunited with his wife in Grenada and would have been able to hear the radio performance of Russell Clardy and his Hillbillies, who had picked up his father's musical mantle and carried it on a weekly basis for Grenada's WGRN radio station.[18]

Until his death in 1983, Russell continued to play at local fiddle contests and a bit at his home. In addition to playing his father's fine fiddle, he played mandolin, guitar, and piano. Unlike Gene, Russell was not known to read music. He learned and played by ear, with no direct instruction from Gene. Gene was said to have paid twelve dollars for his fiddle; much later, Russell had been offered up to a thousand for it. It remains in the family.[19]

—T. DeWayne Moore

All four of Clardy's recorded tunes, with Stan Clements on guitar, are transcribed in this book.

NOTES

1. Tony Russell, *Old Time Music* 20 (Spring 1976): 36.

2. Registration State: Mississippi; Registration County: Carroll; Roll: 1682705.

3. Tony Russell, "Pep-Stepping with the Mings," *Old Time Music* 10 (1974): 15.

4. 1930; Census Place: Beat 2, Carroll, Mississippi.

5. "Fiddlers Contest Was a Big Success," *Winona Times*, November 20, 1931, 8.

6. "Fiddlers Contest Was a Big Success," *Winona Times*, November 20, 1931, 8.

7. "Festival Flashes," Greenwood Commonwealth, 04/3/1934, 5; *Winona Times*, May 1, 1934.

8. Beisswenger and McCann, *Ozarks Fiddle Music* (2008), 129; *Devil's Box* (Winter 1983): 24; Milliner and Koken, *The Milliner-Koken Collection of American Fiddle Tunes* (2011), 302; "Home Brew Rag," 78 rpm recording by Lowe Stokes and His North Georgians, Atlanta, 10/31/1927; Phillips, *Fiddle Case Tunebook: Old Time Southern* (1989), 22; Phillips, *The Phillips Collection of Traditional American Fiddle Tunes*, vol. 2 (1995), 64.

9. Tony Russell, *Old Time Music* 20 (Spring 1976), 37.

10. Harold Clardy telephone interview with Harry Bolick, May 30, 2019.

11. "Hold Preliminary for Dalton Bailey," *Greenwood Commonwealth*, July 10, 1935, 6.

12. "Leflore Man Killed in Fray," *Greenwood Commonwealth*, July 8, 1935, 1.

13. Harold Clardy telephone interview with Harry Bolick, May 30, 2019.

14. "Hold Preliminary For Dalton Bailey," *Greenwood Commonwealth*, July 17, 1935, 1.

15. "Doctor Can't Testify Unless Patient Agrees," *Clarion-Ledger*, Jackson, MS, January 14, 1936, 14.

16. "Governor White Announces Pardon," *Greenwood Commonwealth*, October 28, 1937, 1.

17. "White Suspends Six Convicts," *McComb Daily Journal*, October 29, 1937, 6.

18. "Radio Program Station WGRN," *Greenwood Commonwealth*, July 30, 1938, 8.

19. Harold Clardy telephone interview with Harry Bolick, May 30, 2019.

Harvest Home

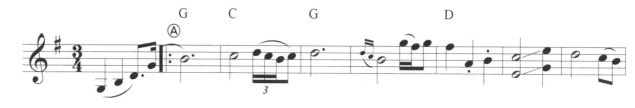

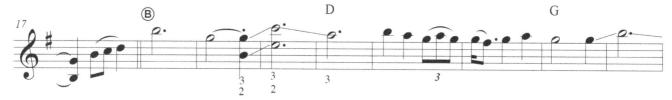

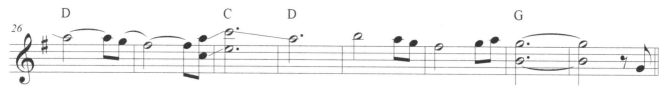

Author's note: This transcription is from Vocalion 5462, recorded Memphis, TN, 02/18/1930. Clardy plays twice through the tune and ends on first part.

Comparable versions: None known

Black Mustache

Author's note: This transcription is from Vocalion 5418, recorded Memphis, TN, 02/18/1930.

Comparable versions:
In this book: "The Little Black Mustache," Nations Brothers, 10/13/1935, Jackson, MS, Vocalion 03152
Vernon Dalhart, Henry Whitter, Ernest Stoneman, and others recorded a song, unrelated except by title.

Moonlight Clog

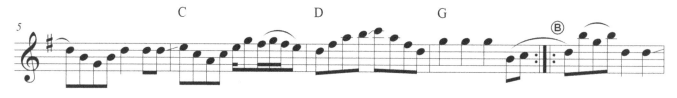

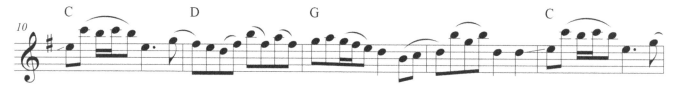

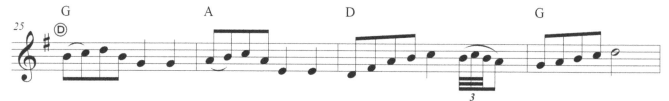

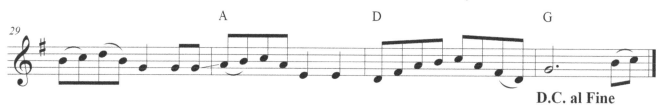

D.C. al Fine

Author's note: This transcription is from Vocalion 5418, recorded Memphis, TN, 02/18/1930. The tune has four parts with the parts repeated AABCDAABCCDAAB.

Comparable versions:
"Nightingale Clog," Cole, *1000 Fiddle Tunes*, 117
"Parkersburg Landing," Ed Haley, Ashland, KY, 1997, Rounder CD 1131/1132
"Rustic Schottische," Cliff [Gross] & Ray, 1938, Vocalion 04204
"Jim Chapman Schottische," Jim Gaskin, 1972/1973, Rounder 0034
"Polka Piquee," Isidore Soucy, 04/1934, Starr 15879
"Moonlight Clog," Angus Chisholm, 11/18/1934, Decca 14004

Sleeping Time Waltz

Author's note: This transcription is from Vocalion 5462, recorded Memphis, TN, 02/18/1930.

Comparable versions: None known

THE COLLIER TRIO

W hen we speak of string band music, we tend to mean the fiddle bands that dominated the Southern record lists between the wars and have consequently been most ardently researched. But string bands took many forms, and the circumstance of them being all lumped together in one "old-time" record catalog shouldn't blind us to the considerable differences of their formations, repertoires, and functions.

In North Georgia, for example, alongside the boisterous fiddle bands like the Skillet Lickers or the Georgia Yellow Hammers were banjo and mandolin groups like the Scottdale String Band. Like the fiddle bands, the Scottdale crew played some of the old breakdowns, but they also favored ragtime and early pop tunes like "St Louis Tickle" and "Silver Bell." The presence of such bands probably did a great deal to keep the music of the ragtime era in the Southern consciousness, and their interaction with the fiddle bands maintained the rich diversity of dancehall and parlor music that characterized Southern string music in general.

Mississippi doubtless had groups on the Scottdale model, but, as elsewhere in the South, such music was usually passed over by the scouts of the record companies, who saw old-time fiddling and singing as their chief business. One band, however, was recorded: the Collier Trio. Their lineup was

Otto, Lucille, and Alsey Collier. Photo courtesy Mike Collier.

somewhat similar to the Scottdale group's—mandolin, tenor banjo, and guitar—and they played waltzes, marches, and popular song tunes. Their music is in quite sharp contrast to that of the Leake County Revelers or Freeny's Barn Dance Band, yet they were from the same neighborhood, and Fonzo Cannon, guitar-player in the Freeny band, sat in with them from time to time.

As their name indicates, the Collier Trio were a family band. Otto Collier (1895–1944) and his older brother William Alsey Collier (1890–1940), the founding members, began playing together in their boyhood, before World War I. In wartime they were stationed at Camp Beauregard, Louisiana, as fulltime army musicians, and they never got to go abroad. Otto played mandolin, banjo, and violin; Alsey played guitar and later drums.

The brothers were born in Meridian but had moved to Leake County by 1920, and spent most of their lives round Carthage. They were never fulltime musicians (after their army days), but made their living as paperhangers or house painters. They played many functions in the area, such as dances, county fairs, American Legion gatherings—but not fiddlers' conventions. As Lucille Collier Lutts, their younger sister, recalled, "My brothers were just—I'll have to say this about them—they called theirselves just a little above the old fiddling, see. You call my brother [Otto], call him a fiddler, he'd tell you right now he wasn't no fiddler—he was a violinist."

Occasionally the brothers would be joined by their younger first cousin William Collier (1904–1984), also from Carthage. William played banjo or guitar. Other musicians would sometimes play with them, like Fonzo Cannon or Lucille Collier's husband Roy Lutts, who remembered doing so in the mid-1920s.

Somehow—nobody can remember how it came about—the Colliers attracted the attention of the Brunswick Record Company, who called them to a recording session in New Orleans in winter 1928, where they played three waltzes and a march. Otto played mandolin, William banjo, and Alsey guitar on all the selections. "Irene Waltz" was a composition by Lucille's piano teacher, Miss Irene Sanders. Lucille had been taking lessons for some time, and played

Unknown and Otto Collier. Photo courtesy Mike Collier.

with her brothers on dates where a piano was available, but she did not attend the recording session.

These initial recordings seem to have been fairly well received, but it was two years before Brunswick recalled them, again to New Orleans. The lineup was the same—and it was a matter of some regret in the family that Otto's violin playing was never put on record, though he appears to have played that instrument both proficiently and often. His preference was for the popular tunes of the period—Lucille instanced "Margie" and "Somebody Stole My Gal"—rather than breakdowns.

The second batch of records came out at a less propitious time and probably did not have very wide sales. Once again, the band played three waltzes and a march. Two of the former were the old favorites "After the Ball" and "When You and I Were Young, Maggie."

One of the Colliers' records, the waltz coupling of "Bluebird" and "Irene," was released in Canada

Otto Collier's mandolin, 2018. Photo by Harry Bolick.

Otto, fiddle; Alsey, guitar, in the Army during WW1. Photo courtesy Mike Collier.

in Brunswick's 52000 series, aimed at the French-Canadian market. The group's name was "translated" into Les Joyeux Montrealais, and the titles likewise converted to French.

No further recording opportunity came the Colliers' way, but they continued to play local functions until Alsey's death on the last day of 1940. As

reported in the *Union* (MS) *Appeal* two days later, he "was found dead on Highway 16 in the corporate limits of Carthage early Wednesday morning with a bullet wound in his forehead . . . [H]e had been carried in a car and his body thrown out."[1] According to the family, he was given drugged whiskey and made away with for the money he had on him. Otto and Lucille were further discouraged by the increasing roughness of the dances for which they played, and eventually quit performing in public. Lucille began to give piano lessons, an occupation she was still following some thirty years later.

The music of the Collier Trio is a valuable testimony of the wide range of styles and repertoire current in the South between the wars. Furthermore, the fact that it could be recorded for, and issued in, a catalog of "Old Time Tunes" shows us how widely that term was interpreted by the businessmen of the record industry. The heritage of the Collier Trio was not rural string bands, with their largely traditional and unwritten repertoire, but rather banjo and mandolin club bands of the early twentieth century— the sort of groups whose photographs fill early twentieth-century instrument catalogs. However, the demands of dance engagements, together with the fact that the band's members did not read music and had to acquire their tunes by ear, preserved in their performances a liveliness that bands more musically literate often lacked.

Tony Russell

A further point of interest about this group is their general similarity to the banjo bands active in Britain at the same time; many amateur or semi-professional combinations with similar instrumentation were playing a comparable repertoire at comparable functions in the 1920s and '30s, and in parts of England one could still hear this tradition in action forty or fifty years later.

—Tony Russell

NOTES

1. "Leake Countian Is Found Slain." *Union Appeal*, Union, MS, January 2, 1941.

After the Ball

Author's note: This transcription is from Brunswick 507, recorded New Orleans, 11/28/1930.

Comparable versions:
"After the Ball," Charles K. Harris, self published 1892
"After the Ball," Vernon Dalhart, 05/13/1925, New York, Columbia 15030-D

Tony Russell

Ben Hur March

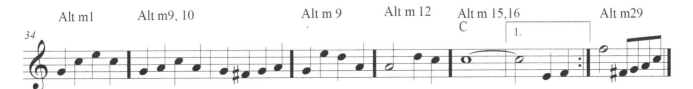

Author's note: This transcription is from Brunswick 288, recorded New Orleans, 09/10/1928. The melody varies a good bit in the
A part and a few of the alt measures are indicated here.

Comparable versions:
"Ben Hur March," F. A. Hall 1892/ E.T. Paull, 1899/ Edward H. Saull, 1916. (Same title, unrelated melody.)

The Bluebird Waltz

Author's note: This transcription is from Brunswick 289, recorded New Orleans, 09/10/1928.

Comparable versions: None known

Tony Russell

Happy Home Waltz

Author's note: This transcription is from Brunswick 550, recorded New Orleans, 11/28/1930. Notes longer than a quarter are played with tremolo.

Comparable versions: None known

Irene Waltz

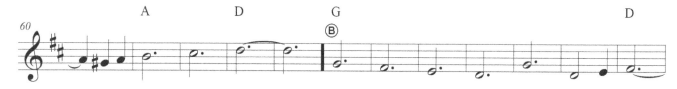

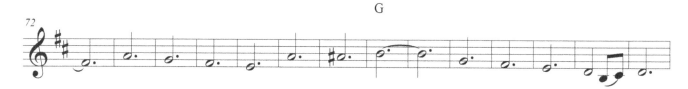

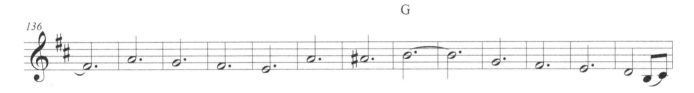

Author's note: This transcription is from Brunswick 289, recorded New Orleans, 09/10/1928.

Comparable versions: None known

Napoleon March

Author's note: This transcription is from the 78 rpm recording, Brunswick 550, recorded New Orleans, 11/28/1930.

Comparable versions: None known

Tony Russell

Over the Waves

Author's note: This transcription is from Brunswick 288, recorded New Orleans, 09/10/1928.

Comparable versions:
Sobre las Olas" ("Over the Waves"), Juventino Rosas, 1888
In this book:
"Winona Echoes," Narmour and Smith, 09/23/1929, New York, OKeh 45414
"Over the Waves Waltz," Kessinger Brothers, 06/24/1929, New York, Brunswick 344
"Over the Waves," Stripling Brothers, 09/10/1934, New York, Decca 5041

When You and I Were Young, Maggie

Author's note: This transcription is from Brunswick 507, recorded New Orleans, 11/28/1930. The second and last time through, the B part is played twice. Mandolin tremolo is played throughout. This is one of the most popular waltzes for Mississippi fiddles, known to be in the repertoire of the Leake County String Band, Hoyt Ming, and I suspect many, many more. George W. Johnson wrote this in memory of Maggie Clark from Glanford, Ontario. George courted and married Maggie in 1864. They moved to Cleveland, OH, where George worked as a journalist. After only a year of marriage, Maggie died of tuberculosis at the age of twenty-three.

Comparable versions:
George W. Johnson, lyrics, J. A. Butterfield, music, 1866
"When You and I Were Young, Maggie," Fiddling John Carson, 11/07/1923, New York, OKeh 40020
"When You and I Were Young, Maggie," Riley Puckett, 09/11/1924, New York, Columbia 15005-D

MIKE COMPTON

Mike Compton (1956–), bluegrass man-dolinist extraordinaire, was born in Meridian, Mississippi, in 1956. While he was growing up, he was the only musician in his family; however, on his paternal grandmother's side, the Galyeans had had a few dance musicians.

Mike's maternal grandfather, Kermit Weeks, played guitar with a local fiddler, Chester Linton. However, the family's music making was all before Mike's time. Mike did hear Chester's sons: fiddler Bernie Linton, who put out at least two cassettes of his bluegrass-style fiddle tunes, and Avil Linton, who played mandolin, guitar, and banjo. He also heard a local bluegrass band led by Raymond Huff-master, who was part of the Mississippi delegation to the 1974 Smithsonian festival. Huffmaster owned the Tin Barn, a honky-tonk north of Meridian near Lauderdale, where Mike met a few local old-time fiddle and guitar players and heard them play Nar-mour and Smith tunes, like "Carroll County Blues."

Mike worked for local farmers during summer vacation in his later teenage years. Some of them were fans of older styles of country music such as the Mom and Dads, Narmour and Smith, Arthur Smith, the Skillet Lickers, and the Leake Country Revelers. One such farmer was Avil and Bernie Linton's "Uncle" Nate Smith, a hobby mandolin player. Mike heard a good amount of the old music on their pickup truck's 8-track player.

Photo of Mike Compton, courtesy Mike Compton.

Mike started out on guitar, with a few unsatisfy-ing lessons from a local teacher. Around age fifteen he began to teach himself mandolin, which he had received as a Christmas present. As a teenager he hung out with his nearby cousin, Jeffrey Moffett, and the two of them pounded out some of the pop songs of the day. Jeffrey eventually inherited the Galyean family fiddle. The only mandolin players in the area that Mike heard were Avil Linton and Ellis Hand, both of whom played old-time tunes. Mike's early progress on mandolin came the hard

Molly Dimple Galyean Benjamin. Photo courtesy Mike Compton.

way, by trial and error. When he moved to Nashville in 1977, he continued to learn on his own simply by playing a tremendous amount.

In Nashville he began to work with former Bill Monroe sideman Hubert Davis. In the mid-1980s he joined the Nashville Bluegrass Band and played to great acclaim for four years. Next he joined John Hartford's string band, performing songs and tunes that catered to Hartford's passionate interest in old-time fiddle tunes. Mike played on six albums and toured extensively with the band until Hartford's death in 2001. Mike's other recording credits are extensive and impressive, but his most widely heard recording is as a member of the "Soggy Mountain Boys" on the Grammy-winning *O Brother, Where Art Thou?* soundtrack.

Mike has been a full-time musician since 2000. Before that he augmented his income with part-time jobs such as cook, industrial floor cleaner, draftsman, landscaper, carpenter's helper, drywall hanger, and pressman. For a while he worked at Hatch Show Print in Nashville.

He continues to tour and perform, as a solo artist and with several duet projects in addition to rejoining the Nashville Bluegrass Band. Teaching since the early 1980s, Mike is much in demand.

His tune "Yankee Gal," from his CD *Rotten Taters*, is included here as it reflects the old-timey side of his music. The notation includes a simplified melody

for old-timey players, and a full bluegrass mandolin version to show what he masterfully plays.

—Harry Bolick

This chapter is based on the author's interview by email with Compton, July 6, 2018.

Recordings

"Yankee Gal" can be heard on Compton's CD, *Rotten Taters*. See mikecompton.net for his extensive discography.

Mike Compton and Norman Blake, "Gallop to Georgia" (Taterbug Records, 2018), contains sixteen tracks of Narmour and Smith tunes.

Yankee Gal

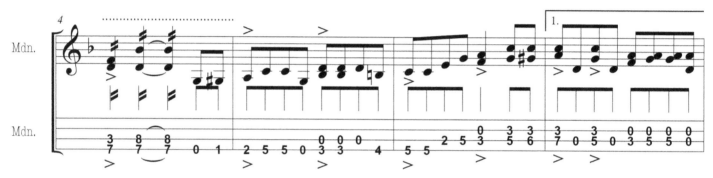

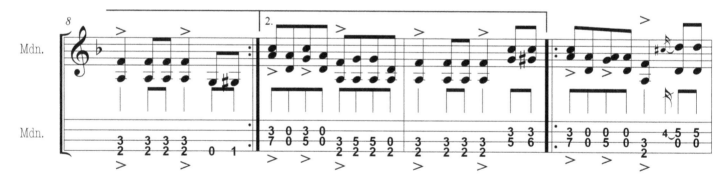

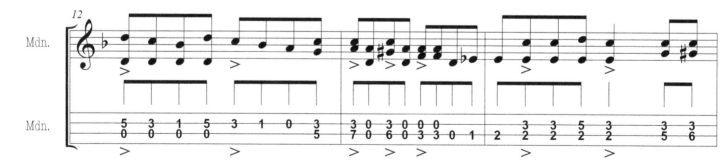

Harry Bolick

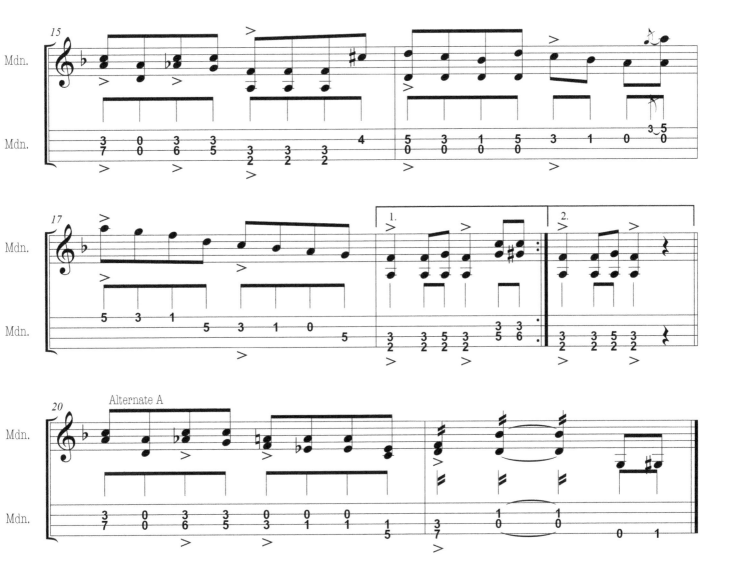

Author's note: Mike's full transcription of his mandolin part is followed by a simplified old-time fiddle version. The tune is by Mike Compton ©Minner Dipper Music, and is used with his permission.

Comparable versions: None known

Yankee Gal

Author's note: This transcription is a simplified old-time fiddle version based on Mike's mandolin version.

LLOYD JEPTHA "JABE" DILLON

Outside of Walthall County, fiddler "Jabe" Dillon (1898–1983) has been largely unknown. But in the county he is fondly and well remembered. He appears a few times in local newspaper accounts, on one extremely rare 78 rpm record, one nearly as rare 45 rpm, and on a precious few home recordings. His strongest pieces, "Brown Skinned Girl," "Memphis Mail," and "Howling Hound," are masterful showpieces: wild, loose, with much variation, verses delivered with abandon, all hovering over the tonic chord carried on relentlessly by the band. On the later solo recording, the 45 rpm record, his feet serve as the accompaniment to his fiddling and singing.

In his own words, Jabe first played fiddle at age seven, starting out on a $1.98 Sears and Roebuck fiddle. He earned the money for the fiddle by helping an old man who was a night watchman at a local sawmill. In a *Times-Picayune* article from October 12, 1969, he is quoted saying he had been playing fiddle since he "sat on my mother's lap and learned on corn shucks." His style appears to be somewhat influenced by African American music, and there was a small African American community in Tylertown. On a family cassette interview from the 1980s, Jabe mentions learning "Refused Love or Brown Skin Baby," from hearing "Old Dennis," an African American fiddler. His wife mentioned

Politician Charlie Sullivan and Jabe Dillon. Newspaper photo courtesy the *Carthaginian*, Carthage, MS, May 13, 1971.

hearing another African American fiddler. Jabe was known to have traveled to nearby New Orleans, where he could have heard many sorts of music. The family doesn't remember him listening to records or even radio.[1] He was a primarily local musician who traveled occasionally for music.

Left to right: Doris Wallis, Either Woody or Howard Hux, unknown, and Jabe Dillon, fiddle, ca. 1969. Photo courtesy Dee McCullough.

He was most active as a musician in the late 1940s and '50s. In addition to local performances at schools and community events, his family remembers his being on concert bills that featured Elvis Presley, Jimmie Rodgers, and Hank Williams. Around the time Jabe and his band recorded the 78 rpm record, perhaps in September 1950 when he performed in New Orleans on a concert bill with Hank Williams, Jabe was offered a generous recording contract from RCA if he would move to Nashville. The family remembers the terms as 6% royalties on records and transportation costs to Nashville for Jabe and his band. The "Jabe Band" consisted of Jabe and his son, Jephthah Lloyd Dillon Jr., known as "J. L.," on lead guitar, and two to four other musicians. The other musicians' names are unremembered. Jabe's response to the offer was, "I

have to go home and dig my potatoes and corn."[2] The rest of the band was not consulted about the offer and did not get to go. His son, J. L., was so disappointed that Jabe turned down the offer that he gave up playing music and broke up the band.

In the summer of 1958, fiddler Obed Magee's nephew, Bob Magee, played guitar and sang in a band with Jabe. One of the Hux brothers was also playing guitar in the band. They played at several movie theatres in Kentwood and Bogalusa, Louisiana. Jabe taught Bob all of the songs that he sang with the band and some Elvis songs. The crowds were small for the band that summer.[3]

A neighbor, Dan Ginn, remembers going to the Dillon household on Saturday evenings in the late 1950s. Family, friends, and neighbors would gather to watch a popular television show early

Harry Bolick

The Jabe Dillon band, likely in Nashville, circa 1950. Lloyd Dillon Jr., guitar, left; Jabe Dillon, fiddle. Other musicians unknown. Photo courtesy Pat Sumrall.

in the evening on the Dillon TV, which was the first, and at that time only, TV in the area. Jabe's wife Myrtle would make a cake or a pie and coffee for everyone. After the television show, Jabe and some boys would play music. The boys were adept at wiring up the early amplifiers and microphones of the era, so Jabe had his own vocal and fiddle microphone. The accompaniment would include mandolin, electric guitar, and drums. They would play only until 10 or 11 p.m., so they would be able to get to church the next morning. Jabe would sing gospel songs, country and western songs, and play fiddle tunes. He would usually sing and play on each number. Although we only know of a few of his pieces, apparently he had a large repertoire. On the 45 rpm recording, canned sound effects are used for the train and dog howls, but on Saturday nights Jabe would vocalize those parts. It's a shame they were not recorded that way.[4] Jabe was not known to play other instruments but would on occasion hold the fiddle like a mandolin and strum the strings. Family members do not recall that any of Jabe's children except J. L. played music.

Jabe was in the local newspapers on a handful of occasions. The *Tylertown Times* in 1951 describes a picnic sponsored by the VFW Post 4812 in the nearby village of Lexie, with music furnished by Guitarist O. L. Hughes and fiddler Jabe Dillon.[5]

In addition to the music, the day was filled with political speeches, baseball, bingo, swimming, hot dogs, hamburgers, soda pop, and cold watermelons. In the January 29, 1953, edition of the *Tylertown Times*, Jabe was sighted playing with his son and Hosea Loflin and others for the Waltham Jaycees Barn Dance at the Tylertown Armory benefit for March of Dimes.[6] In an April 3, 1969, Tylertown newspaper article, Jabe described organizing a band with Woody and Howard Hux and a sixteen-year-old singer, Doris Wallace, sometime after he dissolved the band that included his son.[7] According to an account published in *Bogalusa Daily News* on October 12, 1969, starting in 1963 and for eight years in a row, Jabe won the Fiddlers Contest at the Washington Parrish Fair at Franklinton, Louisiana, about twenty miles from Tylertown. In addition to his known recorded tunes, the article mentions that he played "Fisher's Hornpipe," and that he had played a fiddle contest with one hundred fiddlers and was on stage for thirteen hours before winning first place. A later article credits him with a ninth win, playing "Memphis Mail," "Refused Love," and "Howling Hounds." The number of contestants at the Franklinton contest seems to have varied between four and eight. His unidentified photograph appeared in the *Carthaginian* newspaper of Carthage, MS, on May 13, 1971,

FIDDLIN' JABE . . .
. . . world's greatest fiddler

NOW YOU CAN OWN THESE CLASSICS—
● Memphis Mail   ● Refused Love
● Howling Hound   ● Precious Memories

ONLY $1⁵⁰

Now On Sale At

The Tylertown Times

1972 poster to advertise the
45 rpm recording. Courtesy
Dee McCullough.

where presumably he played for a local event. According to a *Tylertown Times* article interview in 1972, Jabe appeared very early, before records became the norm on radio, on New Orleans radio stations WWL and WESU, playing with Henry Dupree and the River Revelers, Jimmy Wilson, Louie Bono, and Lou Childress.[8] Lloyd Dillon with Jimmy Thornhill, Mrs. Preston Dillon, and the group played at a Tylertown "Walthall Heritage" event for the library on April 8, 1976.[9] Jabe Dillon played violin with a string ensemble at the opening of the East McComb Activities Center after an address by gubernatorial candidate Ross Barnett. Fiddler Obed Magee, who has been described as the three-time fiddling champion of Walthall County, also appeared.

Jabe Dillon in his kitchen, where the 45 rpm was recorded.
Photo courtesy Pat Sumrall.

TO
Progress High School
FRIDAY NIGHT, FEBRUARY 1st — 7:30 P. M.
FIDDLING JABE DILLON
And His Variety Show

Featuring
MISS ALBERTA FUTCH, as Guest Star

LITTLE MISS VESTER MYERS
The Girl that does Everything

MISS CAROLYN BOWMIN
Singer and Performer

MISS JERRY LOU MILEY
Singer and Guitar Player

MISS DORIS WALLACE
Singer and Performer

Fun For All Ages!

Advertising poster ca. 1950s. Courtesy Dee McCullough.

For most of Jabe's later life, he was a largely self-contained and inspired musician, performing solo for local events like the opening of the radio station WTYL,[10] and competing in the Franklinton Parish fair.

In 1972, at age seventy-four, Jabe recorded the music for the 45 rpm record, solo and in his kitchen. Who did the recording and how the recording was produced is unknown, but he did try to sell the 45s locally with a poster advertising their availability at *the Tylertown Times*. In his *Tylertown Times* interview he claims "Refused Love," which he had previously recorded as the "Brown Skin Gal," as his own composition. Perhaps Jabe reworked the tune so much that he considered it a new composition. Curiously, he did not claim to have composed "Howling Hound" and "Memphis Mail." However, those tunes—along with "Old Bill" and the unidentified tune from the family's home recordings—are unique to his playing and likely to be of his own creation.

Jabe Dillon, Myrtle Orvin Dillon, and children.
Courtesy Pat Sumrall.

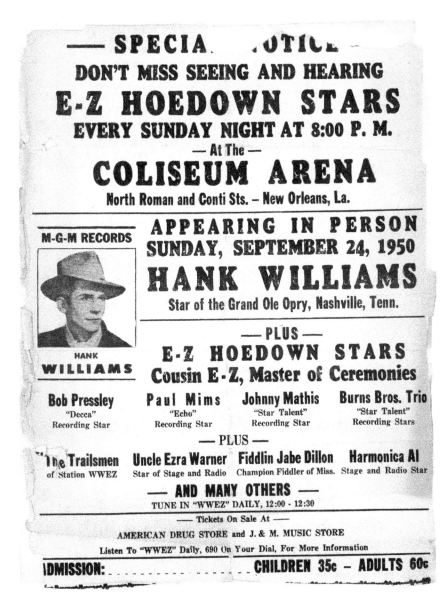

SPECIAL NOTICE

DON'T MISS SEEING AND HEARING

E-Z HOEDOWN STARS

EVERY SUNDAY NIGHT AT 8:00 P. M.

— At The —

COLISEUM ARENA

North Roman and Conti Sts. – New Orleans, La.

M-G-M RECORDS

HANK
WILLIAMS

APPEARING IN PERSON
SUNDAY, SEPTEMBER 24, 1950

HANK WILLIAMS

Star of the Grand Ole Opry, Nashville, Tenn.

— PLUS —

E-Z HOEDOWN STARS
Cousin E-Z, Master of Ceremonies

Bob Pressley
"Decca"
Recording Star

Paul Mims
"Echo"
Recording Star

Johnny Mathis
"Star Talent"
Recording Star

Burns Bros. Trio
"Star Talent"
Recording Stars

— PLUS —

The Trailsmen
of Station WWEZ

Uncle Ezra Warner
Star of Stage and Radio

Fiddlin Jabe Dillon
Champion Fiddler of Miss.

Harmonica Al
Stage and Radio Star

— AND MANY OTHERS —

TUNE IN "WWEZ" DAILY, 12:00 - 12:30

—— Tickets On Sale At ——

AMERICAN DRUG STORE and J. & M. MUSIC STORE

Listen To "WWEZ" Daily, 690 On Your Dial, For More Information

ADMISSION: . . . .   CHILDREN 35c – ADULTS 60c

Poster courtesy
Dee McCullough.

After his death there was a short-lived family controversy over Jabe's violin as the label contained the word *Stradivarius*. However, Jabe's fiddle was a nine-dollar Sears and Roebuck instrument. He owned an equally inexpensive mandolin.

Well liked in the area, with an outgoing and engaging personality, Jabe was also a great storyteller. But David Ginn recalls this "Jabe" story from his own father's telling. In the late 1950s there was a movie theater in Tylertown that showed a variety of movies including science fiction films, with spaceships and alien encounters. UFO sightings were also in the news. One Saturday around lunch, Jabe was in his kitchen when a very alarmed child came running in having sighted a spaceship in the back pasture. Failing to calm the child down, Jabe and several other adults walked out behind the barn to view the "spaceship." In the distance they could see a rounded silvery shape rippling in the sunlight. Now quite alarmed, they rushed back to the house, sent the kids out to the neighbors to spread the news. One of the kids ran a mile down the road to

Sixth from left: Bob Johnson, a friend of Jabe Dillon; seventh from left: Jabe Dillon, at 1926 Franklinton Fiddle Contest.

a neighbor's house where there was a telephone and the Tylertown town police were called.

The police arrived, machine gun in hand, to join the crowd of well-armed neighbors, many of whom were World War II veterans. A horseshoe-shaped military formation was created to approach the "spaceship." One of the men asked, "Why do you think it's moving?" and was answered with, "I think they are unloading." Upon closer inspection the "spaceship" was discovered to be a weather balloon, launched from Denver, Colorado. Fortunately no weapons were fired and no one was injured. For a while after the event, the balloon was displayed in the window of the *Tylertown Times*, so that locals such as David's father could point out the "spaceship" to their children. All of this happened in Jabe Dillon's backyard.

Jabe was a farmer all of his life. He started farming near Tylertown, the county seat of Walthall County, on a good piece of land "near Johnny Stovall's," and worked very hard to make the farm successful. He bought the land with a loan from the Federal Land Bank. Eventually, Jabe paid off the man at the land bank, but got no receipt. The man died the next day and there were no records

of the debt being paid. Jabe lost the land, as he was not able to scrape up the money again. He and his family moved to forty acres that his wife had inherited. He continued to farm and raise cows, but after working so hard and losing the first farm, his heart just wasn't in farming. For a short while, he drove a road grader for the county.

On Sunday afternoons, after church, Jabe would drive his grandkids and other kids to Magee's creek to watch them go swimming. He was a skilled outdoorsman, an excellent fisherman using cane poles and "mudworms" dug from the creek bank for bait. He was noted for building well-crafted cypress fishing canoe-like boats, carved cypress paddles, and fish traps.[11]

Sometime in the mid- to late 1950s, Jabe was the music leader at the Centerville Baptist church. Neither he nor the pianist could read music as they both played by ear. He would lead from the front of the congregation by keeping time with his hands and singing powerfully. He played music at any opportunity that appeared.

An undated newspaper article, very likely from the *Tylertown Times*, has a photo of a smiling Mr.

and Mrs. Lloyd "Jabe" Dillon celebrating their fiftieth wedding anniversary. In the article Jabe said that "he has married many a couple in Walthall during the time he was justice of the peace, then turned right around that night and played for their wedding supper." His wife, Myrtle Orvin Dillon, who was descended from a full-blooded Cherokee mother, was described as having a very happy, easygoing personality. They had four sons together. Though times were hard and money tight, they remained married and content with each other throughout their lives.

There are three recordings each for "Memphis Mail" and "Brown Skin Gal/Refused Love." Each recording has varying lyrics, but utilizes the same bits of melody with varying amounts of rhythmic filler. Jabe seems to be improvising the structure of his collection of tune parts as he plays. It's a wild ride.

—Harry Bolick

This chapter is based on interviews with Dee McCullough, May 14, 2018; Pat Sumrall, September 20, 2018; and a Dan Ginn telephone interview, October 4, 2018.

NOTES

1. May 14, 2018, and May 18, 2018 interviews with Dee McCullough, granddaughter of Jabe Dillon.

2. May 18, 2018 interview with Pat Sumrall, granddaughter of Jabe Dillon.

3. Email from Bob Magee, May 13, 2019.

4. October 4, 2018 Telephone interview with Dan William Ginn, who is the son of one of Jabe's neighbors. Dan has written a novel, *Slim*, about a fictional Tylertown lawyer.

5. "Many Candidates at V.F.W. Picnic," Tylertown *Times*, July 5, 1951.

6. "Time Out for a Gay Time, Had by All, For the Benefit of, March of Dimes," *Tylertown Times*, January 29, 1953.

7. "Noted Fiddling Jabe Dillon, one of the first on the station, will be here Saturday," *Tylertown News*, March 4, 1969.

8. "Old time fiddling captured on Jabe Dillon recording," *Tylertown Times*, October 28, 1972.

9. "Walthall Slating 'Heritage' Event," *McComb Enterprise Journal*, March 31, 1976, 3.

10. "Noted Fiddling Jabe Dillon, one of the first on the station, will be here Saturday," *Tylertown News*, 03/04/1969.

11. Dan William Ginn, *Slim* (Light Switch Press, 2017) 37, 38.

Recordings

Brown Skin Gal/Memphis Mail, Fiddling' Jabe Dillon "Old-time Fiddling" Champion of Mississippi,

Echo 116, 78 rpm, Box 2987, Hollywood 28, California, circa 1950
"Old time Fiddling with Vocal"

Memphis Mail + Refused Love/ Precious Memories + Howling Hound, The World's Greatest Fiddler "Fiddling Jabe," Continental Records: CO-09-15-601, 45 rpm, 1972

Old Bill/Redwing
"Old county fiddling" informal recording recorded 1954 at Osmore's Store and Service Station with Lloyd Dillon, Osmore Dillon, and Willis Alford. Uploaded to archive.org by Sandy Dillon, February 12, 2010.

Jabe and his son with a band, likely called "Jabe's Band" recorded four single-copy 78 rpm discs with eight songs. His family holds the recordings.
   The selections are:

   Brown Skinned Girl (vocal: Jabe Dillon)
   Girl I Left Behind (vocal: Jabe Dillon)
   Tomorrow Never Comes (vocal: J. L. Dillon Jr.) (A composition by Ernest Tubb, lyrics by Johnny Bond, which was a hit in 1945.)
   Unidentified instrumental with no vocal
   Howling Hound (vocal: Jabe Dillon)
   Unidentified song (vocal: unidentified) beginning "Two little girls of my dreams" with unidentified singer
   Yo Yo Blues (vocal: unidentified) (Blind Lemon Jefferson 1929, and Barbecue Bob, 1929 recorded "Yo Yo Blues" but they seem unrelated.)
   Memphis Mail (vocal: Jabe Dillon)

In the 1980s, Frank Dillon recorded a cassette tape with Jabe telling stories and playing the following tunes:

   Miles Standish
   Buggy and a Hoss
   Sally Goodin
   Orange Peeling
   Refused Love
   Memphis Mail

Lamp Lighting Time
Precious Memories
Turkey in the Straw
In the Pines
Silver Haired Daddy of Mine
Howling Hound
Arkansas Traveler
Red Wing
Red River Valley

With permission from his family, all of Jabe's recordings can be heard at: www.mississippifiddle.com

Brown Skinned Girl - Refused Love

Whee   hoo   Good - bye little   love

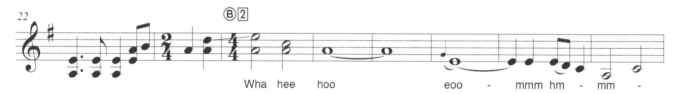

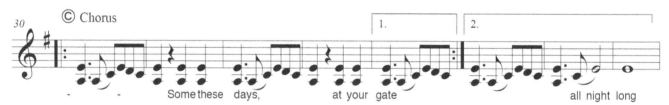

Wha hee   hoo   eoo - mmm hm - mm -

- - Some these days,   at your gate   all night long

Whee   hoo   Good - bye Little   Girl

Harry Bolick

Wha hee hoo   eoo -

- mmm hm - mm   Some these days,   I laid down

Lawd, Lawd

Wha hee hoo

eoo - mmm hm - mm   Mama and Papa,   begged me,

all night long

Ⓕ (From the 45rmp recording)-insert after m22

Author's note: Transcribed from Echo 78 rpm recording. The key is A modal and a "A" chord is played throughout. It's not clear if the guitar is playing Am or A, as the chord is mostly an up-beat "chop."

The repeated measures 30–35 repeat between five and seven times to accommodate the lyrics. M117–23 are from the 45 rpm recording and were not played on the Echo 78 rpm recording; they are inserted on the first pass after M22, when completed, resume playing with M23.

Comparable versions:
"Rocky Road to Dublin," Osey Helton, ca. 1925, Broadway 5122
"Rocky Road to Dublin," Allan Sisson, 02/25/1925, New York, Edison 51559

Lyrics from the 78 recording:

Whee-hoo
Goodbye little love

Wha-hee-hoo-eoo-mmm-hm-mm
Some of these days, at your gate
I'm going home, whiskey straight
Round old house, quiet as a mouse,
All night long

Whee-hoo
Goodbye Little Girl

Wha-hee-hoo-eoo-mmm-hm-mm
Some of the days, I laid down
With your straw, all night long,
freeze to death
Lawd, Lawd

Wha-hee-hoo-eoo-mmm-hm-mm
Mama and Papa, begged me,
begged me, go-on boy,
Go-on boy, county farm
be your home
Lawd Lawd

From the family 78, which has an interesting C part:
Oh Baby, some old day
Old Joe, come on house

Whiskey straight, all night long
Round your house, Lawd, Lawd

Whee-hoo
Fare you well

Wha-hee-hoo-eoo-mmm-hm-mm
Some old days, mighta lay down
With your straw, freeze to death
All night long, Lawd, Lawd

Mama and Papa, begged me,
begged me, go-on boy,
Go-on boy, county farm
be your home, Lawd, Lawd

Lyrics from the 45 rpm recording:

Use my love, bring me down
Lawd Lawd

Wha-hee-hoo-eoo-mmm-hm-mm
Some old day, there lay down
With your straw, all night long,
freeze to death , Lawd, Lawd

Wha-hee-hoo-eoo-mmm-hm-mm
Mama's gone, papa too
Ain't got no sister, ain't got no brother
Lawd, Lawd

Buggy and a Hoss

All I want is a bug-gy and a hoss buggy and a hoss, buggy and a hoss. All I want is a bug-gy and a hoss and sure that we will mar - ry

Author's note: This was transcribed from a Dillon family cassette recording from the 1980s, which can be heard at mississippi-fiddle.com. Dillon was tuned to GDAD. The A part first ending varies, sometimes adding another measure; see "alt first ending." When singing, Dillon simplifies the melody and adds a beat occasionally to draw out a word.

Comparable versions: None known

Jabe Dillon

The Girl I Left Behind Me

Harry Bolick

Author's note: This tune is transcribed from a 78 rpm home recording; listen to it at mississippifiddle.com. First ten measures are played twice, alternating with singer for each of three verses and chorus.

Comparable versions:
See www.tunearch.org for a full discussion of the possible origins of this tune.
It seems to be of eighteenth century Irish and or English origin.
"The Girl I Left Behind Me," Uncle Dave Macon, 4/15/1925, New York, Vocalion 15034
"The Girl I Left Behind Me," Gid Tanner and His Skillet Lickers, 03/29/1927, Atlanta, Columbia 15170-D
"The Girl I Left Behind Me," Doc Roberts and Asa Martin, 03/15/1929, Richmond, IN, Gennett 6826

Lyrics from the 78 rpm home recording:

[The verses are mostly undecipherable but the chorus, the first time only, is:]

Oh that girl, that pretty little girl, that girl I left behind me
Curly hair, the rosy cheeks, the girl I left behind me

Next time the chorus is:

Oh that girl, that pretty little girl, that girl I left behind me
Coal black eyes, rosy red cheeks, the girl I left behind me.

And the third time both choruses are sung, after which, the remaining measures are played.

Howling Hounds

Harry Bolick

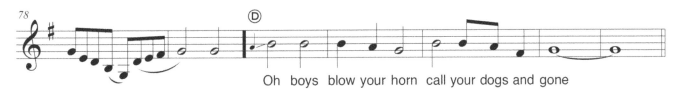

Oh boys blow your horn call your dogs and gone

Jabe Dillon

Harry Bolick

repeat 7 times see m3-35 for variations

Author's note: This is from the family home-recorded 78 rpm disc and varies a good bit from the 45 rpm disc. The vocal on the
45 is mostly a relaxed monotone as opposed to the falsetto one for the 78.

Comparable versions: None known

Lyrics from the 45 rpm recording:

Hey boys blow your horn call your dogs,
put out your fire, the old spark it's done gone

Memphis Mail

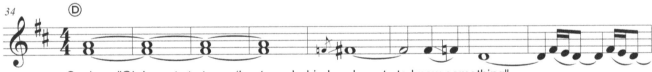

Spoken: "Oh he gets to town 'bout one behind and wants to know something"

Spoken: "Old Jabe is high-balling it. Everything all right"

Harry Bolick

Author's note: This transcription is based on the 45 rpm recording.
The numbers of repetitions of the phases in each part vary on each pass.
The lyrics from the 45 are shown above. M25-M26 has the only two F notes and their pitch is played between F and F#.

Lyrics from the Echo 78 rpm:

Talk about your Southern Pacific, gab about your L&N
Let me tell you about the fastest train ever rolled again
Let her roll, Memphis Mail

One thing is clear, not so long ago
Letting it pour down, the weather turns cold, down that long lonesome road
I says, let her roll, Jimmie, let her roll

Nobody knows what they rode way long ago, sometimes right, sometimes no
Let her roll, boy, let her roll

On the family 78 rpm the lyrics are:
Oh hey, that old Memphis Mail . . .

Miles Monroe Standish

Don't you hear   that lonesome   dove   her   fly from tree   to   tree

Who landed by   his own true   love   And here   they   been   mine

Author's note: This was transcribed from a Dillon family cassette recording from the 1980s, which can be heard at mississippi-fiddle.com. The fiddle is tuned to GDAD.

(The lyrics share verses with many songs, such as "The Blackest Crow" from Tommy Jarrell of North Carolina.)
W. L. Bloomfield, 1853 and/or Raymond, ca. 1850s, lyric and music
Buckley's New Orleans Serenaders, *Song Book for the Parlour* (New York: J. Cozans, 1855)
In this book: "Catahoula Blues," Sylvester Moran
"Take Me Back to the Sweet Sunny South," Da Costa Woltz's Southern Broadcasters, 05/1927, Richmond, IN, Gennett 6176
"Sweet Sunny South," Charlie Poole & The North Carolina Ramblers, 09/1927, Chicago, Paramount 3136

Lyrics:

Don't you hear that lonesome dove
O'er flying from tree to tree
Who landed by her own true love
And here they been mine

Fare you well my own true love
Fare you well for a while
Fare you well, I'm coming back again
If I be ten thousand miles

Ten thousand miles I've saved my love
I've been to England, France or Spain
This frozen breast will never [… ?]
Till you I meet again

I've been false to you my love
Rocks will break and run
Fire will freeze and water will burn
If I no more return

Fare you well my own true love
Fare you well for a while
Fare you well, I'm coming back again
If I be ten thousand miles

And don't you hear that lonesome dove
O'er flying from tree to tree
Who landed by her own true love
And here they been mine

Old Bill

Author's note: The recording, located at archive.org, in very low fidelity, enhanced by straw beating, which produces a sound that approaches undecipherable. The entire short recording is transcribed here. Since no part is repeated, it is unclear what is a part and where the measures of 2/4 are best placed. For example M16–24 could be notated in 2/4. Dillon seems to be organizing his playing in notes grouped over one tap of his foot.

Comparable versions: None known

Old Dan Tucker

Harry Bolick

Author's note: This was transcribed from a Dillon family cassette recording from the 1980s, which can be heard at mississippi-fiddle.com. The fiddle is tuned GDAD.

Comparable versions:
"Old Dan Tucker," Dan Emmett, *Aldophous Morning Glory Songster* (1843), 14
Bolick and Austin, *Mississippi Fiddle Tunes and Songs from the 1930s*: C. M. Coursan, "Big Tom Bailey," 88; Thaddeus Willing-
    ham, "Old Dan Tucker," 388
"Old Dan Tucker," Uncle Dave Macon, 04/13/1925, New York, Vocalion 15033
"Old Dan Tucker," Fiddlin' John Carson, 12/18/1924, New York, OKeh 40263

Lyrics:

Going down the road, with an awful heavy load
[Met a m . . . ?] tack in Mammie's toe
Popped his whip and the lead mule is gone,
Hind mule's popped the wagon tongue

Chorus
Riding up a billy and he led his hound
The old hound barked and the billy jumped
Throwed off Dan right straddle a stump

Chorus
Old Dan Tucker come next day
Rise up [fetching?, sitting . . .], dog at the bone
Old Dan, come up mad
Quit his wife and sold his dog

Orange Peeling

Author's note: This was transcribed from a Dillon family cassette recording from the 1980s, which can be heard at mississippi-fiddle.com.

Comparable versions: None known

Harry Bolick

Unknown Tune

Author's note: This is a one-chord tune in G. The recurring parts may vary by two beats at the end of the phrase. This transcription is of the entire recording. The Nations Brothers were from Lincoln County, which is adjacent to Walthall County where Jabe lived.

Comparable versions:
"Sales Tax Toddle," Nations Brothers, 10/13/1935, Jackson, MS, Vocalion 03184

THOMAS JEFFERSON DUMAS

Tom Dumas's (ca. 1886–1980) grandmother, Clementine Spencer, was born in 1834. Sometime before 1870 she married Wesley Spencer, who apparently adopted her children and gave them his name. They had changed their name back to Dumas by 1880.[1] In 1870 James Dumas was living with his mother Clementine Spencer in Choctaw County.[2] James and Cornelia Dumas married in 1884, just before the birth of their first son Zoda.[3]

My grandmother [Clementine], she was living in North Carolina. And Mr. Dumas, he lived up at Bellefontaine (Mississippi); he was a slavery buyer. He went out there in North Carolina and he bought my daddy's mama and brought her to Bellefontaine. And there was eight of them, was in the family out there and he went out there and bought her. There was four boys and four girls. Her mother and father had eight children. He bought one. And Mr. Parks Spencer that lived over there, little old place called old Slate Springs, about fifteen miles from Bellefontaine. Mr. Dumas put all his folks in an ox wagon and let them go on the Fourth of July over there at Slate Springs, over there at Mr. Spencer's, he give a picnic for them.

My grandmother had three children in slavery times. My daddy [James Dumas] was a slave. . . .

Tom Dumas photo in the William R. Ferris Collection (20367), courtesy of Southern Folklife Collection, Wilson Special Collections Library, University Libraries, University of North Carolina at Chapel Hill.

Tom Dumas, 1974. Photo courtesy *Clarksdale Press Register*.

And so when they closed the war down. Well my grandmother said then it was about six months before they knowed that they was free.[4]

Thomas Jefferson Dumas was born on April 2, 1888, in Bellefontaine, Mississippi, a small community in Beat 1 of Webster County.[5] He was the second oldest son of the couple. In the 1970s, Thomas Dumas recalled his exact birthday:

Mr. Bailey, you know Governor Bailey, he used to be governor here [in Mississippi], he was from a little town called Walthall, just four miles from Bellefontaine. . . . So, me and Tom Bailey, we were raised together, and there was four of us that was the same age, two black and two white. I had an uncle who was born on the 29th of March in 1886. Tom Bailey was born on the 30th of March, 1886. Mr. Artis Branum was born the first day of April in 1886, and I was born the 2nd day of April 1886. We

all lived close together. When the 29th would come, my grandmother would give all four of us a dinner, there were two whites and two blacks, give us a birthday dinner . . . When my birthday would come then my mother would fix dinner and we'd all eat, that's the way we done for years.[6]

Dumas was about nine years old the first time he picked up his father's fiddle. After his parents went to church, Dumas and his brother remained at the house, and they tried to play the fiddle. Even though it "was left there in good tune," his brother never did learn how to play it, but Thomas picked up the fiddle and "commenced playing . . . just as good if [he]'d been playing it fifty years." When his parents returned from church, his sister chortled about their misspent time at the house. She said, "Pa . . . Tom and Fulton playing your old fiddle." According to Dumas, his father handed "it to me and I commenced playing and my daddy, he just had a fit. Well, all right, when we done that then my daddy just took us out and tied us up to a cedar tree and whupped us for messing with the fiddle. Well, he whupped us good."

In a couple of days, his father James and his uncle Sylvester McGhee went somewhere to play that fiddle, every night it seemed. His sister once again opened her mouth and claimed that Thomas "can play the fiddle just as good as you can." With that, his father handed him the instrument, and he began to play that thing in the best rhythm possible since he was too young at the time to pat his foot on the floor. His father was so proud of his clever son that he took him son to play for the white folks at Bellefontaine and Walthall. Pretty soon, he started carrying his son around all the time to play the fiddle. Thomas Dumas explained it this way:

Nobody [taught me how to play the fiddle], I taught myself. I picked it up and went to playing and played just as good when I picked it up as I could. I can't learn nothing. I picked up a banjo done the same thing, picked up a guitar done the same thing, jew's harp done the same thing, tried to blow the french harp for ten years and never could blow a tune on it.[7]

T. DeWayne Moore

Tom Dumas, 1978. Photo courtesy *Greenwood Commonwealth*.

No one had ever seen someone so small play the fiddle. Folks would make requests and he'd cut out and play it.

In the late 1890s, Dumas began performing in a local band. "We got a banjo, a guitar, a mandolin and fiddle," and he exclaimed:

> In the wintertime, why we'd have dances every night. We had dances over there at Eupora, have dances over there at Kilmichael . . . at Houston and Calhoun City. We'd just go out and play for everybody then. We'd get in a wagon and stay there all night long. Just make music all night. I've played a fiddle many a night all night long, what we call the old square dance, one fellow calling the set, letting the people know what to do.

Dumas played the fiddle for his original string band, which played music from about 1898 to 1905. He ended up putting down the band, and he quit the fiddling business. This was the first time he "stowed away his music."

The 1910 census listed Thomas as twenty-two years old and still living at home in 1910.[8] He married and divorced Lena Dumas in October 1915.[9] He registered for the draft on June 5, 1917, and his registration card tells us that he was married and working as a farmer in Walthall.[10] In June 1918, Dumas was living in Tallahatchie County and got called to serve at Camp Grant in Illinois.[11] Another census taker recorded his and his wife Georgia's location in Beat 1 in Webster County in 1920.[12]

Dumas moved to Tutwiler in 1924, and he worked on the farm of Roy Flowers for a long time. It was in Tutwiler that Dumas started to play music again, and he started a little string band around 1930. The group was composed of a guitar, fiddle, and Dumas played the banjo. "[We'd take] trips in wagons to dances that lasted all night. Yessir, we used to have music. We played up there in Vance," Dumas recalled, "out there on the Cagle's Crossing, [and] over there at Shelby. All of these establishments were patronized by white folks." Dumas's group never played for an African American audience in the 1930s. He believed that Black folks in the Delta did not enjoy listening to his country music.

By 1930 Dumas had married a woman named Della, and the couple lived with their children in Tutwiler.[13] By 1940 the Dumas family had moved to Dublin in Coahoma County to work on a farm, but Tom Dumas had connections in Tutwiler, and the couple came back to Tallahatchie County for good sometime thereafter.[14] His father, James "Jim" Dumas, died in 1941. He has a simple, clean headstone at North Union Cemetery in Bellefontaine, Webster County, Mississippi.

Tom Dumas does not show up again in the official record until the late 1960s. In the summer of 1968, folklorist Bill Ferris visited Dumas in Tutwiler. It is from this encounter that we have what until recently had been thought to be the only images of Dumas. It is from this recording session that we have the only recordings of Lee Kizart and Thomas Jefferson Dumas. Ferris recorded Dumas playing several songs on the fiddle and a couple on the banjo.

The next time Dumas made the papers was in the *Sumner* (MS) *Sentinel* in May 1973. The Cotton Carnival made its annual tour to Tutwiler on Monday, April 31, 1973.[15] Dave Jennings III, the Reverend Glen Ray, and Thomas J. Dumas provided "the music, songs, and all."

The Sale of Dumas's Violin

In December 1974, Dumas decided to sell the violin that once had a label inside that read "Italy 1794." According to Dumas, none other than the seventh US president, Andrew Jackson, had gifted it to his grandfather. Not only was Dumas's grandfather once enslaved at the Hermitage, but his family left Tennessee to work for the family of Mississippi governor Tom Bailey.[16] Dumas felt as though he had "no one to hand it down to" except his daughters, and he asked Mrs. Bill Flautt to serve as his agent for the future transaction. She invited all comers to inspect the historic instrument. As to its provenance, Mrs. Flautt explained:

> One of the things that has always interested me about Tom's violin is the well-known fact that

Andrew Jackson's wife, Rachel, loved violin music to the extent that her drive at The Hermitage in Nashville was made in the shape of a violin. One wonders if Tom's grandfather played for Miss Rachel or if, perhaps, she may have handled the instrument itself. It seems likely that Tom's grandfather Dumas might have pleased the Jackson family with some musical effort, which led to their presenting him with the fiddle.

Mrs. Ada Whisenhunt, the supervisor of interpretation and research at The Hermitage, Jackson's home, explained that the cedar trees in front of the house were planted in the shape of a guitar, that Rachel Jackson played the harpsichord and the general a flute, but that there is no record of fiddles.

Dumas sold the violin in 1974 to a Memphis couple, Woody and Juanita Parker, for $250. They had the fiddle evaluated, but they claimed that any value was lost when mice chewed away the little label that read "Italy 1794." They did believe, however, that it very probably did belong to Andrew Jackson.

Although his folk music was the love of his life, Dumas didn't find much appreciation for it in the blues-loving Delta. Quotes taken from two different articles reveal his feelings about music in the Delta: "Where I lived [in the hill country] we had music all the time. But these folks in the Delta, they don't like fiddlin' and banjo music. Well, I'd drink a little whiskey, then I'd go tune up my fiddle and commence playing a little," he said about playing in a Delta tavern in more recent times. They'd have the Seeburgs [jukeboxes] in there and they'd turn them on just as loud as they could:

> dadda-dump dadda-dump dadda-dump, and I'd just pick my fiddle up and walk on out. Because I never did have no use for no Seeburg nohow. All that I did like [on the] Seeburg [wa]s what the white folks played on the Seeburg. You see these white folks still got the old-timey music in them yet, but these other folks hasn't; they done made a change. I have never changed yet.[17]

The Mississippi Federation of Music Clubs honored the memory of W. C. Handy, author of the "St. Louis Blues," and the residents of Tutwiler in July 1976 by presenting a plaque to the little Delta town where Handy first heard that "strange music" known as the blues. Residents turned out for the ceremony in Town Park to hear Tom Dumas's banjo rendition of "John Henry" and for a few to reminisce the times they heard Handy playing that native Delta music.[18] He unwrapped his banjo from its canvas sack and sang his version of "John Henry," the ballad of the railroad spike driver, accompanied by a freight train heading slowly east through Tutwiler, blowing its horn.

Several newspaper reporters from Jackson, Greenwood, and Memphis visited Dumas and wrote articles for their respective newspapers. These writers sought him out for his association with folk music and the blues. After Lee Kizart, he was reported to be last of the blues players of Tutwiler, but one of his granddaughters said that was not true. "No, he didn't play the blues," she said. "He played mostly country and western. He played the banjo and the fiddle."

In April 1978, portrait painter Robert Brougher had several of his works on display at Rarities, a part of the Bluff City Broom Corn Company in Memphis. The prize of the show was a character study of a Black man in overalls: Tom Dumas, a ninety-ish figure in faded Tuf-Nut overalls and a soiled slouched hat. His face was grizzled; his eyes faraway. But one author had the sense that he was a noble man. He had the look of the wisdom of a long life, the certainty of what life was about. Brougher had painted a smaller portrait of Dumas that hung on another wall. Eva Everett believed that Dumas was worth many more paintings, for there was much about him to discover.[19]

Thomas Jefferson Dumas died at a Clarksdale hospital in the first week of December 1980, and he was buried at Oakland Cemetery in Sumner. He was survived by two daughters, Mrs. Fannie Brownlee of Clarksdale and Mrs. Alice Williams of Chicago, along with nine grandchildren, forty great-grandchildren, fifteen great-great-grandchildren, and one great-great-great-grandchild.[20] His music lives on in the field recordings of Bill Ferris and the transcriptions in this book.

—T. DeWayne Moore

NOTES

1. 1880 US Census, Place: Sumner, Mississippi; roll: 664; page: 371C; Enumeration District: 176.

2. 1870 US Census, Place: Township 21, Range 9, Choctaw, Mississippi; roll: M593_725; page: 400B; Family History Library Film: 552224.

3. 1900 US Census, Place: Beat 1, Webster, Mississippi; page: 12; Enumeration District: 0097; FHL microfilm: 1240833.

4. Lonnie Wheeler, "Honest Man: Tom Dumas Has a 'Good Name,' and He Has Everything He Needs," *Clarion-Ledger*, Jackson, MS, November 12, 1976, 33.

5. The 1900 census, 1910 census, and his World War I registration card all list 1888 as the year of his birth.

6. Steve Burtt, "Folk Musician Tom Dumas of Tutwiler dies at 94," *Charleston Sun Sentinel*, Charleston, MS, December 11, 1980, 1.

7. David Brown, "The Man Who Played Jackson's Fiddle," *Charleston Sun Sentinel*, Charleston, MS, July 8, 1976, 12.

8. 1910 US Census, Place: Beat 1, Webster, Mississippi; toll: T624_756; page: 11A; Enumeration District: 0105; FHL microfilm: 1374769.

9. *Webster County Times*, October 25, 1915.

10. US, World War I Draft Registration Cards, 1917–1918, Ancestry.com, 2005.

11. US Lists of Men Ordered to Report to Local Board for Military Duty, 1917–1918, Ancestry.com, 2013.

12. 1920 US Census, Place: Beat 1, Webster, Mississippi; roll: T625_899; page: 11B; Enumeration District: 110.

13. 1930 US Census, Place: Tutwiler, Tallahatchie, Mississippi; page: 12A; Enumeration District: 0020; FHL microfilm: 2340902.

14. 1940 US Census, Place: Coahoma, Mississippi; roll: m-t0627–02017; page: 13B; Enumeration District: 14–34.

15. "Tutwiler News," *Sumner Sentinel*, Sumner, MS, May 3, 1973, 2.

16. "Legendary Violin Offered for Sale," *Clarksdale Press Register*, Clarksdale, MS, December 11, 1974, 3.

17. David Brown, "The Man Who Played Jackson's Fiddle," *Charleston Sun Sentinel*, Charleston, MS, July 8, 1976, 12.

18. "Tutwiler Becomes Official Home of the Blues," *Greenwood Commonwealth*, Greenwood, MS, July 29, 1976, 1.

19. Eva Everett, "Brougher Portraits Now on Exhibit in Memphis," *Press Register*, Clarksdale, MS, April 18, 1978.

20. Steve Burtt, "Folk Musician Tom Dumas of Tutwiler Dies at 94," *Charleston Sun Sentinel*, Charleston, MS, December 11, 1980.

Recordings

Mississippi Sawyers: A Collection of Old-Time Mississippi Fiddling (LP, Sawyer Productions, 1980): Cotton–Eyed Joe.

William Ferris field recordings: SFC Audio Open Reel FT-20367/10242, in the William R. Ferris Collection (20367), Southern Folklife Collection, Wilson Special Collections Library, University Libraries, University of North Carolina at Chapel Hill.

Burden Down

Author's note: Transcription from William Ferris field recording, see appendix A. The fiddle is tuned to AEAE and tuned low.
   Tom Dumas said, "I been knowing this song since 1897."

Comparable versions:
(Related to: "Will the Circle Be Unbroken," "Battle Hymn of the Republic")
"Since I Laid My Burden Down," The Elders McIntorsh and Edwards' Sanctified Singers, Chicago, 12/04/1928

Cindy

Dig them Irish Potatoes, then roast them in the sand   If I can't eat

them all,   save for Juli - anne   Get along   home, Cindy,   Get along

home   Get along home,   Cindy,   One   more   night   and   day

Author's note: Transcription from William Ferris field recording, see appendix A. The fiddle is tuned AEAE and tuned low. The grace notes indicate unison slide in to the high E, so that two strings sound E.

Comparable versions:

Bolick and Austin, *Mississippi Fiddle Tunes and Songs from the 1930s*: Charlie Addison, "Want to Go to Meeting," 41;
 Mrs. R. C. Clifton, "Miss Cindy," 79; B. M. Guilette, "Liza Jane," 111; Mrs. Joe McCoy, "Her Cheeks Are Like a Cherry," 142;
 Rev. J. E. Williams, "Cindy Waltz," 206; John Brown, "Cindy," 227; Enos Canoy, "Where'd You Get Your Whiskey," 247;
 W. E. Claunch, "Cindy," 255; Frank Kittrell, "Cindy Jane," 308; Hardy Sharp, "Liza Jane," 339; Thaddeus Willingham, "Miss
 Cindy," 384
"Cindy in the Meadows," Samantha Bumgarner & Eva Davis, 4/22/1924, New York, Columbia 167-D
"Cindy," Riley Puckett and Clayton McMichen, 04/02/1927, Atlanta, Columbia 15232-D
"Get Along Home, Miss Cindy," Pope's Arkansas Mountaineers, 02/06/1928, Memphis, TN, Victor 21577

Lyrics:

Dig them Irish potatoes, then roast them in the sand,
If I can't eat them all, save for Julianne

Chorus:

Get along home, Cindy, Get along home
Get along home, Cindy, one more night and day

Possum up that simmon tree, raccoon on the ground
Raccoon told that possum, shake them Simmons down

Going downtown the buggy, what want me bring you back
Got more to say, good old gal, put in that paper sack

I wish I was an apple just a hanging on a tree
Every time Cindy came by, she'd take a bite of me

When I was a pretty little boy sixteen inches high
I would court pretty little gals, and make the old 'uns cry

I would not marry a yaller gal and I'll tell the reason why.
Her neck is is long and strainy, I'm afraid she'll never die

Cindy in the summertime, Cindy in the fall,
I can't get Cindy, don't want none at all.

Cotton-Eyed Joe

Had not met Cotton Eyed Joe, I'd been married seventy years ago. What ya going

do, what you going go, what you going do with Cotton Eyed Joe.

Author's note: Transcription from William Ferris field recording, see appendix A. Fiddle is tuned to AEAE and tuned below A440.

Comparable versions:
Bolick and Austin, *Mississippi Fiddle Tunes and Songs from the 1930s*: Allen Alsop, "Cotton-Eyed Joe," 44; Rev. J. E. Williams, "Cotton-Eyed Joe," 207
In this book: "Cotton-Eyed Joe," Carter Brothers & Son, 11/22/1928, Memphis, TN, Vocalion 5349
"Cotton-Eyed Joe," Dykes' Magic Trio, 07/1927, New York, Brunswick 120
"Cotton-Eyed Joe," Pope's Arkansas Mountaineers, 07/1928, Memphis, TN, Victor 21469
"Cotton-Eyed Joe," Gid Tanner & His Skillet Lickers, 10/1928, Atlanta, Columbia 15283-D

Lyrics:

Had not met Cotton Eyed Joe, I'd been married seventy years ago
What ya going to do, what you going go, what you going do with Cotton Eyed Joe

Old Dan Tucker was a good old man, washed his face in a frying pan
Stuck his head in a wagon wheel, died with a toothache in his heel

Way down yonder in a hollow log, led my horse and fucked us all.
If he lives, ride him again, if he dies, I'll tan his skin.

Old-time gal pickin' that cotton, cotton's all out and the feeds all rotten,
Heeeeyyyyyahh, What ya going do, what ya going say, What ya going do with Cotton Eyed Joe

I fell down bumped my toe, wouldn't broke it all that Cotton Eyed Joe
Cotton Eyed Joe, wouldn't broke it all that Cotton Eyed Joe

John Henry

John Henry was a little bitty boy, was no bigger than the palm
of your hand Picked up a hammerand a little piece of steel, I'll make a
steel driving man....

Author's note: Transcription from William Ferris field recording, see appendix A. The fiddle is tuned to AEAE and low.

Comparable versions:
In this book: Sid Hemphill, "John Henry"
"John Henry Blues," Fiddling John Carson, 03/1924, Atlanta, OKeh 7004
"Death of John Henry," Uncle Dave Macon, 04/14/1926, New York, Vocalion 15320
"John Henry," Ernest V. Stoneman, 06/21/1926, New York, Edison 5194
    Lyrics:
    John Henry was a little bitty boy, was no bigger than the palm of your hand
    Picked up a hammer and a little piece of steel, I'll make a steel driving man ...

    John Henry hammered in the mountain, till his hammer caught on fire
    The last words I heard John Henry say, want a cool drink of water before I die

    John Henry got sick and he had to die, buried him in the sand
    Every time that the train passed by, there laid a steel driving man

Old Hen Cackled

Thomas Jefferson Dumas

Author's note: Transcription from William Ferris field recording, see appendix A.

Comparable versions:
Bolick and Austin, *Mississippi Fiddle Tunes and Songs from the 1930s*: Mrs. M. B. Brister, "Old Hen Cackled on the Pot," 66; John Brown, "Old Hen Cackled," 73; W. M. Collom, "Rabbit in a Ditch," 82; Jim Gooch, "Old Hen Cackled," 110; Dr. Frank Smith, "Old Hen Cackled," 179
In this book:
"Cackling Hen," Hoyt Ming and His Pep Steppers, *New Hot Times* (Homestead LP 103, 1973)
"The Old Hen Cackled and the Rooster Is Going to Crow," John Carson, 06/14/1923, Atlanta, OKeh 4890
"Hen Cackle," Gid Tanner & Riley Puckett, 03/08/1924, New York, Columbia 110-D
"Cackling Hen," J. D. Harris, 1925, Asheville, NC, OKeh 45024

Pretty Little Girl

Author's note: Transcription from William Ferris field recording, see appendix A.

Comparable versions:
"Dandy Jim of Caroline," Thomas "Daddy" Rice of the Virginia Minstrels, A. Fiot, Philadelphia, 1844
Bolick and Austin, *Mississippi Fiddle Tunes and Songs from the 1930s*: Allen Alsop, "Pretty Little Girl in the County," 50;
W. A. Bledsoe, "Purtiest Little Girl in the County," 222
"Prettiest Little Girl in the County," Gid Tanner & His Skillet Lickers, 04/10/1928, Atlanta, Columbia 15315-D
"Little More Sugar in the Coffee," Fiddlin' John Carson & His Virginia Reelers, 12/09/1930, Atlanta, OKeh 45542

Sally Goodin

Had a piece of pie, had a piece of pudding Love that gal,

love that pudding Love that gal called Sally Goodin

Author's note: Transcription from William Ferris field recording, see appendix A. The fiddle is tuned AEAE and tuned low.

Comparable versions:

Bolick and Austin, *Mississippi Fiddle Tunes and Songs from the 1930s*: J. E. Shoemaker, "Sally Goodin," 173; Miss Mae Belle Williams, "Bear Creek," 204; John, Brown, "Sally Goodin," 234; W. E. Claunch, "Sally Goodin," 272, 252; Thaddeus Willingham, "Sally Goodin," 395

In this book: "Sally Goodin," Claude Kennedy

"Sally Goodwin," Ira Ford, *Traditional Music of America* (New York: E.P. Dutton, 1940), 64, 209 (calls), 419 (verses)

"Sally Gooden," Eck Robertson, 07/01/1922, New York, Victor 18956

"Old Sally Goodman," Fiddlin' John Carson, 11/07/1923, New York, OKeh 40095

"Sally Goodin," Kessinger Brothers, 02/05/1929, New York, Brunswick 308

FREENY'S BARN DANCE BAND AND
THE FREENY HARMONIZERS

Freeny's Barn Dance Band first put down roots around 1913, when William Leslie Freeny (1898–1957), fiddler, and A. F. "Fonzo" Cannon (1900–1967), guitarist, began to work together at square dances. Leslie Freeny was from Freeny community, some five miles southeast of Carthage in Leake County, as was his cousin Charles Hendrix Freeny (1907–1975), who soon joined them to play tenor fiddle parts. Fonzo Cannon was born in the small community of Edinburg, northeast of Carthage. Among the trio's best tunes were the waltzes "Sweet Bunch of Daisies" and "Wednesday

(Ira Ellis?, guitar), Sadie Freeny Chamblee, and Carlton Freeny, banjo, ca. 1920s. Photo courtesy Beth Alford.

Carlton Freeny, 1941. From the collection of Tony Russell.

Leslie Freeny, age 17. From the collection of Tony Russell.

Night Waltz." They continued to play at functions around Leake County, and in the mid-1920s were occasionally joined by Hendrix's young cousin Samuel Carlton Freeny (1912–1987).

Carlton, who was also from Freeny community, had begun playing guitar young, ordering his first instrument from Sears and Roebuck in Memphis, and learning chords from Hendrix. He also played a Gibson tenor banjo. Meanwhile, his sister Sadie was learning the piano, which she was later to play in one of the family bands.

Leslie Freeny and Fonzo Cannon married sisters and continued to be close friends and playing companions. Cannon heard, and was impressed by, the records of Riley Puckett, and he tried to follow his style of playing on tunes like "Sally Gooden" and "Low Down Hanging Around." He also liked to sing, and would urge Leslie to play "background music" while he did so, but Leslie always demurred.

It was through Fonzo Cannon that the group came to make records. He contacted H. C. Speir, the Jackson music store owner who was instrumental in getting many local performers on to records with various companies.[1] The Leake County Revelers were one of Speir's bands. He also discovered blues singers such as Tommy Johnson, Son House, and Skip James, and had a hand in an early recording of sermons by the Rev. C. M. Grayson of Magee, Mississippi. Speir operated for the Victor, Columbia, and Paramount companies, but he was acting for OKeh Records when he held an audition with Cannon and the three Freenys in his store on Friday, November 21, 1930. Speir suggested the numbers that he thought would be best, and Carlton noted in his diary, "We got the contract."

His diary entry for Tuesday, December 16, reads: "Cloudy today & rain. Went to Jaxon today. Made 3 records. For OKeh company. Got back here about eleven o'clock." "We made suggestions as to the numbers to be recorded," Carlton remembered years later. "The recording team listened and made suggestions and final selections." Carlton always described the recording lineup as a quartet, but other accounts suggest that it was in fact a quintet, with another cousin, Cleveland Freeny (1905–1982), on mandolin.

Tony Russell

Freeny orchestra of 1930–32. Left to right: Hendrix Freeny, Sadie Freeny, O. Ellis, Tessie Lee Ellis, Benson Mills, Herbert Cagle, S. Carlton Freeny, Ira Ellis. From the collection of Tony Russell.

Fonzo Cannon with his wife Ruby, son Hubert, and daughter Faye, 1929. The car is Fonzo's 1926 Chrysler roadster. Photo courtesy Carl Fleischhauer.

Carlton Freeny diary entry
of December 16, 1930. Photo
courtesy Beth Alford.

Carlton Freeny and Sadie Freeny Chamblee, Christmas
1972. From the collection of Tony Russell.

"Sullivan's Hollow," the Freenys' masterpiece, is a strange, bittersweet tune, full of bluesy slurs, somehow both somber and gay at the same time. The unison fiddling of Leslie and Hendrix is remarkable—hollow, shimmering, almost ghostly. As a melody, "Sullivan's Hollow" is no more than an over-and-over strain, remaining on the tonic chord nearly all through its course. The reel tempo is laid down by Cannon's drumming, hypnotic chords and

Carlton's precise strum. All together, the performance is a superb display of timing and its rewards.

The beauty of the tune belies its history. Sullivan's Hollow is an area in Smith County, some way south of Leake. Carlton was sure the tune came from there. He wrote: "As a kid I used to be afraid to go through the area as a result of the many tales told."

According to the 1938 WPA guide to Mississippi, "The Hollow, a long narrow valley lying south of Mize, has been the source of so many tales of feuds and bloodshed that it is now impossible to separate fact from legend. Every Mississippian knows of it and uses its name as a synonym for lawlessness. It was first inhabited by nine Sullivan brothers, fierce Irishmen who brought with them from the South Carolina mountains the clannish customs of that section...."[2]

A few years later, a lurid feature in *Collier's* magazine, purporting to "unfold the bang-bang history of Mississippi's most legendary family, and how they got that way," documented "terrible tales... of fighting and feuding, of ambuscades and revenge for deeds done a generation before.... Sullivan's Hollow is a common-place synonym for general lawlessness, covering everything from murder to moonshining and resisting arrest."[3]

The waltz "Don't You Remember the Time" is more melancholic, with the fiddles contributing

Hendrix Freeny, 1943. From the collection of Tony Russell.

Fonzo Cannon, guitar; Hubert Cannon, mandolin; Leslie Freeny, fiddle; Arnold Freeny. The two little girls are Hubert's sisters. Carthage, MS, ca. 1930. Photo courtesy Carl Fleischhauer.

a sobbing melody. "The Leake County Two Step" is paced much like "Sullivan's Hollow." "Croquet Habits," a mildly suggestive song from the family of "Take a Drink on Me," "Take a Whiff on Me," and so forth, elicits a tough, bluesy sound from Leslie Freeny, and Fonzo Cannon delivers the lyrics with gusto. As so often in the band's music, you feel a tension between the steady rhythm of banjo and guitar, and the fiddles straining to tear things up.

Finally, in the two tunes titled "Mississippi Square Dance," on which Fonzo Cannon calls the sets, the fiddlers have an opportunity to be a little wilder. "Sally Ann" ("Mississippi Square Dance–Part 2") combines the familiar sound of a traditional fiddle tune and the unusual approach that Leslie and Hendrix brought to it. Their way, it seems, was to work within a narrow compass, using relatively few notes, but wringing everything out of them.

These were very fine records, with a firm, stamping rhythm, always considered one of the band's strengths—quite different from the approach of the

better-known Leake County Revelers, whose lineup of fiddle, mandolin, banjo, and guitar achieved a lighter, airier sound, lilting rather than stomping.

◆ ◆ ◆

Several other Mississippi performers were present at that series of sessions in Jackson. On the Monday of that week the Mississippi Sheiks were at hand; Tuesday, the Black singers Charley McCoy, Slim Duckett, and Peg Norwood; then the Freeny band; then the Newton County Hill Billies, and the Black preacher Elder Curry. Uncle Dave Macon and Sam McGee appeared on Wednesday to cut ten songs. The rest of the week saw a couple of gospel quartets, the return of the Sheiks and Elder Curry, and a vocal group called the Magnolia Trio.[4] In five days almost a hundred masters were successfully made. Whether because of good planning, or excellent performances, or merely a sense of economy in Depression times, over three quarters of these Jackson recordings were commercially issued.

Among this flood of releases were all six of Freeny's Barn Dance Band's sides, but times did not favor the phonograph record. Sales were poor, and the discs are consequently rare. OKeh soon had to wind up its old-time series. The Freeny band nevertheless received a flat fee of $75 for each release.

The failure of the records to make the band's name much more widely known may have been one of the reasons the group came to look back on another event as perhaps the most exciting of their career. In the spring of 1930, some nine months before the recording session, the trio of Leslie, Hendrix, and Fonzo—Carlton was in high school—was playing at a Carthage general store, the People's Wholesale Company. The store was on the ground floor of a hotel and the hotel was currently entertaining a distinguished visitor.

The news broke in the local newspaper on Thursday, March 13: Jimmie Rodgers was to play three evening concerts at the Fox Theatre. Rodgers was at the height of his popularity, and the three shows cost the theatre owner, George Chadwick, $1,500. Chadwick charged a dollar a head admission—"which amounted," as Fonzo's son Hubert Cannon pointed out, "to two days' work for a laboring man at that time." And Rodgers was in extremely poor health, incapable of playing for very long at a stretch. So, hearing the music coming up from the ground floor of his hotel, he invited the trio up for drinks, explained his problem, and asked for their assistance.

The Thursday and Friday concerts were sellouts. The Freeny–Cannon trio played a couple of tunes with Rodgers singing, then a couple of fiddle tunes with him joining in on guitar. Rodgers rested a good deal of the time, but gave his one-man show as long as he could, finally calling the band out on stage to relieve him while he went back. Hubert Cannon, then six years old, was in the audience with his mother. "I remember how thin and pale Jimmie looked and also the big diamond ring he wore on his finger." Hubert also recalled a couple of Rodgers's jokes, which "were a little naughty at my age."

That Saturday morning Rodgers had a hemorrhage, and a local doctor, Dr. W. S. Martin, advised him to stay in bed in case he suffered another. The evening show was cancelled and Rodgers refunded Chadwick a third of his payment. The trio probably got no payment for their part but, Hubert Cannon remembered, "They considered it a great honor and of course it was. My father told me that Jimmie was very grateful and just kept telling them how much they had helped him. My father always thought of him as a fine gentleman and a common man even though he was very famous at this time."

◆ ◆ ◆

About the end of 1930, the Freeny circle took in some more musicians, becoming more of a show band and playing at fairs and contests as well as dances. Hendrix and Carlton were members, playing fiddle and trombone respectively, and Carlton's sister Sadie played drums. Ira Ellis, Benson Mills, and Herbert Cagle all played trumpet; O. Ellis, saxophones; and his wife Tessie Lee Ellis, piano. This band lasted about a year, and then took new shape as the Freeny Harmonizers.

The Harmonizers were normally Ira Ellis, now on lead fiddle; Hendrix Freeny, lead or tenor fiddle; Carlton Freeny and Neal Babb (guitars); Clyde Finklea (banjo), and Sadie Freeny (piano). But, according to Carlton, "when playing for fairs and large dances, etc., Ira Ellis played trumpet with me on tenor sax and we used drums. We played a thirty-minute spot each Sunday afternoon over the radio station in Kosciusko, for quite a while. We never made much money, but did have lots of fun." Carlton also recalled that the band's theme tune was "Memories."

Meanwhile, Fonzo Cannon had forsaken the life of a sharecropper for the more comfortable one of owning and operating a service station. He introduced his son to string band music, and Hubert recollected: "I remember playing with the band when I was seven to ten years old. I started on a ['tater-bug] mandolin because it was small enough for me to hold. I later played the guitar. We played for a dance in a neighbor's home from 8 p.m.

until 2 a.m. and a hat was placed in the floor at the intermission and the dancers dropped the money in the hat. For our nightly work we collected $4.75 for five of us. I remember they divided the money and I got the 75 cents, but I also remember that everyone enjoyed themselves."

Fonzo Cannon also played with the Collier Trio, appearing at the Fox Theatre before shows and during intermissions, and at dances.

The larger Freeny orchestra, with brass and reeds, was never recorded, but a rather diminished Freeny Harmonizers group did appear at a recording session in 1935. ARC–Brunswick had a team in Jackson from October 10 to 22, recording gospel groups, blues singers, and old-time musicians of various kinds, principally for its Vocalion label, among them the Nations Brothers. The Harmonizers' date certainly involved Ira Ellis (fiddle), Neal Babb (guitar), and Carlton Freeny (tenor banjo), who appear to be the only musicians audible on the issued titles. But it is possible that Hendrix Freeny was also present on second fiddle, though not in a favorable enough position for the microphone to pick him up well. All Carlton's diary entry for Sunday, October 20, states is: "Went to Jaxon today. Made 3 records. Took Sady down. Got back at 8.30."

The unissued titles from this session include the bluesy-looking "How Come You Do Me Like You Do?" and "It's Tight Like That," and the popular tunes "Roll On, Mississippi, Roll On" (from 1930) and "Ain't She Sweet" (1927). The cuts selected for release were "Podunk Toddle," a hard-driving medley of hoedown tunes, and a bluesy vocal number sung by Babb, "Travellin' Blues."

The band's sound is now a long way from that of 1930. Ira Ellis is a fine hot fiddler, but lacks the distinctiveness of Leslie and Hendrix Freeny, and his performances do not have the peculiar regional quality of the Freeny's Barn Dance Band sides. While "Sullivan's Hollow" has central Mississippi written all over it, "Podunk Toddle," good and hearty though it is, might have been made almost anywhere in the South.

With this single Vocalion release, the Freeny circle bowed out of the recording scene, but the musicians within it continued to perform at one

function or another. For instance, Hubert Cannon remembered: "I accompanied Leslie Freeny at a fiddlers' contest at Madden, Mississippi, about 1939. I played the guitar while he played fiddle. We competed against Mr. Ira Ellis . . . and others. Mr. Ellis won first prize with Leslie winning second. I think because of my poor guitar playing. I understand that was the only time Mr. Ellis beat him in contest and they competed many times."

Fonzo Cannon went on to become a used-car dealer and enjoy a good living. "He taught me," said his son, "everything that he knew how to do, including how to play the guitar. He loved good music of any kind, Bill Monroe was his favorite, especially when he had Chubby Wise fiddling for him." Hubert's own sons also took up music for enjoyment, and Fonzo would join them and their father to make a three-generation band. "He could still play good guitar and his timing was great." For the latter part of his life he suffered from emphysema, and eventually he died from it. In Hubert's words, he was often "very poor, but always managed to have plenty to eat and lots of fun in life."

Ira Ellis of the Harmonizers died in 1962, Clyde Finklea in 1968, and Neal Babb in 1971. Babb "was a very good friend and buddy of mine," said Hubert Cannon; "he taught me more guitar than anyone else." But the Freeny circle was by no means broken. Carlton and his sister (now Mrs. Sadie Freeny

Chamblee) remained at the homeplace, while Mrs. Leslie Freeny and Mrs. Fonzo Cannon, as well as Hubert Cannon and his family, were in the Carthage area. Hendrix moved to California, where he played organ and piano in his local church and sometimes violin solos. In the fall of 1975, he journeyed down to Roosevelt Lake to meet Morgan Gilmer and sat in with his Leake County String Band. Sadly, he was unable to play for long and had to return home sick. He died of a heart attack at his home in California City shortly afterward. Carlton continued to play into the '80s, sometimes with the Leake County String Band. "We play once or twice each week, at state parks—rest homes—churches etc.," he wrote to Pat Conte,[5] eight months before his death.

—Tony Russell

NOTES

1. For an account of Speir's activities as a talent scout for record companies, see David Evans, "An Interview with H. C. Speir," *JEMF Quarterly* VIII:3, no. 27 (Autumn 1972): 117–21.

2. Mississippi: The WPA Guide to the Magnolia State (New York: Viking Press, 1938).

3. Harry Henderson and Sam Shaw, "The Sullivans of Sullivan's Hollow: Mississippi's Most Legendary Family," *Collier's*, March 17, 1945.

4. Possibly associated with the Magnolia State Male Quartet of Jackson, reported as singing on WJDX in the *Greenwood Commonwealth*, Greenwood, MS, January 24, 1930.

5. S. Carlton Freeny, letter to Pat Conte, December 2, 1986.

Croquet Habits

Author's note: This transcription is from OKeh 45524, recorded Jackson, MS, 12/16/1930. The harmony part indicated is only a representative one of a constantly varying accompaniment.

Comparable versions:
"Take a Whiff On Me," Publications of the Folk-Lore Society of Texas, Austin, TX, 1916, #2. 63
"Take a Drink On Me," Charlie Poole & the North Carolina Ramblers, 07/25/1927, New York, Columbia 15193-D
"Cocaine Habit Blues," Memphis Jug Band, 05/17/1930, Memphis, TN, Victor V38620

Lyrics:

Well the croquet habit is mighty bad
But these old habits I've always had
Oh, hey, honey, won't you come out tonight?

Well, way down yonder in the sunny south
Where the sun shines warm in my honey's house
Oh, hey, honey, ain't you comin' out tonight?

Well, I seen my honey goin' across the field
She's windin' and twistin' like an automobile
Oh, hey, honey, don't deny your name

Well, I got a good woman and she lives in town
And when I'm gone she wears a mourning gown
Oh, hey, honey, can't you come out tonight?

Well, you got a nickel and I got a dime
If you don't mind, it'll all be mine
Oh, hey, honey, ain't you comin' out tonight?

But if you don't believe I'll treat you right
Just follow me down to my shack tonight
Oh, hey, honey, can't you come out tonight?

Don't You Remember the Time

Author's note: This transcription is from OKeh 45508, recorded Jackson, MS, 12/16/1930. The second fiddle part varies a bit each pass. Two variations are shown.

Comparable versions:

"Don't You Remember the Time," W. R. Williams, words and music, 1919

"Don't You Remember the Time," Clayton McMichen [Bob Nicols] & Riley Puckett, 11/06/1929, Atlanta, Columbia 15114-D

"Don't You Remember the Time," Callahan Brothers, 01/05/1934, New York, Banner 33103

Tony Russell

The Leake County Two Step

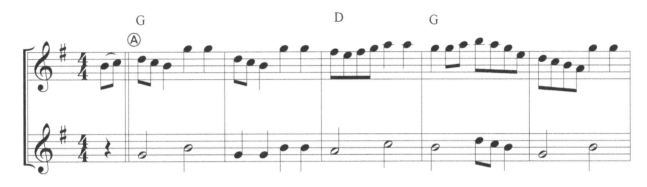

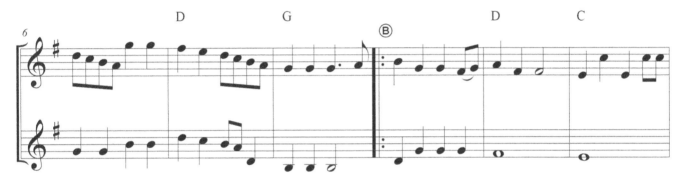

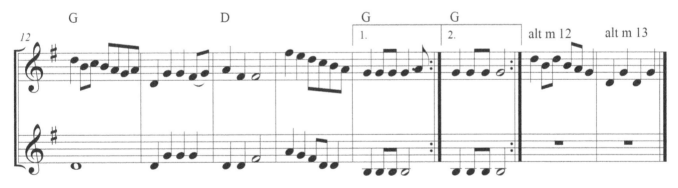

Author's note: This transcription is from OKeh 45524, recorded Jackson, MS, 12/16/1930.

Comparable versions: None found.

Mississippi Square Dance–Part One

Author's note: This transcription is from OKeh 45533, recorded Jackson, MS, 12/16/1930.

Comparable versions:
"Fire In the Mountain," Fiddling John Carson & His Virginia Reelers, 11/21/1926, Atlanta, OKeh 45068
"Hogeye," Pope's Arkansas Mountaineers, 02/06/1928, Memphis, TN, Victor V21295
"Sal Let Me Chaw Your Rosin," Gid Tanner & His Skillet Lickers, 04/11/1928, Atlanta, Columbia 15267-D

Tony Russell

Mississippi Square Dance–Part Two

Author's note: This transcription is from OKeh 45533, recorded Jackson, MS, in 12/16/1930.

Comparable versions:
"Sally Ann," The Hill Billies, 01/15/1925, New York, OKeh 40336
"Sally Ann," Fiddling John Carson, 06/24/1925, New York, OKeh 40419
"Sally Ann," Fiddlin' Doc Roberts Trio, 03/05/1931, New York, Banner 32176

Podunk Toddle

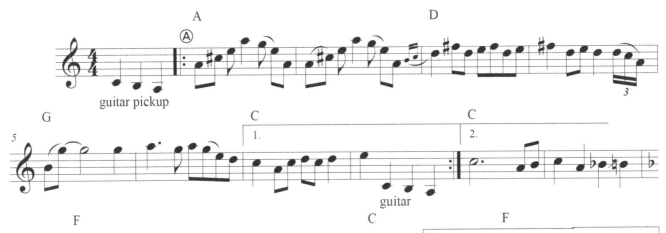

Tony Russell

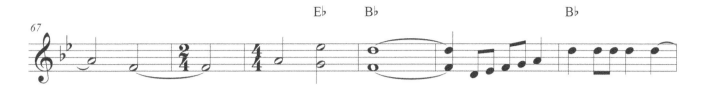

Author's note: This transcription is from Vocalion 03140, recorded Jackson, MS, 10/20/1935. A and B parts are played twice in their entirety, and then played through as written in the order: ABABCDE.

Comparable versions:
"Hickman Rag," The Hillbillies, 05/21/1926, New York, NY, Vocalion 15377 (loosely comparable)

Sullivan's Hollow

Author's note: This transcription is from OKeh 45508, recorded Jackson, MS, 12/16/1930. Part B2 is played alternately with B.

Comparable versions:
(Compare M20–26 with M21–26 of "Sweet Milk and Peaches" by Narmour and Smith in this book. "Sullivan's Hollow," here in the key of C, is often played in the key of D, which makes the similarity more apparent.)

Travelling Blues

Author's note: This transcription is from Vocalion 03140, recorded Jackson, MS, 10/20/1935.

Comparable versions: None known

JOHN STUDIVAN GATWOOD

As the winner of a local Mississippi fiddle contest, John Gatwood (1903–1964) was asked to record by Columbia Records. On December 15, 1928, at a hotel in New Orleans, Gatwood recorded a total four of fiddle tunes: "Crawford March" and "Engineer Frank Hawk" with the Rainey Old Time Band, "Shear the Sheep Bobbie," and "Third Party" with the Gatwood Square Dance Band.

The Gatwood Square Dance Band consisted of John Gatwood on fiddle, his brother Jim [James Louis] (1909–1981) on guitar, and an unidentified

Bill Gatwood (holding fiddle), John Gatwood (holding Charlie's bass), and Charlie Ward with his foot on the bass. Photo courtesy Sue Reano.

Sue Gatwood, John Wayne Gatwood (guitar), John Gatwood (fiddle), at the home of Frank Burns, who is in the background, ca. 1955. Photo courtesy Sue Reano.

Forrest County Ramblers, ca. 1945. Left to right: Archie Nobles, guitar; F. M. Smith, steel guitar; John Gatwood, fiddle; Uncle Charley William Ward Sr. (holding guitar but usually playing bass). Second row: John's nephew, Louis Gatwood, standing on running board of the car; young Charley William Ward Jr. at the wheel. Photo courtesy Sue Reano.

L to R: Junior Gatwood (John Gatwood's nephew), steel guitar; Bonnie Gatwood, age 14, guitar; John Gatwood, fiddle, and young John Wayne. Photo courtesy Sue Reano.

mandolin or banjo-mandolin player. The Rainey Old Time Band consisted of John Gatwood on fiddle, a second, unidentified fiddler on "Crawford March," Jim Gatwood on guitar, and an unidentified mandolin or banjo-mandolin player. Marion Allen Rainey (1885–1969) and John Gatwood are the speakers on "Engineer Frank Hawk." Rainey does the dance calls on "Third Party." "Third Party" is a term locally used to describe someone who was trying to steal one's sweetheart. It isn't clear whether Rainey played any instrument; he probably wasn't the mandolin player. He may be the second fiddler on "Crawford March."

In addition to composing all of the four tunes recorded in 1928, Gatwood also composed one song, "Johnnie Boy Blues." An untitled fiddle tune from a 1958 family recording included here may

be the melody for "Johnnie Boy Blues." The lyrics remain unknown.

For his recordings, Gatwood's bands were paid $500 in lieu of accepting royalties. He used his share of the money to pay for the birth expenses of his first child, Bonnie. The records were popular locally for years; as his daughter Bonnie said in a 2016 interview, "all the jukeboxes had the records."

John Gatwood was born in Lucedale, George County, to James Phillip Gatwood and Lillie Mae (Louis) Gatwood, who was originally from Alabama. John lived his life largely in the southeastern quarter of Mississippi, residing in Lamar, Jeff Davis, Forrest, Clarke Jones, and Scott counties.

Initially learning to play from an older neighbor by the name of "Skinner," John was the first in his family to be a musician and play the fiddle.

Harry Bolick

He played entirely by ear, in some cases learning tunes from records. His children remember him playing "Corrina, Corrina," endlessly, along with the Victrola. He also played guitar, sounding much like Jimmie Rodgers. That is the style that he taught to his children. Gatwood was hardly alone in admiring Rodgers's recordings, but according to the family, there was a personal connection. Gatwood and his brother Jim met Jimmie Rodgers, and hopped a train from Meridian to Memphis with him.

John's family warmly remembers him as both a musician and as a loving father. John first taught his wife to play guitar, then his daughter Bonnie when she was about ten years old. All of the kids had to learn to "second" on guitar because "he had to play that fiddle." He just expected them all to play. His teaching method was straightforward; he would demonstrate the chord shapes and count out the rhythm, loudly. John would "peck them on the head" with his bow if the new guitarist was not keeping good time or played the wrong chords.

In 1923 John, on horseback, first met his future wife, Dovie Estell Mabry, then aged thirteen and riding in the back of a wagon. He said that she looked like a "big red apple" to him. She was born in Laurel, Mississippi, where she received some schooling, adding to her own common sense and intelligence. Although he was good with numbers and careful with measurements, John did not learn to read or write. Dovie would read for him and take dictation from him for his letters. Together they had eight children: Bonnie Jean, James Rudolph (who died as a child), Mack William, Joyce June, Shirley Mae, John Wayne, Janie Sue, and Dorothy Ann. Most of the children sang and/or played guitar, piano, or accordion. Sue became a professional country singer for thirty years and of all the children, most took after her father's musical calling. On one occasion, he said to her: "Sue, one day you gonna go far, far in this world. Honey, you love it [music] as much as I do."

John worked as a farmer and was a fine carpenter. As a carpenter, at times he worked for local lawyers, the governor, and for the military at Camp Shelby, a military post south of Hattiesburg. He built two local Pentecostal churches, one at Petal and the other in Purvis, using the same plan. The Purvis church was only a few blocks from the Gatwood home. At the church, John enjoyed the music but not the preaching. After the music, and before the preaching, John would sneak out of church, leaving the rest of his family in the pews. The preacher in Petal, Jessie Slade, played piano for church services; his wife sang, John played fiddle and there would be a guitar player. They also played "street services" in the courthouse squares in surrounding towns to bring the church to the people and to add new church members. John's daughters, Shirley, at about age twelve, and Sue, about age seven, began singing for church and street services. Brother John, who was three years older, would play guitar.

John's music circle extended to family and a few close friends and neighbors. His sister Bessie learned to play fiddle and piano. His brothers Jim and Millard learned to play guitar. His brother-in-law, Charlie William Ward Sr., played upright bass. Charlie William Ward Jr. played steel guitar. John also played with Jimmie Swan, a local guitarist and singer who went on to make country records and had a career in country music. Gatwood's band, the 1945 Forest County Ramblers, included John Gatwood on fiddle, Jim Gatwood on guitar, F. M. Smith on steel guitar, Archie Nobell on guitar, and Charlie William Ward Sr. on bass. On occasion and certainly in 1945, John attended meetings of the Forrest County Fiddlers Association, which met in Hattiesburg.[1] There is more information about those meetings in the chapter "Communities of Fiddlers in Mississippi."

John played for the public, sometimes as often as three or four nights a week in bands consisting of family and friends. Although not a touring artist, he would on occasion travel as far as Louisiana, Alabama, and Texas for a single appearance. John was an entertainer, a cutup, and a magnetic personality who always had a surprise. He moved around while playing but did no trick fiddling. In a low-fidelity home recording, a sample of John fronting the band and introducing the number can be heard. He is jovial and engaging and his medley of "Tennessee Wagoner" and "Over the Waves" is well rehearsed, tight, and professional. He was remembered as very hospitable and sociable, always happy to see

company. With friends and relations, there would be hugs both coming and going, and he would often say, "If y'all are ever down my way, you stop and see me," and he meant it.

John performed in a variety of local venues from fiddle contests to yard parties and home dances to an inauguration party for Gov. Theodore Bilbo at his Hattiesburg house. Most often John played and sang for dances at the American Legion or Veterans of Foreign Wars (VFW) halls for World War II veterans. To judge by the ads in the *Hattiesburg American* newspaper, in 1943 the "Gatwood Brothers String Band of Petal" played weekly at the American Legion Hall in Hattiesburg for at least July through October.[2] They would play two-steps, waltzes, the jitterbug, reels, and the Virginia Reel. Although grounded in the old-time fiddle style, John kept his ears open and learned new tunes and songs, keeping current with the musical taste of his audience and dancers. In one instance his daughter Bonnie remembered being paid seven dollars to play guitar for the American Legion dance at a time when a postage stamp was three cents. This was likely sometime after 1938 or soon thereafter. When he played some events he thought inappropriate, his band would not include his children.

For a while in the late 1950s, John, his daughter Sue, and her brother John appeared weekly on *McCaffrey's Show Time*, a thirty-minute TV show broadcast on WDAM in Hattiesburg. The sponsor, Red McCaffrey, had a big local grocery store. John also played often on the Hattiesburg radio stations WBKH and WFOR.

Although he had some awareness of his failing health, John was active to the very end. On March 16, 1964, he met a friend who was down on his luck. John helped the man move and gave him his last five dollars. The next day, when John was supposed to go to the hospital, he instead insisted on going to see Charlie William Ward Jr., the steel guitar player. John began to feel ill. His daughter, Joyce, said, "Daddy, let's go straight to the hospital," but he insisted on going to see Charlie. He said, "We'll get there on the way home, I need to see Charlie." Minutes later, in Hattiesburg, he had a heart attack, slumped over the wheel, hit a telephone pole, and left this world. The family service was held at home in a house that John had built. The funeral was held in the church in Purvis that he built. John is buried in Purvis in Lamar County, along with his wife Dovie and other family members.

John's fiddle is still in the family, in the possession of his great grandson, Riley T. Finley, who used it while studying at the Young Musicians program at University of California, Berkeley. John would have been proud to know that Riley made it to Carnegie Hall, playing there with a youth orchestra at age twelve. John had always wanted to play at the Grand Old Opry, and in 2013, Riley's sister, Brynna sang with a choir at the Opry in Nashville, Tennessee.

—Harry Bolick

This essay is based on an extensive interview with Sue Reano, August 10, 2016, Boston, and access to her copy of the 1958 home recordings.

NOTES

1. "Fiddlers Play Next Dec. 1," *Hattiesburg American*, November 5, 1945, 7.

2. *Hattiesburg American*, Hattiesburg, MS, July 26, August 2, 16, 23, 30, September 16, 20, October 4, 25, 27, 1943.

John Gatwood's known repertoire

Tunes remembered by family or from family recordings:

Alabama Gals
Alabama Jubilee
After the Ball
Aunt Nellie's Quilting Party
Bile Them Cabbage Down
Carroll County Blues
Dance All Night
Down Yonder
Georgia Camp Meeting
Listen to the Mockingbird
Little Old Log Cabin in the Lane
Make Me a Pallet on the Floor
Old Shanty Town
Over the Waves
Red River Valley
Redwing
Rose of San Antonio
Sitting on Top of the World
Tennessee Wagoner
Under the Double Eagle [John on guitar]
Wednesday Night Waltz
Waltz You Saved for Me
Wang Wang Blues

Recordings

All four of Gatwood's 78-era recordings are transcribed in this book.

In 1958 the Gatwood family had the loan of a reel-to-reel tape recorder for about a year. These home tapes of family and band performances contain Jimmie Rodgers songs, country, and pop tunes (like the Everly Brothers' "Bye, Bye, Love") performed by John and his bands and his children at home. Sue played piano and accordion on the tape. John played fiddle, guitar, and sang. Three tunes—"Carroll County Blues," "Sitting on Top of the World," and an unknown tune, possibly "Johnnie

Boy Blues"—from this home recording can be heard at mississippifiddle.com.

A tape of John's record collection includes recordings by Narmour and Smith ("Where the Southern Crosses the Dog"), the Delmore Brothers, Doc Watson, Jimmie Rodgers, and more modern country pop singers.

John shared a fondness for the song "Old Shanty Town" with Alvis Massengale, who also played it. "In a Shanty in Old Shanty Town" was a pop song published and recorded in 1932.

John's daughter Sue Reano, a guitarist and singer, composed and recorded a fine album of gospel songs, *Have You Heard: The Story of Jesus*, under her stage name Sue Reno.

Carroll County Blues

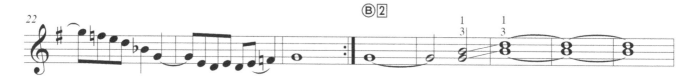

Author's note: This was transcribed from the 1958 home tape; listen at mississippifiddle.com

Comparable versions:
In this book:
"Carroll County Blues," Narmour & Smith, 03/11/1929, Atlanta, OKeh 45317
"Carroll County Blues," Doc Roberts Trio, 02/03/1933, New York, Banner 32713
"Tennessee River Bottom Blues," Mike Shaw & His Alabama Entertainers, 12/10/1930, Atlanta, OKeh 45518

Harry Bolick

Crawford March

Author's note: This was transcribed from Columbia 15675-D, recorded New Orleans, 12/15/1928.

Comparable versions: None known.

Engineer Frank Hawk

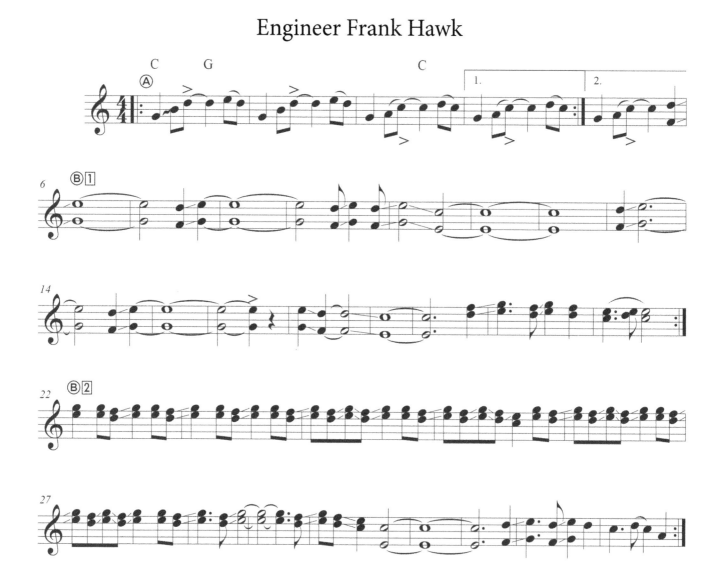

Author's note: This was transcribed from Columbia 15675-D, recorded New Orleans, 12/15/1928. The B part is played eight times. All are similar except for the harmony note G, which is voiced either above or below the E melody note except for the seventh pass, which is shown as B2.

Comparable versions:
No melodic similarities, but see "Railroad Blues" by the Nations Brothers in this book for another tune featuring train sounds.

Harry Bolick

Shear the Sheep Bobbie

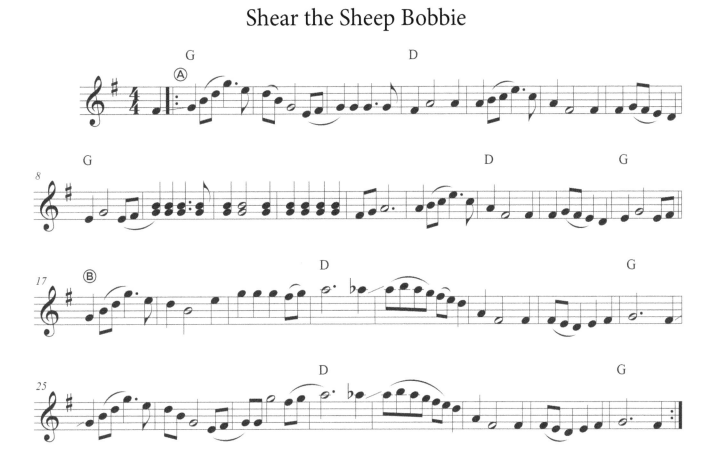

Author's note: This was transcribed from Columbia 15363-D, recorded New Orleans, 12/15/1928. M9–15 get doubled on some passes through the tune.

Comparable versions:

Bolick and Austin, *Mississippi Fiddle Tunes and Songs from the 1930s*: Ruby Costello, "I Want to Go to Meeting," 87; W. E. Claunch, "Chicken Pie," 254, and "Miss Sally at the Party," 265; John Hatcher, "Old Miss Sally," 298; Charles Long, "Jones County," 324, and "Steamboat," 330; Hardy Sharp, "Great Big Yam Potatoes," 337

H. M. Belden and Arthur Palmer Hudson, *The Frank C. Brown Collection of North Carolina Folklore, Vol. 3: Folk Songs* (Durham, NC: Duke University Press, 1952), 510, 565

"Shear the Sheep Bobbie," Gatwood Square Dance Band, 12/15/1928, New Orleans, Columbia 15363-D

In this book:

"Been to the East Been to the West," Leake County Revelers, 04/27/1928, New Orleans, Columbia 15318-D

"Share 'Em," Scottsdale String Band, 08/10/1928, Atlanta, OKeh 45256

"Take Me Back to Tulsa," Bob Wills & His Texas Playboys, 02/25/1941, Dallas, OKeh 06101

Sitting on Top of the World

You come here

Harry Bolick

ri-der,   holding out your hand   I can get a wo-man just like   you can get   a man

But she's   gone   and   I don't   worry, cause I'm sitting on top of the world

Author's note: This was transcribed from the 1958 home tape; listen at mississippifiddle.com. There is a second, garbled second verse in this low-fidelity recording that is played over M57–85; M86–94 are played before the abrupt ending of the home recording.

Comparable versions:
"Sitting on Top of the World," Mississippi Sheiks, 02/17/1930, Shreveport, LA, OKeh 878
"Sitting on Top of the World," Scottsdale String Band, 12/01/1930, Atlanta, OKeh 45509
"Let My Peaches Be," Riley Puckett, 02/01/1939, Rock Hill, SC, Brunswick B8037
"Sitting on Top of the World," Ken Bloom (on bottleneck concert zither,) Clifftop 2012 festival, https://www.youtube.com/watch?v=gRgFSRdyIQs

Third Party

Author's note: This was transcribed from Columbia 15363-D, recorded New Orleans, 12/15/1928. Carl Carmer, in his 1934
book *Stars Fell on Alabama*, describes a fiddle contest in DeKalb County, Alabama (about four hundred miles from where
Gatwood lived), where "Third Party" was played. Family members described a "third party" as someone trying to steal the
affections of one's partner.

Comparable versions: None known.

Harry Bolick

Untitled Tune

Author's note: This was transcribed from the 1958 home tape; listen at mississippifiddle.com. The tune was untitled on the recording but may be Gatwood's composition "Johnnie Boy Blues."

Comparable versions:
"Hamilton's Special Breakdown," Wyzee Hamilton, 01/02/1927, Chicago, Paramount 33186
"G Rag," Georgia Yellow Hammers, 08/09/1927, Charlotte, NC, Victor 21195

HOMER CLYDE GRICE

omer Grice (1910–1994) of Kilmichael, Mississippi, was an accomplished musician on fiddle and guitar and a fine singer. Beginning around age ten, he learned old-time fiddle by ear from his father, including the use of several fiddle tunings. By age twelve he was playing for dances. During the Depression, he played "with a band of young boys around Meridian nightspots."[1] He was quite active in the 1920s and '30s. In an interview with H. T. Holmes in 1973, he recounted that he had been asked to prepare for a commercial 78 rpm recording, most likely in Memphis in 1930. There was some last-minute change and he and his band did not go. Other than Grice on fiddle, the unnamed band consisted of Leroy Ellis on tenor banjo and Wilson Bingham on guitar.[2] I suspect that his composition, "Dead Cat on the Line," would have been a tune that they would have recorded. He also remembered playing in Meridian on the courthouse square in the 1930s and being offered a spot on the Grand Old Opry, sponsored by a tobacco company. However, he was content to have missed the opportunities to be a professional musician, preferring to remain and play near home. He played for county square dances where he could make $1.50–2.00 a night. At the time, that would buy groceries for the week. He entered many fiddle contests, often winning first place. At Kosciusko on one occasion, his prize money was twenty-five dollars. A few years before

1982, Grice won first place in the state fiddle contest in Jackson.[3]

Grice also played with Pete Herring, who recorded with the Mississippi Possum Hunters. Later bands with Grice included the musicians Dewitt and Clayton Tyler, Leroy Ellis, Buck Turner, and "Joe the Wrangler." In the 1952 Kilmichael fiddle contest, Grice came in second on fiddle and second with his string band with Clayton Tyler, Pete Herring, and Grover O'Briant.[4] In 1957 he played a square dance at the Poplar Springs Community Club with Clayton Tyler, Lonnie Ellis, and Wilson Bingham.[5] A few weeks later he played there again with Lonnie Ellis, Maxie Ellis, Wilson Bingham, and Jody Bridges.[6] Grice played dances in Winona with Tyler for over forty years.[7] He competed in the Kosciusko fiddle contest many times, as early as 1932[8] and in the final one in the 1990s. He often visited and played with Grover O'Briant of Kilmichael, who organized the later versions of the Kosciusko contest. In addition to old-time fiddle tunes, Grice played in styles that he referred to as "jazz," "classical," and "Lawrence Welk," all of which he considered easier to play on fiddle than hillbilly. His guitar playing was heavily influenced by his favorite guitarist, Riley Puckett.

In the 1970s and 1980s Homer Grice played at home, at local dances, and concerts with his wife, Mary Marjette, who played mandolin and guitar; and with his neighbors, Mr. and Mrs. James Ward,

Homer Grice and Pete Herring, ca. 1930s. Photo courtesy of Tempie Woods.

who played guitar and piano. Mary said, "I just love waltzes and gospel. I've been playing guitar for some forty-six years. I had to. I had to live with him."

Grice worked for twenty-three years as a picture framer with the J. A. Olson Co. In retirement, he applied his woodworking skills to violins. Self-taught, learning the craft from a book, Grice made over twenty-five violins, some with local woods.[9]

Clayton Tyler (1919–1986) was a longtime musical partner with Grice and had a varied musical career. He began to play guitar at age sixteen and went on to become an accomplished songwriter and performer. The Ray Brothers recorded Tyler's song, "Got the Jake Leg Too," in 1930. In 1938 he toured in the South with the Lou Childress Band in a medicine show, playing in schoolhouses and

theatres. He was unhappily stuck with the stage name of "Mississippi Sawyer," until he wrote his song "The Mississippi Tadpole," which gave him a nickname he preferred.[10] Tyler boarded in Meridian with Jimmie Rodgers's brother, Tallmadge, and became a friend of Jimmie's. Tyler performed with Rodgers, and later on radio and television on his own. In his own words, "I had a few high hopes but I was no star and never would be. It takes all sorts of folks to make up a world." He described country music this way in an interview: "Well, it's an original expression of deep emotions. It's also a bit nostalgic. It should always stay in the range of beautiful sound. It should sing things that happen to people but on a high enough plane that it is uplifting and will prompt a person to high thoughts. That's country music, plain and simple."[11]

Tyler recorded an LP of his songs, *Down Home*, in Tupelo with fiddler Johnny Gimble as a sideman. Tyler worked as a professional photographer in his later years.

Homer Grice, French Camp, MS, 1975. Photo by Carl Fleischhauer.

—Harry Bolick

Lee Jackson and Homer Grice, French Camp, MS, 1975. Photo by Carl Fleischhauer.

Clayton Tyler

Clayton Tyler, 1985. Photo courtesy *Winona Times*.

Clayton Tyler and friend

Clayton Tyler, 1979. Photo courtesy *Winona Times*.

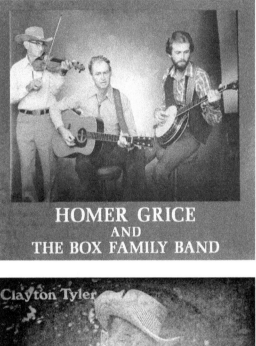

Homer Clyde Grice

[195]

NOTES

1. "Fancy Fiddlin,'" *Clarion-Ledger*, Jackson, MS, August 9, 1981, 1E.

2. 1973 taped audio interview by H. T. Holmes, on deposit at Mississippi Department of Archive and History.

3. "Kilmichael's Homer Grice . . . Taking Up Where Stradivarius Left Off," *Winona Times*, June 3, 1982, 1.

4. "Record Crowd Turns Out for Talent Show," *Winona Times*, January 5, 1953, 1.

5. "Square Dance at Poplar Springs for Polio Fund," *Winona Times*, January 25, 1957, 1.

6. "Poplar Springs Dance Boosts Polio Fund," Winona Times, February 1, 1957, 1

7. "Kilmichael's Homer Grice . . . taking up where Stradivarius left off," 1.

8. "Old Fiddlers in Attala Compete," *Clarion-Ledger*, Jackson, MS, October 16, 1932 12.

9. "Fancy Fiddlin,'" *Clarion-Ledger*, Jackson, MS, August 9, 1981, 1E.

10. Spoken intro to his song "Mississippi Tadpole," on his LP *Down Home*, Statue Records, ca. 1970s.

11. "Country Musician Clayton Tyler Reveres Jimmie Rodgers," *Winona Times*, May 3, 1979, 7.

Homer Grice's known repertoire

After the Ball
Boil Them Cabbage Down
Bye, Bye, My Honey I'm Gone
Call Me Back to Your Heart [sung with guitar]
Carroll County Blues
Charleston 1 and 2
Crawdad Song
Dead Cat on the Line
Devil's Dream [from his father]
Empty Chair [sung with guitar]
Goodnight Waltz
He's with Me All the Way [sung with guitar]
Ida Red [tuned: GDGB]
Kinnie Wagner
Kirby Jail
Little Black Mustache
Mexicali Rose
Moonlight Clog
Muddy Wagoner
Old Joe Clark [tuned: GDGD] [from his father]
Radio Mama

Sally Goodin [tuned: GDGD]
When You and I Were Young Maggie

Recordings

Homer Grice and the Box Family Band, LP, Riverside
    Recording NR14197, Kilmichael, MS, 1982
Faded Love
Fifty-Year Waltz
Carroll County Blues
Dead Cat on the Line
Stone Rag
Moon Light Waltz
Leather Britches
Over the Waves
Muddy Wagon
San Antonio Rose

Field tape, 1973, interview by H. T. Holmes, on deposit at Mississippi Department of Archive and History.

September 21, 1977, interview and field tape, from collection of Tony Russell.

Clayton Tyler Recording

Down Home, Status Records NR6874, no date
Rocking Along in an Old Rocking Chair
Mississippi Tadpole
Casey Jones
Memories of Jimmie Rodgers
Mother's Lullaby
Somebody's Been Using My Shoes
Money Molder
Long Black Veil
Lamp Lighting Time in the Valley
The Homebrew Song

Bye, Bye, My Honey I'm Gone

Author's note: Transcribed from a 1977 tape session with Tony Russell, from the collection of Tony Russell.

Comparable versions: None known

Dead Cat on the Line

Harry Bolick

Author's note: Transcribed from his 1982 LP, which had very limited distribution.

See mississippifiddle.com to hear this track. The structure of this tune is loose and somewhat improvised in feeling. It's not clear what Grice's title refers to. An article in the *Miami News*, May 1, 1982, offers these possibilities: "When someone is trying slip up behind you or deceive you"; "A third party eavesdropping on a telephone party line"; "When a fisherman is using a trotline and does not check it everyday, a dead catfish on the line suggests that the fisherman is having some sort of problem." Rev. Gates preaches on his recording, "If a child is no way like his father, there's a dead cat on the line. . . ."

Comparable versions: None known

"Dead Cat on the Line," Rev. J. M. Gates, 03/18/1929, Atlanta, OKeh 8684

Ida Red

Author's note: Transcribed from a 1977 taped interview with Homer Grice, June 16, 1973, interviewed by H. T. Holmes. The interview is located at the Mississippi Department of Archives and History (call number AU 863). Grice played this tune in GDGD, cross tuning in the key of G; I have notated it in A to match the fingering to the tuning AEAE. Tune the fiddle down to GDGD and use the same fingering to play in G. The F# note in m12–14 is actually pitched a bit sharp, between F# and G. Lyric sung over the first part of the tune:

"Doctor said I'm sick and out of my head but I'm just a fool about Ida Red."

Comparable versions:
"Ida Red," Fiddling Powers & Family, 08/19/1924, Camden, NJ, Victor 19434
"Ida Red," Riley Puckett, 04/22/1926, Atlanta, Columbia 15102-D
"Ida Red," Tweedy Brothers, 03/1928, Richmond, IN, Gennett 6529

Kennie Wagner

Author's note: Transcribed from a 1977 recording session with Tony Russell, from the collection of Tony Russell. Arnold Hudson in *Folksongs of Mississippi* includes the lyrics to two versions of a ballad about Kennie Wagner. Preceding his crime spree, Wagner was a trick-shot artist in a circus. In one of his several altercations with the law, he killed Sheriff McIntosh of Greene County while escaping. He fled to Arkansas, where he murdered another officer. He was captured by a woman sheriff in Arkansas and then tried in Mississippi, where he was imprisoned and made several escapes and was recaptured. Wagner was still living when Hudson published his book in 1936.

Comparable versions: This melody is not related to the recordings listed below. However, the lyrics all refer to the same events.
"Kennie Wagner" (music and lyrics Andy Jenkins, 1926), Vernon Dalhart, 02/16/1926, New York, Columbia 15065-D
"Kennie Wagner's Surrender" (music and lyrics, Andy Jenkins, 1926), Vernon Dalhart, 09/11/1926, New York, OKeh 40685
"Kennie Wagner's Surrender," Ernest V. Stoneman, 02/01/1927, New York, Gennett 6044

SIDNEY HEMPHILL SR.

"He was a music man. Then he learnt all of us. He learned us. Good as ever been through here, Panola County," declared Lucius Smith, talking about his longtime playing partner and musical mentor, Sid Hemphill (1876–1961).[1] "He'd play down to an organ, down to a piano, down to a Jew's harp." Alan Lomax exclaimed that his blindness was "the last thing you'd recall about him. His face blazed with inner light. He ran rather than walked everywhere. He could never wait for his wife to bring something, but always darted up to find it himself. His speech, which could not keep pace with his thoughts and designs, had become telegraphic and brusque."[2] Hemphill was central to the music community in northern Mississippi during his lifetime, coming from a family of musicians and leaving a family of musicians in his wake.

The Hemphill family is similar in some ways to and contemporaries of the Chatmon family when it comes to African American musical legacies in Mississippi. Both of the families boasted recording artists who achieved legendary status in the annals of American music. Both families descended from fiddle-playing patriarchs who certainly had some old-time fiddle music in their repertoires, but Sid Hemphill was the first musician to record as the leader of a fife and drum outfit. Though most commentators seized upon his perceived musical connections on the other side of the Atlantic Ocean, this essay concerns itself with the full range of music, instrumentation, and experiences that constitute the legacy of a "music man," Sid Hemphill.

Jared Snyder and Colin Larkin, in their respective entries for the *Encyclopedia of the Blues*, tell us that Sid Hemphill—the vocalist who played fiddle, guitar, drums, piano, Jew's harp, harmonica, ten-hole quills, and banjo—was the son of a "slave fiddler" named Dock Hemphill, who was indeed born enslaved in 1848.[3] The family musical traditions of the Hemphill family go back to a contemporary of Henderson Chatmon (also born 1848), who his son Sam claimed "worked in the field [and] played music in slavery time." As I explain in the section on the Chatmon family, Henderson was not yet a teenager when the war broke out and it's doubtful that he played the fiddle during "slavery times."[4] The same is most likely true of Dock Hemphill, who, according to Sid, "got all his tunes from his colored cousin. Down in south Mississippi. An awful fiddle player."[5] According to Jim O'Neal, in a more recent article based on the notes of folklorist Alan Lomax, his father's cousin lived in Choctaw County.

Dock Hemphill had come from Georgia, according to the death certificate for his son Jim, sometime after emancipation and married a woman named Fannie Hubbard (b. 1853).[6] The couple had their first

Sid Hemphill, fiddle; Lucius Smith, banjo. Photo courtesy Alan Lomax Collection at the American Folklife Center, Library of Congress, courtesy of the Association for Cultural Equity.

child, Jennie, around 1870, and around 1873, they had another daughter named Mary. On September 13, 1876, the couple gave birth to one of the most amazing and versatile musicians to ever pick up a fiddle in Mississippi. Sid Hemphill was presumably born at the Pleasant Mount precinct of Panola County, where the Hemphill family lived in 1880.[7] Out of the seven children by the elder Hemphill, six played music and formed a family band that lasted until the boys got married, and, influenced by their wives, quit playing. As a youth, Sid had a cane "stuck" in his eye and went blind. He later developed a cataract in the other eye while working as a blacksmith's apprentice.[8]

In 1900 Sid Hemphill moved to Beat 3 of Choctaw County, where he lived with his wife, Maggie, his mother-in-law Lizzie Buck, and his brother-in-law Arthur Buck. Considering that on the same census page are Ben (b. 1835), Peter (b. 1942), and James (b. 1881) Hemphill, and, according to Jim O'Neal, Dock Hemphill had learned to play the fiddle from his cousins in Choctaw County, Sid must have learned a few things from his uncles and cousins at this time. Dock also may have been around Choctaw County, as he disappears from the 1900 Census. The roots of some musical traditions that Sid Hemphill later passed down to his children and other artists such as Fred McDowell had developed in the crucible of the larger Hemphill family at the turn of the century. Considering that that particular section of the state produced such old-time fiddling phenoms as Hoyt Ming and the Choctaw Playboys, Choctaw County very well may have been the staging ground for what would be one of the most novel outpourings of creative energy ever unleashed in musical form in Mississippi. It certainly seems an appropriate setting for musical education in a range of styles.

In 1910, Dock and Fannie Hemphill show up in Beat 2 of Tate County, but Sid is nowhere to be found. Regardless, between 1900 and 1904, Sid had moved back to the hill country and started to write songs. Hemphill composed songs celebrating local events and people. Some of his songs had lyrical stanzas running into twenty-one or more verses, most often with live accompaniment on fiddle or the banjo. Several of them were written at the behest of locals who played a role in the events. In fact, these individuals are responsible for John W. Work III not getting to hear the recordings of Hemphill when he was writing his book. In the section on "Ballads" in his untitled manuscript, Work III informs us that Hemphill's ballads were "not available" at the time of his writing, "because they referred largely to persons living at present in his area."[9]

Hemphill composed "The Roguish Man," for example, at the behest of an African American named Jack Castle. According to Hemphill, the man he knew as Jack Castle was "raised right up yonder in the hills around Cypress Corner" in Tate County, a section known for the practice of "whitecapping" as a deterrent to any African Americans thinking of moving into the neighborhood.[10] Castle "wanted to be a bad nigger," Hemphill explained, and he wanted Hemphill to valorize him as a "Bad Negro," a hero figure in Black folklore who committed crimes in defiance of apartheid and got away so smooth he never got caught.[11] Castle had heard another one of Hemphill's original compositions and exclaimed: "Oh, by God, make one about me now, what I done." Castle seems to have cherished his reputation as a bad man and wanted his rough-and-tumble exploits celebrated in song. If such men did get caught in open defiance of white supremacy, the sentiments of most Americans during Jim Crow demanded restoration of the community's confidence.

The unquestioned prestige and honor in meting out extralegal justice is the theme of his song "The Strayhorn Mob," a song with lyrics objectively written by an African American about a mob of whites and Blacks from the Strayhorn community who raided the Senatobia jail to lynch a white man named Jim Whitt. He had allegedly killed one of the men from Strayhorn with a double-barreled shotgun. Due to Whitt's removal to Jackson, no lynching ever occurred outside the Senatobia jail. Sam Howell, the member of the Strayhorn mob who solicited Hemphill to come up with the song, was wounded in a shootout with Tate County Sheriff

J. M. Poag on April 12, 1905, and one of the excited Strayhorn men shot and killed the sheriff, which set them all to flight. A posse later arrested nine suspected members of the Strayhorn mob, "five of them being white and four of them negroes."[12] Howell and two other defendants underwent a jury trial at Holly Springs that resulted in an acquittal, and subsequent trails in Oxford and Batesville also ended in the acquittal of the other members.[13] In response to the surprise jury verdict, Judge J. B. Boothe declared, "For some reason, unknown to this court, you have disregarded your oaths and trampled the law under your feet."[14] Such perversions of justice, one *New Orleans Times-Picayune* correspondent noted, "are responsible for a large number of lynching's. The accuracy of this statement cannot be questioned."[15]

Though some scholars who have examined "The Strayhorn Mob" story have sought to silence the involvement of African Americans and discount the many ways that race dictated the outcome of the ordeal, the acquittal of the Strayhorn Mob belies the lack of faith in the courts to carry out justice swiftly as a justification for lynching. The merits of mob justice outweighed the life of a county sheriff in northern Mississippi.[16] Of course, had the alleged murderer been African American instead of white, the sheriff very well might have lived; the Black suspect might have very well been hanged, too.

Mississippians between 1900 and 1909 lynched more African Americans than citizens in any other state. Indeed, the amount of Black lynching victims rose to previously unseen heights in the 1890s, while whites were lynched far less after the 1880s. The crystallization of racial stereotypes, such as the Jezebel and the Black Beast, Black disfranchisement under the 1890 state constitution, and the Supreme Court's decision in *Plessy v. Ferguson* that codified racial segregation into the law made lynch mobs and lynching so synonymous with the violent deaths of Black men that most leaders in Black communities began to denounce lynching and discourage the participation of African Americans.[17] In fact, one of the last instances of Black-on-Black lynching occurred in Panola County in 1899.[18] One hundred forty-one Black men and a few Black women were lynched in Mississippi during the initial decade of the twentieth century, plenty of them in north Mississippi counties, and only eleven whites in the whole state. Perhaps singing a refrain for the slain sheriff of Panola County and all the victims of extralegal justice, Hemphill focused his words on the victim at the end of the song and exclaimed, "They laid him low." He was indeed the twelfth white victim of extralegal violence during the period.

Another one of Hemphill's ballads, "The Carrier Line," told the story of a train wreck on the Sardis & Delta Railroad. Buffalo, New York, native and lumberman Cassius M. Carrier owned a logging company and in 1901 built the Sardis & Delta Railroad, called simply Mr. Carrier's line in the song. The line's central purpose was to haul logs to Sardis in Panola County from Bobo Lake (later renamed Lake Carrier), twenty-two miles to the west in the Delta. Carrier incorporated the Carrier Lumber and Manufacturing Company in Sardis, and his son Robert Carrier helped keep the logs rolling until it was sold to the Yazoo & Mississippi Valley Railroad in 1906. Though the road was ripped spike, tie, and rail from its moorings as the lumbermen in the 1920s retreated from the woods they cut out in the early twentieth century, the song about the road lives in the field recordings of Hemphill. James Silver, the chair of the history department at the University of Mississippi, wrote about the Carrier Line in the *Journal of Mississippi History*.[19] For his 1954 article, "Paul Bunyan Comes to Mississippi," he interviewed Robert Carrier, for whom Carrier Hall was named on the campus of the University of Mississippi, and conducted oral histories with former lumbermen who had once worked for him. Silver located the blind leader of a five-piece string band living about four miles from Senatobia. "His gray hair and bent body belied the vigor of a tremendous voice," Silver wrote, and "he played his own accompaniment on a fiddle held together by nails and a couple of pieces of bailing wire."[20]

Local newspapers for this period never mention a train wreck at Malone's Trestle. But some of the other lyrics provided better leads. Though not enlightening about the wreck, local newspapers revealed that one of the engineers was indeed named Dave Cowart. Hemphill described him as a "rough engineer." In the song, Carrier warns Cowart not to run the train so fast, and he finally transferred Cowart to another engine and apparently fired Cowart after he wrecked at Malone's Trestle. In March 1909, Dave Cowart worked as an engineer for the Lamb Fish Lumber Company. According to the *Tallahatchie Herald*, Cowart ran "his engine from Effie to the logging plant in an estimated eleven minutes" when a woman needed medical aid. Though the woman had died five minutes prior to his arrival, Cowart's swift work as an engineer was dubbed a "heroic effort" nonetheless.[21]

Cowart continued to work as an "engineer" until 1910, when he decided to parlay his reputation for speed into a political career and an automobile dealership in the Tallahatchie County seat of Charleston. The *Tallahatchie Herald* asserted that the "hustling Ford man ... would make the town a good officer and it would be hard to do better than to elect him as one of its alderman" in 1910.[22] For his support in the 1920 election for governor, Lee Russell gave him the title of Major and appointed him part of his staff. He later became the road commissioner in the 1940s and one of the most successful business owners in Tallahatchie County.

Not all of Hemphill's music was original. He was also fond of singing traditional ballads, such as "Joe Turner," "The Boll Weevil," "John Henry," "Old Blue," and "Casey Jones." Hemphill performed his ballads in a string band, a type of ensemble soon to be extinct in the area. This fact undoubtedly contributed to the disappearance of the repertoire of songs associated with such bands.

Sid Hemphill is missing from the 1910 Census, but due to the songs we know he lived near Senatobia around 1905. Sid Hemphill lost his wife Maggie sometime between 1913 and January 1920, when he shows back up in Beat 2 of Panola County. The widower and farmer lived with his three daughters, Virgie (thirteen), Rosa Lee (eleven), and Cindy, or Sidney Lee (eight).[23] Sid Hemphill continued to live in Panola County in 1942, when he became the last artist to record in the final session of the historic 1941–42 expeditions of the Library of Congress and Fisk University. Sociologist Lewis Jones and folklorist Alan Lomax were the two men who heard about Hemphill from Turner Junior Johnson, another blind musician from Panola County, who played on the corner for tips in Clarksdale. In his 1994 book, Lomax recalled that Johnson referred to Hemphill as the "best musician in the world." Jones and Lomax, therefore, took off one day to find him at a picnic in Sledge. It proved a particularly unpleasant excursion for Lomax. His notes from the trip tell about "driving for hours" to find "a dreary picnic" with "nothing to eat or drink." Lomax setup his equipment and recorded from 3:00 p.m. to 9:00 p.m. on August 15, 1942. He recorded twenty-two songs and an interview with Hemphill and his string band, which consisted of Hemphill on fiddle, Alex "Turpentine" Askew on guitar, Lucious Smith on banjo, and Will Head on bass drum. Their ages, according to the 1940 Census, were sixty, fifty-eight, and fifty-six respectively.

The performances recorded by Lomax and Jones included several up-tempo ballads in string band format featuring Hemphill on fiddle. Other numbers in fife and drum style and some with quills (homemade panpipes crafted from local bamboo cane, as were the fifes) replacing the fife were also recorded. This group's remarkably broad repertoire encompassed fife and drum tunes, reels, marches, waltzes, turn-of-the-century pop hits, church songs, and ballads.

Hemphill possessed equally impressive talents as an instrument maker, maestro, and rural impresario, and he may have managed a stable of bands that he sent to various events over an area of several counties in the hills, the Delta, and Tennessee. Hemphill told Lomax and Jones in 1942: "Well, I can play .. . a guitar, fiddle, mandolin, snare drum, foe [fife], bass drum, quills, banjo, pretty good organ player." Heavy burlap sacks were hung in his smokehouse and filled not with meat but with instruments, many of which he had made himself. And he did all this as a blind man. In his notebook Lomax described him as "blind, creative, bubbling with energy."

While our concern in this book is primarily his work in a string band setting, the group also identified as a fife and drum outfit and played music infused with European military drumming traditions and African polyrhythms. Though the blues ballads, which were so full of local lore and history, held the primary interest of Lomax at the time, he later wrote that "Devil's Dream," played on the quills, was "the strangest and most primitive Afro-Am. [*sic*] sound I've ever heard." On this basis, he concluded that Hemphill had "introduced me to the main find of my whole career—the African fife-and-drum dance bands of the Mississippi Hills."[24]

Lomax celebrated his discovery of Sid Hemphill's fife and drum band music for its perceived "African roots," a vague and subjective descriptor sometimes attached to musical traditions that seem more primitive. This assertion has been one of the most repeated conclusions about the importance of Lomax's field trips to the state, but ethnomusicologist David Evans maintains that Hemphill's fife and drum tracks don't sound "African" at all. Bill Ferris and his French-born wife, Josette, shot a 16-millimeter documentary on a fife and drum band near Como whose sound, in Ferris's opinion, was the "most African" in this country.[25] A performance of the northern Mississippi fife and drum music, somewhat like what Sid Hemphill would have presided over, can be seen at a little over eight minutes into Worth Long and Alan Lomax's 1978 film *The Land Where the Blues Began*. Despite the race-based assertions about some essential African primitive nature, Hemphill continued to teach his particular musical traditions to his children and grandchildren. "E'er since I was nine years old, I played drums with my grandfather," Jessie Mae told folklorist Alan Lomax in 1978, as quoted in *The Land Where the Blues Began*. "But when my granddaddy was alive, he could play anything. He made me a drum, he made me a fiddle. And he could play all this music that we had. Every music that we had, he could play." David Evans believes that any strongly "African" element is largely confined to the quills tracks, which aligns with the conclusions of Jared Snyder, the author of Hemphill's entry in the *Encyclopedia of the Blues*, who stated that Hemphill's "quill playing was highly syncopated and displayed the closest ties to African music."[26]

By the time Hemphill and his band stopped playing, Lomax was "perishing of asthma—the dust and heat & fatigue finally got" to him. So Jones and Lomax packed up their equipment and headed back to Clarskdale, where they departed for Nashville forthwith. Lomax recorded two further tracks with Hemphill on the quills when he revisited him in 1959.

Sid Hemphill's 1942 recordings were not among the first recordings issued on 78 rpm discs by the Library of Congress. While some material from the 1942 sessions in Mississippi came out on disc eventually, the music of Hemphill remained unissued until ethnomusicologist David Evans compiled several of the Hemphill tracks in the 1970s for the Testament LP *Traveling Through the Jungle* and the Library of Congress LP *Afro-American Folk Music from Tate and Panola Counties, Mississippi.*

Sid Hemphill never made a single commercial recording of any of his songs. His two field sessions with Lomax were made more accessible in 2013, when Mississippi Records of Portland, Oregon, released the first full album by Hemphill, *Devil's Dream*. Other members of the Hemphill family also became musicians, including his daughter Rosa Lee Hill and his paternal granddaughter, Jessie Mae Hemphill. Sidney Hemphill Sr. and his daughter Rosa Lee Hill are buried at New Salem Baptist Church Cemetery in Senatobia, Tate County, Mississippi. Jessie Mae Hemphill is not far down the road in Senatobia.

Jim O'Neal claims that Sid Hemphill "was not a bluesman in the sense we often define Hill Country blues today," but O'Neal did not elaborate on his meaning behind the definition.[27] The contemporary popular concept of the "hill country blues" musician is a product of the racial stereotype–based A&R practices at Fat Possum Records, whose policies extend from the segregation of sound during the early days of the recording industry, when A&R men buttressed the idea that racial segregation was natural by limiting the recording opportunities of African Americans to blues music. The segregation of sound remains a powerful influence, particularly on the young white men who found financial success recording African American artists on Fat Possum Records.[28] According to one student of hill country blues, Jacqueline Sahagian, Fat Possum's "rebel identity actually makes [them] have a lot in common with other white guys from the past who have sought to explain and present the blues to white audiences.... Although Fat Possum's work seems edgy and new, it really shows that blues marketing has not changed much since the race records era."[29]

Sid Hemphill, as an African American and as a musician, reflects the sort of dynamism and versatility that was indicative of so many other African Americans born in the wake of the Civil War, who defied the gendered cultural construct of the "hill country blues" man, and every other construct of a blues man for that matter. According to music critic Amanda Petrusich in her review of *The Devil's Dream*, "Hemphill's work incorporates attributes of the Mississippi Hill Country's better-known traditions ... mastered by [Fred] McDowell, R. L. Burnside, and Junior Kimbrough, and the fife-and-drum music practiced by Otha Turner, Napoleon Strickland, and Hemphill himself."[30] Sid Hemphill performed from here to hell and gone, and he could certainly play old-time. All his recorded fiddle tunes with the string band are transcribed in this book.

—T. DeWayne Moore

NOTES

1. Jim O'Neal, "Sid Hemphill: Hill Country Patriarch," *Living Blues* 253:49:1 (February 2018): 38.

2. Alan Lomax, *The Land Where the Blues Began* (New York: New Press, 1993), 315.

3. Dock Hemphill was enumerated for the 1880 Census on June 14 at Enumeration District 153, Pleasant Mount precinct, Panola County, Mississippi, with wife Fannie (twenty-seven) and children Tommie (eleven), Mary (seven), Sid (four), and Henry H. (five months, born February). All six had been born in Mississippi, as had their respective parents, except that the state of birth of Dock's parents was unknown.

4. T. DeWayne Moore, "Bo Carter: Genius of the Country Blues," *Blues and Rhythm* 330 (May 2018): 14–24.

5. "Aweful," in this context, means highly skilled and almost obsessed; see Lomax, *The Land*, 315.

6. The maiden name of Fannie Hemphill comes from the death certificate of Jim Hemphill; Tennessee, Death Records, 1908–1958, Ancestry.com, 2011.

7. 1880 US Census, Pleasant Mount, Panola, Mississippi; Roll: 661; Page: 55C; Enumeration District: 153.

8. O'Neal, "Sid Hemphill," 38.

9. John W. Work III, "Untitled Manuscript," in *Lost Delta Found: Rediscovering the Fisk University–Library of Congress Coahoma County Study, 1941–1942* (Nashville, TN: Vanderbilt University Press, 2005), 92.

10. "Whitecapping in Tate," *Jackson Daily News*, January 8, 1916.

11. Lawrence Levine discusses several archetypes of African derivation in the culture of African Americans. These archetypes include the "Bad Man," a merciless killer who lacks remorse; "the moral hard man" who possesses the strength and courage to flout the limitations of white society; and the "tricksters," who attain their goals through wit and guile rather than power and authority. The "moral hard man" develops from concepts of the warrior in the folk culture of Central Africa, whereas the trickster archetype is more tied to West African origins. Lawrence Levine, *Black Culture and Black Consciousness: Afro-American Folk Thought from Slavery to Freedom* (Oxford: Oxford University Press, 1977), 367–440. For more on the warrior, see Clyde W. Fords, *Hero with an African Face* (New York: Bantam, 1999), 68–94; Akinwele Umoja, *We Will Shoot Back*: Armed Resistance in the Mississippi Freedom Movement (New York: New York University Press, 2013), 21.

12. "Nine Men Arrested," *Jackson Daily News*, April 13, 1905, 1.

13. "Are Not Guilty," *Jackson Daily News*, September 12, 1905.

14. "Sign of the Times," *Natchez Democrat*, May 2, 1906.

15. "Sign of the Times," *Natchez Democrat*, May 2, 1906.

16. Tom Freeland and Chris Smith, "That Dry Creek Eaton Clan: A North Mississippi Murder Ballad of the 1930s," in *Nobody Knows Where the Blues Come From: Lyrics and History*, ed. Robert Springer (Jackson: University Press of Mississippi, 2006), 126–50.

17. Karlos Hill, *Beyond the Rope: The Impact of Lynching on Black Culture and Memory* (New York: Cambridge University Press, 2016), 30.

18. *Vicksburg Herald*, June 21, 1899.

19. James W. Silver, "Paul Bunyan Comes to Mississippi," *Journal of Mississippi History* 19 (1957): 93–119.

20. Silver, "Paul Bunyan Comes to Mississippi," 98.

21. "Young Woman Killed," *Tallahatchie* (MS) *Herald*, March 10, 1909, 5.

22. *Tallahatchie* (MS) *Herald*, August 3, 1910, 3.

23. As Sid Hemphill, he was enumerated in the 1930 Census at Beat 2, Panola County, in Mississippi. He was a roomer with Sallie Sykes (forty-two, widow, having married at twenty) and her sons, Warren (twenty-one) and Oscar (eighteen).

24. O'Neal, "Sid Hemphill," 39.

25. Billy Skelton, "Folklore Specialist Tours State Recording Heritage," *Clarion-Ledger* (Jackson, MS), June 6, 1971, C1.

26. Jared Snyder, "Sid Hemphill," in *Encyclopedia of the Blues*, ed. Ed Komara (New York: Routledge, 2006), 419.

27. O'Neal, "Sid Hemphill," 39.

28. Jacqueline Sahagian, "The Same Old Blues Crap: Fat Possum Records' Matthew Johnson and How White Masculinity Continues to Shape the Blues," paper presentation at the Southern Music Symposium at the Center for the Study of Southern Culture at the University of Mississippi, February 26, 2018.

29. Hannah Reed, "Southern Music Symposium to showcase history, beauty, sound of the South tonight," February 26, 2018, *Daily Mississippian*, https://thedmonline.com/southern-music-symposium-showcase-history-beauty-sound-south-tonight/, accessed March 30, 2019.

30. Amanda Petrusich, review of Sid Hemphill's *The Devil's Dream: Alan Lomax's 1942 Library of Congress Recordings*, Pitchfork.com, March 28, 2013, https://pitchfork.com/reviews/albums/17862-sid-hemphill-the-devils-dream-alan-lomaxs-1942-library-of-congress-recordings/, accessed June 23, 2019.

T. DeWayne Moore

Arkansas Traveler

Hello   fiddler,   hello   self

Well, hello fiddler, hello   self   I'm just a fiddler, if anybody asks

Author's note: Transcribed from Alan Lomax's recordings online at research.culturalequity.org. Hemphill is tuned about three half steps low and has a relentless shuffle. The second part is played once; the number of repeats on the first part varies with his singing. After his first verse, Hemphill sings many of the standard verses of the Arkansas Traveler skit.

Comparable versions:
Only the first half of the first part of this version is comparable to the sources below.
"The Arkansas Traveler," *The Arkansas Traveler's Songster* (New York: Dick & Fitzgerald, 1864), 5–9
Bolick and Austin, *Mississippi Fiddle Tunes and Songs from the 1930s*: W. E. Claunch, 251; John Hatcher, 284; Stephen B. Tucker, 344; all titled "Arkansas Traveler"

In this book:
"Arkansas Traveler," Enos Canoy
"Arkansas Traveler," Henry C. Gilliland and A. C. "Eck" Robertson, 06/30/1922, New York, Victor 18956
"Arkansas Traveler," Fiddlin' John Carson & His Virginia Reelers, 03/1924, Atlanta, OKeh 40108
"Arkansas Traveler," Kessinger Brothers, 02/11/1928, Ashland, KY, Brunswick 247

Boll Weevil

T. DeWayne Moore

Author's note: Transcribed from Alan Lomax's recordings online at research.culturalequity.org. This tune is a mix of "Frankie and Johnny" with the "Boll Weevil" songs. alt M1–4 are played when the melody is played without singing.

Comparable versions:
"Dixie Boll Weevil," Fiddlin' John Carson, 03/1924, Atlanta, OKeh 40095
"Boll Weevil Blues," Gid Tanner, 03/07/1924, New York, Columbia 15016-D

Lyrics:

I gonna sing you something
Play it from my home

Well darn boll weevil
It's trying to take our home,
It take our home, take our home

The farmer went to the merchant
Merchant, I'll tell you the facts

I'll come and kill the boll weevil
If you'll give me you Stetson hat.
I'll have a time.

The farmer cut the boll weevil
And rolled him up in the sand
And when he seen that morning
He's acting like a man
He's had a time

That farmer went back to the merchant
Merchant, I'll tell you a certain fact
That murderer killed the boll weevil
Now give me a [parting?] sack
I'll have a time.

Then the farmer went to the merchant
Merchant, I don't have no more
Give her my coffee, started on my car[?]
I'll have a time

That farmer said now boll weevil, you are doing it wrong
Eating all this cotton and started on this farm
I'll have a time

And the farmer went to the boll weevil and
Said, boll weevil, where in the world your home?
I've stayed on in Texas won't be there very long
I'll have a time

That farmer went out and see one more
Them boll weevils flying in the air

Went out there an had a feeling
He'd move his family there
I'll have a time

That farmer said boll weevil
What the world you trying to do?
I'm trying to cast this roving eye
Kill em all, can't you[?]
I'll have a time

That farmer said boll weevil
Boll weevil, I thought I buried you in the sand
I'll be back next spring with you
Buried up your land
have a time

That farmer said boll weevil
How come you help me
You know your farm of cotton there
Trying to kill the kid[?]
But I'll have a time

The farmer went to the merchant
For to get his wife a dress
No you cannot farmer
Cause you've got the debt
have a time

And farmer went to his merchant then
For some dipping and chewing
Boll weevil tell, now farmer
Ain't nothing doing here
have a time

[Instrumental twice]
The farmer went to his merchant then, boys
For to get him a bucket of lard
But he gets nothing farmer
Boll weevil's got the job
You have the time

[Instrumental]
The farmer went to his field the next morning
And bo weevils were lying in there
Went out there next evening done moved his family there

That farmer asked the boll weevil
What you trying to do
I'm trying to catch this road in mine
Give me all you can too[?]
You have the time

[Instrumental]

Carrier Line

Nobody   had a nickle,   you couldn't get a   dime.   If you want to make your money,

boys,   work   on Mr. Carrier's   time.   Oh,   huh

T. DeWayne Moore

Author's note: Transcribed from Alan Lomax's recordings online at research.culturalequity.org. The lyrics have previously been printed in the booklet notes to Library of Congress LP L67 (reissued as Rounder CD 1515) and James Silver quoted a version in an article he published on the logging industry in Mississippi.

Comparable versions: None known

Lyrics:

Nobody had a nickel, you couldn't get a dime.
If you want to make your money, boys, work on Mr. Carrier's time.
Oh, my honey babe . . .
[Refrain repeated after each stanza]

Mr. Dave Cowart went on Mr. Carrier's engine;
Mr. Carrier he looked and laughed.
"Tell you, Dave Cowart, don't run my train too fast."

Mr. Dave told Mr. Carrier, "Man, don't you know I know your rule.
Tell you, Mr. Carrier, a train ain't no mule."

Mr. Dave Cowart went down to Baptist;
Mr. Carrier stood on the railroad track.
"Send back Dave Cowart, get Mr. Bailey back."

Mr. Dave told Mr. Carrier, "Man, fire me if you will.
Every time it come a shower of rain, he can't run it up Johnson Hill."

Mr. Carrier said, "Dave Cowart, see what you have done.
You left Sardis at twelve o'clock, done made it back at one."

Mr. Dave said, "Well, Mr. Carrier, let me have my way.
Let me run this Seven Spot, I'll make three trips today."

Mr. Carrier said, "No, Dave Cowart, tell you in time.
Can't let you run the Seven no more." "Well, I'll have to run the Nine."

Everybody around Sardis said, "Mr. Carrier, I know you got your way.
Mr. Bailey's much too old a man to run your train like Dave."

Last one Monday morning, it come a shower of rain.
Nine come to Ballentine blowing like a fast train.

When the Nine got over to Sardis with a large load of logs,
Mr. Carrier told the people at the plant, "Yonder train off the Yellow Dog."

They said to Mr. Carrier, "Man, ain't you 'shamed?
Looking out the window, don't know your own train?"

Mr. Carrier went to Dave Cowart, "Dave, I done told you so.
Train costs too much, you can't run my train no more."

Mr. Carrier's timbermens quit too. Thought they all was mad.
They didn't like his paydays cuz he's paying 'em off in brass.

Mr. Carrier's timbermen left, thought they was going home.
Stopped down the railroad, farming at Malone's.

Mr. Carrier went down to Malone's, he didn't mean no harm.
He didn't know his timbermen knowed how to farm.

Oh he couldn't pay 'em no greenbacks, couldn't pay 'em no gold,
Couldn't pay 'em no silver. All his banks done closed.

Mr. Carrier's engine left Sardis then; she left there mighty hot.
Got down to Malone's Trestle where he could wreck that Seven Spot.

Well, they telephoned to Mr. Carrier. "Don't you think it'd be nice?
Telephone to Sardis and get Dr. Rice."

Mr. Carrier said to Dave Cowart, "Man, ain't you 'shamed?
You done wrecked my Seven Spot, done scald the preacher's hand."

Mr. Carrier said to the conductor, 'ductor [doctor?], thank you for saving his life.
Conductor says he's a lazy man, he won't hardly die.

He wore a mighty fine coat, boys. Mighty fine shirt.
Ride that train every day. He didn't never work.

I played on Mr. Carrier's railroad, Sardis on Main and Beale.
I made dollars down there without working in the field.

Well they carried him down to Emma's. Aunt Emma hollered and screamed.
"Needn't cry, Miss Emma, but he got scalded by the steam."

Eighth of January

You can't eat, you can't write You can't eat no sup - per tonight

You can't eat you can't stay Dawn break on your way

T. DeWayne Moore

Author's note: Transcribed from Alan Lomax's recordings online at research.culturalequity.org. Hemphill is tuned about three half steps low and has a relentless swinging shuffle. He begins with the second part and then plays the tune mostly as shown. His repeats of parts vary.

Lyrics:

You can't eat, you can't write
You can't eat no sup-per tonight
You can't drink you can't shine
You can't talk to that gal of mine.

You can't eat, you can't write
You can't eat no sup-per tonight
You can't drink you can't shine
You can't eat before suppertime.

You can't eat …
You can't eat …
You can't eat …
You can't eat …

Comparable versions:
Ira Ford, *Traditional Music of America* (New York: E.P. Dutton, 1940), 63
Bolick and Austin, *Mississippi Fiddle Tunes and Songs from the 1930s*: Charlie Edmundson, "Eighth of January March," 95;
    F. Ezell, "Eighth of January Waltz," 104; Enos Canoy, "Eighth of January," 238; W. E. Claunch, "Eighth of January," 258;
    John Hatcher, "Eighth of January," 291; Hardy Sharp, "Eighth of January," 336; J. A. Moorman, "Eighth of January," 150
In this book: "Dunkirk," Claude Kennedy
"Eighth of January," Arkansas Barefoot Boys, 02/11/1928, Memphis TN, OKeh 45217
"Eighth of January," Fox Chasers, 06/11/1930, San Antonio, TX, OKeh 45496
"Eighth of January," Ted Gossett's Band, 09/16/1930, Richmond, IN, Champion 16160

John Henry

T. DeWayne Moore

Author's note: Transcribed from Alan Lomax's recordings online at research.culturalequity.org. Hemphill is tuned about three
    half steps low. The first sixteen measures are the fiddle introduction. The second sixteen measures are roughly what he sings,
    and the second instrumental version between verses.

Comparable versions:
In this book: Tom Dumas, "John Henry"
"John Henry Blues," Fiddlin' John Carson, 03/1924, Atlanta, OKeh 7004
"Spike Driver Blues," Mississippi John Hurt, 12/28/1928, New York, OKeh 8692
"John Henry," Ernest V. Stoneman, 06/21/1926, New York, Edison 5194

Lyrics:

Take this hammer, killed John Henry
Laid him low, laid him low
Take this hammer, killed John Henry
Laid him . . .

Take your hammer to the captain
Tell him he's gone, tell him he's gone

When you hear that bulldog barking
Somebody around, somebody 'round
When you hear that bulldog barking
Somebody around, somebody 'round

When you hear that peafowl a hollering
Gonna rain, gonna rain
When you hear that peafowl hollering

Hammer, hammer, killed John Henry
Don't you see, don't you see?
Hammer, hammer, killed John Henry

I don't like no red-black woman
Like myself, like myself
I don't like no red-black woman
——

This is the hammer killed John Henry
Don't kill me, don't kill me
This is the hammer killed John Henry
—[?]

Take this hammer, carry it to Captain
Tell him he's dead, tell him he's dead
Take that hammer, carry it to Captain
He's —[?]

This is the hammer killed my brother
He is gone, he is gone
This is the hammer killed my brother
—[?]

Hammer, hammer killed John Henry
He's gonna need, he's done need
Hammer, hammer killed John Henry
—[?]

Keep My Skillet Good and Greasy

If I

can,   don't know   wh - en,   Gonna make it to my shanty   if I   can,

Bought them   chickens in my   sack Got the hounds on my track   Gonna make it to my shanty if I   can

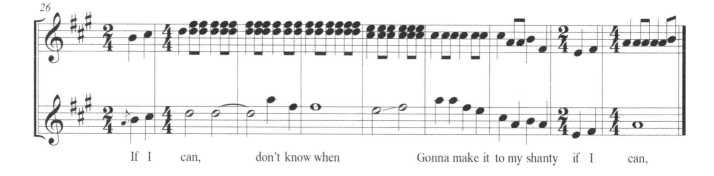

If I   can,   don't know when   Gonna make it to my shanty   if I   can,

T. DeWayne Moore

Author's note: Transcribed from Alan Lomax's recordings online at research.culturalequity.org.

Comparable versions:
"Keep My Skillet Good and Greasy," Uncle Dave Macon, 07/08/1924, New York, Vocalion 14848
"Bootlegger's Blues," Mississippi Sheiks, 06/12/1930, San Antonio, TX, OKeh 8820
"Keep My Skillet Good and Greasy," Henry Whitter, 11/14/1924, New York, OKeh 40296

Lyrics:

If I can, don't know when
Gonna make it to my shanty.

Times are getting hard, gonna buy a bucket of lard
Keep my skillet greasy if I can.
If I can, don't know when.

If I can, don't know when.
Well the rooster's a setting high
I'm gonna catch him on the fly
Keep my skillet greasy If I can.

If I can, don't know when.
Well, I'm going to New Orleans, I'm gonna get a pot of turnip greens,
I'm gonna keep my pot a-frying if I can.
If I can, don't know when.

Well that chicken's setting high, boys go catch while him I do try
To keep your skillet greasy if I can
If I can, don't know when
I'm gonna make it to my shanty, if I can.

I got a rabbit in the log, I ain't got no rabbit dog
Don't you never let my rabbit get away.
Get away, get away.

I done felled him, smelled him had my hands on him
Don't you never let my rabbit get away.
Get away, get away.

I'm going to town to buy me a bloodhound
Keep my skillet good and greasy.

If, I can, I don't know when.
If, I can, I don't know when
Gonna take it to my shanty if I can.

Leather Britches

Author's note: Transcribed from Alan Lomax's recordings online at research.culturalequity.org. This transcription is from the first pass of the tune, where the sound is the clearest.

Comparable versions:

"Lord McDonald's Reel," Niel & Nathaniel Gow, *Third Collection of Niel Gow's Reels* (ca. 1792), 9

"Leather Breeches," Cole, *1000 Fiddle Tunes*, 22

Bolick and Austin, "*Mississippi Fiddle Tunes and Songs from the 1930s*: Mr. J. H. Wheeler, "Leather Breeches," 202; John Hatcher, "Leather Britches," 295; Hardy C. Sharp, "Leather Britches," 338; Stephen B. Tucker, "Leather Britches," 359

In this book: "Leather Breeches," Carter Brothers & Son, 11/22/1928, Memphis, TN, Vocalion 5295

"Leather Breeches," Leake County Revelers, 04/13/1927, New Orleans, Columbia 15149-D

Rye Straw

Author's note: Transcribed from Alan Lomax's recordings online at research.culturalequity.org. Hemphill is tuned three half
  steps low. His repeats for the parts vary, but the first part is always longer.

Comparable versions:

Bolick and Austin, *Mississippi Fiddle Tunes and Songs from the 1930s*: Frank T. Kittrell, "Rye Straw," 314; Charles Long, "Ala-
  bama Waltz," 319; Stephen B. Tucker, "Joke on the Puppy," 358
"Rye Straw," Uncle Am Stuart, 06/1924, New York, Vocalion 14843
"Rye Straw," Clayton McMichen & Riley Puckett, 10/29/1929, Atlanta, Columbia 15524-D
"Rye Straw," Doc Roberts & Asa Martin, 01/13/1930, Richmond, IN, Gennett 7221

So Soon I'll Be at Home

Author's note: Transcribed from Alan Lomax's recordings online at research.culturalequity.org.

Comparable versions: None known.

T. DeWayne Moore

CLAUDE KENNEDY

Claude Kennedy (1908–1980) of Mendenhall in Simpson County, Mississippi, was not a widely known musician outside of his community. However, his band, the Six Towns Band, traveled to Washington in July 1974 to perform at the Smithsonian Folklife Festival as representatives of the state of Mississippi. In usual Mississippi networking fashion, they had been recommended for the performance by one of Claude's cousins, who had a relative working for the Smithsonian.

The land that is now Simpson County was originally part of the territory of the Six Towns tribe of the Choctaw Nation. In 1910 an early version of the Six Towns Band consisted of Monroe Kennedy, Bob and Annie Cockrell on fiddle, Fannie Patterson on guitar, Louisa Brown on mandolin, and Mattie Patterson on banjo.[1] Monroe Kennedy's son Claude led the later version of the band that appeared in Washington. A 1937 newspaper announced:

Claude in Washington, 1974. Photo courtesy Claudette Kennedy.

> The Six Town Singiness-Swinginess Fiddle Band will appear on program at Shivers School Friday, Sept 17th at 8 pm and at Martinsville on Sept 18th at 8pm. The admission price is 25 cents and 15 cents. This Band broadcast over WJDX in Jackson on Monday, Wednesday and Friday at 11:15 am and features male and female vocal duets, Violin duets,

Guitar and Mandolin solos, Black-faced Comedian and Band Concert. The characters are Ruby and Rena, Songbirds, Blackie, the Violinist; Lazy Bones, Pianist and the Black-Faced Comedian.[2]

Claude worked primarily as a farmer or rancher, raising cotton at first and then converting to raising cattle around 1949. He also worked as a substitute mail carrier. Early on he traded cattle in New Orleans, later moving his trade to Hattiesburg and Jackson. Early in the 1940s he traveled to do construction in Panama. After marriage and the birth of his children, his interests were home, music,

Claude Kennedy. Photo courtesy Claudette Kennedy.

cattle, and church. His daughter, Claudette, recalls no traveling for family vacations and that he was very careful with expenses.[3]

He married Dell Edwards in 1946 and became a father for her two children from her previous marriage. Their daughter Claudette was born in 1948. Before his marriage he played for dances, incurring the disapproval of his church and was "churched" or banished from the church. After a time he was readmitted, and became a song leader for the choirless congregation. In later years he would occasionally play a hymn on the fiddle in church. When Claudette was old enough, he insisted that she learn to play piano so that she could play for the church, which she has done to this day. Claudette learned to play from notation but not by ear. Claude eventually took a few lessons and learned to read music notation, but by far the bulk of his music was learned by ear.

Claude and Claudette, beyond a few early attempts, never played together.

Claude played music with family and friends, occasionally appearing in public. The Six Towns Band played locally at church programs, reunions, amateur contests, and nursing homes. It's likely that Claude learned at least some of his music from his father. Early in his life, he played with his brother Aubrey who played mandolin, before Aubrey moved to Kentucky. He continued to play with his sister Ruby, a piano player. Members of the Six Towns Band, Dewitt Flint on piano and R. T. Gardner on guitar, would often come to Claude's house to play instrumental versions of popular songs, but not square dance music.

Claude entered the state fiddle contest in Jackson several times, placing second on one occasion. Claude's version of the Six Towns Band seems to

APPEARING IN PERSON
THE SIX TOWN BAND

SMITHSONIAN
INSTITUTION
Site of the
American
Folklife
Music
Festival

The famous SIX TOWN BAND will bring a music concert to the people consisting of Country, Dixieland, Western and Gospel music.

The SIX TOWN BAND was chosen by the Smithsonian Institution in Washington, D. C., along with other high-scale musicians from the State of Mississippi, to entertain 5 million people on the mall between the Lincoln Memorial and the Washington Monument.

THE WASHINGTON POST described the American Folklife Music Festival from the State of Mississippi as the biggest and greatest and best that was ever held in Washington, D. C. The festival was held from July 3 through July 7, 1974.

Don't miss this music concert when it comes near you. THE SIXTOWN BAND will appear in person at the time and place listed below.

If you want this concert in your community, call or write Robert D. Flint, Mendenhall, Mississippi, (601) 847-3156.

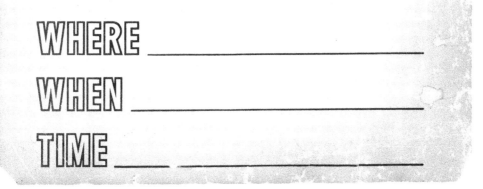

WHERE _____

WHEN _____

TIME _____

Promotional poster for Six Town Band, ca. 1975. Courtesy Claudette Kennedy.

have formed in the early 1970s, perhaps inspired by the invitation to go to the Smithsonian festival. The band at that time, all from Mendenhall, consisted of Claude Kennedy on fiddle, R. T. Gardner on guitar, Dewitt Flynt on piano, Jimmie Ray Weathersby on bass, and Mims Gregory on rhythm guitar. The only other appearances of the band that are remembered were in 1976 when they played at a church in Athens, a Mississippi Sesquicentennial event, and a free concert inside the Mendenhall court house. In 1977 they won Best Overall Band at the first bluegrass festival in Monticello. Claude played up until a few months before he passed away in 1980.

"Claude's Dream" is a tune that came to him in a dream. He woke up, practiced till he finished it, and recorded it on a cassette. He has no other known compositions. However, his seven home cassette recordings of the tune "Soggy Bottom" all vary

Claude Kennedy, ca. 1970s. Photo courtesy Claudette Kennedy.

Page 6, Section One   The Magee Courier, Magee, Miss., June 20, 1974

Six Town Band. Left to right: Mims Gregory, Jimmy Ray Weathersby, Dewitt Flynt, R. T. Gardner, Claude Kennedy.
Courtesy *Magee Courier.*

The late Monroe Kennedy plowing his fields located out from Legion Lake.

Monroe Kennedy. Courtesy Claudette Kennedy.

Original female members of the Six Town Band. Left to right: Fannie Patterson, Mattie Patterson, Louisa Brown, Annie Cockrell. Courtesy Claudette Kennedy.

considerably and suggest that he was composing and working out its structure.

Claude's nephew, Jack Magee, a fine Mississippi fiddler in his own right, has preserved Claude's music, making the home recordings available. He has learned and performs some of his tunes, most notably "Claude's Dream." See appendix B for information on Jack's recording. The only other recordings of Claude or of the Six Towns Band are from the 1974 Smithsonian Folklife Festival and are in the Ralph Rinzler Folklife Archives and Collections, Center for Folklife and Cultural Heritage, Smithsonian Institution in Washington, DC.

For many of the tunes transcribed here, there were no titles for the recordings. Titles of closely related tunes are indicated in the heading in parenthesis. The recordings are posted at mississippifiddle.com, with our thanks to Jack Magee for sharing them with us.

—Harry Bolick 2019

NOTES

1. *Magee Courier*, Magee, MS, June 20, 1974, 1.
2. "Six Town Singers Feature Musical Entertainment," *Simpson County News*, September 16, 1937, 10.
3. Author's interview with Claudette Kennedy Weldon, Magee, MS, May 16, 2017.

Claude Kennedy Six Towns Repertoire List circa 1976

Old-time Tunes

A Bird in a Gilded Cage
A Bicycle Built for Two
Alabama Jubilee
Are You from Dixie?
Arkansas Traveler
Beautiful Ohio
Beer Barrel Polka
Bill Cheatham
Birmingham Jail
Boil them Cabbage Down

Bully of the Town
Canadian Sunset
Carroll County Blues
Carry Me Back to Old Virginia
Chicken Reel
Claude's Dream
Correna, Correna
Darling Nellie Gray
Dark Town Strutters Ball
Deep Ellum Blues
Deep in the Heart of Texas
Dixie
Dixie Darling
Don't Fence Me In
Down Yonder
Faded Love
For Me and My Gal
Four-Leaf Clover
Get along Home Cindy
Guitar Rag
Hold That Tiger
Home Sweet Home
Hot Time in the Old Town Tonight
Indian Love Call
I Want a Buddy, Not a Sweetheart
It Is Sweet to Be Remembered
It's a Long, Long Way to Tipperary
Jelly Roll Blues
Just Because
Let Me Call You Sweetheart
Listen to the Mockingbird
Love Letters in the Sand
Make Me a Pallet on the Floor
Mama Won't You Please Come Home
Maple on the Hill
Memories
Mexicali Rose
Mollie Brown
My Bonnie Lies Over the Ocean
My Buddy
My Wild Irish Rose
My Old Kentucky Home
Oh Susanna
Over the Waves Waltz
Plain-Wang Blues

Play Wolly Doodle

Ragtime Annie

Red River Valley

Red Wing

Release Me

Roll Out the Barrel

Sallie Goodwin

St. Louis Blues

Salty Dog

San Antonio Rose

Satisfied Blues

Silver Bells

Silver Threads among the Gold

Smile the While

Soggy Bottom

Soldiers Joy

Springtime in the Rockies

Suwanee River

Sweet Bunch of Daisies

Sunrise Serenade

Take Me Back to Tulsa

That Silver-Haired Daddy of Mine

Tenting Tonight

Tiger Rag

Turkey in the Straw

Under the Double Eagle

Wabash Blues

Wabash Cannon Ball

Walk Easy

Way Down Yonder

When It's Peach Picking Time in Georgia

When You and I Were Young Maggie

When You Wore a Tulip

Whistling Rufus

Wildwood Flower

Yankee Doodle

Yellow Rose of Texas

You Are My Sunshine

Waltz Tunes

Bill Myer's Waltz

Festival Waltz

Forty Years Waltz

Good Night Waltz

Merry Widow Waltz

Missouri Waltz

Oklahoma Waltz

Over the Waves Waltz

Tennessee Waltz

The Waltz You Saved for Me

Wednesday Night Waltz

Untitled No. 1 (Bill Cheatham)

Author's note: Transcribed from family home recordings shared by Jack MaGee. The tunes were not identified by name. Listen to them at mississippifiddle.com

Comparable versions:

"Quayside Hornpipe," Keith Norman McDonald, *The Skye Collection of the Best Reels and Strathspeys Extant* (1887; reprinted 1979 by S. Cranford), 174 (only the "A" part of the tune)

Bolick and Austin, *Mississippi Fiddle Tunes and Songs from the 1930s*: W. A. Bledsoe, "Bill Cheatham," 219

"Brilliancy Medley," Eck Robertson, 10/11/1929, Dallas, Victor 40298

"Bill Cheatem," James Cole String Band, 06/1928, Indianapolis, IN, Vocalion 5226

"Bill Cheatham," Blind Joe Mangrum & Fred Schriver, 10/06/1928, Nashville, Victor 40018

Untitled No. 2 (Casey Jones)

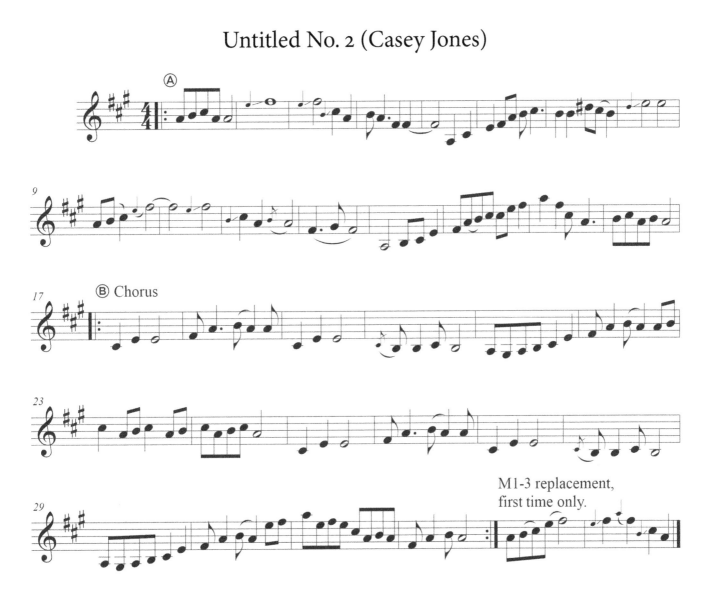

Author's note: Transcribed from family home recordings shared by Jack MaGee. The tunes were not identified by name. Listen to them at mississippifiddle.com. Only on the first pass of the tune, M33 and M34 replace the first two measures. On subsequent passes through the tune, play as written.

Comparable versions:
The second part of this tune is related to the chorus of the song "Casey Jones."
"Casey Jones," Fiddling John Carson, 11/07/1923, New York, OKeh 40038
"Casey Jones," Mississippi John Hurt, 02/14/1928, Memphis, TN, OKeh unissued
"Casey Jones," Gid Tanner & His Skillet Lickers, 03/28/1927, Atlanta, Columbia 15237-D

Untitled No. 3 (Clarinet Polka)

Author's note: Transcribed from family home recordings shared by Jack MaGee. Listen to them at mississippifiddle.com. After M51, repeat the C part and end with the C part.

Comparable versions:
"Dziadunio Polka," or "Dziadek Polka" (Grandfather Polka), Karol Namyslowski, copyright 1913
"The Clarinet Polka," Frank Przybylski, 1915, Columbia
Cole's Universal Library-Favorite Polkas, Cole, fol (1943), p 1 (Toodle Oodle Melody)

Claude's Dream

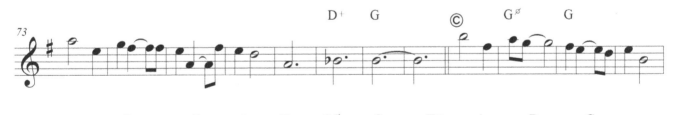

Author's note: Transcribed from family home recordings shared by Jack MaGee. Listen to them at mississippifiddle.com. Transcription is thanks to Jo Miner.

Comparable versions: None known

Untitled No. 4 (Devil's Dream)

Author's note: Transcribed from family home recordings shared by Jack MaGee. The tunes were not identified by name. Listen to them at mississippifiddle.com.

Comparable versions:
Elias Howe, *Howe's School for the Violin* (Boston: Oliver Ditson, 1851), 29
Bolick and Austin, *Mississippi Fiddle Tunes and Songs from the 1930s*: T. W. Cooper, "Untitled," 86; W. E. Claunch, "Devil's Dream," 256; Stephen B. Tucker, "Devil's Dream," 352
In this book: "Devil's Dream," Grover O'Briant
"Devil's Dream," Kessinger Bros, 02/10/1928, Ashland, KY, Brunswick 256
"Devil's Dream," Clayton McMichen, 06/01/1931, New York, Decca 2649

Dunkirk

Author's note: Transcribed from family home recordings shared by Jack MaGee. Listen to them at mississippifiddle.com.

Comparable versions:

Ford, *Traditional Music of America*, 63

Bolick and Austin, *Mississippi Fiddle Tunes and Songs from the 1930s*: Charlie Edmundson, "Eighth of January March," 95; F. Ezell, "Eighth of January Waltz," 104; Enos Canoy, "Eighth of January," 238; W. E. Claunch, "Eighth of January," 258; John Hatcher, "Eighth of January," 291; Hardy Sharp, "Eighth of January," 336; J. A. Moorman, "Eighth of January," 150

In this book: "Eighth of January," Sid Hemphill

"Eighth of January," Arkansas Barefoot Boys, 02/11/1928, Memphis TN, OKeh 45217

"Eighth of January," Fox Chasers, 06/11/1930, San Antonio, TX, OKeh 45496

"Eighth of January," Ted Gossett's Band, 09/16/1930, Richmond, IN, Champion 16160

Untitled No. 5 (Golden Slippers)

© (golden slippers)

Author's note: Transcribed from family home recordings shared by Jack MaGee. The tunes were not identified by name. Listen to them at mississippifiddle.com. The last four measures seem to be a fifth part that Kennedy couldn't fully remember and is incomplete.

Comparable versions:

James Bland, lyric and music, 1880

"Golden Slippers," Dykes Magic City Trio, 03/11/1927, New York, Brunswick 128

"Golden Slippers," H. M. Barnes & His Blue Ridge Ramblers, 1/28/1929, New York, Brunswick 313

"O Dem Golden Slippers," Roy Harvey, Jess Johnston & the West Virginia Ramblers, 06/03/1931, Richmond, IN, Champion 16757

Untitled No. 6 (Paddy on the Turnpike)

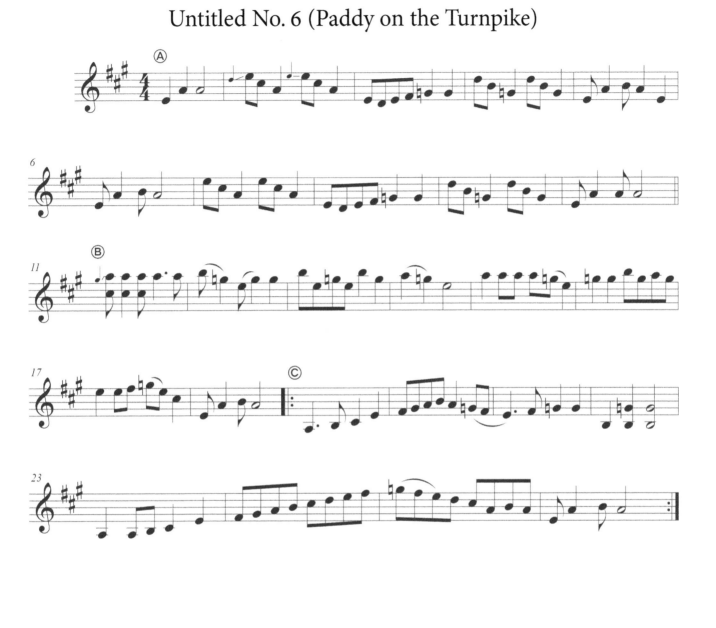

Author's note: Transcribed from family home recordings shared by Jack MaGee. The tunes were not identified by name. Listen
to them at mississippifiddle.com.

Comparable versions:
"Colonel Crockett," George Knauff, *Virginia Reels,* Vol. 3 (Baltimore: George Willig Jr., 1839)
"Jack Smith's Favorite Reel," Cole, *1000 Fiddle Tunes*, 40
In this book: "Jenny on the Railroad," Carter Brothers & Son, 11/22/1928, Memphis, TN, Vocalion 5297
"The Gal on the Log," Cap. Moses J. Bonner, 03/17/1925, Houston, Victor 19699 (A and B parts only)

Untitled No. 7 (Rachael)

Harry Bolick

Author's note: Transcribed from family home recordings shared by Jack MaGee. The tunes were not identified by name. Listen to them at mississippifiddle.com. The first part is played once and in terms of timing, quite loose. On subsequent passes through the tune, Claude plays the simpler version indicated as the third part.

Comparable versions:
The second part is the Revelers Mississippi Breakdown, which they play in C, or "Rachael" or "Texas Quickstep" usually played in the key of D.
Also known as "Rachael."
"Strawberry Blossom," Francis O'Neill, *O'Neill's Music of Ireland: Eighteen Hundred and Fifty Melodies* (Chicago: Lyon and Healy, 1903), 253
Bolick and Austin, *Mississippi Fiddle Tunes and Songs from the 1930s*: Stephen B. Tucker, "Circus Tune," 250
In this book: "Wednesday Night Waltz," Leake County Revelers, 04/13/1927, New Orleans, Columbia 15189-D
"Texas Quickstep," Red Headed Fiddlers, 10/18/1928, Dallas, Brunswick 285
"Cherokee Polka," Ed Haley, *Vol. 2: Grey Eagle* (Rounder, 1998)

Sally Goodin

Author's note: Transcribed from family home recordings shared by Jack MaGee. The tunes were not identified by name. Listen to them at mississippifiddle.com. I have marked each pass in this string of variations as a new part, but it really is theme and variation applied to the same basic melody. But what a long string of variations!

Comparable versions:
Bolick and Austin, *Mississippi Fiddle Tunes and Songs from the 1930s*: J. E. Shoemaker, "Sally Goodin," 173; Miss Mae Belle Williams, "Bear Creek," 204; John Brown, "Sally Goodin," 234; W. E. Claunch, "Sally Goodin," 272, 252; Thaddeus Willingham, "Sally Goodin," 395
"Sally Goodwin," Ford, *Traditional Music of America*, 209 (square dance calls), 419 (verses)
In this book: "Sally Goodin," Tom Dumas
"Sally Gooden," Eck Robertson, 07/01/1922, New York, Victor 18956
"Old Sally Goodman," Fiddlin' John Carson, 11/07/1923, New York, OKeh 40095
"Sally Goodin," Kessinger Brothers, 02/05/1929, New York, Brunswick 308

Soggy Bottom

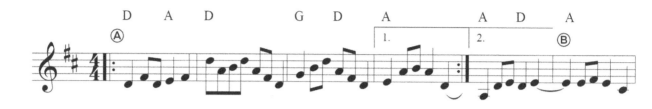

Author's note: Transcribed from family home recordings shared by Jack MaGee. Listen to them at mississippifiddle.com. This transcription follows version three of the solo fiddle recordings. Suggested chords are indicated. With the multiple recordings of this tune, I suspect that Kennedy was composing the tune and trying out different ideas.

Comparable versions: None known

Harry Bolick

Untitled No. 8 (Tom and Jerry)

Author's note: Transcribed from family home recordings shared by Jack MaGee. Listen to them at mississippifiddle.com.

Comparable versions:

Bolick and Austin, *Mississippi Fiddle Tunes and Songs from the 1930s*: John Hatcher, "Tom and Jerry," 304 (resembles Kennedy's D part); Stephen B. Tucker; "Tom and Jerry," 367 (shares title but not the melody)

"Tom and Jerry," Smith's Garage Band, 10/29/1929, Dallas, Vocalion 5375 (resembles Kennedy's D part)

"The Lost Child," Stripling Brothers, 11/15/1928, Birmingham, AL, Vocalion 5321 (resembles Kennedy's D part)

Untitled No. 9 Waltz

Harry Bolick

Author's note: Transcribed from family home recordings shared by Jack MaGee. Listen to them at mississippifiddle.com.

Comparable versions:
None known.

THE LEAKE COUNTY REVELERS

The Leake County Revelers were the most famous string band to come out of Mississippi in the 1920s. Through their broadcasts on WJDX in Jackson, their personal appearances, and their many records, in particular their bestseller "Wednesday Night Waltz," they became household names in central Mississippi and were known in several adjacent states. At a time of poor communications and widespread rural poverty, this was real acceptance.

In the mid-1920s, Leake County and the counties adjoining it were neither wealthy nor modernized. Electricity was just coming to the towns, and farmers out in the country were still using kerosene lamps. The countryside itself was open, with few major highways or railroad lines, and much uncleared land still in the Pearl River bottoms.

The true home of the Leake County Revelers was not really in Leake County at all. Sebastopol lies just over the county line in Scott County, close to the point where Leake and Scott abut Neshoba and Newton respectively, so that the town lies almost at the center of a four-county block. It was in Sebastopol that the four men who were to make up the Revelers first got together, and in the four counties around that they played much of their music.

The oldest member of the group was Robert Oscar Mosley (1884–1931), who played mandolin.

He was always known as R. O. He owned a hardware store in Sebastopol, with a sideline in phonograph records. Some time during the 1920s, he started playing with a couple of Leake Countians with whom he'd become acquainted, Jim Wolverton and Will Gilmer. Wolverton (1895–1969) was a farmer and played five-string banjo; he came from a musical family and had several musician brothers, and was also a good bass singer. William Bryan Gilmer (1897–1960) could play banjo (his first instrument) and guitar, but the fiddle became his first love. He worked at Dr. Thomas Underwood's drug store next door to Mosley's shop, and did a little extra business selling Victrolas.

The band was completed when Dallas Jones (1889–1985) joined as guitarist. He too was a Scott Countian. He met the other three one evening after work and was soon playing with them regularly on Saturday afternoons. He had started out as a fiddler, learning from one of his brothers, and had had a string band in his teenage years with a couple of cousins. But he had also played guitar since he was twelve, and he went back to that instrument when joining the Revelers-to-be.

The band had been playing as a unit for about a year before they attracted the notice of a record company. The Jackson talent agent H. C. Speir was himself from the band's area, and when he heard

Dallas Jones, R. O. Mosley, Jim Wolverton, Will Gilmer. Publicity photo from collection of Tony Russell.

reports of their music, he recommended them to Frank B. Walker of Columbia Records. Walker was later to tell a story about this.

I happened to be up in Leake County, Mississippi. I think it's probably one of the most—well, one of the poorest counties in the United States of America. It's poverty stricken. The people are removed from education and from all sorts of social contacts. And I found a little group that had been playing together—four people—they interested me, so I gave them a name. I called them the Leake County Revelers—a very high-sounding name and they were a pretty good-sounding group. But they played things that didn't have any sense to them at all. They just played and played and played, in schoolhouses for practically nothing. So you have to figure out something that would give it some sort of quality to what they were doing, and then you'd have to give it a name.

So we thought that this was a grand idea, and they made their first record. And on one side we called it "Courtin' Waltz" [*sic*]. Well, that means that, down in the South, of course, you just don't go dating a girl. You court her. And when do you court her? Well, it's usually Wednesday night. Maybe on Sunday, but Wednesday night was the courting night. So we had "Courtin' Waltz" on one side of the record and on the other side we had "Wednesday Night Waltz." It became one of the biggest-selling records of all time.[1]

The band made its first recordings, including the waltz hit, in New Orleans in April 1927. Thereafter they recorded twice yearly, in spring and winter, through 1929, with a final session in winter 1930. Altogether they released twenty-two records.

According to Dallas Jones, it was Speir, not Walker, who gave them their recording name. Either way, it was not an entirely accurate sobriquet:

Dallas Jones, Jim Wolverton, R. O. Mosley, Will Gilmer. Publicity photo courtesy of Carl Fleischhauer.

From Columbia catalog, 1928. Collection of Tony Russell.

Mosley and Jones were from Scott County, and Wolverton, though originally from Leake, was by then living and farming in Neshoba. They might just as easily have been the Scott County Revelers.

Throughout their recording days the Revelers made many personal appearances in central and southern Mississippi. A typical report reads: "The Leake County Revelers will give a program at Sulphur Springs school house Saturday night, March 10, [1928,] with the aid of the music and expression teacher of Sebastopol. Come and get your money's worth. Admission fee, 15 cents for children; and 25 cents for adults."[2]

They performed not only as a four-piece but in various smaller combinations: Gilmer and Wolverton would play fiddle–banjo duets, Jones and Wolverton guitar–banjo pieces, and Jones would sing with just his own guitar accompaniment. The band would play many Saturday-night dances in private houses. Jones remembered that, in his younger days,

Tony Russell

breakdowns were the favorites, but later the waltz came in, and the band had a certain reputation for waltzes. They also attended fiddlers' contests and gave entertainments in schools, including comic sketches, with Gilmer playing a blackface part, Jones the "silly kid" in a clown suit, and Wolverton the straight man.

The band seems never to have gone to the Kosciusko fiddlers' contest, but did enter one held at Morton. Jones remembered winning first prize in the singing section with "Rock All Our Babies to Sleep," and was also successful with "Shanty in Old Shanty Town." Gilmer used to play a breakdown like "Leather Breeches" or "Sally Gooden," then a waltz or a blues.

Radio developed slowly in Mississippi. Whereas WSB in Atlanta was broadcasting old-time music regularly from the mid-1920s, and was being echoed by stations in Texas, Mississippi stations seem not to have been active in that way, or at all. According to Mumford Bean, WELO in Tupelo was broadcasting old-time music in the late 1920s, but no station in that city was listed in *Radio Digest* during 1929–30. If the *Digest* is to be relied upon, the longest established station in Mississippi was WCOC in Meridian, which opened in February 1927 with the slogan "Down in the old Magnolia State." By 1930 WCOC was a 1,000-watt station, rivaled only by the newer and equally powerful WJDX in Jackson, which had come on air in December 1929.[3] Other stations were rarely above 100 watts, and Hattiesburg's WRBJ in 1930 was a mere ten watts.

"Much Mississippi talent is coming to the front at Station WJDX, Jackson," reported a paper in Yazoo City in January 1930. "Only last week it was discovered that the Leake County Revelers, a string band quartet, had been Columbia recording artists since 1927. They have made 20 records. The Revelers were on the air through WJDX for an hour recently."[4] They had a regular hour-long Saturday-evening program, usually 7–8 p.m. or 8–9 p.m., sponsored by Mississippi Power & Light, and made their broadcasts from a studio high up in the Lamar Life Building, under the clock. On the first anniversary of their broadcasting debut, a baker who had his store near the studio baked

LEAKE REVELERS ON AIR TONIGHT

WJDX Program Saturday Includes Many Favorites of Radio Fans

The Leake County Revelers of Sebastopol, Miss., known as "the finest interpreters of old waltz melodies in the southland," will go on the air at WJDX for an hour's broadcast tonight at eight o'clock.

The personnel of the Leake County Revelers is as follows: W. B. Gilmer, violin; D. L. Jones, guitar; R. O. Mosley, mandolin, and J. M. Wolverton, banjo. These artists have been making records for the last two years for the Columbia Phonograph company, having completed fourteen records, and are just beginning their second two-year exclusive contract with them.

The Revelers, who have become favorites among artists of station WJDX, will play many beautiful old southern airs tonight. It is fitting that such selections will be broadcast since this is the birthday of George Washington, first president of our United States.

Clarion Ledger, February 22, 1930.

a huge cake for them, with "Happy Anniversary Leake County Revelers" in icing on the top. That evening they were invited to dine with Governor Connor in his mansion across the street from the Lamar Building.

They had many requests from listeners—165 in a week was the record, said Jones—and these came not only from Mississippi but from farther southwest: Arkansas, Louisiana, Texas. The station could even be picked up as far away as Hawaii.

Carlton Gilmer, 1975. Photo courtesy Carl Fleischhauer.

The announcer for the Revelers' program, J. S. "Mac" Howell, sometimes traveled with them. One time, Howell set up a tour for the group, which took them eastward into northern Alabama and Georgia. This, according to Jones, was a mistake, for they found themselves in devoted Skillet Lickers country, and met with less success than they might have merited. They did play a few guest radio dates, for example in Montgomery and Atlanta. They also ran into the Skillet Lickers themselves; Jones remembered meeting Clayton McMichen, Riley Puckett, and Gid Tanner.

The band also played a part in regional politics, as Frank Walker recalled.

> A gentleman in the South by the name of Huey Long . . . when he was running for lieutenant governor [*sic*] of Mississippi [*sic*], I was perhaps instrumental in getting him to hire the Leake County Revelers to go up through North Louisiana and so forth to play for him at schoolhouses. And they attracted the crowd, and after they had the crowd

there, Huey used to speak to them about what a wonderful lieutenant governor [*sic*] he'd make, and he was elected hands down. But really the Leake County Revelers won the election. Then after that, that same pattern was adopted by some others . . .[5]

◆ ◆ ◆

It would be a mistake to think of the Revelers as a full-time unit, or of its members as playing only in that context. Neither the region nor the times permitted that sort of concentration—nor, quite possibly, did the temperaments of the band's members. No doubt each of the Revelers played on his own, or with entirely different musicians, from time to time. Will Gilmer in particular did so, and many memories of him as an individual quite apart from the Revelers were retained by Carlton Gilmer (1914–1985) of Walnut Grove.

Will was kin to Carlton's father, Ed Gilmer, and being a single man saw a good deal of them, even living with them for a spell. Carlton had traded a

Dallas Jones, 1975. Photo courtesy Carl Fleischhauer.

bicycle for a guitar, and Will showed him his first chords. Later Carlton took up the fiddle and learned some of Will's tunes, and how to play second parts. Will taught him "Moonlight on the Bay" on guitar, and various waltzes and blues on fiddle. "The Waltz You Saved for Me" and "Sweet Bunch of Daisies" were a couple of Will's favorites. He also composed and taught to Carlton a sort of follow-up to "House of David Blues" called "House of Morgan Blues." By and large, as Carlton remembered, Will preferred blues and waltzes to breakdowns.

Will Gilmer liked to ramble, and he traveled in several states, often with outfits such as Dr. Simpson's medicine show. (According to his cousin Morgan Gilmer, the whole band sometimes played for this show.)[6] Carlton would drive Will to the nearest railroad station to start his ramblings. Will, he said, had friends in virtually every town in Mississippi and the neighboring states—many of them women friends. He never married.

One of Will's frequent associates, when he was performing apart from the other Revelers, was a

Smokey and the Ghost

Uncle Will was fully dressed and actin' straight, and he was out on the stage, you know, and they was just talkin', and he told Smokey that there was a real nice place there, but, he said, "I got a feelin' I gotta move on, because," he says, "they tell me that exactly at twelve o'clock every night there's a ghost walks through here."

And old Smokey—Black, you know—"Oh, no, sir," [he] says, "I don't believe in that ghost stuff." Says, "Ain't no such thing as a ghost. I don't believe that."

And they kept watchin' the clock that was up there and it got pretty close to twelve, them carryin' on. And Uncle Will says, "I'm goin'. You gonna stay here?"

"Yes, sir, I'm gon' stay here. There ain't no such thing as a ghost."

And Will left out, you know, and old Smokey's mutterin' away, say, "Them goin' on about a ghost. There ain't no such thing. I'll stay here. I'll give it to you, I'm not scared." And he got him a newspaper and sat down in a rockin' chair and got all comfortable, you know.

Uncle Will got back there and got all wrapped up in a sheet, all dressed up, you know, and he come through and just tapped him on the shoulder. And he looked around—well, Will had done gone this way, you know, and missed him. But he had a spooky feelin'. You could tell he's getting scared all the time.

And directly Will come back and touched him, you know. And he said, "I don't know what that is. I'm sure somethin' touched me." Said, "I know there ain't no such thing as a ghost." And directly he sat down, readin' this paper.

And he cast his eye up there and it was exactly twelve o'clock.

So Uncle Will, he just laid his arm around him, you know, all wrapped up. And he looked up there and he seen that arm over here, you know, and he had that newspaper, and him sittin' there in that chair. And I've never seen nobody that could put on like he could—his feet, his legs, his whole body was just shakin', all . . .

Now he could throw a fit!

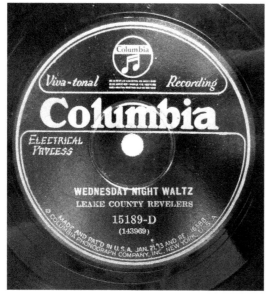

blackface comedian who called himself Smokey Cole. The two had met on a traveling show; Smokey was not a local man. They would do comedy sketches between acts at school plays and the like. Carlton would often sell tickets at these shows, and, while Smokey was blacking up, would play the fiddle while Uncle Will danced. Carlton recalled one of Will and Smokey's routines in some detail.[7]

There are Will Gilmer stories to be heard all over the Revelers' old stamping grounds. The time he "stole" a fellow's billfold by sucking it out of his pants pocket with a vacuum pump. The time he took a long drink out of the skimmin's barrel at Wes Thomas's syrup mill, and took three days to recover. Or the time when Mosley kept on playing a certain record in his shop next door. "It was just an old crazy record," said Carlton, called "Dead Cat on the Line."[8] "Uncle Will said that he heard that record until he just wanted to scream when Mosley put it on." So he got hold of a cat, soaked its fur in kerosene, set light to it, pushed it in at the back door of Mosley's store, and let it go about its business.

◆ ◆ ◆

The death in 1931 of R. O. Mosley, the oldest member of the group (and, according to some, the leader), does not appear to have driven the Leake County Revelers into retirement. They do seem to have been dropped from the WJDX schedule during 1931, but they continued to fill engagements. They played, for instance, at an "Old-Fashioned Country Dance" at Jackson's University Club in November 1932,[9] and there are occasional sightings of them in the local press as late as 1935. Perhaps they recruited a new member to replace Mosley. They also earned themselves a namecheck in the 1938 WPA guide to Mississippi, which, in its paragraph on Carthage, remarked, "The town is known throughout the State because of the Leake Co. Revelers, a group of local musicians who are keeping alive the old folk songs of the section." (It then added, incomprehensibly, "Their instruments vary from the saw to the harmonica.")[10]

Their recording career, however, ended in 1930. At that time, record companies were discarding all but their most popular artists, and the Revelers' sales had fallen off considerably since their excellent start in 1927. While the shake-up in the record industry during the Depression years, and the rather new look of the business when it recovered somewhat in the mid-1930s, would probably have sealed the fate of the Revelers as a recording band even had the group stayed intact, the loss of Mosley would have changed the character of their music radically, for not only was his delicate mandolin-playing an intrinsic part of their sound, but he also seems to have been responsible for selecting a good deal of their material.

Jim Wolverton carried on farming after the group broke up, and sang bass in the Scott County Quartet. Will Gilmer lived on in bachelorhood and contented solitude, his fiddle laid aside. Dallas Jones was the only ex-Reveler to pursue a musical career at all actively. For a time he played with the Cleve Bass band, which replaced the Revelers on WJDX, under the aegis of their predecessors' old sponsor, Mississippi Power & Light. The outfit, which was based in Jackson, included Oswald Boyd, Ruby Bishop (vocal and ukulele), Gracie Tackett (piano), and the leader on fiddle. Jones then went north, to Detroit. By 1940 he had returned to Sebastopol, but soon afterward he moved to Jackson and took a job as a bellboy in the large Heidelberg Hotel downtown. He remained there, working up to superintendent of service, for thirty-one years, until the hotel closed down in 1974 and he retired. In these later years he had little to do with music, though he would occasionally call for square dances.[11]

◆ ◆ ◆

When the old bands pass on, their music too often passes with them, to be revived—if at all—only by people who are separated from it not only by several generations but generally by a wide cultural gap. But there are instances of a band's legacy being handed down to kinfolk and acquaintances, and living again in its homeland. The music of the Leake County Revelers survives in this way, in the playing of the Leake County String Band.

Forty or fifty years ago, this part of central Mississippi, and in particular the four-county square of Leake, Scott, Neshoba, and Newton, was a region of great musical riches, home to a number of fine bands that coexisted without rivalry or envy. But in the depth of their recorded repertoire and the reach of their radio programs and personal appearances, the Leake County Revelers earned a special place in the annals of Mississippi music. Thanks to those recordings, their revels are not, and need never be, ended.

—Tony Russell

NOTES

1. Frank Walker and Mike Seeger, "Who Chose These Records? A Look into the Life, Tastes, and Procedures of Frank Walker," in Josh Dunson and Ethel Raim, eds., *Anthology of American Folk Music* (New York: Oak Publications, 1973), 8–17. Walker's memory was at fault: the reverse side of "Wednesday Night Waltz" was titled "Good Night Waltz." The Revelers did not record "Courtin' Days Waltz" until their penultimate session in December 1929.

2. *Union Appeal*, Union, MS, March 8, 1928.

3. "Celebration of the first birthday of WJDX broadcasting station of the Lamar Life Insurance Company will begin Sunday at 1 p.m.," *Daily Clarion-Ledger*, Jackson, MS, December 7, 1930.

4. "State Talent Is Coming to Front At Station WJDX," *Yazoo Herald*, Yazoo, MS, January 21, 1930.

5. Walker and Seeger, "Who Chose These Records?"

6. Morgan Gilmer, letter to Tony Russell, March 8, 1973.

7. Carlton Gilmer, interviewed by Tony Russell, Walnut Grove, MS, October 20, 1975.

8. This can only refer to the popular OKeh record of 1929 "Dead Cat on the Line," a sermon by the African American minister Rev. J. M. Gates. (Or conceivably the cover version made the following year for Victor by Rev. F. W. McGee.)

9. "Annual Old Style Barn Dance For Week-end At The University Club. 'Ye Olden Time' Costumes To Be Worn in Celebration of Bidding Goodbye to Hard Times and Depression—Music By The Leake County Revelers," *Clarion-Ledger*, Jackson, MS, November 17, 1932.

10. Mississippi: The WPA Guide to the Magnolia State (1938).

11. Dallas L. Jones, interviewed by Tony Russell, Jackson, MS, October 22, 1975.

THE LEAKE COUNTY REVELERS ON RECORD

For their first session with Columbia, in New Orleans in April 1927, the Revelers, or their producer Frank Walker, picked a safe foursome: two breakdowns and two waltzes, with nothing particularly out of the ordinary about them. The breakdowns "Johnson Gal" and "Leather Breeches," coupled to form their debut release, gave a good introduction to Will Gilmer's agile fiddling and the delicate sound of the band as a whole. "Johnson Gal" was unusual in having a vocal refrain by Gilmer, perhaps the only solo he committed to record.

The coupling "Wednesday Night Waltz"/"Good Night Waltz" was an extraordinarily influential record, so its origins are all the more interesting. "Wednesday Night Waltz" is certainly older than the Revelers' recording. Will told Carlton Gilmer that he learned it "out in Texas somewhere," and the tune is to be found on early western recordings, e.g., by Otto Gray's Oklahoma Cowboy Band, under its (perhaps original) name of "Cowboy Waltz." The incorporation of passages in breakdown tempo, however, seems to have been Will Gilmer's idea; the tune thus introduced is "Saturday Night Breakdown," which the Revelers later recorded in its own right.

Many artists recorded "Wednesday Night Waltz" in the Revelers' wake—not just fiddlers like Clark Kessinger, Doc Roberts, and Charles Stripling, but Hawaiian groups like the North Carolina Hawaiians (OKeh, 1928) and Walter Kolomoku's Honoluluans (Victor, 1929). Words were composed for the tune within a couple of years, and it was recorded as a vocal number by Bud and Joe Billings (Frank Luther and Carson Robison) (Victor, 1929), the Cruthers Brothers (OKeh, 1929), and Riley Puckett (Bluebird, 1934).

Advance orders for the two records from this session appear to have been promising for a new band, and over 5,000 of each had been subscribed to before release. The first issue (the breakdowns) went on to sell 35,703 copies by 1931, when the Columbia "Old Familiar Tunes" catalog was closed, and later in the 1930s it was reissued on Vocalion. It proved to be the Revelers' second-best seller, but it was still far behind the waltz coupling, which scaled astonishing sales heights for the period and area and eventually reached a total of 195,717 copies sold. It too was reissued on Vocalion, staying in that catalog until at least the end of the '30s, and after World War II was twice more released, on red-label Columbias. Over about a quarter of a century, "Wednesday Night Waltz"/"Good Night Waltz" must have sold well over 200,000 copies.

The band's second session, in Atlanta in October 1927, differed considerably from the first. While the earlier date had been dominated by Gilmer's fiddling and composed of largely traditional material, the Atlanta one drew on composed tunes, employed more elaborate vocal parts, and often placed Mosley's mandolin in a joint leading role with the fiddle. The result was to make the Revelers seem a much more versatile band than their first two records would have implied, and at the same time to test their appeal on a variety of selections.

"My Wild Irish Rose" seems to have been sung by Mosley or Wolverton, with trio harmonizing on the refrain. The normal composition of the Revelers' vocal trios was apparently Jones (lead), Gilmer (tenor), and Wolverton (bass), but it is quite possible that they practiced variations on this; certainly it is not always Jones who sings lead.

"My Bonnie Lies Over the Ocean," similarly in waltz time, was a glee-club favorite of the later nineteenth century, but originated as a stage-Irish song, "Barney."[1] Here the lead voice does seem to be Jones's. Also from the close-harmony tradition, and again in waltz tempo, "In the Good Old Summertime" has Jones as lead singer and a strong chorus harmony.

"Listen to the Mocking Bird" is one of the oldest composed pieces in the band's repertoire, and one that can be compared with numerous recorded versions, by the country fiddlers Arthur Smith and Curly Fox, the Texan harmonica player W. W. MacBeth, and several French-Canadian musicians. It became a trick piece above all, its trills and whistling effects being reproducible on both fiddle and harmonica, and it has made its share of impressions over the years at fiddlers' contests. The Revelers' treatment is much more sober, with just some whistling, perhaps by Wolverton.

"The Old Hat" and "Monkey in the Dog Cart" were two excellent fiddle breakdowns to round off the session. The former, though known by that name in the region, is more often called something like "Going On Down Town," and was recorded as such by the Skillet Lickers. Much later, Grandpa Jones was successful with a primarily vocal version. "Monkey in the Dog Cart" takes us back to the

fiddle-dominated sound of the first session. "You better look out there, Will!" cries Wolverton at one point. "You gonna break your arm!"

These fiddle tunes were the first to be released from this session, and they eventually sold 22,906 copies. "My Bonnie Lies Over the Ocean"/"In the Good Old Summertime" reached 14,131. The remaining two titles were held back until 1931 and released as the Revelers' last record, shortly before the demise of the "Old Familiar Tunes" list. It sold much less well than its session-mates, perhaps no more than a few hundred copies.

Returning to New Orleans in April 1928, the band continued the fiddle-favoring mood of their last recorded performances. "Been to the East—Been to the West" is a bluesy fiddle number with a rather subsidiary vocal part. "Crow Black Chicken," a piece evidently unique to the Revelers, is also essentially a fiddle tune, though decorated with a vocal arrangement in which one singer handles the verses, the other the refrains; neither sounds like Jones, but it may be he who terminates the performance by knocking on his instrument and giving out some hearty crowing. Ry Cooder revived the tune by performing it on his 1972 album *Boomer's Story*.

"Make Me a Bed on the Floor" is more bluesy fiddling, with a vocal limited to the title phrase sung over and over, probably by Jones and Gilmer. "Merry Widow Waltz" had previously been recorded by the North Georgia fiddler A. A. Gray. "They Go Wild Simply Wild Over Me" is a jolly little song, which Jones thought he got "off the music." "Put Me in My Little Bed" would seem to be a precursor of "Put My Little Shoes Away."

Sales of records from this session: "Make Me a Bed on the Floor"/"Merry Widow Waltz," 27,904; "They Go Wild Simply Wild Over Me"/"Put Me in My Little Bed," 9,212; and "Been to the East—Been to the West"/"Crow Black Chicken," 12,024.

The Revelers' fourth session, in New Orleans in December 1928, commenced with a popular traditional fiddle tune, generally known as "Dance All Night with a Bottle in Your Hand" or similar, but on the Revelers' recording titled "Bring Me a Bottle," the phrase taken from the verse that the singer delivers four times during the recording: "Bring me a bottle of I don't care what . . ." The Revelers play it in a way that clearly expresses their confidence as recording artists, ending with a Skillet Lickers tag. The singer does not sound like Jones, and might be Gilmer.

"Birds in the Brook" is one of the most musically elaborate of the Revelers' tunes. The mandolin takes the lead and lends an airy, jaunty flavor to a tune whose measured tempo recalls the Irish set dance. But any Irishness about it is probably factitious, since it was a composed piece of the late nineteenth century. Jones credited Mosley as the source of the tune.

"Rockin' Yodel" is the same song as Jimmie Rodgers's "Rock All Our Babies to Sleep," but the Revelers' recording predates his by almost four years, and was probably derived (if from a record at all) from Riley Puckett's 1924 recording. Jones's ability as a Rodgers interpreter is noted in a report of an August 1929 engagement in Taylorsville: "The Leak [sic] County Revelers, a musical company composed of a yodeler and black faced comedian, presented a program at the high school auditorium on Friday evening. A number of Jimmy Rodgers's favorite yodeling pieces were sung with guitar accompaniment by a yodeler very much like Jimmy Rodgers himself."[2]

"Memories," "Magnolia Waltz," and "Julia Waltz" are elegant tunes in the time signature for which the band was becoming known. "Julia" had been recorded at the April 1928 session and rejected. Carlton Gilmer remembers playing a second part to it behind his uncle on many occasions.

"Molly Put the Kettle On," a breakdown with a repeated vocal section (probably sung by Jones, but it might be Gilmer), was also recorded by the Skillet Lickers (almost three years later) but was otherwise not particularly common on record at this time.

Sales of these issues were: "Rockin' Yodel"/"Julia Waltz," 10,339; "Bring Me a Bottle"/"Molly Put the Kettle On," 6,632; and the somewhat later released "Birds in the Brook"/"Magnolia Waltz," 1,602. This last coupling was also issued in Australia on the Regal label, credited to "The Alabama Barnstormers."

The April 1929 Atlanta session, somewhat like the previous date in that city, got under way with some vintage popular numbers: "Memories Waltz," "Where the Silv'ry Colorado Wends Its Way," "Georgia Camp Meeting," and "I'm Gwine Back to Dixie." "Memories Waltz" was a puzzling choice for recording, since it's the same piece as "Memories" from the previous session; possibly, at the time, Frank Walker judged the earlier recording unfit for release and called for a remake. "Silv'ry Colorado" is an early example of the citybilly genre; Jones sings just one verse and chorus and the rest is instrumental. "Georgia Camp Meeting," by contrast, is music all the way, the mandolin sparkling through the old ragtime-era piece, which over the years has been interpreted by military bands, then old-time string bands, then ragtime finger-picking guitarists. The mandolin stays upfront for "I'm Gwine Back to Dixie," which has Jones singing the verses and trio harmonizing on the refrain. This Old South song would be difficult to put across today, but in the Revelers' time it was probably accepted at face value.

"Dry Town Blues" is a slightly ragtime tune, evidently unique to the Revelers, that twice slips into the "How Dry I Am" melody. The full-length version of "Saturday Night Breakdown"—previously available only in part, tucked away inside "Wednesday Night Waltz"—moves with exemplary lightness and is one of the best of the group's breakdown performances.

"Good Fellow," another piece presently known only from the Revelers' recording, has singing probably by Jones, with trio refrains and a spot of twin whistling, very likely by Jones and Gilmer. I suspect the Revelers had been listening to a contemporary string band from north Georgia, the Georgia Yellow Hammers, whose manner they quite effectively pastiche here. "Uncle Ned," with its neat vocal arrangement, was another of the Revelers' recordings to be released in the UK and Australia in the early 1930s under the pseudonym "Alabama Barn Stormers." Somehow Dallas Jones heard about this, because he remarked to the author in 1975, "Somebody over in England, they copied a bunch of these records and sold them under another name."[3]

Sales of "Georgia Camp Meeting"/"I'm Gwine Back to Dixie" were 5,153; "Memories Waltz"/"Where the Silv'ry Colorado Wends Its Way," 5,737; "Dry

Town Blues"/"Good Fellow," 4,341; and "Saturday Night Breakdown"/"Uncle Ned," 5,574.

The entirely instrumental session held in New Orleans in December 1929 had a strong waltz emphasis but also produced a pair of graceful blues, or rather blues titles, since "Lonesome Blues" is not strictly a blues at all. "Leake County Blues" was based on a theme Gilmer heard somewhere and rearranged. "Sweet Rose of Heaven" was very likely borrowed from the recording by Taylor-Griggs' Louisiana Melody Makers (Victor, 1928); the piercingly beautiful waltz is there credited to the fiddler and co-leader F. R. Taylor. Gilmer's fiddle gives a little room to the mandolin for "Beautiful Bells," and Mosley achieves an appropriate tinkling effect in this attractive waltz. Neither "Mississippi Moon Waltz" nor "Courtin' Days Waltz" appears to have been recorded by any other group of the period. All together, though a rather circumscribed session, this produced disciplined music that cannot have failed to please the Revelers' devotees. "Sweet Rose of Heaven"/"Beautiful Bells" sold 4,790; "Leake County Blues"/"Lonesome Blues," 4,836; "Mississippi Moon Waltz"/"Courtin Days Waltz," 3,068.

The band's final session, at the Edwards Hotel in Jackson in December 1930, was held during a weeklong stay by OKeh Records. It would be the last recording session held in Mississippi until 1935.

"Thirty-First Street Blues," a relatively recent composition, may have been derived from the blues singer Clara Smith's 1924 recording. "Picture No Artist Can Paint" was found in an old songbook by Jones, who sang lead on it. Lines like "Picture the gum that she used to chew—chew it a while and hand it to you" suggest that this is a parody of a more serious model. "When It's Springtime in the Rockies" was a new song, published the previous year, and the Revelers were among the first to record it, ahead of Gene Autry, the Ranch Boys and numerous others.

The remainder of the session was entirely instrumental. "Mississippi Breakdown" was the Revelers' version of what is generally known as "Texas Quickstep" (though Narmour and Smith's "Mississippi Breakdown" was not), and may have been a deliberate cover of the Red Headed Fiddlers' 1928

Brunswick record. "Texas Fair," "Lazy Kate," and "Jungle Waltz" have no exact parallels on old-time recordings. "Jungle Waltz" was claimed by Jones as his composition, and one assumes that the unissued "Gilmar [*sic*] Waltz" was Will's.

These releases were low sellers by comparison with the 1927–28 ones; "When It's Springtime in the Rockies"/"Jungle Waltz" reached 1,956; "Thirty-First Street Blues"/"Mississippi Breakdown," 914; and "Picture No Artist Can Paint"/"Texas Fair," 790. "Lazy Kate" was paired with "Memories" from the December 1928 session; Frank Walker either forgot that he had issued the 1929 remake, "Memories Waltz," or didn't think it mattered. The coupling was released in 1931, when few records were selling, and sold few copies.

Due to copyright restrictions, "When It's Springtime in the Rockies" (Columbia 15648-D, recorded Jackson, MS, on 12/18/1930) does not have a transcription included in this book. The English recording label Document Records has produced a complete set of the Leake County Revelers recordings and the song may be heard there.

—Tony Russell

NOTES

1. Compare a version by the English folk group The Watersons on Topic 12TS265.

2. "Leake County Revelers. Musical Pair Entertain a la Jimmy Rodgers," *Daily Clarion-Ledger*, Jackson, MS, September 1, 1929.

3. Dallas L. Jones, interviewed by Tony Russell, Jackson, MS, October 22, 1975.

Beautiful Bells

Author's note: This transcription is from Columbia 15501-D, recorded New Orleans, 12/10/1929. The harmony fiddle part varies on each pass, but I have indicated a basic version.

Comparable versions:
George A. Russell, music, 1869
"Beautiful Bells," Fiddlin' Bob Larkin & His Music Makers, 02/22/1928, Memphis, TN, OKeh 45229

Tony Russell

Been to the East, Been to the West

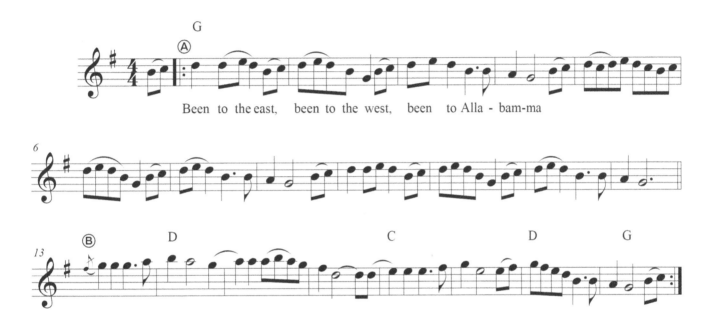

Been to the east, been to the west, been to Alla - bam-ma

Author's note: This transcription is from Columbia 15318-D, recorded New Orleans, 04/27/1928.

Comparable versions:

Bolick and Austin, *Mississippi Fiddle Tunes and Songs from the 1930s*: Ruby Costello, "I Want to Go to Meeting," 87; W. E. Claunch, "Chicken Pie," 254, and "Miss Sally at the Party," 265; John Hatcher, "Old Miss Sally," 298; Charles Long, "Jones County," 324 and "Steamboat," 330; Hardy Sharp, "Great Big Yam Potatoes," 337

Belden and Hudson, *Frank C. Brown Collection of North Carolina Folklore, Vol. 3: Folk Songs*, 510, 565

In this book: "Shear The Sheep Bobbie," Gatwood Square Dance Band, 12/15/1928, New Orleans, Columbia 15363

"Share 'Em," Scottsdale String Band, 08/10/1928, Atlanta, OKeh 45256

"Take Me Back to Tulsa," Bob Wills & His Texas Playboys, 02/25/1941, Dallas, OKeh 06101

Lyrics:

Been to the east, been to the west, been to Alabama

Old man gave me nothin for to eat but the leg of a yella hammer

Prettiest little girl I ever did see, lives in Alabama

Wanna know her name? I'll tell ya what it be it ain't but Suzy-anna

Birds in the Brook

Author's note: This transcription is from Columbia 15625-D, recorded New Orleans, 12/13/1928. The mandolin plays the melody. The recording repeats in the order of ABCBAB. In the third part, I have indicated minor chords where I hear the guitar playing only the bass notes D and E respectively.

Comparable versions:
"Birds in the Brook," by Robert Morrison Stults, 1893
"Birds in the Brook," Metropolitan Orchestra, 10/15/1901, Victor 1022
"Birds in the Brook," Arthur Pryor Orchestra, 04/30/1906, Victor 2766

Tony Russell

Bring Me a Bottle

Bring me a bottle of I don't care what, don't care what, don't care what

Bring me a bottle of I don't care what,

Alt: m7,8 when sung

get all rid of that pain I've got.

Author's note: This transcription is from Columbia 15380-D, recorded New Orleans, 12/12/1928.

Comparable versions:
In this book: "Give Me a Bottle of I Don't Care What," Newton County Hill Billies, 12/16/1930, Jackson, MS, OKeh 45544

Similar A parts:
"Dance All Night with a Bottle in Your Hand," Gid Tanner & His Skillet Lickers, 11/02/1926, Atlanta, Columbia 150108-D
"Dance All Night with a Bottle in My Hand," Stripling Brothers, 08/19/1929, Chicago, Vocalion 5395

Similar B parts:
"Jenny Lind Polka and Waltz," Robert Kelley (New York: William Hall and Son, 1848)
Bolick and Austin, *Mississippi Fiddle Tunes and Songs from the 1930s*: Charlie Edmundson, 97
"Jenny Lind Polka," Henry Whitter's Virginia Breakdowners, 07/22/1924, New York, OKeh 40211
"Heel and Toe Polka," Henry Ford's Old Time Dance Orchestra, 12/02/1926, Dearborn, MI, Victor 19909
"Dance with a Girl with a Hole in Her Stocking," Doc Roberts & Asa Martin, 05/15/1928, Richmond, IN, Gennett 6495
In this book: "Heel and Toe Polka," W. T. Narmour & S. W. Smith, 02/14/1929, Memphis, TN, OKeh 45276

Courtin' Days Waltz

Author's note: This transcription is from Columbia 15569-D, recorded New Orleans, 12/10/1929.

Comparable versions: None known

Tony Russell

Crow Black Chicken

Author's note: This transcription is from Columbia 15318-D, recorded New Orleans, 04/27/1928.

Comparable versions: None known

Lyrics:

Chicken crow for midnight, chicken crow for day,
Along comes an owl, ooh-haa! Knocked that chicken away.

Chorus:
Crow black chicken, crow today, crow black chicken, fly away
Crow black chicken crow today, I like chicken pie.

I went up on the mountain to give my horn a blow
I thought I heard a pretty girl say, "Yonder comes my beau."

North Carolina Chicken, take me to my grave
Thought he hear my sweetheart say my chicken gone away.

Dry Town Blues

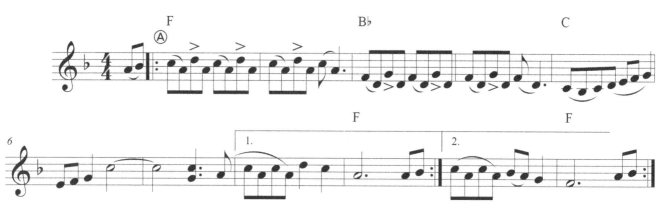

Author's note: This transcription is from Columbia 15441-D, recorded Atlanta, 04/16/1929. This tune was played with the repeats: AAAABBBBAAC.

Comparable versions: None known
The recording quotes "How Dry I Am" twice, interjecting it with the main melody.
"How Dry I Am," Wise String Orchestra, 08/27/1929, Knoxville, TN, Vocalion 5360

Tony Russell

Georgia Camp Meeting

Author's note: This transcription is from Columbia 15409-D, recorded Atlanta, 04/16/1929. The tune is played with the repeats of ABABC ending on B part. Along with this tune, Kerry Mills also wrote "Red Wing" and "Whistling Rufus."

Comparable versions:
"At a Georgia Camp Meeting," Kerry Mills, words and music, 1897
"Choctaw County Rag," Ray Brothers, 05/28/1930, Memphis, TN, Victor V40313
"Georgia Camp-Meeting," Carolina Mandolin Orchestra, 12/1927, New York, OKeh 45191
"Georgia Camp Meeting," McLaughlin's Old Time Melody Makers, Memphis, TN, Victor 21286

Good Fellow

Author's note: This transcription is from Columbia 15441-D, recorded Atlanta, 04/16/1929. On the second time through, the verse is skipped. The chorus is whistled in harmony and then sung. On the third time, the verse is played and the chorus is sung. The fiddle does not play during the chorus.

Comparable versions: None known

Tony Russell

Goodnight Waltz

Author's note: This transcription is from Columbia 15189-D, recorded New Orleans, 04/13/1927.

Comparable versions:

Bolick and Austin, *Mississippi Fiddle Tunes and Songs from the 1930s*: Edward Kitrell, "Good Night Waltz," 128; Alvis Massengale, "Good Night Waltz," 415

"Good Night Waltz," Kessinger Brothers, 02/11/1928, Ashland, KY, Brunswick 220

"Poor Girl's Waltz," Reese Jarvis & Dick Justice, 05/20/1929, Richmond, IN, Gennett, unissued

"The Moonshiner's Waltz," Scottsdale String Band, 03/14/1929, Atlanta, OKeh 45352

In the Good Old Summertime

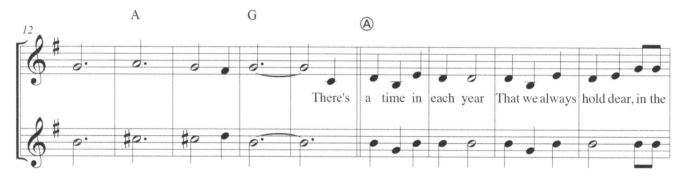

Tony Russell

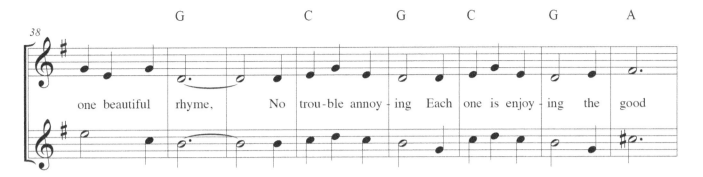

one beautiful rhyme, No trou-ble annoy-ing Each one is enjoy-ing the good

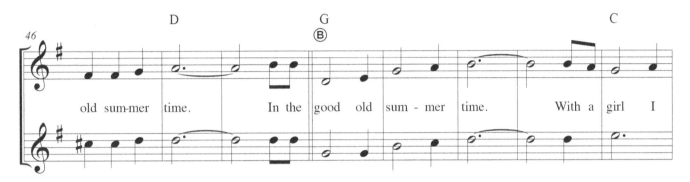

old sum-mer time. In the good old sum - mer time. With a girl I

see in the home And we would al - ways claim a kiss when ever a

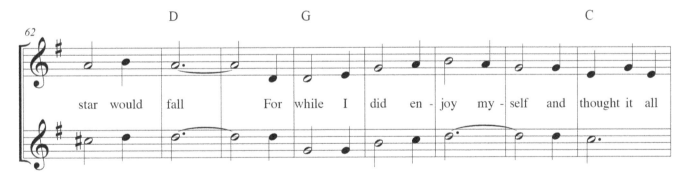

star would fall For while I did en - joy my - self and thought it all

ve - ry fine When we began rain - ing in lightening bugs in the good old

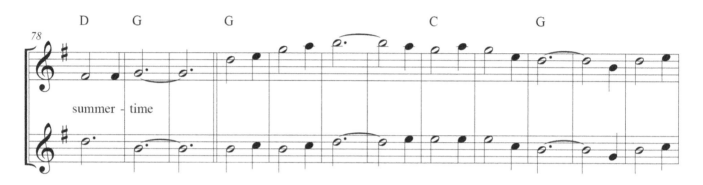

Tony Russell

Author's note: This transcription is from Columbia 15227-D, recorded Atlanta, 10/25/1927.

Comparable versions:
"In the Good Old Summer Time," published 1902, music by George Evans, lyrics by Ren Shields
"In the Good Old Summer Time," Uncle Dave Macon, 09/08/1926, New York, Vocalion 15441
"In the Good Old Summer Time," Hugh Gibbs & His String Band, 04/1927, Chicago, Paramount 3004
"In the Good Old Summer Time," Humphries Brothers, 06/10/1930, San Antonio, TX, OKeh 45489

Lyrics:

There's a time in each year
That we always hold dear,
in the good old summertime
And the birds and the trees
And sweet scented breezes,
Good old summertime
When your day's work is over
then you are in clover,
And life is one beautiful rhyme,
No trouble annoying
Each one is enjoying
the good old summertime.

In the good old summertime.
With a girl I see in the home
And we would always claim a kiss whenever a star would fall
For while I did enjoy myself and thought it all very fine
When we began raining in lightening bugs in the good old summertime

To swim in the pool,
You'd play "hooky" from school,
In the good old summertime;
You'd play "ring-a-rosie"
With Jim, Kate, and Josie,
In the good old summertime,
Those days full of pleasure
We now fondly treasure,
When we never thought it a crime
To go stealing cherries,
With face brown as berries,
In the good old summertime

In the good old summertime,
In the good old summertime,
With Georgia would go riding and we'd have a jolly time.
Now Georgia only has one arm and that's a very good sign
That I have two for driving in that good old summertime

I'm Gwine Back to Dixie

Tony Russell

Author's note: This transcription is from Columbia 15409-D, recorded Atlanta, 04/16/1929. The recording begins with an instrumental chorus, which is repeated after each chorus.

Comparable versions:
"I'se Gwine Back to Dixie," C. A. White, 1874
"I'se Gwine Back to Dixie," *Willie E. Lyle's Great Georgia Minstrels Songster*, 1875
"I'se Gwine Back to Dixie," Uncle Dave Macon & His Fruit Jar Drinkers, 05/19/1927, New York, Vocalion 5157
"I'se Gwine Back to Dixie," Hayden Quartet, 1901, Victor 657

Lyrics:

I'm going back to Dixie, no more I'm gwine wander
My heart turns back to Dixie, I can't stay here no longer
I miss the old plantation, my home and my relations
My heart turns back to Dixie, and I must go

I'm going back to Dixie, I'm going back to Dixie
I'm goin where the orange blossoms grow
I hear the children calling, I see their sad tears fallin'
My heart turns back to Dixie, and I must go

I mowed in the fields of cotton, I worked up on the river
I use to think if I got off, I'd never go back, no never
But times have changed the old man, his head is bending low
His heart turns back to Dixie, and he must go.

I'm traveling back to Dixie, my steps are slow and feeble
I pray the Lord to hep me and keep me from all evil
And should my strength forsake me and I pray the lord to take me
My heart turns back to Dixie, and I must go.

Johnson Gal

Don't care where in the world I go   Can't get around with the calico

---

Author's note: This transcription is from Columbia 15149-D, recorded New Orleans, 04/13/1927. The repeats are quite loose in this recording. M10 signals the coming chord change in the C part and perhaps there was a visual signal for the D part.

Comparable versions:

Bolick and Austin, *Mississippi Fiddle Tunes and Songs from the 1930s*: Frank Kittrell, "Want to Go to Meeting and I Got No Shoes," 315 (Similar "A" part)

"Texas Farewell," Fiddlin' Jim Pate, 10/16/1929, Dallas, Victor V40170 (similar "A" part)

Lyrics:

Don't care where in the world I go,
Can't get around with the calico.

Oh my honey can't you see,
Never get to heaven 'less you do like me.

Want to go to heaven, yes I do
Want to go to heaven with the Johnson crew.

Want to go to heaven, want to go straight
I want to walk through them pearly gates.

See those girls, dressed so fine
Ain't a-got Jesus on their mind.

Julia Waltz

Author's note: This transcription is from Columbia 15353-D, recorded New Orleans, 12/13/1928.

Comparable versions: None known

Jungle Waltz

Author's note: This transcription is from Columbia 15648-D, recorded Jackson, MS, 12/18/1930. In a 1975 interview with Tony Russell, Dallas Jones said that he composed this waltz.

Comparable versions: None known

Tony Russell

Lazy Kate

Author's note: This transcription is from Columbia 15767-D, recorded Jackson, MS, on 12/18/1930.

Comparable versions:

The A part is closely related to the low part of "Soldier's Joy"

Bolick and Austin, *Mississippi Fiddle Tunes and Songs from the 1930s*: Dalton Brantly, 65; Charlie Edmondson, 102; W. E. Ray, 162; W. E. Claunch, 273; John Hatcher, 301; Stephen B. Tucker, 364, all titled "Soldier's Joy"; Rev. J. E. Williams, "Ricket's," 211; and W. A. Bledsoe, "Farewell Mary Anne," 220

Aird, James, *A Selection of Scotch, English, Irish and Foreign Airs* Vol. 1, No. 109 (1778)

"Soldier's Joy," Fiddlin' John Carson & His Virginia Reelers, 06/30/1925, Atlanta, OKeh 45011

"Soldier's Joy," Taylor's Kentucky Boys, 06/27, Richmond, IN, Silvertone 5060

"Soldier's Joy," Kessinger Brothers, 02/05/1929, New York, Brunswick 341

Leake County Blues

Author's note: This transcription is from Columbia 15520-D, recorded New Orleans, 12/10/1929. On the recording the A and B parts are played three times before playing the C part.

Comparable versions:
The C part quotes the song "Careless Love."
"Careless Love," Ernest Stoneman & The Dixie Mountaineers, 04/24/1928, New York, Edison 52386
"Careless Love," Byrd Moore & His Hot Shots, 10/23/1929, Johnson City, TN, Columbia 15496-D
"Careless Love," Riley Puckett, 03/29/1931, Atlanta, Columbia 15747-D

Leather Breeches

Author's note: This transcription is from Columbia 15149-D, recorded New Orleans, 05/13/1927. M29 is sometimes substituted for M8.

Comparable versions:
"Lord McDonald's Reel," Niel & Nathaniel Gow, *Third Collection of Niel Gow's Reels* (ca. 1792), 9
"Leather Breeches," Cole, *1000 Fiddle Tunes*, 22
Bolick and Austin, *Mississippi Fiddle Tunes and Songs from the 1930s*: Mr. J. H. Wheeler, "Leather Breeches," 202; John Hatcher, "Leather Britches," 295; Hardy C. Sharp, "Leather Britches," 338; Stephen B. Tucker, "Leather Britches," 359
In this book: "Leather Breeches," Sid Hemphill
In this book: "Leather Breeches," Carter Brothers & Son, 11/22/1928, Memphis, TN, Vocalion 5295

Listen to the Mocking Bird

Tony Russell

Author's note: This transcription is from Columbia 15776-D, recorded Atlanta, 12/10/1927. The verses are sung an octave lower than the fiddle part shown above. The last verse does not appear in the Septimus Winner sheet music.

Comparable versions:
Alice Hawthorn, Septimus Winner, 1855
"Listen to the Mocking Bird," Sam Long, 02/23/1926, Richmond, IN, Gennett 3255
"The Mocking Bird," Tweedy Brothers, 07/17/1928, Richmond, IN, Gennett 6604
"Mocking Bird," Arthur Smith Trio, 1/22/1935, New Orleans, Brunswick B5843

Lyrics:

I'm dreaming now of Hally, sweet Hally, sweet Hally
I'm dreaming now of Hally for the thought of her is one that never dies
She's sleeping in the valley, the valley, the valley
She's sleeping in the valley, and the mocking bird is singing where she lies

Ah well I yet remember, remember, remember
Ah well I yet remember, when we gather'd in the cotton side by side
'Twas in the mild September, September, September
'Twas in the mild September and the mocking bird was singing far and wide.

When the charms of spring they weaken, they weaken, they weaken
When the charms of spring they weaken and the mocking bird is singing on the bough
I feel like one forsaken, forsaken, forsaken, forsaken
I feel like one forsaken since my Hally is no longer with me now.

Lonesome Blues

Author's note: This transcription is from Columbia 15520-D, recorded New Orleans, 12/10/1929.

Comparable versions:
"Lonesome Road Blues," Henry Whitter, 12/10/1923, New York, Vocalion 14809
"Going Down the Road Feeling Bad," The Hillbillies, 10/23/1926, New York, Vocalion 5021
"Lonesome Road Blues," Ernest V. Stoneman's Trio, 01/27/1927, New York, OKeh 45094

Tony Russell

Magnolia Waltz

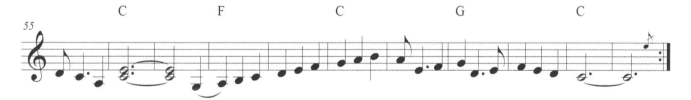

Author's note: This transcription is from Columbia 15625-D, recorded New Orleans, 12/13/1928. Note the indicated fingerings for the position shift from first to second positions.

Comparable versions:
"Magnolia Waltz," Cherokee Ramblers, 07/11/1935, New York, Decca 5162

Make Me a Bed on the Floor

Make me a pallet out near the door

Alt m1-4

Author's note: This transcription is from Columbia 15264-D, recorded New Orleans, 04/27/1928. The alternate measures act as a B part to this single part song. The part is played twice and then played with the alternate measure twice. When sung, the lyrics are sung on consecutive passes through the tune.

Comparable versions:

Bolick and Austin, *Mississippi Fiddle Tunes and Songs from the 1930s*: Unknown, "Make Me a Bed On the Floor," 189

"Make Me a Pallet on De Flo," Howard W. Odum and Guy B. Johnson, *The Negro and His Songs* (Chapel Hill: University of North Carolina Press, 1925), 183 (lyrics only)

"Pallet on the Floor," Stripling Brothers, 03/12/1936, New Orleans, Decca 5267

Lyrics:

Make me a pallet right near the door.
Make me a pallet down in the floor.

Memories

Memories, memories Dreams of love so true O'er the sea of memory

I'm drifting back to you Memories, memories Dreams of love so true

O'er the sea of memory I'm drifting back to you Round me at twilight come stealing

Shadows of days that are gone Dreams of the old days revealing Mem'ries of love's golden dawn

Author's note: This transcription is from Columbia 15767-D, recorded New Orleans, 12/13/1928 (and rerecorded as "Memories Waltz," on Columbia 15427-D, recorded Atlanta, 05/16/1929). They play the A part instrumental introduction, then sing verse/ chorus structure.

Comparable versions:
"Memories," music, Egbert Van Alstyne; lyrics, Gus Kahn, 1915, published in *Our Boy's Songster* 6 (New York: Delaney & Co., 1917)
"Memories," John Barnes Wells, 02/03/1916, Victor 17968A
"Beautiful Memories," Arthur Smith Trio, 08/03/1937, Charlotte, NC, Brunswick B7203

Lyrics:

'Round me at twilight come stealing
Shadows of days that are gone
Dreams of the old days revealing
Mem'ries of love's golden dawn.

Memories, memories
Dreams of love so true
O'er the sea of memory
I'm drifting back to you.

Childhood days, wild wood days
Among the birds and bees
You left me alone, but still you're my own
In my beautiful memories.

Merry Widow Waltz

Author's note: This transcription is from Columbia 15264-D, recorded New Orleans, 04/27/1928.

Comparable versions:
Bolick and Austin, *Mississippi Fiddle Tunes and Songs from the 1930s*: Jerry Larco, "Merry Widow Waltz," 131
"Merry Widow Waltz" (from the operetta *The Merry Widow* by Franz Lehár), Victor Dance Orchestra, 07/15/1907, Victor
    16577
"The Merry Widow Waltz," A. A. Gray, 03/20/1924, Atlanta, OKeh 40110

Tony Russell

Mississippi Breakdown

Author's note: This transcription is from Columbia 15668-D, recorded Jackson, MS, 12/18/1930.

Comparable versions:

(The tune is also known as "Rachael")

"Strawberry Blossom," Francis O'Neill, *O'Neill's Music of Ireland, Eighteen Hundred and Fifty Melodies* (Chicago: Lyon and Healy, 1903), 253

Bolick and Austin, *Mississippi Fiddle Tunes and Songs from the 1930s*: Stephen B. Tucker, "Circus Piece," 350

In this book: "Wednesday Night Waltz," Leake County Revelers, 04/13/1927, New Orleans, Columbia 15189-D

In this book: "Untitled (Rachael)," Claude Kennedy

"Texas Quickstep," Red Headed Fiddlers, 10/18/1928, Dallas, Brunswick 285

"Cherokee Polka," Ed Haley, *Vol. 2: Grey Eagle* (Rounder, 1998)

Mississippi Moon Waltz

Author's note: This transcription is from Columbia 15569-D, recorded New Orleans, 12/10/1929. The recording repeats in the order: AABBAA.

Comparable versions: None known

Molly Put the Kettle On

Molly put the kettle on, Sally put the dinner on Molly put the kettle on, and we'll

all take tea

Author's note: This transcription is from Columbia 15380-D, recorded New Orleans, 12/13/1928.

Comparable versions:

"Molly Put the Kettle On," Charles White, *White's New Illustrated Melodeon Song Book* (New York: H. Lond & Brother, 1851), 29

Bolick and Austin, *Mississippi Fiddle Tunes and Songs from the 1930s*: Mr. T. W. Cooper, "Mollie Bring the Kettle," 85; John Brown, "Molly Put the Kettle On," 72; J. E. Shoemaker, "Ladies Fancy," 170

"Sourwood Mountain Medley," Uncle Dave Macon, 09/08/1926, New York, Vocalion 15443

"Molly Put the Kettle On," Gid Tanner & His Skillet Lickers, 10/24/1931, Atlanta, Columbia 15746-D

Lyrics:

Molly put the kettle on, Sally put the dinner on
Molly put the kettle on, and we'll all take tea.

Molly put the kettle on, Sally put the dinner on
Molly put the kettle on, Daddy come home.

Monkey in the Dog Cart

Author's note: This transcription is from Columbia 15205-D, recorded Atlanta, 10/25/1927. The sliding double stop indicated once in M17 is to be used throughout that second part of the tune.

Comparable versions:

(Perhaps distantly related to "Liza Jane")
"Monkey in a Dog Cart," Hoyt Ming and His Pep Steppers, *New Hot Times!* (Homestead LP 103, 1973)

(right page)

Author's note: This transcription is from Columbia 15227-D, recorded Atlanta, 10/25/1927.

Comparable versions:
Uncertain origin, published 1881, by Charles E. Pratt, music, Samuel N. Mitchell, lyrics
"Bring Back My Bonnie to Me," Hayden Quartet, 11/13/1901, Philadelphia, Victor 123

Lyrics:

My Bonnie lives over the ocean My Bonnie is over the sea
My Bonnie is over the ocean, so bring back my Bonnie to me.
Bring back, bring back, bring back my Bonnie to me, to me
Bring back, bring back, oh bring back my Bonnie to me

Oh blow you winds over the ocean, Oh blow you winds over the sea (repeat)
and bring back back my Bonnie to me.

The winds that blow over the ocean, the winds that blow over the sea (repeat)
have brought back my Bonnie to me.

Chorus:
Brought back, brought back my Bonnie to me....

My Bonnie Lies Over the Ocean

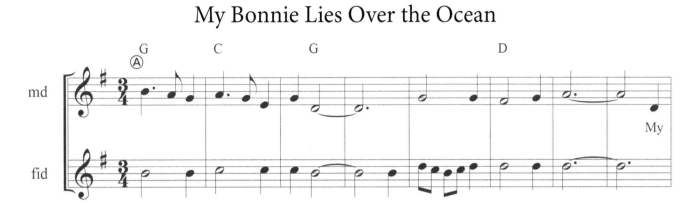

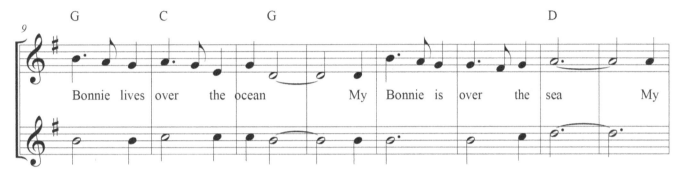

Bonnie lives over the ocean My Bonnie is over the sea My

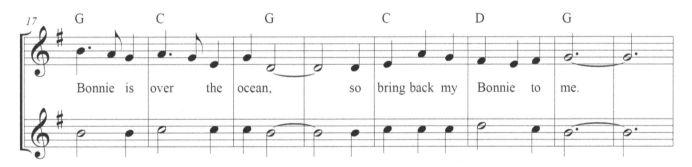

Bonnie is over the ocean, so bring back my Bonnie to me.

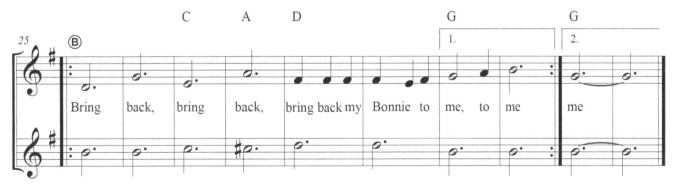

Bring back, bring back, bring back my Bonnie to me, to me me

My Wild Irish Rose

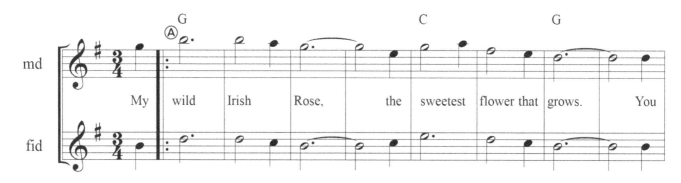

My wild Irish Rose, the sweetest flower that grows. You

may search everywhere, but none can com-pare with my wild I-rish Rose. My wild

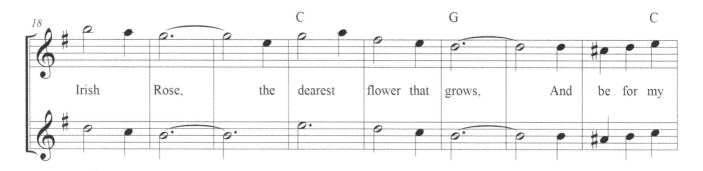

Irish Rose, the dearest flower that grows, And be for my

sake, she may let me take the bloom from my wild Irish Rose. If

Tony Russell

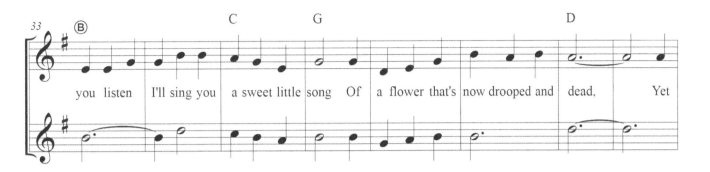

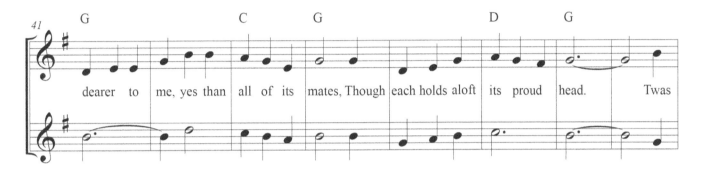

Author's note: This transcription is from Columbia 15776-D, recorded Atlanta, 10/25/1927. The recording begins with an instrumental version of the chorus with the mandolin playing an octave lower than indicated. The verse is sung, followed by a vocal chorus, and then an instrumental chorus ending with a vocal chorus.

Comparable versions:
Chauncey Olcott (born John Chancellor Olcott), song and lyrics, 1899
"My Wild Irish Rose," Lester McFarland & Robert Gardner, 12/13/1927, New York, Vocalion 5191
"My Wild Irish Rose," Hugh Cross & Riley Puckett, 04/12/1928, Atlanta, Columbia 15266-D

The Old Hat

When you hear your cow a lowin', You'll know it's milkin' time   So back your leg, old   Jersey   And

let your milk come down.   Gwine   on   down   town   Gwine   on   down   to   town   I'm

going on down to Vicksburg town   To   make   my   banjo   sound.

Tony Russell

Author's note: This transcription is from Columbia 15205-D, recorded Atlanta, 10/25/1927. This is basically a one-part tune with a repeated eight-measure phrase. When sung, the fiddle part is initially simplified to the vocal part, labeled B, but is then varied with the A1 and A2 parts. The order of A1 and A2 varies. About halfway through the alt M1 and 2 are used fairly consistently to the end.

Comparable versions:
Bolick and Austin, *Mississippi Fiddle Tunes and Songs from the 1930s*: Thaddeus Willingham, "Going On Down Town," 380
"Going Down to Lynchburg Town," Blue Ridge Highballers, 03/24/1926, New York, Columbia 15096-D
"Lynchburg Town," The Highlanders, 05/1929, New York, Paramount 3171
"Going On to Town," Salem Highballers, 10/18/1929, Richmond, VA, OKeh 45455

Lyrics:

When you hear your cow a lowin',
You'll know it's milkin' time
So back your leg, old Jersey
And let your milk come down.

Chorus:
Gwine on down town, Gwine on down to town
I'm going down to Vicksburg town to make my banjo
sound.

I went up to shoo-fly's house
Shoo-fly wasn't home
I ain't gonna look too fuzzy
When shoo-fly's at home

Devil saw the monkey
and he told him to leave this town
and he couldn't start out to see him
and he threwed them pumpkins down

(Chorus)
Raccoon up the 'simmon tree
Possum on the ground
And the possum said to the raccoon
Shake some 'simmons down.

(Chorus)
Raccoon on the main line
Possum on the switch
The rabbit ain't no railroad man?
He's a runnin' son of a gun

(Chorus)
(Chorus)

Picture No Artist Can Paint

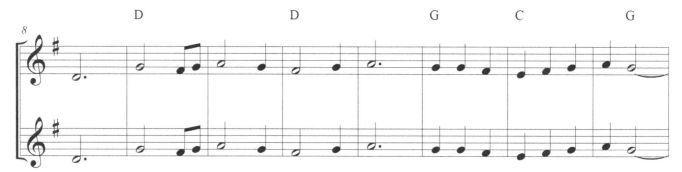

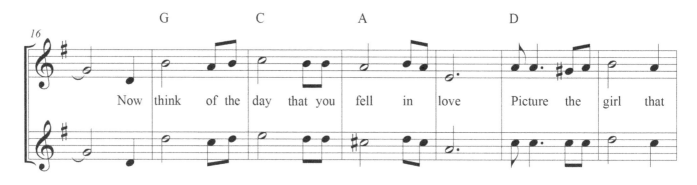

Now think of the day that you fell in love Picture the girl that

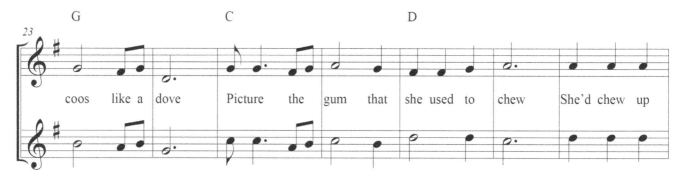

coos like a dove Picture the gum that she used to chew She'd chew up

Tony Russell

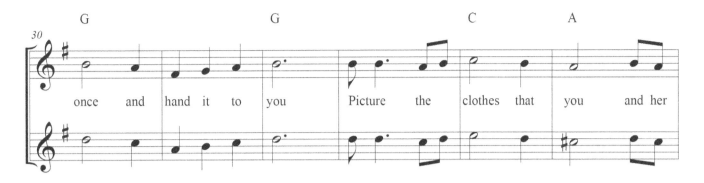

Author's note: This transcription is from Columbia 15691-D, recorded Jackson, MS, 12/18/1930.

Comparable versions:
J. Fred Helf, words and music, 1899, "A Picture No Artist Can Paint"; new lyrics by the Leake County Revelers, perhaps based on Will. F. Denny's parody, 04/07/1900, Berliner 01 161
"A Picture No Artist Can Paint," Lester McFarland & Robert A. Gardner, 6/16/1929, New York, Brunswick 350

Lyrics:

Now think of the day that you fell in love
Picture the girl that coos like a dove
Picture the gum that she used to chew
She'd chew up once and hand it to you

Picture the clothes that you and her wore
Didn't care if they happened to be poor
Sew on a patch and wear them some more
That's a picture no artist can paint

Now picture an old maid when she's thirty-eight
Comes in home early 'cause she can't stay out late
Goes to her room when her supper she's eat
Pulls off her shoes and washes her feet.

Folds up her clothes with the greatest of care
Two little shoes, she sits in a chair
Looks under her bed t'see if a man is under there
That's a picture no artist can paint.

Now picture a man—I'll give you a hint
Don't come in home a-till the night is half spent
Greatest of care he pulls off his socks
Puts one in the churn, the other in the wood-box
Clothes he don't hang on the back of a chair.
Don't look under his bed to see if a woman was there
If fifty was there, he wouldn't care
That's a picture no artist can paint.

Put Me in My Little Bed

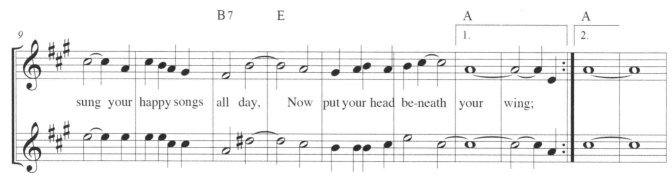

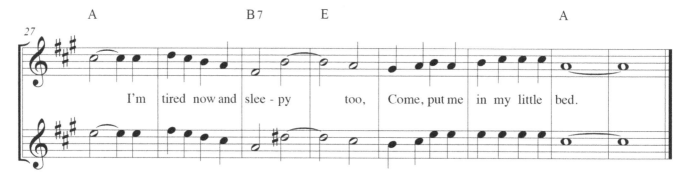

Tony Russell

Author's note: This transcription is from Columbia 15292-D, recorded New Orleans, 04/27/1928.

Comparable versions:
"Put Me in My Little Bed," Lyrics by Dexter Smith, music by C. A. White, Boston: White, Smith & Perry, 1870
"Put Me in My Little Bed," Uncle Dave Macon & Sid Harkreader, 06/20/1929, Chicago, Vocalion 5397

Lyrics:

[Instrumental of the verse]
1. Oh! birdie, I am tired now,
I do not care to hear you sing;
You've sung your happy songs all day,
Now put your head beneath your wing;
I'm tired now and sleepy too
And sister, when my pray'r is said,
vI want to lay me down to sleep,
Come put me in my little bed.

Chorus:
Come, sister, kiss me good night,
For I my evening pray'rs have said;
I'm tired now and sleepy too,
Come, put me in my little bed.

[Instrumental of the verse]
2. Oh! sister, what did mother say,
When she to Heaven was called away?
She told us always to be good,
And never, never go astray;
I can't forget the day she died,
She placed her hand upon my head,
She whisper'd softly, "keep my child,"
And then they told me she was dead.

Chorus 2: Come sister, hear me now,
For I, my evening prayer am saying,
I'm tired now and sleepy too,
Come put me in my little bed.

[Instrumental of the verse]

Rocking Yodel

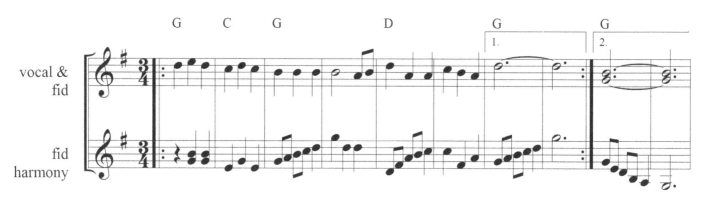

Tony Russell

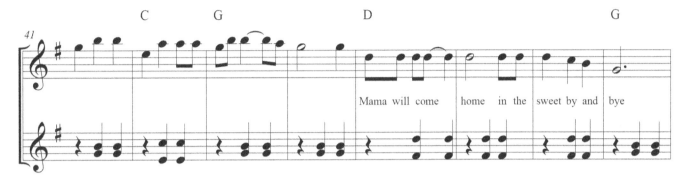

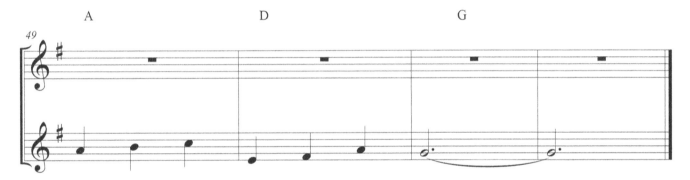

Author's note: This transcription is from Columbia 15353-D, recorded New Orleans, 12/13/1928.

Comparable versions:
"Rock all our babies to sleep, Hush-a-bye, Baby," June Keen, words and music, 1893, L. W. Lipp
"Rock All Our Babies to Sleep," George Riley Puckett, 03/18/1924, New York, Columbia 107-D
"Tossing the Baby So High," Uncle Dave Macon, 09/09/1926, New York, Vocalion 15452
"Rock All Our Babies to Sleep," Jimmie Rodgers, 08/11/1932, Camden, NJ, Victor 23721

Lyrics:

Show me that girlie that has never has had
Her dear little baby boy
Nary this child that never has cried
Made up and pleasured and glad.

Some folks seek pleasures away from the home
But I no pleasures can see
My wife, she a-goes roaming away from the house
While I rock the babies to sleep.

[Yodeling]
Mama will come home in the sweet by and bye.
I'm just thirty-five and my dear little wife
Jesting as younger than me
She's full of enjoyments funny as could be
Oft times to laughter a-spree.

She leaves me behind, the babies to mind
Then I'll be alone as can be
Then she'll go roaming away from the home
While I rock the babies to sleep.

[Yodeling]
Mama will come home in the sweet by and bye.
One night when I'd rocked the babies to sleep
I did venture a walk down the street
There before my eyes to my surprise
my wife and a policeman six feet.

I passed her by. I flung her a smile.
Saying I had been taken with thee
They'd been hugging and kissing all of this while
While I rocked the babies to sleep

[Yodeling]
Mama will come home whenever she wants to.

Saturday Night Breakdown

Author's note: This transcription is from Columbia 15470-D, recorded Atlanta, 04/16/1929.

Comparable versions:
In this book: "Mississippi Breakdown," Mississippi Possum Hunters, 05/28/1930, Memphis, TN, Victor 23595
In this book: "Nine O'Clock Breakdown," Newton County Hill Billies, 12/16/1930, Jackson, MS, OKeh 45544

Tony Russell

Sweet Rose of Heaven

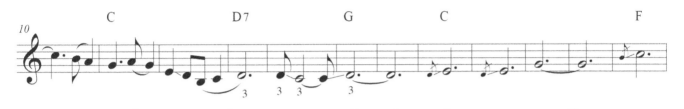

Author's note: This transcription is from Columbia 15501-D, recorded New Orleans, 12/10/1929.

Comparable versions:
"Sweet Rose of Heaven," Taylor-Griggs Louisiana Melody Makers, 09/13/1928, Memphis, TN, Victor 21768

Texas Fair

Author's note: This transcription is from Columbia 15691-D, recorded Jackson, MS, on 12/18/1930.

Comparable versions: None known

Tony Russell

They Go Simply Wild Over Me

hate to talk about my-self, but here's the time I must, Your con-fi-dence I'll trust, I

have to speak or bust It's fun-ny how I get the girls, I nev-er try at

all, I seem to hip-no-tize them, I'm bound to make them fall

They go wild sim-ly wild o-ver me, They go mad just as mad as they can

be, No ma-ter where I'm at, All the lad-ies thin or fat, The

tall ones the small ones, I grab them off like that, Ev-ry night how they fight o-ver

me, I don't know what it is that they can see The la-dies look at me and

sigh, In my arms they want to die, They go wild sim-ply wild o - ver me.

Author's note: This transcription is from Columbia 15292-D, recorded New Orleans, 04/27/1928.

Comparable versions:
Lyrics, Joe McCarthy, music, Fred Fisher, published by McCarthy and Fisher Inc. of New York, 1917

Comparable versions:
"They Are Wild Over Me," Wesley Long, 02/19/1937, Bluebird B-6891
"They Go Wild Simply Wild Over Me," New Dixie Demons, 12/16/1936, Decca 5320

Lyrics:

I hate to talk about myself, but here's the time I must,
Your confidence I'll trust, I have to speak or bust
It's funny how I get the girls, I never try at all,
I seem to hypnotize them, I'm bound to make them fall

They go wild simply wild over me,
They go mad just as mad as they can be,
No matter where I'm at,
All the ladies thin or fat,
The tall ones the small ones,
I grab them off like that,
Every night how they fight over me,
I don't know what it is that they can see
The ladies look at me and sigh,
In my arms they want to die,
They go wild simply wild over me.

I got so many pretty girls, I'll give a few away,
They bother me each day, they're leading me astray,
There's lots of fellows get a girl, but never get her drift,
I always get the women, it's just a natural gift.

Chorus 2:
They go wild simply wild over me,
They go mad just as mad as they can be,
No matter where I'm at,
All the ladies thin or fat,
The tall ones the small ones,
I grab them off like that,
Every night how they fight over me,
I don't know what it is that they can see
I can never be alone
I have to choke the telephone
They go wild simply wild over me.

Tony Russell

Thirty-First Street Blues

blues   Can't lose them, got those thirty-first street   blues

Do ya know the part that's crazy? Something else will save you   Yo-ti-la-hee-o   -   lay-hee-ti -

D   G

o   Some say it's the   sweetness in the sugar, can't you see?   Yo-ti-la-hee-o   -   lay-hee-ti -

D   G   D   G

o   Now, if only I could think of it   Yo-ti-la-hee-hoo   Yo-la-hee-hoo   Yo-ti-la-hee-hoo

Just a   little   more   of it...   Yo-ti - la - hee-hoo   Yo - ti - la - hee-hoo-lay - tee - hoo

Author's note: This transcription is from Columbia 15668-D, recorded Jackson, MS, 12/18/1930.

Comparable versions:
"31st Street Blues," named after a popular thoroughfare in Chicago, published by Joe Davis, and reportedly featured by Josie
    Miles in the show *Runnin' Wild*.
Written by Wendell Hall and Harry Geise and published in 1924.
"31st St. Blues," Clara Smith, 01/31/1924, New York, Columbia 14009-D
(The Revelers kept Smith's chorus and then added and altered lyrics, added barbershop harmony and yodeling.)
"Railroad Take Me Back," Bowman Sisters, 10/23/1929, Johnson City, TN, Columbia 15621-D
"Mississippi Freight Train Blues," Kid Smith & Family, 12/02/36, New York, ARC 7–03–52
"31st Street Blues," Leon's Lone Star Cowboys, 03/13/1936, New Orleans, Decca 5280

Lyrics: Chorus instrumental with the last line sung:
                                                             . . . Railroad take me back, got the Thirty-First Street Blues
Chorus instrumental
La di-diddly-di-de-do, La di-diddly-di-de-do,   Do ya know the part that's crazy?
[Spoken with yodel instrumental vamp underneath]   Something else will save you Yo-ti-la-hee-o-lay-hee-ti-o
Stop that singin', boys, stop that singin'   Some say it's the sweetness in the sugar, can't you see? Yo-
Haven't I done told you that I was blue? (how come? how   ti-la-hee-o-lay-hee-ti-o
come?)   Now, if only I could think of it, Yo-ti-la-hee-hoo (un-huh)
Well, because, I can't decide   Yo-ti-la-hee-hoo (oh that's sweet), Yo-ti-la-hee-hoo
                                                             Just a little more of it . . . Yo-ti-la-hee-hoo
I just crazy, ain't myself, I feel all bad inside   Yo-ti-la-hee-hoo-lay-tee-hoo
And whenever every a freight train possesses me, it se-
duces me to ride   Railroad, take me back, got the Thirty-First Street blues
And it's go right along, Doo-doo dee doo, right along   Please don't jump the track, I ain't got no time to lose
Toward my hometown, Doo-doo dee doo, my hometown   Got lot of biscuits, got my loaf of bread
                                                             None is like the Thirty-First, I heard 'em say
Chorus sung: Railroad, take me back, got the Thirty-First Street blues
Railroad, take me back . . .   Can't lose them, pass the keg and so can you

Uncle Ned

Author's note: This transcription is from Columbia 15470-D, recorded Atlanta, 04/16/1929.

Comparable versions:
Stephen Foster, Lyrics and music, 1848
"Old Uncle Ned," Fiddlin' John Carson, 12/18/1924, New York, OKeh 40263
"Uncle Ned," Uncle Dave Macon, 09/09/1926, New York, Vocalion 15450
"Old Uncle Ned," Al Hopkins and His Buckle Busters, 12/20/1928, New York, Brunswick 300

Lyrics:

There was an old darkie and his name was Uncle Ned and he died long ago, long ago
He had no wool on the top of his head, in the place where the wool ought to grow.

Then lay down the shovel and the hoe, hang up the fiddle and the bow,
There's no more work for good old Ned, he's gone where the good darkies go.

His fingers was long like the cane in the brake, he had no eyes for to see,
He had no teeth for to eat the hoecakes, so he had to let the hoe cakes be.

One cold frosty mornin', Well Ned he did decline
The tears poured like the rain, for they knew that old Ned was laid in the grave
We'll never see the like again.

Wednesday Night Waltz

Author's note: This transcription is from Columbia 15189-D, recorded New Orleans, 04/13/1927.

Comparable versions:

A part:

"Wednesday Night Waltz," Kessinger Brothers, 02/11/1928, Ashland, KY, Brunswick 220

"Wednesday Night Waltz," Fiddling Doc Roberts Trio, 06/03/1931, New York, Banner 32203 and other issues

"Wednesday Night Waltz," Stripling Brothers, 09/10/1934, New York, Decca 5018

B part, also known as "Rachael":

"Strawberry Blossom," O'Neill, *O'Neill's Music of Ireland, Eighteen Hundred and Fifty Melodies*, 253

Bolick and Austin, *Mississippi Fiddle Tunes and Songs from the 1930s*: Stephen B. Tucker, "Circus Piece," 350

In this book: "Mississippi Breakdown," Leake County Revelers, 12/18/1930, Jackson, MS, Columbia 15668-D

In this book: "Untitled (Rachael)," Claude Kennedy

"Texas Quickstep," Red Headed Fiddlers, 10/18/1928, Dallas, Brunswick 285

"Cherokee Polka," Ed Haley, *Vol. 2: Grey Eagle* (Rounder, 1998)

Where the Silv'ry Colorado Wends Its Way

For the flowers creep no more' Round my cheerless cabin door Where the silver Col - o - rado wends its way

---

Author's note: This transcription is from Columbia 15427-D, recorded Atlanta, 04/16/1929. After first ending in M58, there is an instrumental chorus and two verses, ending on M59.

Comparable versions:
"Where the Silvery Colorado Wends Its Way," C. H. Scroggins and Charles Avril, 1901
"Where the Silvery Colorado Wends Its Way," Emry Arthur & the Cumberland Singers, 06/22/1928, Indianapolis, IN, Vocalion 5225
"Where the Silvery Colorado Wends Its Way," Carter Family, 06/09/1936, New York, Decca 5263

Tony Russell

THE LEAKE COUNTY STRING BAND

Although far less well known and influential than the Leake County Revelers, the Leake County String Band has the distinction of being the longest lived of all of the Mississippi string bands. Early versions of this local Leake County string band under the leadership of George Gilmer date from the 1930s, or perhaps the 1920s. Except for concerts during its most visible period in the 1970s and a single recording in 1971, the band played close to home, mostly socially in their homes, nursing homes, and churches. Throughout most of its long life, this band seems to have been more a collection of friends playing local, well-loved tunes than a professional or even semi-professional band. They usually had two fiddles, often playing in harmony, particularly on favorite waltzes. Their repertoire, which is listed at the end of this article, largely consisted of well-known tunes, many recorded by the Leake County Revelers. Judging from Shelby Sanders's large collection of band rehearsal cassettes, George Gilmer's composition the "Mississippi Shuffle" seems to have been played nearly every time the band got together. With changes in personnel, the band continued until June 27, 1991, making it the longest-lived Mississippi string band.

The earliest version of the band was referred to as the Old Leake County String Band, to differentiate it from the Leake County Revelers, and that early band was likely the Madden Community Band described later in this essay. George Gilmer may well have led that version of the band. George and Morgan Gilmer, fiddlers and distant cousins of the Leake County Revelers' fiddler Will Gilmer, revived the Leake County String Band in 1969. During this period, Morgan Gilmer fronted the band as George's health began to fail. George passed away in 1973 and Morgan passed in 1978.

After George Gilmer died, Morgan fronted the band during its most active and visible period.

They performed at the 1974 Smithsonian Folk Festival in Washington and a large bicentennial event in Philadelphia in 1976, which led to their appearance in a movie and on its soundtrack LP, *Ode to Billy Joe*, in 1976. Morgan died in 1978. In 1980 the surviving members of the Freeny and Leake County String Bands, led by Carlton Freeny, joined forces under the name the Leake County String Band.

Various fiddlers from the band entered the Mississippi state fiddle contest in Jackson for many of the years between 1984–98 and the Kosciusko fiddle contest at least in 1990. In 1983 they played for fellow Leake Countian, Governor Ross Barnett, at the Hitching Rail. Other locations where they performed were the Sebastopol Opry, the Pickin' Place in Prentiss, the Agriculture Museum in Jackson, Union County Day in 1986, and at the Center for Southern Folklore's festival in Memphis in the late 1980s.

Their bass player, Roy Alford, recalled playing all weekend at the Mississippi Trade Mart for the Craftsman's Fair to celebrate the bicentennial. "I taped my fingers real good," Alford said, "but the string wore clean through and tore 'em all up again."[1]

Shelby Sanders, who played rhythm guitar and then bass, joined the band in the mid-1980s and is the last surviving member. During his tenure, he remembers the gigs, mostly nursing homes, VFW or American Legion halls, as poorly attended. Twenty would have been a good crowd. However they all enjoyed playing for an audience. All were members of local churches and careful about avoiding events where there would be dancing or drinking. However according to the local newspaper, they did play a square dance for a county sesquicentennial at the Carthage Coliseum in 1984. One year they played seventy performances. The most promising concert was for the opening of the Tennessee/Tombigbee Waterway on May 31, 1985, but publicity was nonexistent and virtually no one attended. The band played many local events where there would be other bands playing popular music of the area—bluegrass, western swing, gospel, and country—some of which made its way into their repertoire.[2]

In a local newspaper, the *Carthaginian*, dated June 27, 1991, there is a short statement of the band's demise.

The personnel on their 1971 recording were George and Morgan Gilmer on fiddles, Sam Alford on lead guitar, and Howard Smith on rhythm guitar. Other members or guests of the band over the years were Alvis and Cartis Massengale, Carlton Freeny, Smith Freeny, Hendrix Freeny, Cleveland Freeny, Hayward and Shelby Sanders, Roy Alford, Ollie Brown, Grover Babb, Roscoe Moore, Bud Jones, Joe Cox, Drane Adams, Sam Alford, and Howard Smith.

George Dewey Gilmer (1900–1973) was the eldest son of William Archable "Bill" Gilmer and Callie Fredonia (Jones) Gilmer, who were sharecropper farmers. In the late 1800s, three of Callie's brothers, Billy, Johnny, and Joe Jones, formed a string band, which played at various events in Leake County. Her oldest brother, Arthur Elonzo Jones, would take up his fiddle, late in the afternoon, and play hymns while sitting on his front porch. George's younger brother Curtis was playing guitar by age twelve. George and Curtis would play, the five sisters sang, and Mrs. Gilmer played spoons or danced. George and Curtis played locally for dances and events.

In the early 1920s, when George was in his early twenties, he would sometimes get his daughter Jackie out of bed before sunup, bundle her in a quilt, carry her to the fireplace, place her in a rocker next to the fire and play the fiddle for his audience of one.

George quit school in the fourth grade to help with the family farm work and spent the rest of his life doing hard physical work. During the Depression George worked for the WPA, digging ditches alongside roads, to provide for his wife and five children. The family was sharecropping until 1934, when they were able to buy a farm. Around 1946 George added a tiny country store to the family's businesses. He also bought and sold scrap metal, bought and sold trees to cut for lumber. He would clear the trees and with hired help and mules, clear the logs from the land, one at a time. As a carpenter, he built several houses, including his own.

George married Lona Wright in January 1919, and by 1945 they had had six children. From the 1920s till around 1936, George and Lona with their

Sherri Gilmer, Georgia Gilmer Snowden, George Gilmer, 1968. Photo courtesy Georgia Gilmer Snowden.

"Dub" Gilmer, George Gilmer, Jackie Gilmer, 1937. Photo courtesy Georgia Gilmer Snowden.

George Gilmer on bed with fiddle. Photo courtesy Georgia Gilmer Snowden.

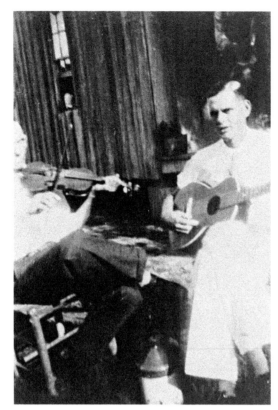

Russell family photo, may be Grover Russell and Grady Russell. Possibly "Uncle Lee Russell and Grover, LA, 1932." Photo courtesy Carl Fleischhauer.

Russell family photo, Madden MS, 1932. Brothers and sisters, front row: Grover, Grady; back row: Annie Maude, Bonnie Ruth. Photo courtesy Carl Fleischhauer.

children attended informal jam sessions on Saturday nights, when they weren't performing elsewhere. Those sessions were held at their home and other homes in the area. Removing the furniture from the room would make space for dancing and for the players. Anyone who could play joined in. Children would play games; women would make a supper and visit while the music rolled on.[3]

The Old Leake County String Band, as some area musicians called it, flourished in the 1930s. George Gilmer, a well-spoken-of fiddler, was a key member. In December 1933, George composed his sole instrumental fiddle piece, which he called "The Mississippi Shuffle."[4] Thurman Ware also played fiddle. The other members, Grady Russell (1907–1981), who played guitar, fiddle, and banjo, and his brother, guitarist Grover Russell (1912–1980), had learned to play when they were quite young. The band played at various functions in and around the

Scott-Leake-Neshoba County area. Grady Russell remembered that they could put on a good program, with singing, playing, and sketches. Thurman Ware and Grady would do a haunted house routine, with Grady in blackface.

The Russells both lived out their lives in the Carthage area and continued to play with each other from time to time, sometimes accompanied by Howard Smith, a later guitarist with the Leake County String Band. They had a number of Jimmie Rodgers–styled compositions of their own composing. In 1935, through the efforts of H. C. Speir, they recorded six of their own Rodgers-styled duets and solos.

The Old Leake County String Band (or part of it; the personnel are uncertain in the ARC record company logs) recorded on one occasion, as the Madden Community Band. Madden is in southeastern Leake County. The instruments were fiddle,

Harry Bolick

Russell family photo. Thought to be Grover's father, Albert Russell. Photo courtesy Carl Fleischhauer.

Russell family photo. Thought to be Grady with a child. Photo courtesy Carl Fleischhauer.

piano, mandolin, and guitar, with vocal. The tunes recorded but unissued by ARC in Hattiesburg MS, on July 24, 1936, were "Going Down Town" and "Pallet on the Floor."

Presumably George Gilmer or Thurman Ware was on fiddle, possibly Grady Russell on banjo rather than mandolin, and Grover Russell on guitar. George's brother, Curt Gilmer, who may have been present at the session, recalled a Black musician called "Mooney" on piano, who the session director, W. R. Callaway, brought in. There can be little doubt that this was the celebrated Cooney Vaughan, who is known to have been from around Hattiesburg and was certainly at this session, and had recorded in several lineups such as the Mississippi Jook Band, just a few days previously. Grady Russell confirms

Russell family photo. Bonnie Ruth, Lee Russell (an uncle), and unknown guitarist at Lee's; before Lee moved to Louisiana in 1932. Photo courtesy Carl Fleischhauer.

Front, left to right: George Gilmer, Morgan Gilmer. Rear, left to right: Howard Smith, Sam Alford, ca. 1971. Photo courtesy Virginia Gilmer.

the name Cooney and clearly recalls him being around as a sort of session musician, though he doesn't think he played with the Madden Community Band.

The recordings were done at the Forest Piano House, and according to Curt Gilmer the musicians had to stop in the middle of a performance to let trains go by. The sides were never released, but people claim to have heard them, probably on test pressings that were sent to the artists. The tunes are common to the region. The Leake County Revelers recorded "Going Down Town" as "The Old Hat" and "Pallet on the Floor" as "Make Me a Bed on the Floor."[5]

After the recordings, George continued to play close to home and with his family. George's son, William Jasper, nicknamed Dub, started to learn

mandolin, an instrument his size, starting at age five. Two years later, in 1932, with the proceeds from the cotton harvest, George bought a mandolin for Dub and a Silvertone guitar for his daughter, Flossie Jack, nicknamed "Jackie." George insisted that they learn to play. Dub won a contest at age eight, becoming the "Mississippi Champion Mandolin Player." Forming a trio, the family trio performed for dances, fiddlers' contests, house sessions, and other events during the 1930s. George and Dub would enter fiddle contests with Dub often taking the money for best fiddler under thirty and George for best fiddler over thirty.

In 1938 Tom Bailey made an unsuccessful campaign for governor. He had heard of the trio, especially young, thirteen-year-old Dub, and wanted them to play to attract crowds to campaign events.

Sam Alford, guitar; Barney Ellis, mandolin; Roy Alford, bass; Morgan Gilmer, fiddle; Howard Smith, guitar. Photo courtesy Virginia Gilmer.

Morgan Gilmer and children. Photo courtesy Virginia Gilmer.

Morgan Gilmer. Photo courtesy Virginia Gilmer.

Jackie wrote Mr. Bailey's campaign song when she was a seventeen-year-old senior in high school. When Jackie graduated high school and moved to Union to find a job, she stopped playing. Dub continued to perform, sporadically, for the rest of his life.

In the late 1940s and early '50s, Dub played country music with his uncle, "Curly Q" Curtis. The band dressed in cowboy attire and played at country schools and other venues in Leake and surrounding counties. In the 1960s, Uncle Curt and his band had a radio show on WMAG in Forest, Mississippi.

By the 1950s fiddle contests and weekly home sessions had faded, with the home sessions occurring only when married children would come to visit. George continued to play at home for himself and his family. In 1969 he and a cousin, Morgan Gilmer, joined to revive the Leake County String Band. However, due to failing health, George was only able to play with them for a few years. Usually the band would come to his house to play while the wives visited.[6]

In 1971 they recorded a self-titled LP that had a plain white cover and very limited distribution, perhaps only one or two hundred copies.

The year after George's death in 1973, the Leake County String Band was invited to perform at the Smithsonian Institute's Festival of American Folk Life in Washington, D.C. That performance caught the eye of someone working on the movie *Ode to Billy Joe*, which was set and filmed in Mississippi. The band was asked to perform in a segment of the film and they excitedly agreed. George's daughter, Georgia Glimer Snowden, described the band's reaction to the movie:

> The movie premier[e], in Greenwood, Mississippi, was a huge deal for those country folks. Cousin Morgan, the other band members and their wives got all gussied up and proudly attended the showing. However, they were mortified when they realized that during their playing, the film would cut to the back of the barn where prostitutes were entertaining their clientele. There they were in their Panama hats, with red, white, and blue headbands, playing their hearts out, while the devil was loose

in the back room. They were born and raised in hard-shell Southern Baptist country; therefore the scandalous public presentation didn't set well with those God-fearing men. They left the premier[e] fully expecting to be expelled from the church. Cousin Morgan was a deacon, for gosh sakes. I'll bet Daddy was looking down grinning, shaking his head, and thanking the Almighty that he'd missed that one ill-fated performance.[7]

Morgan Kelly Gilmer

Morgan Gilmer (1908–1978) spent his life in Leake County as a farmer, carpenter and fiddler. We know little about him prior to 1969, with the revival of the string band, though it seems likely that he had been playing with George Gilmer previously. Roy Alford recalled that the first tune that Morgan learned was "The Old Hat," also called "Going Down Town."

During a tornado in 1966, Morgan was seriously injured and his first wife, Aileen Scott Gilmer, was killed.[8] His bandmate Howard Smith was deeply affected by Morgan's near-death experience and developed a lifelong aversion to bad weather, occasionally canceling a gig due to threatening weather. Morgan had recovered from his injuries by 1969 when he courted and married Virginia Brittain. Both had long lived in the area but had not known each other till they began to date. In the first years of their marriage, Morgan and Virginia lived in the town of Rosebud, before moving to Walnut Grove, where they jointly ran a dry cleaning business for a few years. Morgan loved to dance, although Virginia didn't. The band, with its rehearsals, concerts, along with church, was their social life. The band performed often and rehearsed once or twice a week.

Morgan played one of Will Gilmer's fiddles. He was also known to play piano and "any kind of instrument," but only played fiddle in the band. Morgan's daughter, Mildred, played piano for the church. Morgan occasionally would play a hymn on the fiddle in church. He primarily played by ear but could read "the notes."

Morgan was a showman in the band. He or Howard Smith would talk to the audience. On stage,

Leake County String Band, April 30, 1985. Left to right: Sam Alford, Carlton Freeny, Howard Smith, Haywood Sanders, Smith Freeny, Shelby Sanders, Joe Cox. Photo courtesy Beth Alford.

Freeny Harvest Day, United Methodist Church, 1983. Shelby Sanders, Carlton Freeny, Smith Freeny, Haywood Sanders, unknown mandonlinist, Sadie Freeny Chamblee at piano. Photo courtesy Beth Alford.

Morgan would tell jokes, sometimes on Virginia who would be in the audience, which embarrassed her a little bit but was not a source of friction between them.

1976 was a big year for the band, with many performances around the state for the national bicentennial. Along with other bands they played the Temple Theatre in Meridian every Saturday night. They also played at local flea markets.

Morgan continued to play until his heart attack in 1978. He had been a heavy smoker. According to Virginia, "He was the happiest when he was playing that fiddle."[9]

Samuel Carlton Freeny

Carlton (1912–1987) recorded with the Freeny Barn Dance Band in 1930, the Freeny Harmonizers in 1935, and played with various versions of the Freeny Band from the 1920s until 1980, when the Freeny and Leake County String Bands combined.

Carlton was a very outgoing person, comfortable in public, and thus became the front man for the band.

Carlton played off and on with versions of the Freeny band over the years. But by the 1970s, he had been inactive musically for years, due to family and work. Inspired by Tony Russell's interest and research of Mississippi fiddle music, he began to play again in 1972.

Carlton served in World War II and Korea, and returned to become a well-known and well-liked member of the community in Carthage as a Mason, a Shriner, a fixture in the Methodist church, and as a local weatherman. He worked for, and eventually managed, the Central Power Association in Carthage until he retired in 1977.

See the Freeny Barn Dance Band chapter for more information about Carlton and his music.

Cartis Massengale

From at least 1980[11] through 1982,[12] Alvis Massengale played with the Leake County String Band

Cartis Massengale. Photo by Gil Ford, used for 1980 *Mississippi Sawyers* LP cover.

but is better known for his 1930s recordings with the Newton County Hill Billies. Cartis Massengale (1928–2000) grew up hearing the fiddle music that his father Alvis played. By age twelve, Cartis was backing Alvis on guitar. He picked up the fiddle while in the Navy in the 1950s during the Korean conflict.[13] He played fiddle for a few years in the later version of the Leake County String Band. He recorded the tune, "Rocky Mountain Goat," for the 1980 *Mississippi Sawyers* LP. Robert Alford, Joe Cox, and Howard Smith of the Leake County String Band provided accompaniment for the fiddlers on the LP. As late as 1996 he was still hosting at the monthly country music get-togethers in Sebastopol.[14]

Royal ("Roy") Chadwick Alford

Around 1972 Sam Alford asked his brother Roy (1919–2006), who was living in Jackson, to join the Leake County String Band. In Sebastopol, Roy found and acquired an upright bass and then had to learn to play it at the band's Friday night jam sessions. Band practice was every Saturday night, playing until eleven or midnight, unless they had a gig. They would start the evening with a meal in a cafe and then adjourn to practice at a house in Standing Pine. Roy remembered that at the time, you could only hear country music out in the country and small towns, not Jackson, so it was necessary for him to travel out to the Carthage area for music.

In the Alford family the musicians came from his mother's side of the family. Roy started on rhythm guitar. He began by experimenting with his older brother's guitar. Around age sixteen he got his own mail order $19.98 guitar. His brother Sam taught him to play. Sam had learned to play from Jimmie Rodgers records and from Gene Autry, Roy Rodgers, and the Delmore Brothers songbooks.

While growing up, Roy would walk ten to twelve miles to listen to the Grand Old Opry on the radio at a neighbor's house. For entertainment when he was young in Leake County, there would be weekend hayrides or folks would gather in a big pasture to "roast weiners and things." There would be picking and singing around a campfire. When people would visit other parts of the United States, they would bring back a song or tune that they had learned. Sometimes they would learn a new song from a movie. Seeing a movie was an exciting, once- or twice-a-year event for young Leake County folks in the 1930s.

In the 1930s, Roy was in a band with Sam on guitar and a friend named Horace on fiddle. They would often play at a schoolhouse as part of an evening of entertainment, where there would be a play with the children dressing up in old-time clothes. For twenty-five to fifty cents apiece the band would play an instrumental and a song between the acts of the play. Another chance to perform would be a "Pound Supper." Ladies would bake a cake, which would then be sold to the highest bidder, with the proceeds going to the church or the school. The band would play. Then a cake would be auctioned. This sequence would be repeated until the cakes were gone. Occasionally they would play

for dances, which would be supervised by parents. Square dances had gone out of style. Roy did not describe the kinds of dances for which he did play.

When he got a little older, Roy was in another local string band with four boys that would go to local fiddle contests. A fiddle contest was a fairly big event for these small communities. To get to the next town, a group of people would rent a school bus for thirty-five cents a seat. Local merchants sponsored the contests and the prizes were nothing fancy. Roy remembers winning a free haircut, a pair of overalls, and an oil-change, even though he did not have a car. The contestants would play a hoedown, a waltz, and a free tune. If the fiddler won, perhaps he would share a dollar of the prize money with the guitarist who backed him up. Roy did not remember seeing any banjo players, just guitar and fiddle.[15]

Roy worked for the Mississippi State Highway Department as a map salesman.

The band credits in the photos in this article are the best indicator of the band's changes in personnel over the band's long life.

—Harry Bolick

NOTES

1. Linda Thorsby, "Bass Fiddler Strums America Into 3rd Century," *Clarion-Ledger*, Jackson, MS, July 11, 1976, 6B.

2. Interview with Shelby Sanders, Carthage, MS, May 17, 2017.

3. Telephone interview with Georgia Gilmer Snowden, July 6, 2017, and access to her unpublished manuscript for a book about her father and family.

4. Telephone interview with Georgia Gilmer Snowden, July 6, 2017, and access to her unpublished manuscript for a book about her father and family.

5. Tony Russell, *Old Time Music* 20 (Spring 1976): 39, 40.

6. Telephone interview with Georgia Gilmer Snowden, July 6, 2017, and access to her unpublished manuscript for a book about her father and family.

7. Georgia Gilmer Snowden, from her unpublished manuscript for a book about her father and family.

8. James Bonney, "Still More Dead Found in Rubble Left in Tornado's Destructive Path, 61 Known Dead, 497 Injured, 19 Critical," *Clarion-Ledger*, Jackson, MS, March 5, 1966, 1, 12.

Front, left to right: Ollie Brown, Smith Freeny. Rear, left to right: Howard Smith, Shelby Sanders, Heywood Sanders. Photo courtesy Tim Freeny.

9. Interview with Virginia Gilmer at her home in Forrest, MS, May 17, 2017.

10. Interview with Beth Alford, Freeny, MS, May 17, 2017.

11. "Fourth Annual Country Day Saturday," *Union Appeal*, Union, MS, August 20, 1980, 1.

12. Mary Anne Wells, "Union's Alvis Massengale, Still fiddlin' around," *Union Appeal*, Union, MS, July 14, 1982, 5.

13. "Mr. Cartis L. Massengale," *Union Appeal*, Union, MS, January 3, 2001, 9.

14. "Sebastopol News," *Scott County Times*, July 10, 1996, 5B.

15. Roy Alford interview, Jackson, August 12, 1975, by Stephen Cook, MDAH call number AU 605.

Recordings

The Leake County String Band (Field Recorders Collective FRC 730; a reissue of the 1971 LP with additional tracks)

1971 Leake County String Band self-produced LP:

    Morgan Gilmer, first fiddle

    George Gilmer, second fiddle

    Sam Alford, lead guitar

    Howard Smith, rhythm guitar

Down Yonder

Silver Bells

Ragtime Annie

Wen I'm Gone, Don't Grieve After Me

Wednesday Night Waltz

Mr. and Mrs. Used To Be (Judy Gilmer, vocal)

Maggie

Merry Widow Waltz

Nellie Moore

Dry Town Blues

My Waltz (Morgan Gilmer)

Mississippi Shuffle (George Gilmer)

Ode to Billy Joe, 1976, movie in which they played "Ragtime Annie" and "Bug Dance"

On the movie soundtrack LP Morgan Gilmer played "Standing Pine Breakdown."

Memphis's Center for Southern Folklore's Festival CD *A Slice of Southern Music* has one track by the Leake County String Band from 1988 or 1982: "Cat Fight/Leather Britches."

Howard Smith, Joe Cox, and Robert Alford appear as back-up musicians on *Mississippi Sawyers: A Collection of Old-Time Mississippi Fiddling* (LP, Sawyer Productions, 1980).

Leake County String Band Repertoire:

(A listing of tunes from home tapes and Smithsonian Folk Festival recordings)

Alabama Jubilee
Amazing Grace
Anniversary Waltz
Arkansas Traveler
Beautiful Dreamer
Bile Them Cabbage Down
Bill Bailey
Bully of the Town
Cacklin' Hen
Caissons Go Rolling On
Chinese Breakdown
Cindy
Columbus Stockade
Copper Kettle
Dixie
Doughboy Rag
Down Yonder
Dry Town Blues
Eighth of January
Faded Love
Fifty-Year Waltz
Fireball Mail
Flop Eared Mule
Floyd Collins
Foggy Mountain Breakdown
Fraulein
Golden Slippers

Good Night Waltz
Good Old Mountain Dew
Great Speckled Bird
Hot Time in the Old Town Tonight
House of Morgan Blues
I Don't Love Nobody
I'll Be All Smiles Tonight
I'll Fly Away
I'm Thinking Tonight of My Blue Eyes
In the Garden
In the Sweet Bye and Bye
Jack and Joe
John Henry
Johnson's Old Grey Mule
Just Because
Kentucky Waltz
Leather Britches
Liberty
Listen to the Mockingbird
Little Star
Live and Let Live
Lonesome Road Blues
Make Me a Pallet
Merry Widow Waltz
Mississippi Sawyer
Mississippi Shuffle
Mockingbird Hill
Monkey in the Dogcart
Mr. and Mrs. Used to Be
My Own Home Waltz
My Waltz (Morgan Gilmer)
Nellie Moore
Nobody's Business But Mine
Old Hat
Old McDonald
Old Red Wagon
Old Rugged Cross
Old Shep Waltz
Old Spinning Wheel
Over the Waves
Peekaboo Waltz
Pop goes the Weasel
Precious Memories
Ragtime Annie
Raunchy Grande or Spanish Two Step ("El Rancho Grande")

Red Fox Waltz

Red River Valley

Redwing

Rocky Mt. Goat

Rubber Dolly

Sallie Goodin'

San Antonio Rose

Sebastopol

She'll Be Coming 'Round the Mountain

Silent Night Waltz

Silver Bells

Smoke on the Water

Soldiers Joy

Somebody Touched Me

Standing Pine Breakdown

Sweet Bunch of Daisies

Sweet Hour of Prayer

Take Me Back to Tulsa

Tennessee Waltz

Twinkle Little Star

Uncloudy Day

Under the Double Eagle

Using My Bible for a Road Map

Wabash Cannonball

Waltz Across Texas

Wednesday Night Waltz

Weeping Waltz

Westfalia Waltz

When I'm Gone Don't You Grieve After Me

Whistlin' Rufus

Wild Irish Rose

When My Blue Moon Turns to Gold Again

When You and I Were Young, Maggie

Where, Oh Where Has My Little Dog Gone?

Year of Jubilo

El Rancho Grande

Newspaper advertisement for 1940 Gene Autry movie *Rancho Grande*.

Author's note: This transcription is from a Shelby Sanders home tape. Starting with M11, this is a unique example of what happens to a popular tune in Mississippi. They take a tune that is rhythmically regular and reject such a pedestrian approach.

Comparable versions:
"Allá en el Rancho Grande" is a 1920s Mexican song written for a musical theatrical work; it appeared in the 1936 Mexican motion picture *Allá en el Rancho Grande*, sung by Tito Guízar
"El Rancho Grande," Bing Crosby, 04/03/1939, Decca 1752
"El Rancho Grande," Gene Autry, in the 1939 film *Mexicali Rose* and a commercial recording

Mississippi Shuffle

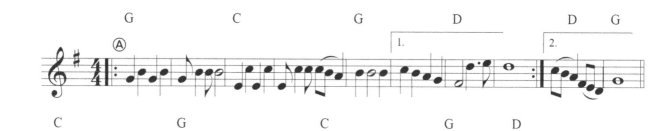

Alt m 27-36 Double stops or Harmony fiddle:

Alt m 11-169 Double stops or Harmony fiddle:

Author's Note: George Gilmer of the Leake County String Band composed "Mississippi Shuffle" in 1931. This transcription is based on their self-produced LP, *Leake County String Band*, Walnut Grove, MS, 1971.

Comparable versions: None known

Harry Bolick

My Waltz

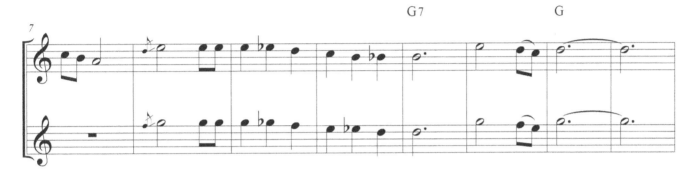

Author's note: Morgan Gilmer composed "My Waltz." This transcription is based on their self-produced LP *Leake County String Band*, Walnut Grove, MS, 1971.

Comparable versions: None known

Precious Memories

Author's note: This transcription is from a Shelby Sanders home tape. As usually played, M7 and M14 would be doubled, but on the home recording of this Morgan and George Gilmer duet it is only held for one measure.

Comparable versions:
J. B. F. Wright, words and music, 1925

Harry Bolick

SENATOR GEORGE CECIL McLEOD

By the time that he recorded his instrumental LP *The Fiddling Senator* in 1979, McLeod (1927–2011) was playing in the bluegrass style. However, many of the tunes on that recording were well known old-time tunes such as "Billy in the Lowground," "Ragtime Annie," and "Lost Indian." As a child, what he heard and what inspired him to want to play were old-time fiddlers. His Uncle, M. L. Griffin, was an active dance fiddler playing for family gatherings and house dances when McLeod was young. In an interview with Chris Goertzen, McLeod recalled hearing those first fiddle tunes:

Uncle M. L. Griffin, who married my Daddy's sister; they had eight children, all of them older than I was. They were all talented musically, and my uncle played the fiddle. And that's where the young folks up in Leakesville would gather up on Saturday night to dance. They'd clear the furniture out of one room and the hall, and Uncle M. L. would play, with some of the children accompanying him, some on guitar, and some of the girls would sometimes play piano [or] accordion. They danced in the bedroom and in the hall connecting. Momma and Daddy enjoyed dancing. They'd carry my brother and sister [and me] to the dance.

Highway sign in Greene County, MS. Photo by Harry Bolick.

Lee Fulcher and Senator George C. McLeod. Photo by James Fulcher, ca. 1980s.

I can remember sitting on a little stool or a little box behind the door, in the corner, listening to my uncle play. Some of the tunes would just thrill me out of my mind. The hairs would stand up on the back of my neck and chills would go up and down my back. And on occasion, the fiddle still causes that sensation on selected tunes, and on rare occasions I've even had that experience while I was playing, but not on a regular basis.[1]

McLeod got his first fiddle when he was a tenth grader taking violin lessons from the school band director. His lessons ended after six months when the director was drafted. But he continued to listen to the radio, to shows like the Grand Old Opry, and absorbed as much as he could. His strongest early influence came from his much older close neighbor, the highly regarded local fiddler, Jody Denmark, whom he pursued for lessons. It is likely that the

Harry Bolick

Box Denmark, ca. 1920. Photo courtesy Lea Sprague Winfield.

two transcriptions included here are based on tunes that he learned from Jody.

McLeod was born near Leakesville in Greene County. Just after World War II he served in the US Navy, and on his return finished his studies and graduated from Mississippi State College. He married Elaine Kendrick, a piano teacher from Hazlehurst, in 1951. They often played music together. Due to the demands of his dairy and farm, he quit playing from 1961 through 1966, but took it up again as it was helpful when he entered politics. He ran unsuccessfully in 1967 and then was elected state senator in 1970. In 1973 he performed as a guest with Bill Monroe at the Grand Ole Opry. He continued to mix politics and music for the rest of his life.[2] He lived most of his life in Leakesville and in his obituary was described as a retired farmer.

The Denmark family fiddlers of Greene County, MS

James Allen "Box" Denmark

"Box" (1859–1937) was a left-handed fiddler. In an Alabama fiddle contest, perhaps near Jackson, Alabama, he was in the final round. After he played his first tune, another fiddler who played "Listen to the Mockingbird" and seemed to be winning followed

him. In response, for his final tune, "Box" announced that he would also play "Listen to the Mockingbird," but that it was such a simple tune that he would play it left-handed. Apparently no one noticed that he had played his first tune left-handed, and "Box" won the contest. Box married Sabrina Beech and together they raised ten children.

Joseph W. (Jody) Denmark

Jody (1891–1972) married Lydia Bell Dueitt in 1914 and they had four boys and a girl. He . . .

> had a little farm . . . maybe worked some turpentine and logged wood some. He repaired instruments a good bit. He had home-made [repair tools]; he'd take a can, and he had it fixed to where he could heat it on the stove, and direct the steam through a little tube where it would loosen up the glue on a fiddle. I had a double barrel gun . . . that the stock got broken in. [Denmark] made a stock for it out of cherry. He was gifted at carving, and making things of that sort, and repairing this and that. He wasn't noted as much especially during the time that I knew him for work as he was for three things that he was par excellent in: hunting, fishing, and fiddling.[3]

He was an excellent hunter and fisherman and was handy with tools. He carved turkey, duck, and crow calls and made his own fishing poles from bamboo that he grew near his home. Out behind his house, he packed worms and dirt in an old Coca-Cola cooler to keep the worms good and cool.

Jody had an unusual fishing technique. He would lay the fishing pole in the water on the edge of the bank. When he got a bite, he would slide the pole backward and pull the fish out. Another sideline was carving new gunstocks and repairing guns.

To add more entertainment to accompany his fiddling, Jody constructed a foot-operated contraption with several African American dancing dolls. A simpler version of this device is called a "limberjack." People would come from quite a distance to hear him play and operate the gizmo. Eudora Welty took a beautiful photo at the 1937 state fair in Jackson, MS, of a seated fiddler playing for two boys along the side of a road among the parked cars.[4] On the ground in front of him, he has his foot on a limberjack matching the one that Jody Denmark was known to use. The fiddler strongly resembles a family photo of "Box" Denmark, shown here.

Due perhaps to his strenuous outdoor life, Jody was still a "real limber" fiddler in his eighties, and still able to run and hurdle.

Elvin Ray Denmark

Elvin Ray (1915–2002) married Dorothy Vanosdol and they raised two children. Both Elvin Ray and Jody worked for themselves for most of their lives: farming, hunting, fishing, building things, working on fiddles, and of course, playing music for pleasure.

Elvin Ray started out on guitar, backing up his brother, Garner, and Jody at local barn dances or "Frolics." Garner Wayne Denmark played both fiddle and guitar. He and Elvin Ray would swap out accompanying each other. As teenagers they would catch a watermelon truck down to New Orleans and play fiddle and guitar duets of fiddle breakdowns on the streets for tips.

After the Korean War, someone in the family came back with a reel-to-reel recorder and made recordings of Jody and Elvin Ray. Sadly, these recordings have not been heard or made available outside the family.

Elvin Ray Denmark, ca. 1950. Photo courtesy Randy Miller.

During his pre-teen and early teenage years, Randy Miller spent a lot of time with his grandfather, Elvin Ray, learning to play guitar with him. When he first started on guitar, Jody Denmark told him, "You ain't gonna never learn to play nothing." This had the effect as Jody intended, making Randy determined to learn to play. I've heard this traditional method of "teaching" described as "hillbilly Suzuki." Randy received little direct teaching to learn guitar. He was shown the chords and taught to "keep good time." If he got out of time, Elvin Ray would pull off his cap and lightly swat Randy with it. They all just "picked it up," by watching and by ear.

When Randy got good enough on guitar to back up Elvin, they would sit close together on straight chairs in the living room and play every night of the week. Elvin would practice and learn or remember Jody's tunes. He would play them a bit different, but long years of backing up Jody had cemented many of the tunes into his memory. Elvin Ray would come home after work, after Randy returned from school, and Elvin would say, "Get your guitar, son, let's go." They would get in the truck and go to George Cecil McLeod's or maybe somewhere in Alabama. They would play wherever they went visiting. Most of the time, Randy did not know the people, and only Elvin Ray and Randy would play music. On Saturday nights they would play for parties for Elvin's friends, playing, just the two of them till maybe 2 a.m. Favorite tunes were "Carroll County Blues," "Hen Cackle," "Boil Them Cabbage," "Billy in the Lowground." Nothing made Elvin Ray happier than the two of them playing a tune right the first time. Elvin was not concerned with winning fiddle contests; his goal was to introduce Randy to music. The only music Randy knew while growing up was Merle Haggard and fiddle tunes.

One day, Randy's mom told Elvin Ray, "Randy had got school tomorrow and he's got to do his homework." She told Randy, "I don't care what Elvin Ray says, you stay home or I'll wear you out!" When Elvin Ray came in from work that day, he told Randy, "You get your guitar and get in the truck." Randy said his mother wouldn't let him go. Elvin insisted and drove them to his daughter's house and telling Randy, "Don't even get out of the truck. I'll take care of this." Randy watched Elvin Ray and his mother talk on the porch of her house. Elvin Ray got his way; Randy never got a whipping or heard any more about it. Elvin Ray made his point: music was more important than algebra. Randy said, "He was my idol all my life till I got grown."

When Randy moved away from home, he quit playing for several years; when he started back he, got an electric guitar and sat on the front porch, playing music. "It was as normal as breathing."[5]

—Harry Bolick

NOTES

1. Chris Goertzen, *Southern Fiddlers and Fiddle Contests* (Jackson: University Press of Mississippi, 2008), 15.

2. Liner notes from 1970 LP *The Fiddling Senator*.

3. Chris Goertzen, George Cecil McLeod, Mississippi's Fiddling Senator, and the Modern History of American Fiddling, American Music Series (Urbana: University of Illinois Press, 2004).

4. Eudora Welty, *Photographs* (Jackson: University Press of Mississippi, 1989), 127.

5. Author's telephone interview with Randy Miller, November 20, 2018.

Recordings

1979 Self-produced LP, *The Fiddling Senator*, with his wife, Elaine McLeod on piano, his longtime accompanist Lee Fulcher on guitar, and the accomplished violinist Mickey Davis on bass. Tunes on the LP: "Billy in the Lowground," "Happy Time Waltz," "Medley of Buffalo Gal, Senaca Square Dance and The Girl I Left Behind Me," "Sugarfoot Rag," "Red-Wing," "Bonaparte's Retreat," "Good Night Waltz," "Amazing Grace," "Ragtime Annie," "Roxanna Waltz," "What's the Reason," "Stone's Rag," "Black Velvet Waltz," "Lost Indian," "Maiden's Prayer," and "What a Friend We Have in Jesus."

Mississippi Sawyers: A Collection of Old-Time Mississippi Fiddling (LP, Sawyer Productions, 1980): "Mississippi Sawyer," "John Henry," and "Golden Slippers"

1974 Smithsonian Festival recordings in the Rinzler Archive:

McLeod announced the bands and called a square dance during the festival.

"Joe Turner's Blues" (with the Six Towns Band), "Billy in the Lowground," "F Waltz," "Ragtime Annie," and "Maiden's Prayer."

A home rehearsal tape with guitarist Chris Goertzen is my source for the transcriptions and "Confederate March."

For more information on Senator George C. McLeod, see Chris Goertzen, *Southern Fiddlers and Fiddle Contests* (Jackson: University Press of Mississippi, 2008).

Harry Bolick

Civil War March

Author's note: Transcribed from Chris Goertzen's field recording, with Elaine McLeod on piano.

Comparable versions: None known

THE MERIDIAN HUSTLERS

This three-piece string band, consisting of fiddle, banjo, and guitar, recorded for Paramount—the only known old-time act from Mississippi to do so—in Chicago in June 1929. "I'd Rather Stay Out in the Rain" is a version of "I Don't Work for a Living," a humorous hobo song recorded by a few other country artists and perhaps most widely circulated in a recording by Frank Luther under the pseudonym Pete Wiggins (OKeh, 1930).[1] The song is still under copyright and we are not including a transcription here. "Queen City Square Dance" is an interesting treatment of "Flop Eared Mule," taken rather slower and more deliberately than usual southeastern sets (e.g., by the Blue Ridge Highballers, Robinette and Moore, Kahle Brewer with Ernest Stoneman, and many more). The fiddling is identifiably Mississippian, a little sour in pitch and with a slight shake on high notes. There's a ragtime guitar break, something in the manner of Urias Bouchillon, the Greenville, South Carolina, guitarist who accompanied his brother, the talking bluesman Chris Bouchillon. Note the yodeling refrains, which prompt the listener to think of Meridian's most famous son.

In September 1929, the Meridian Hustlers placed first in the Band category at a Labor Day rodeo on the Meridian fairgrounds. (An otherwise unidentified "Leake County Band" placed second.)[2] In February 1930, *Radio Digest* reported that the "Meridian Hustlers Orchestra from Meridian, Miss." were

broadcasting on WAPI Birmingham, Alabama.[3] These fugitive sightings apart, little has been discovered about this band.

—Tony Russell

NOTES

1. It was also recorded by the popular Irish American singer James J. Mullan of Philadelphia, with the Four Provinces Orchestra (Columbia 33324-F), Mullan being given joint composer credit with the Orchestra's leader, pianist Edward Lee.

2. *Meridian News-Review*, Meridian, MS, September 6, 1929.

3. "Who's Who in Broadcasting," *Radio Digest* (February 1930).

Queen City Square Dance

Author's note: This transcription is from Paramount 3173, recorded Chicago, June 1929. The basic pattern is four As and four Bs, repeated but alternating passes of the A part, use one of the alt Ms indicated in the transcription. The first pass has only two As, four Bs, one alt A, then a 16M solo guitar part.

Comparable versions:
"The Long Eared Mule," Emmett Lundy & Ernest V. Stoneman, 05/27/1925, New York, OKeh 40405
"Long Eared Mule," The Hill Billies, 04/30/1926, New York, Vocalion 15368
"Ranger's Hornpipe," Stripling Brothers, 08/19/1929, Chicago, Paramount 3173

MILNER AND CURTIS WITH THE MAGNOLIA RAMBLERS

(Luther Milner (1886–1961), Luther Curtis (1908–1991), fiddles; Homer Ellis, mandolin; Leo Ellis, guitar)

Doc Bailey of Winona recommended this group to the Vocalion Record Company. They recorded two tunes, "Evening Shade Waltz" and "North East Texas," in Memphis in February 1930. On the record label, both Milner and Curtis were misidentified as "Luke." Lonnie Ellis remembers Milner and Curtis as Attala County residents both around fifty years of age at the time they recorded.[1]

Both Milner and Curtis were occasional fiddle contestants in the Kosciusko fiddling convention. The *Star Herald* newspaper of Kosciusko briefly described two contests. On March 3, 1916, Milner wrote to thank the organizers of the contest for his second place prize, a cake.[2] On November 10, 1916, Milner took fifth place and won a fine leather pocketbook. Curtis in sixth place won a shirt.[3]

The third contest was the following year in October. Sustained applause greeted the thirty-six fiddlers as they marched in to the stage. "Old Attala sustained her reputation, for having more and better fiddlers in her borders than can be found anywhere else in the universe."[4] The fiddlers were accompanied by straw beaters and a guitarist. Both Milner and Curtis secured prizes.[5]

Milner and Curtis also placed and won prizes in 1919 at Kosciusko: A Stetson hat, a pair of eighteen-karat shoes, a suit pressing, a haircut and shave, and twelve cold drinks from a grocery store.[6]

"Among the most enjoyable features of the programme was the fiddling and dancing of a four-year old boy who handled both the fiddle and his feet dexterously, the clog dancing (fifty-seven distinct movements) of Mr. Dave Atwood while Mr. Luther Milner fiddled a typical jig and Mrs. J. Clifton Lucas egged him on with patting which would have made the adept at a negro dance envious. This performance evoked applause that was prolonged and deafening," [7]

They also attended a fiddlers' contest, along with the Freeny Harmonizers in Ethel, Mississippi, in 1936.[8]

Homer Ellis was an older brother of Lonnie Ellis of the Mississippi Possum Hunters. Leo Ellis was Homer's son. For more information on the Ellis family, see the Mississippi Possum Hunters

Luther Milner and his grandson, Don. Photo courtesy Don Milner.

and Grover O'Briant chapters in this book. Little is known of Luther Curtis.

Luther Benson Milner (1886–1961) was born on the family property located in Northeast Attala County, Mississippi, approximately six miles south of French Camp, Mississippi, and one mile west of the Natchez Trace Parkway. The nearest town is McCool. He was known throughout the area as "Lute."

Lute's grandfather migrated from Jefferson County, Alabama, and settled in Attala County about 1846. Lute's father, George Washington Milner, was also a fiddler. He was born about 1848 and served with the Confederacy during the American Civil War.

Lute built a house on the family property in 1908. He then married Annie Blanche Ramsey and moved her into the house where she lived until her death in 1981. She was remembered as saying, "Lute would go somewhere and play that fiddle all night, come home at dawn, eat breakfast, then hitch up

his mule and plow the crops all day." She grew up just outside the village of French Camp, Mississippi. Her sister, Birdie, was married to a fine fiddler, John Holloway, of the Mississippi Possum Hunters.

Lute worked most of his life as a farmer, raising cotton, but was elected to county tax assessor twice for two four-year terms. In his fifties he began work for the Mississippi Highway Department. He bought land from farmers for the department. He had a good rapport with the farmers, knew real estate values, and was good at it.

Luther Doy, Lute's youngest son, was thirteen when he died in 1932. He had become an accomplished guitarist at that early age and had played with Lute. After his death, Lute put away the fiddle for a long time.

Lute's grandson, Donald E. Milner, grew up about 100 yards away from Lute's house in a house built by his father in 1937. Lute remained reluctant to play; Don only heard him play on a handful of times with John Holloway on the front porch. "One of my favorite memories that I recall, was in early evening, usually in the summer, when cows were milked, mules fed, and chores completed. We would gather on the front porch, he would break out the old fiddle and serenade us along with the chirping of the crickets and the singing of the June bugs."[9]

—Harry Bolick

NOTES

1. Tony Russell, *Old Time Music* 20 (Spring 1976): 40.

2. "An Appreciation," *Star-Herald*, Kosciusko, MS, March 3, 1916, 1.

3. "Fiddler's Contest a Great Success," *Star-Herald*, Kosciusko, MS, November 10, 1916, 1.

4. "Fiddler's Contest a Perfect Success," *Jackson Daily News*, Jackson, MS, October 19, 1917, 1.

5. "Fiddler's Contest a Perfect Success."

6. "The Fiddlers Contest," *Star-Herald*, Kosciusko, MS, November 7, 1910, 1.

7. "Fiddler's Contest a Perfect Success."

8. "Ethel School News: The Fiddlers Contest," *Star-Herald*, Kosciusko, MS, November 19, 1936, 8.

9. Email interview with Don Milner, May 11–12, 2013.

Evening Shade Waltz

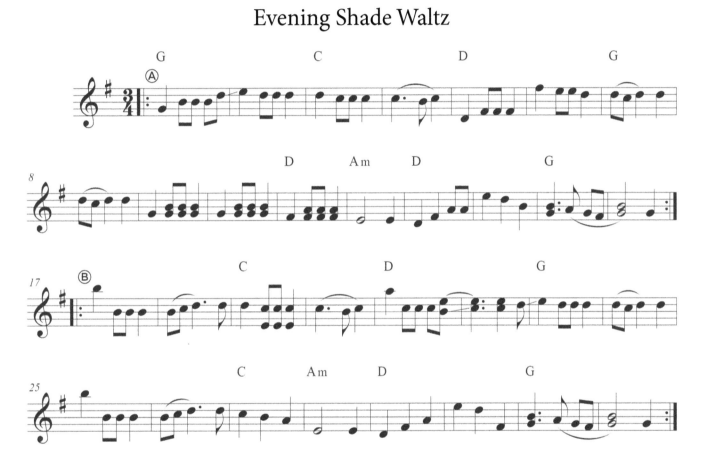

Author's note: This transcription is from Vocalion 5426 recorded Memphis, TN, 02/18/1930. The Am chord in M12 and M28 sounds like Curtis was playing a C chord and just lifted his finger that had held down the C note, so the A note sounds.

Comparable versions: None known

Northeast Texas

Author's note: This transcription is from Vocalion 5426 recorded Memphis, TN, 02/18/1930.

Comparable versions:
"The Hero," Knauff, *Virginia Reels* II #5 (Baltimore, 1839)
Bolick and Austin, *Mississippi Fiddle Tunes and Songs from the 1930s*: W. E. Claunch, "Wagoner," 277; Stephen B. Tucker,
    "Texas Wagon," 365
"Waggoner," Uncle Am Stuart, 06/1924, New York, Vocalion 14840
"Kentucky Wagoners," Allen Sisson, 02/25/1925, New York, Edison 51720
"The Waggoner," Fiddlin' Doc Roberts Trio, 03/05/1931, New York, Banner 32309

HOYT AND ROZELLE MING

The name was as intriguing as the music. Chinese? Indian? Neither seemed really likely, but then, the music of Floyd Ming and his Pep Steppers on those old Victor records was strange enough to justify some rather wild speculation.

The origins of the Mings were not quite so exotic, but we can at least trace them back a long and interesting distance. A James Menge, perhaps of German origin, had settled in James City County, Virginia, by about 1650. A later James Menge, his grandson, was in North Carolina in the 1720s, and

Rozelle and Hoyt Ming. Photo courtesy Carl Fleischhauer.

Hoyt Ming and His Pep Steppers promotional photo. Front, left to right: Hoyt, Rozelle, and Troy Ming. Rear: Andrew D. Coggin, dance caller. Photo courtesy Carl Fleischhauer. The band had its portrait taken by J. J. Huffman of Tupelo a few days after the recording session, at the request of a local record dealer. The picture was then used for newspaper advertising.

Newspaper ad for Ming's Pep Steppers. Photo courtesy Carl Fleischhauer.

one of his descendants, probably a grandson, was included in the South Carolina census in the 1770s. It seems to have been in this generation or the next that the spelling changed to Ming.

That was certainly the form of the name borne by Charles Ming (b. 1804), who took a branch of the family into Mississippi, settling during the 1840s as an overseer in Winston County. One of Charles's six children, Clough Ming (1859–1934), went to live in Choctaw County. When his son Hoyt was born, the family had been Choctaw County residents for over twenty years.

Hoyt Ming (1902–1985) grew up in a musical family. Of the seven boys, three or four learned instruments. His own beginnings he remembers quite well.

I first started—I was about fifteen years old, and my daddy invited a string band over home one night to play, you see. And they were good. And somehow I liked the fiddler, the way he played his fiddle. So I began to think, well, I'd like to play a fiddle. So I managed to get hold of a secondhand fiddle—I just call it fiddle—and in learning I'd pick out a simple piece, like, say, for instance, "Shortenin' Bread," something like that . . . you know, easily accomplished. And I'd just pick out— the tune'd be in my head—and find the note on the fiddle. I'd just pick it out till I got it just like I wanted it.

I'd keep on—instead of jumping from that to some other piece and mixing up so many, I'd first learn one simple piece as well as I could. Then I'd learn another. Maybe it'd be a little bit harder, but I just kept on till I'd worked every piece out at a time. 'Cause if you go to jumping, sometimes

Hoyt Ming scrapbook. Photo courtesy Carl Fleischhauer.

maybe half accomplish one tune and then get on to some other, you can't get anywhere.... And I'd always select the pieces that I thought were good. If there was some piece that I didn't care about the kind of music, I wouldn't try to learn it. But the pieces I liked, that's the kind I'd try to play.

The Ming boys started to play together as a band—Hoyt on fiddle, his brothers Troy on mandolin and Ethel on guitar—and were invited to local dances and parties. Hoyt became a keen visitor to

fiddlers' contests, and told Gus Meade that he often stayed up all night learning new tunes.

In January or February 1928, Ralph Peer of Victor came to audition a bunch of musicians in East Tupelo. Hoyt overheard somebody talking about it and enquired at the Troy Drug Store, where Victrolas were sold. The druggist told him the time and location of the audition.

By this time, Hoyt generally played with his wife Rozelle (1906/7–1983), whom he had married in 1924. Originally schooled in violin and piano,

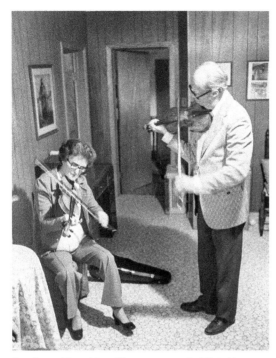

Rozelle and Hoyt Ming. Photo courtesy Carl Fleischhauer.

Hoyt Ming at potato bin. Photo courtesy Carl Fleischhauer.

Hoyt Ming at French Camp Fiddlers Contest, 1975. Photo courtesy Carl Fleischhauer.

Tony Russell

Rozelle began to play guitar with her husband, initially with her sister on mandolin. In his sister-in-law's absence, Troy Ming would play in her place, and this was the trio that appeared for the audition. They also brought along a caller, Andrew D. Coggin (1890–1977) of Nettleton. The band satisfied Peer, and about a month later, in mid-February, they traveled up to Memphis, where Victor had established a recording station.

Other bands from Lee County, where the Mings were then living, had attended the audition but failed to win a recording opportunity. In fact Hoyt's band was one of the first from Mississippi to get on records. The Leake County Revelers had started about a year earlier, while Narmour and Smith made their first sides two days later than the Mings—also in Memphis (for OKeh), though Hoyt didn't encounter them at that time.

On February 13 the band recorded four numbers. "Indian War Whoop" was Hoyt's specialty and he often won fiddlers' contests with it. He originally knew only two other fiddlers who played it: his cousin Pearl Burdine (1887–1977), who was then living in Choctaw County, and Emmett Conner (1889–1969), of Kosciusko. The striking feature of the tune is the hollering, which chimes in with the high notes at the end of phrases. Burdine and Conner used to do it, but Hoyt's hollering was different, and indeed he didn't always do it exactly the same way himself, as you can tell from the two takes that were issued. (The original coupling of "Indian War Whoop" and "Old Red" on Victor used the second take of each tune, but later on, in the 1930s, the first take of each appeared on Bluebird.) Some years later Hoyt met another fiddler, from Longview in Oktibbeha County, who knew the piece, too. But Hoyt's was the only version ever recorded by a Mississippi fiddler.

The notion of a whooping or hollering Indian somewhere inside a fiddle tune wasn't unique. Hiter Colvin, a Louisiana-born fiddler then living in southern Arkansas, recorded an "Indian War Whoop" for Victor the year after Hoyt. It's an entirely different tune, but Colvin inserts a holler in much the same fashion. At least some fiddlers think of part of the tune "Lost Indian" as embodying the same idea.

"Old Red" came from a Choctaw County fiddler named Tommy Quarles, and secondarily from Emmett Conner and Tom Bowen (who also knew "Pallet on the Floor," which Hoyt played). "White Mule" was a retitling by Peer of what Hoyt knew as "Whoa Mule," and it too came from Emmett Conner. Both "Old Red" and "White Mule" have dance calls by Coggin.

"Tupelo Blues" came from a Longview fiddler, Forest Quinn (1900–1991), whom Hoyt met when he was at agricultural high school there. Quinn was also the source of "Drafting Blues" and "New Hot Times," which Hoyt recorded on his 1975 Homestead LP. "Tupelo Blues" was originally known to Hoyt as "Florida Blues," but Peer thought it appropriate to give the tune a more local name. This, as we shall see, was to be a far-reaching decision on Peer's part.

Gus Meade, describing Hoyt Ming's fiddling, wrote that he "was among the earliest of the Mississippi fiddlers to make such effective use of double stops and to achieve so much spirit with such a long bow. Many dance fiddlers favor a short bow for the drive that music for dancing demands. Hoyt has an interesting little wobble . . . which adds a jauntiness and the required drive."[1]

One of the features of the Mings' music that most appealed to Peer was the foot-tapping with which Rozelle accompanied her guitar-playing, and he had her stamping away as loudly as possible when the recordings were cut. This was an extraordinary departure from his usual practice of muffling musicians' feet or having them take their shoes off while recording, a tale told by many of the people he recorded. It did in fact give the music an infectious rhythm—though Rozelle always thought it ruined it—and it further suggested the name of Pep Steppers, which Hoyt thought up when Peer pressed him for a suitable band credit. It sounded like stepping, and it felt peppy.

Not content with changing some of the tunes' names, Victor in the end altered Hoyt's too, though no doubt by a mere misreading: he ended up on the disc labels as Floyd Ming.

◆ ◆ ◆

The band returned from Memphis with a fee of $25 a tune plus expenses, and carried on with the musical activities the recording session had briefly interrupted: fairs, picnics, political rallies, fiddlers' contests, a few dances. The usual problems affected them. Heavy drinking in the dancehalls kept them away from playing that sort of function. Hoyt and Rozelle had three young children to raise. It was even difficult to keep enough players together. Troy Ming had married and was less available for dates, and then Rozelle's sister stopped playing with them. It was always easier to find guitar players than mandolin players, so Rozelle switched to mandolin.

In the late 1920s and '30s, however, Hoyt and Rozelle did feature prominently in their region's music scene. Like many Mississippi musicians they regularly attended the big fall contest at Kosciusko. Hoyt won first prize among fifty-six contestants in 1928; he tied with a Kenneth Whitmire, and the decision was made by drawing straws. This win put him in the champion category in subsequent years. He remembers seeing Willie Narmour at Kosciusko in 1929 or 1930, and also Alvis Massengale (of the Newton County Hill Billies), who played "Give the Fiddler a Dram" with a straw-beater accompanying him.

While in Kosciusko, one time the Mings also broadcast over a station there. Years afterward, when the main fiddlers' contest had moved to Jackson—the Kosciusko affair died in the mid-1930s—they broadcast out of the Robert E. Lee Hotel there. But radio was never a particularly attractive prospect for them, since it would have meant time away from their children. In the mid-1930s, Hoyt played with Kelly Draper, Carl Woods, W. C. Gillis Jr., and G. M. Collier in a band called the Choctaw Playboys, which on at least one occasion broadcast over WNBR in Memphis.[2]

◆　◆　◆

Emphasizing their musical career tends to make one forget that the Mings were never full-time musicians. Hoyt's livelihood was farming, and his main crop potatoes. He sold direct to farmers, and to some cooperatives, with buyers as far away as Virginia, West Virginia, and Kentucky. During the

selling season, from April to late July, he would advertise in farm papers, initially the *Mississippi Market Bulletin* out of Jackson, then *Southern Agriculturist* and *Progressive Farmer*. Plants sold for sixty-five cents a thousand, postpaid. When help was hard to get, Hoyt and Rozelle would do everything themselves; once they counted and bunched 30,000 plants in a day. Seed potatoes remained their chief source of income, though they had a few head of cattle on their forty-acre holding. Their return to music in the 1970s brought them unexpected further income.

Hoyt always liked old-time music, and in his most active playing days he kept up with what other local musicians were doing. He bought records, including some by Jimmie Rodgers and various ones by string bands. He especially enjoyed the Leake County Revelers:

> That fiddler, he was a good soft fiddler. And the rhythm, and the kind of instruments they had as a band, that really was my favorite.
>
> Now for two-piece music—and that's all they had—and you know what, the fiddle he played on was a homemade fiddle—and that was Narmour and Smith. And I believe the best piece he [Narmour] put out was "Charleston No. 1." I played the "Charleston No. 2" and some of "Carroll County Blues." I can play "Charleston No. 1" but I can't play it like he played it. Somehow he's got a little something in there that I just don't get in like he does, you know. But that "Charleston No. 1" is hard to beat. And I know everybody that I've heard that talked about his playing of the records, they'll mention that "Charleston No. 1."

(Incidentally, Hoyt confirmed what had been said elsewhere, that the "Charleston" tunes Narmour played had nothing to do with the Charleston dance but took their name from the town of Charleston in Tallahatchie County.)

Blues—the feel of the blues—colored almost everything Hoyt Ming played.

> A blues is a kind of a—I call it sort of a lonesome . . . there's another name for it, kind of a haunting

sort of a little . . . Like a fellow say, "Blue, down and out," you know, they have a little different sound music from others. And I think that's where they get it, you know, the time back in the war days and all, during the 1918, they were going off to the war and things were kind of blue and so on, and they just began to put out pieces they call the blues. Say if you're off somewhere, way away from home, get lonesome, and you write a song, it'll have a blues, like, kind of, 'cause you're blue, you know. And they fix a song that way, go to singing it, they'll call it a blues and it'll be a different type, come under a different name.

But when it got started, why, it just began to spread, you know. And of course all the blues didn't sound alike. Maybe some of the blues didn't sound so haunting or lonesome like. But it became so popular that some of them would name it the blues anyway. So that's a whole lot the way the blues got started.

Hoyt used to pick up blues sometimes from other fiddlers, sometimes from records. A white fiddler from Louisville, Mississippi, Wayne Jones, was by way of being a blues specialist. The blues records Hoyt listened to were mostly of blues singing, like "St Louis Blues" or "Down in Black Bottom Blues"; he remembered hardly any Black blues fiddlers, either on record or in person. The Mississippi Sheiks, for instance, though they were well known on records,

and (one would assume) in person, at any rate in central Mississippi, he didn't remember at all. In his teens there was a Black string band around Ackerman led by a fiddler named Coleman; this was the only Black fiddler he could remember seeing.

◆ ◆ ◆

Hoyt and Rozelle played less and less over the years, and by the 1950s they were finding it hard to keep a band together. Hoyt let his fiddle get into a poor state, and by about 1957 or '58 the Mings were definitely in retirement from music.

Fifteen years passed. A solitary old recording, the "Indian War Whoop," was available all this time on Harry Smith's Folkways *Anthology*, delighting and puzzling old-time music fans, but apart from this the recorded heritage of Mississippi was very scantily represented on LP records, and the area was out of fashion among fiddle music buffs. True, there was Bill Mitchell, the "fiddling sheriff" of Tupelo, and Merle Taylor from Saltillo, but their music was of the bluegrass generation.

One day in February 1973, Hoyt was going through some old things and came across the 1928 photograph of the original band. Without quite knowing why, he kept it out, and put it on his desk. A few days later came a letter from David Freeman of County Records, asking about the old band and the records and everything. Hoyt was struck by the coincidence, and then observed that two anniversaries were at hand: it was fifteen years since his musical retirement, and forty-five since the Victor recording session. It seemed somehow a good sign.

Freeman visited the Mings that summer, on a research trip with Richard Nevins and Gus Meade. Hoyt and Rozelle were living near Ackerman in Choctaw County, some seventy-five miles south of Tupelo on the Natchez Trace Parkway. Impressed by the Mings' undiminished capabilities, the visitors took back a good enough report to secure Hoyt and Rozelle a booking for the 1973 National Folk Festival. While out east they cut an album for Freeman's Homestead label with their son Hoyt B. Ming and James Alford on guitars. The following year they represented Mississippi at the Smithsonian Festival of American Folklife, and also played a prestigious "Mississippi Folk Voices" concert at the State Historical Museum in Jackson. In 1975 they played on the soundtrack of the locally made movie *Ode to Billy Joe*, based on Bobbie Gentry's country hit.

The Mings also played at local concerts, folk festivals, and the like, with a couple of youngsters, Ricky Morgan (guitar) and Wayne Dawkins (bass guitar). Rozelle generally played mandolin, but did some twin-fiddle numbers with Hoyt like "When You and I Were Young, Maggie" or "Ozark Waltz" (which they learned from a 1930 recording by the

Morrison Twin Brothers String Band from Arkansas, reissued on one of Freeman's County LPs). The new Pep Steppers brought the Mings' music a little closer to the present day, without compromising its integrity, and for friends and admirers of Hoyt and Rozelle it was a truly heartening experience to hear them and their unique old tunes, all sounding as vivid and remarkable as ever.

And none of this might have come about, had not an astute recording man thought that "Florida Blues" was an odd name for a Mississippi tune, and decided on "Tupelo Blues" instead—giving researchers decades later a clue where to start looking for the Mings.

—Tony Russell

NOTES

1. Gus Meade papers, Southern Folklife Center, University of North Carolina, Chapel Hill.

2. *Choctaw Plaindealer*, Ackerman, MS, April 13, 1934. The Choctaw Playboys are also mentioned in the *Choctaw Plaindealer* on May 18 and July 27, 1934.

Recordings

Hoyt Ming and His Pep-Steppers, *New Hot Times!* Homestead 103, 1975

Beautiful Texas

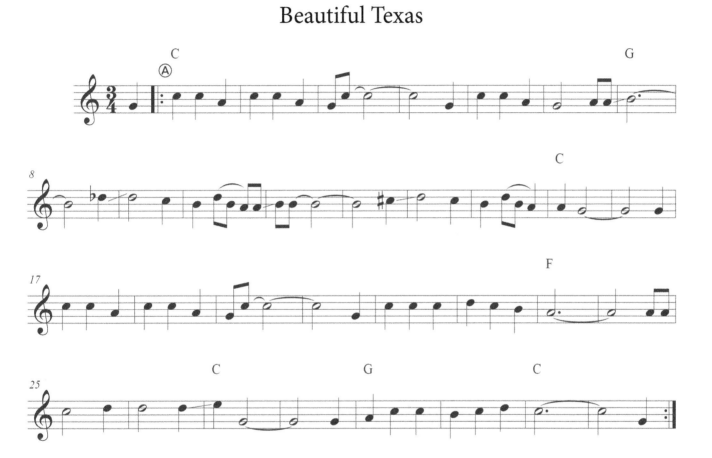

Author's note: This transcription is based on an unused take from the 1975 LP.

Comparable versions:
"Beautiful Texas," The Westerners (Massey Family), 06/11/1934, Chicago, Conqueror 8437
"Beautiful Texas," Milton Brown & His Brownies, 01/28/1935, Chicago, Decca 5071

Bonny Blue Flag

Author's note: This transcription is based on the 1975 LP version.

Comparable versions:
"The Bonnie Blue Flag" is an 1861 Confederate marching song.
"The Bonnie Blue Flag," Harry McCarthy, lyrics with the melody taken from the song "The Irish Jaunting Car," introduced in Jackson, MS, in 1861
"The Bonnie Blue Flag," A. E. Blackmar, New Orleans, published six editions between 1861 and 1864.

Tony Russell

Cackling Hen

Author's note: This transcription is based on the 1975 LP version. The B part varies with each pass of the tune.

Comparable versions:

Bolick and Austin, *Mississippi Fiddle Tunes and Songs from the 1930s*: Mrs. M. B. Brister, "Old Hen Cackled on the Pot," 66; John Brown, "Old Hen Cackled," 73; W. M. Collom, "Rabbit in a Ditch," 82; Jim Gooch, "Old Hen Cackled," 110; Dr. Frank Smith, "Old Hen Cackled," 179

In this book: "Old Hen Cackled," Tom Dumas
"The Old Hen Cackled and the Rooster Is Going to Crow," John Carson, 06/14/1923, Atlanta, OKeh 4890
"Hen Cackle," Gid Tanner & Riley Puckett, 03/08/1924, New York, Columbia 110-D
"Cackling Hen," J. D. Harris, 1925, Asheville, NC, OKeh 45024

Charleston #2

Author's note: This transcription is based on the 1975 LP version.

Comparable versions:
In this book: "Charleston #2," Narmour & Smith, 09/23/1929, New York, OKeh 45377

Chicken Reel

Author's note: This transcription is based on the 1975 LP version.

Comparable versions:

Joseph M. Daly, music, 1910

"Chicken Reel," Tweedy Brothers, 06/14/1924, Richmond, IN, Gennett 5488

"Slow Buck," Gid Tanner & His Skillet Lickers, 04/11/1928, Atlanta, Columbia 21567-D

"Chicken Reel," Kessinger Brothers, 09/16/1930, New York, Brunswick 480

Cripple Coon

Author's note: This transcription is based on the 1975 LP version. The offensive title for this tune would not be acceptable today, but at the time of this recording was unfortunately in common usage.

Comparable versions: None known

Tony Russell

Drafting Blues

Author's note: This transcription is based on the 1975 LP version. Fiddler Forest Quinn was Ming's source for "Drafting Blues."

Comparable versions: None known

Indian War Whoop

Author's note: Hoyt recorded "Indian War Whoop," as Floyd Ming & His Pep Steppers on 02/13/1928 in Memphis, TN, (Victor 21294) and again in 1973. Hoyt's version was a personal one but based on versions played by his older cousin Pearl Burdine and Emmett Connor of Kosciusko. There is a photo of Burdine in the section, Communities of Fiddlers in Mississippi. I've notated the 1973 version above but it varies as noted below:

The A part is repeated twice all times.
1: first long note is 5 beats, 5 riffs, second long note is 10 beats, 3 riffs
2: first long note is 4 beats, 4 riffs, second long note is 10 beats, 3 riffs
3: first long note is 5 beats, 4 riffs, second long note is 8 beats, 3 riffs
4: first long note is 4 beats, 3 riffs, second long note is 11 beats, 2 riffs
5: first long note is 4 beats, 3 riffs, second long note is 6 beats, 0 riffs

1928 version:
1: 4 A parts, first long note played and sung 14 beats, alt M12 played, 11 riffs, second long note played and sung 11 beats, 7 riffs
2: 3 A parts, first long note played and sung 9 beats, 7 riffs, second long note 12 beats, 4 riffs, second long note repeated 9 beats, 9 riffs
3: 3 A parts, second long note played and sung 10 beats, 8 riffs, second long note 11 beats, 4 riffs
4: 3 A parts, second long note played and sung 10 beats, 6 riffs, second long note 8 beats, 0 riffs

Comparable versions: None known, although there are many tunes with this name.

Tony Russell

Mississippi Sawyer

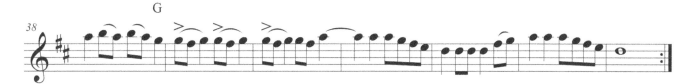

Author's note: This transcription is based on a tune from the 1975 LP.

In M1 Ming plays the first note on a down-bow, then for the next three measures rows the bow in a tight circle accenting each A note on an up-bow. On the quick down-bow, readying the bow for the next stroke, not much is heard. This creates a part of his distinctive sound. M12 incudes the D drone under the alternating notes played over it. M13 is played the same, but is indicated without the drone for clarity.

Comparable versions:

"Love from the Heart," Knauff, *Virginia Reels*, Vol. IV (Baltimore, 1839), Part 4 #4

Bolick and Austin, *Mississippi Fiddle Tunes and Songs from the 1930s*: Sinclair Crocker, 91; E. Shoemaker, 171; J. H. Wheeler, 203; Rev. J. E. Williams, 209; W. E. Claunch, 264; Hardy C. Sharp, 340; Stephen B. Tucker, 360, all titled "Mississippi Sawyer"

"Mississippi Sawyer," Gid Tanner and His Skillet Lickers, 04/08/1929, Atlanta, Columbia 15420-D

"Mississippi Sawyer," Kessinger Brothers, 02/05/1929, New York, Brunswick 309

"Old Time Corn Shuckin' Part 1," Ernest Stoneman & the Blue Ridge Corn Shuckers, 07/27/1927, Bristol, TN, Victor 20835

New Hot Times

Author's note: This transcription is based on a tune from the 1975 LP.
Fiddler Forest Quinn was Ming's source for "New Hot Times."

Comparable versions:
"A Hot Time in the Old Town Tonight," Theodore Metz, music and lyric, 1896
"There'll Be a Hot Time in the Old Town Tonight," Gid Tanner & His Skillet Lickers, 10/29/1929, Atlanta, Columbia 15695-D

Tony Russell

Old Red

Author's note: This transcription is based on the tune from the 1975 LP. The B part repeats only on the first pass of the tune.
   Ming's version of "Old Red" came from neighboring fiddlers Tommy Quarles, Emmett Connor, and Tom Bowen.

Comparable versions: None known
"Old Red," Floyd Ming & His Pep Steppers, 02/13/1928, Memphis, TN, Victor 21294

Pep Steppers Waltz

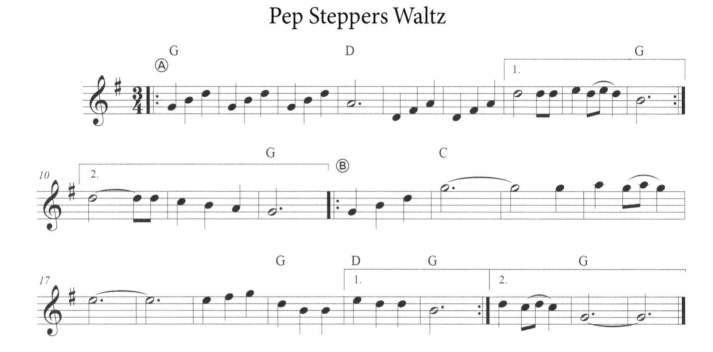

Author's note: This transcription is based on a home recording made by Hoyt Ming Jr., of Hoyt and Bert Ming

Comparable versions: None known

Tony Russell

Rattlesnake Daddy

Author's note: This transcription is based on the 1975 LP version.

Comparable versions:
"Rattlesnake Daddy," Bill Carlisle, 24/07/1933, New York, Vocalion 25020
"Rattlesnake Daddy," Callahan Brothers, 08/17/1934, New York, Banner 33414

Tupelo Blues

Author's note: This tune is transcribed from Ming's 78 rpm recording. Hoyt learned it from fiddler Forest Quinn. Alt M2 shows how he played that phrase on the 1975 LP. Ming is not consistent with the number of beats in the beginning of this tune. In the recording less than half of the time, he adds a beat after M3 and or M8, an eighth rest and an E on the upbeat. The E as played in M1 should be played through M12. The quarter note E is played unison on the open E string and fingered on the A string. The open E string rings over the fingered slide out of the E on the A string, creating a sort of yelp.

Ming said the original title for the tune was "Florida Blues," but the title was changed at the recording date. Jim Ewing, "Musician from Ackerman has been fiddlin' for years," *Jackson Daily News*, Jackson, MS, August 28, 1984, C1.

Comparable versions: None known

"Tupelo Blues," Floyd Ming & His Pep Steppers, 02/13/1928, Memphis, TN, Victor 21534

Turkey in the Straw

Author's Note: This transcription is from a Hoyt Ming Jr. home recording of Hoyt and Bert Ming.

Comparable versions:

"Zip Coon," J. B. Farrell, lyric and music, 1834 / Mr. Dixon, 1834

"Zip Coon," Thos. Birch, New York, 1834 (http://www.loc.gov/item/sm1834.360780/)

"Natchez on the Hill," Knauff, *Virginia Reels*, Vol. 1 (Baltimore: George Willig Jr., 1839), http://dc.lib.unc.edu/cdm/ref/collection/sheetmusic/id/9230

Bolick and Austin, *Mississippi Fiddle Tunes and Songs from the 1930s*: Berlon Flynt, "Old Zip Coon," 105; Mrs. Della Patterson, "Turkey in the Straw," 158

"Turkey in the Straw," Henry Gilliland & A. C. "Eck" Robertson, 06/30/1922, New York, Gennett 4974

"Turkey in the Straw," Dr. D. Dix Hollis, 06/1924, New York, Paramount 33153

"Turkey in the Straw," Fiddlin' John Carson, 08/27/1924, Atlanta, OKeh 40230

White Mule

Author's note: This transcription is from Victor 21294, recorded Memphis, TN, 02/13/1928. M8–9 are not played the first time
through but then they are played on every other pass through the tune. In an article by Jim Ewing ("Musician from Ackerman has been fiddlin' for years," *Jackson Daily News*, Jackson, MS, July 28, 1984), Ming said the original title for the tune was
"Whoa Mule, Let Me Put the Saddle on You."

Comparable versions:
"The Kicking Mule," Fiddlin' John Carson, 11/08/1923, New York, OKeh 40071
"Buckin' Mule," Gid Tanner & George Riley Puckett, 03/18/1924, New York, Columbia 110-D
"Ride That Mule," Al Hopkins & His Buckle Busters, 05/16/1927, New York, Brunswick 186

Tony Russell

THE MISSISSIPPI POSSUM HUNTERS

One day in 1930, in the middle of a busy recording session set up by Victor in downtown Memphis's Ellis Auditorium, four fiddle tunes were recorded, to be issued later on a couple of records credited to the Mississippi 'Possum Hunters. Forty years later, as people began to collect and talk about these old records, a few listeners noticed that the two couplings attributed to this group were remarkably different from each other. One pair of tunes, the first to be recorded and the first to be issued, "Possum on the Rail" and "Mississippi Breakdown," were straightforward breakdowns played by a fiddler with guitar and cello accompaniment. But the other pair, recorded later that day, showed the hand of a flashier performer, with a strong ragtime sense. These two, "The Last Shot Got Him" and "Rufus Rastus," had guitar and mandolin accompanying the fiddle.

The differences between the selections and, even more, the approaches and mannerisms of the fiddlers prompted those inquisitive listeners to doubt whether the same lineup could have been responsible for both pairs of tunes. And in that suspicion, as it happens, they were both right and wrong.

The Mississippi 'Possum Hunters were three men from round Winona: Lonnie Ellis, John Holloway, and Pete Herring. They were talent obtained for Victor by the local record-store owner and veterinarian Dr.

Pete Herring, ca. 1930. Photo courtesy Tempie Woods.

A. M. Bailey. Ellis remembered their recording name having been thought up by Bailey, but Doc was uncertain about it; in any case, it's likely that the inspiration was a band then popular on the Grand Ole Opry, Dr. Humphrey Bate and His Possum Hunters.

Lonnie Ellis (1895–1976) was originally from Friendship, about twenty miles east of Winona. His father was a fiddler, and four of his five brothers were musicians too. (One, Homer, recorded with Milner and Curtis.) Lonnie grew up learning such tunes as "Chicken Reel," "Old Joe Clark," "Sally Goodin,"

"Fisher's Hornpipe," "Bill Cheatham," "Goodnight Waltz," and "Wednesday Night Waltz." He worked as a farmer or sawmill operator. In the 1930s, he sold his sawmill business and went to the Delta to farm, in the Itta Bena–Moorhead area. Cotton was an unrewarding crop at that time, and it was impossible to make much of a living, but there were at least musical acquaintances to be struck. Homer and Robert Hatcher, who played fiddle and guitar respectively, lived on Ellis's place for a year. Their mother, he remembered, was a girlfriend of Fiddlin' Arthur Smith.

Ellis often attended the big fiddlers' contest at Kosciusko, where he once won second place, and another time third. He met there such prominent fiddlers of his region as Willie Narmour, Luke Milner, and Luke Curtis.

He also played country dances and gave entertainments at private houses, often in company with Holloway and Herring. He had a first cousin who was a good caller, as was another acquaintance, Jake Townsend.

John M. Holloway was a few years older than Lonnie Ellis. (He may be the John Holloway who around the time of the recordings was living in the community of Bethsaida in Neshoba County.) As a young man he was a good fiddler—Ellis praised his command of faster tunes—but in later years he more or less gave up playing. Then he lost a finger of his left hand in an accident with a saw (his occupation was carpentering).

Arnold Perry "Pete" Herring (1911–1983) lived at different times in the Clear Creek, Pine Bluff, and Poplar Creek communities around Winona. In 1931 the *Winona Times* reported that he "entertained with music, guitar and voice" at a birthday party for Ms. Frances Weeks at Wesley Chapel in Carroll County.[1] He continued to play music into the late 1950s, and in April 1959, entered the Kilmichael Lions Club Fiddlers' Contest in the categories of singing-with-guitar and accordion; he placed second with his guitar, and also second in the string band section, accompanying Homer Grice, Grover O'Briant, and Clayton Tyler.[2] According to his obituary, he worked as a piano tuner.

Lonnie Ellis remembered in some detail that recording session in 1930. He and Holloway were required by the A&R man, Ralph Peer, to play separate audition pieces. These were accepted, and shortly afterward recorded. The order of the session was as follows: Ellis (fiddle), Herring (guitar), and Holloway (cello) played "Mississippi Breakdown" and "Possum on the Rail"; Herring, accompanied by his own guitar, sang "I've Got a House in Chicago" and "Take a 'Tater and Wait," which were never issued; and then, after a break in which other acts recorded, the 'Possum Hunters reconvened as Holloway (fiddle), Ellis (mandolin), and Herring (guitar) to play "The Last Shot Got Him" and "Rufus Rastus."

Ellis's "Possum on the Rail" came from his brother Homer. "Mississippi Breakdown" came, he said, from an old record of the Leake County Revelers: not, as one would first assume, their own recording under that title (which wasn't made until six months after Ellis's), but the tune the Revelers recorded in April 1929 as "Saturday Night Breakdown." This would have been on the market some months before the Victor session: time enough, certainly, for Ellis to work up a version.

Holloway's tunes have a more diverse background. "The Last Shot Got Him" was known in the region, Ellis claimed (though he himself didn't play it), but it turns up also in Texas, where Chenoweth's Cornfield Symphony Orchestra, a string band from the Dallas area, recorded it in 1925. A song with a related title, "The First Shot Missed Him," was known to and recorded by the Black songster Mississippi John Hurt, from next-door Carroll County. The change in title proves to be merely a folk variant; Hurt's tune is identifiably the one Holloway plays, and the opening verse that he sings is "The first shot missed him, a mile away, / The last shot got him, so they say." Ellis, however, didn't recall any words associated with the tune, and it's probable that both he and Holloway regarded it as a fiddle number and no more.

"Rufus Rastus," too, was originally a song, first published in 1905: "Rufus Rastus Johnson Brown, / What you goin' to do when the rent comes 'round?" Harry Von Tilzer, who composed the sprightly ragtime tune, claimed he heard that second line used by a Black woman, berating her husband, at the railroad station in Miami once. His frequent

Tony Russell

1. *Winona Times*, Winona, MS, May 1, 1931.
2. *Winona Times*, Winona, MS, May 1, 1959.

collaborator Andrew Sterling incorporated it into the song lyrics, and in fact "What You Goin' to Do When the Rent Comes 'Round?" was the original published title. It was a great favorite of the coon-song era, and is fondly recalled in works of popular music history like Sigmund Spaeth's *Read 'Em and Weep* and Ann Charters's *The Ragtime Songbook*. Holloway treated it simply as a ragtime fiddle piece.

When the trio had made their six tunes, the whole batch was played back to them, and they were paid for their work—$50 apiece for everything. Ellis says he also received a half-a-cent royalty rate on his own pair of tunes, from which he claims he earned, over about fifteen years, some three or four hundred dollars. It is interesting that each fiddler received composer-credit for both his performances; this was by no means the rule with Victor, particularly where non-vocal recordings were concerned.

In later years, when the powerful Mexican border radio stations could be heard in Mississippi, Ellis was surprised to hear his half-forgotten Victor record played on XERA, Del Rio—not once but several times.

When interviewed in 1975, he was still listening in for fiddling on the radio, and would tape Kenny Baker's playing whenever he could. When the Opry was on, he used to get out his fiddle and play along, but after a severe illness in 1975 he played little.

—Tony Russell

The Last Shot Got Him

Author's note: This transcription is from Victor 23644, recorded Memphis, TN, 05/28/1930.

Comparable versions:
"First Shot Missed Him," Mississippi John Hurt, This recording was made at the *Last Sessions*, Vanguard VSD 79327, recorded 1966, released 1972

Mississippi Breakdown

Author's note: This transcription is from Victor 23595, recorded Memphis, TN, 05/28/1930.

Comparable versions:
In this book: "Saturday Night Breakdown," Leake County Revelers, 04/16/1929, Atlanta, Columbia 15470-D
In this book: "Nine O'Clock Breakdown," Newton County Hill Billies, 12/16/1930, Jackson, MS, OKeh 45544

'Possum on the Rail

Author's note: This transcription is from Victor 23595, recorded Memphis, TN, 05/28/1930.

Comparable versions:
"Raccoon on a Rail," Home Town Boys, 10/26/1931, Atlanta, Columbia 15762-D

Tony Russell

Rufus Rastus

Author's note: This transcription is from Victor 23644, recorded Memphis, TN, 05/28/1930. This melody of a minstrel-era song
   contained racially stereotypical lyrics, not sung on this recording, that would not be acceptable today.

Comparable versions:
Andrew B. Sterling, lyrics, Harry Von Tilzer, music, 1905
"Rufus Rastus Johnson Brown," Frank Novak & His Rootin' Tootin' Boys, 04/26/1937, New York, Vocalion 03751
"What You Gonna Do When the Rent Comes 'Round," Louise Massey & the Westerners, 06/11/1940, Chicago, OKeh 05650

THE MISSISSIPPI SHEIKS

The Mississippi Sheiks were perhaps the most commercially successful recording artists from Mississippi prior to World War II. Yet they fit none of the stereotypes about country music or the blues. The primary members of the Mississippi Sheiks on recordings were Alonzo (Lonnie) Chatmon and Walter Vinson with other brothers Armenter (Bo) (who recorded as Bo Carter) and Sam Chatmon, with the musicians Charlie McCoy and Eugene Powell at times augmenting the band. Harry Chatmon was also active musically. As the offshoot of a string band that catered to dance audiences and the resort vacation crowds, the Sheiks performed and recorded more country music than any popular country blues recording stars. Their work drew favorable comments from many Mississippi musicians such as Houston Stackhouse and Son House. House even preferred their playing to that of Charley Patton. The Mississippi Sheiks recorded some of the most enduring and widely copied country blues melodies of the prewar period. Each of the members was steeped in old-time country music and their music occasionally was marketed to white audiences in the Hill Billy series. While the Sheiks' tunes transcribed in this book were not widely played by white fiddlers, they are in the format for, and would have been played for, country dances.

The professionalism of the Mississippi Sheiks, as well as the group's affinity for country music, reflects the guiding influence of Lonnie Chatmon. His fiddle playing shaped their sound while his opportunism paved the way for their success. In later interviews, Vinson offered fantastic tales of Lonnie's musicianship: "He didn't make no mistakes; he didn't play no discords ... he was just a violin player. Got the record all the way through Mississippi ... as the best violin-player." The breadth of their repertoire, the reliable standards of musicianship, and the varied use of keys and rhythms was how the Sheiks caught the interest of their audience and sustained it. The songs "Jailbird Love Song" and "Yodeling Fiddling Blues" were no doubt influenced by the work of Meridian native Jimmie Rodgers. Hokum blues such as "Shake Hands and Tell Me Goodbye" and "She Ain't No Good" (also done by Charlie McCoy) were obvious crowd favorites.

Utilizing liner notes, interviews, government documents, newspapers, and conducting field research in the town of Bolton, Mississippi, this essay centers on Lonnie Chatmon. It also details the experiences, history of the Chatmon family, the Mississippi Sheiks, Henderson and Harry Chatmon, and a prodigious young musician by the name of Charlie McCoy. Through growing up on a farm near the small town of Bolton, marrying an older woman with several

OKeh Records advertisement.

Brunswick Records advertisement.

Brunswick Records advertisement, February 15, 1930.

children, settling down to farming near Vicksburg, playing in a hotel orchestra in Jackson, recording for OKeh Records in Atlanta, and operating a café in Glen Allan, Mississippi, Lonnie Chatmon was the brother that everyone looked to for leadership. As the leader of the Mississippi Sheiks, he had the foresight to recruit a pair of talented accompanists, Charlie McCoy and Walter Vinson, whose prodigious abilities and broad repertoires included blues, popular music, ballads, and old-time tunes.

Drawing on previously undiscovered interviews with Lonnie Chatmon's older sister and younger

T. DeWayne Moore

brother, Josie and Larry Chatmon, we now know that McCoy and Vinson developed their talents initially under the tutelage of fiddler and pianist Harry Chatmon, the youngest son of Henderson and Eliza Chatmon, whom the duo backed in a string band in the late 1920s. Moreover, we conclude that the fiddler heard in the recordings of Alec Johnson and Chatmon's Mississippi Hot Footers is not Bo Carter, as previously believed, but rather Harry Chatmon, who remained employed as a musician in a hotel orchestra in Jackson throughout the Great Depression. The influence of Harry Chatmon on the music of the younger musicians, as well as Lonnie's ability to recruit them away from his youngest brother, set the stage for the recording of all the Sheiks tunes transcribed in this book. While the decisions of record companies to limit African American artists to the blues seems to have dictated the nature of their releases after 1930, the diverse musical offerings of the Sheiks and their cohorts prior to 1931 demonstrate the sort of dynamic and rich musical traditions that developed in African American string bands in Mississippi.

Ralph Lembo and the birth of the Mississippi Sheiks

The broad repertoire of the Mississippi Sheiks beyond blues may have been due to Lonnie Chatmon and Walter Vinson's experience of performing in Itta Bena for Ralph Lembo, an Italian American record store proprietor and talent scout. Lembo's influence on the course of popular music was at its height in the late 1920s. Lembo had recently auditioned Lonnie's brother Bo Carter (Armenter Chatmon) and sent him to record in New Orleans, a discovery that led to the Mississippi Sheiks.[1] Lembo probably heard about the excellent fiddle-playing musicians in the Chatmon family from Bo Carter or Charlie McCoy.

Toward the end of the year, he offered to pay a couple of the songsters ten dollars each to come play one evening at his store in Itta Bena. In the late 1920s, almost any of the Chatmons could have entertained a crowd to much satisfaction in Itta

Bena, but Lembo wanted the fiddle of Lonnie Chatmon, who had recently decided to tour around the Delta with a talented local musician, Walter Vinson. Vinson had made a name for himself among the musicians living near Bolton, and he caught the attention of Lonnie Chatmon around the same time of the invitation to perform in Itta Bena. According to Vinson, Lonnie simply approached him one day and declared, "I want you to play with me." Chatmon wanted a skilled accompanist on his upcoming tour through the Delta. He wanted to make as much money as possible. Although he did not know it yet, he made an excellent decision in recruiting Vinson as the other member of the Mississippi Sheiks.

Lonnie Chatmon also made a pivotal decision "to play for this fellow [who] was running a furniture store" in Itta Bena.[2] From February 1927 to the winter of 1930, Itta Bena merchant and Italian immigrant Ralph Lembo "was responsible for virtually all the recordings of the early Delta Blues."[3] Lembo discovered Charley Patton, Bo Carter, Rubin Lacy, the Graves Brothers, the Mississippi Sheiks, and Booker Washington (Bukka) White, and perhaps others. He also invited several artists to perform at one of his three stores, including Blind Lemon Jefferson, Jim Jackson, and Mississippi John Hurt. In the late 1920s, the small Delta town of Itta Bena became sort of a magical locus for a host of talented African American recording artists.[4]

Walter Vinson claimed that he composed the famous "Sitting on Top of the World" on the morning after they played a white dance in Greenwood, while they were en route to Itta Bena. He believed that the song would be a "sure success" after an African American walking by the two men heard it and immediately placed nineteen dollars into the tip bucket. Having only just then come up with the song, he must have felt so great that he hollered out, "I'm sitting on top of the world!" This was the type of song that piqued the interest of Ralph Lembo, and he recognized the songwriting talent and broad repertoire of the string band duo.[5] Vinson explained it:

> So I went down to Itta Bena to play for this fellow who was running a furniture store. He paid us ten

dollars apiece to play for two and half hours for him. Lonnie said to me, "See boy, we can get ten dollars apiece everywhere they go play." I liked that ten dollars for a couple of hours. So this fellow in Itta Bena wrote to P. C. Brockman in Atlanta, Georgia. He got in touch with Polk Brockman, and he wanted us to come to San Antonio to do some recording. Lonnie said, "How many records you want us to make?" Brockman said, "You all can make me two or three dozen." Lonnie said, "How much will that pay?" [Brockman] said, "How much do you want?" "For three dozen records," Walter Vinson declared, "I want a thousand dollars a day." Brockman said, "Well, we will pay you that."[6]

In February 1930, Lembo sent Lonnie Chatmon and Walter Vinson to what turned out to be the most important recording session of their career. At the session for OKeh Records in Shreveport, Louisiana, Atlanta-based talent scout Polk Brockman set up the equipment. Vinson and Chatmon walked right up and presented themselves to him. Polk Brockman requested that they come up with a "fancy" name for the band. In tribute to the pop hit "Sheik of Araby," someone suggested "The Mississippi Sheiks." And thus the Sheiks were born. This was the February 17, 1930, session in which "Sitting on Top of the World" (403806-A) was recorded and paired for release with "Lonely One in this Town" (403806-B).[7] Other songs from this session also became big hits: "Stop and Listen," and "Alberta Blues." For this very successful and profitable session, the Sheiks recorded a total of eight sides that were later released on the OKeh label.[8]

The session also solidified the association of Lonnie Chatmon and Walter Vinson. In fact, it became "so cliquish" that they addressed each other as "Bruno" and referred to other musicians as "Doc." Sam Chatmon recalled how the duo often had issues between them, but the problems outside of music were never enough to break up their musical partnership. "Sometimes their pants would get a little thing behind 'em," Sam stated, "but still they'd stay together."[9] Walter felt his singing made him indispensable to Lonnie, but he valued Lonnie's violin so highly that he silently suffered

his partner's habit of surreptitiously pocketing the tips he collected at their performances.

The Recordings of the Mississippi Sheiks

Prior to World War II, record companies recorded relatively few Black string bands for either their series of race or hillbilly records, often operating under the assumption that this older African American string-band music had little commercial appeal or that blues and gospel records sold better to African American audiences, or both. Charles Wolfe, a string band scholar, estimated that record companies released only fifty records of prewar Black string-band music, while releasing about twenty thousand records of blues and gospel music. Though Wolfe's figures are certainly too low, the number of prewar commercial recordings of Black string-band music is still small even if we count all fiddle-based bands, including duos, trios, and jug bands. That puts us at five hundred records, and the actual number may be closer to one thousand. Wolfe's point, however, is an important one: as a result of A&R men's aesthetic and commercial considerations, African American string bands were greatly underrepresented on prewar commercial phonograph recordings, which makes the handful of surviving performances of these neglected bands on hillbilly records valuable for understanding a once flourishing African American musical

Bo Carter, Lonnie Chatmon, Walter Vinson. Photo courtesy Document Records, UK.

tradition. Not only are their recorded performances important but so are the historical context of their lives, recording sessions, live performances, homes, occupations, births, and deaths.[10]

One student of the Sheiks has recently argued that we will never know how many African American string bands were not recorded. "From this historical distance and without much evidence to go on," he complains, "we cannot know" much more about African American musicians, the attitudes of A&R men toward them, and the extent to which these attitudes shaped the careers of the musicians. In 2019 the growing number of digitally archived documents available online for researchers hold precious bits of information that have the power to end these silences, put names to recordings, empower these forgotten figures from the American past and tell their stories.

The Sheiks had their busiest year of recording sessions in 1930. After the first session in Shreveport in February, they had a summer session in San Antonio. Bo took his brothers Sam and Lonnie Chatmon to San Antonio, Texas, in June 1930 to record for OKeh Records. On June 9, Bo and Sam recorded behind Texas Alexander as the Mississippi Sheiks. The next day, Bo and Lonnie Chatmon recorded behind Walter Vinson on several sides, including "Sheiks Special," issued as "Walter Jacobs and the Carter Brothers." Later that day, Bo was the featured artist, accompanied by Sam. Although the first title indicates only two performers in the title, "We Are Both Feeling Good Right Now," Lonnie and Walter Vinson may have been present for some sides. The OKeh files give "Bo Carter" as performer credit for most titles, and Bo uses his steel-bodied National style N guitar on June 12, 1930, when, still at San Antonio, Bo and Sam recorded for OKeh as the "Mississippi Sheiks." The two Chatmon brothers possessed "almost a country and western purity in their singing," according to Samuel Charters, "and pieces like 'Jail Bird Love Song,' sung as a duet, were very effective in their imitation of white singing and accompaniment style."[11] The records from this session demonstrate the dynamic abilities of Bo Carter to not only reach his audience through erotic symbolism but also appeal to white hillbilly audiences.

This book contains transcriptions of "The Sheik Waltz" and "The Jazz Fiddler" from the February 17 OKeh session in Shreveport; "Sheiks Special," "Mississippi Lowdown," and "That's It" from the June 10 session in San Antonio; and "Jackson Stomp," "Alma Waltz (Ruby Waltz)," "Vicksburg Stomp," "Sunset Waltz," "The Farewell Waltz," and "Morning Glory Waltz" from the December sessions in Jackson at the King Edward Hotel.

For the recording sessions of the Sheiks, the song arrangements of each recorded side had been pre-designed by Lonnie and rehearsed in live settings. "He'd teach him [Walter] his chords," Sam recalled. Lonnie would "tell 'em what note to make, if it wasn't right he'd tell him . . . [might] sit down with Walter and all but put Walter's hands on the strings." Vinson proved an adept pupil, however, and he learned Lonnie's method of sight-reading. Vinson somewhat idealized the violin as "the king of string instruments," which partly led him to conceive of his role as secondary. He felt obliged to strum most of his accompaniments, and he never even attempted to back him up on the mandolin, an instrument he played proficiently yet regarded as a redundant lead. Vinson claimed to have taught mandolin to Charlie McCoy at some point.

The characteristic sound of Lonnie's fiddle playing and Walter Vinson's vocals and guitar mark the Sheiks' recordings in the Edwards Hotel in December 1930. The duo recorded more than fifteen tunes on December 15 and 19.[12] Bo is most likely playing guitar behind Charlie McCoy on December 15 and 16, and Bo recorded his first sides under his nom de plume Bo Carter on December 15 as well. Walter Vinson was second vocalist for two sides, but Walter did not play guitar for the Bo Carter sides.

Charlie McCoy showcased his mandolin work on the recordings as the "Mississippi Mud Steppers" in Jackson at the King Edward. After this session, the record companies never again released any of the recordings of the Sheiks in their hillbilly series. All these sides were released in the white hillbilly series, and you will find each one of them transcribed in this book.

"Jackson Stomp" was based on Cow Cow Davenport's "Cow Cow Blues." McCoy even recorded it again at the same session, adding a vocal part and calling it "That Lonesome Train Took My Baby Away." The song is a dazzling, virtuoso mandolin performance. McCoy further showcases his versatility on a trio of waltzes, playing mandolin on "Alma Waltz (Ruby Waltz)" and banjo on two other numbers. The various waltzes that McCoy and Vinson recorded are both highly technically proficient and unusual.

On the same day, McCoy proved his versatility by singing the sentimental "Always in Love with You" and "I've Been Blue Ever Since You Went Away." Charlie McCoy sang two duets with Bo Carter on December 19, 1930. "The Northern Starvers Are Returning Home" and "Mississippi I'm Longing for You" were both extraordinary songs (utilizing the melody of "Corinne Corinna") intended to invoke homesickness through the theme of northern migration.

Neither I nor Australian blues chronicler Bob Eagle can locate Charlie McCoy in the 1930 Census. His brother Wilber "Joe" McCoy appears, working as a musician in a "dance orchestra" at Ward 11 in Memphis, where he lives with his wife "Memphis" Minnie, his mother Alice, and his older sister Bessie.[13] He may have already been taking part in the Great Migration in 1931. In January he recorded for Brunswick in Chicago as one of the Mississippi Blacksnakes. Early in 1932, he turns up in New York, recording for Vocalion a catchy, if melancholy, little song called "Too Long." The Mississippi Sheiks had recorded it about four months earlier, but it sounds more characteristic of Charlie McCoy, whose voice, by this time, had lost its sharp edges and acquired the characteristic vocal inflections of a Depression-era blues singer.

For the OKeh session in Atlanta on October 25 and 26, 1931, Lonnie is the fiddler on Bo's recording of "Baby, How Can It Be?" as well as the recordings cut under the name Mississippi Sheiks at that two-day session, which feature Walter Vinson on guitar. Bo is the singer and guitarist who recorded the song "I Want You to Know," which guitar instructor Woody Mann argues is "the most sophisticated song found" in a collection of tunes he compiles and examines by *Six Early Blues Roots Guitarists*.[14]

On some sides, Vinson ignored his straitjacketed role and his fingerpicked guitar parts shine brightly. "The World Is Going Wrong" features some fine picking in G with variations such as the stunning double-time, syncopated run in G at the end of each verse or the way he rolls up the G note in the bass. These songs work out to ten bars, including the bridge, which includes the true resolution of the verse line. Vinson's playing technically resembled that of Charlie McCoy, who also recorded the song.

In "I've Got Blood in My Eye," Vinson plays in F, a key engaged with by only experienced guitarists. Most of his accompaniment is straight up. In the break, however, he shows a high degree of imaginative flat-picking and the stunning double-time fiddling of Lonnie Chatmon is somewhat unusual. The origins of songs such as "Please Baby" and "Honey Babe Let the Deal Go Down" may have their origins in popular music. "Stop and Listen No. 2" is very similar to Tommy Johnson's "Big Road Blues," but contains more variation in its guitar part. The song is one of the most recorded themes in the blues, and the blending of Vinson's guitar and Chatmon's fiddle represents the Sheiks at their finest. Vinson's lyrical display is especially expressive in this version of the song. No strangers to sexual themes, the Sheiks may have been inspired by Bo Carter and attempted to capture some of his randy essence in the song "Ramrod Blues."

Lonnie Chatmon and Walter Vinson recorded sixteen sides in Grafton, Wisconsin, in 1932 as the Mississippi Sheiks for Paramount Records. An unknown pianist plays on "I'll Be Long Gone." The Sheiks may have been present when the young white men of Edwards, Mississippi, hosted a dance on July 31, 1932, and the performance of "Chatmon's orchestra" may have been led by Harry Chatmon. Scholars previously estimated that the Paramount sessions had occurred in July, which would have meant the Sheiks had only recently returned in time for their performance.[15] The recent discovery of the session cards, in the John Steiner Collection at the University of Chicago, confirms that Lonnie Chatmon and Walter Vinson were the composers of the music as well as the performers on the records of the Sheiks.[16]

Left to right, seated: Liza, Henderson, Lula, Armenter (Bo), and Lonnie Chatmon. Standing: Irene, Willie, and Ferdinand Chatmon. The two boys, standing, are Larry and Sam Chatmon, ca. 1910.

The Mississippi Sheiks waxed their final sides for OKeh Records in Chicago in June 1933, but only one record was ever released from that session. Sam Chatmon accompanied the Sheiks on a trip to Chicago but did not join the group in the studio. The additional musicians, he explained, came along to fill out the sound for the live shows that filled their time on the way up to Chicago and on the way back to Mississippi.[17]

Lonnie Chatmon recorded twelve sides for Bluebird in San Antonio, Texas, in March 1934.[18] He plays fiddle along with Walter Vinson on second guitar and his brother Bo singing and playing guitar. The Sheiks recycled "Corrine Corrina" in the song "Sweet Maggie," replacing the name of the woman and keeping the melody. The original recording of "Queen Bee" was almost certainly the inspiration for the similarly titled song of John Lee Hooker.

Bo recorded twelve sides in New Orleans on January 19, 1935, with his pianist brother Harry Chatmon. The sides recorded by the Mississippi Sheiks at that session were the last to feature the group under that name. Bo is probably the guitarist who backs Harry "Carter" Chatmon at that session, and Bo may have also been the guitarist for the sides

recorded by Harry Chatmon at Jackson in October 1935 for Vocalion 03143.

"When we went to make the records in Jackson," Bo shared with Paul Oliver, "the engineer apparently overstepped his technical role in the session in trying to show the musicians how to 'stop and start the records.'" He tried "to tell us when we got to begin and how we got to end," Bo asserted, "and you know, I started not to make 'em!" We "traveled all over and we made records and we played just about anywhere you could name," he reasoned, "so how could he tell me how to stop and start the song?" The session proved to be the last for Harry Chatmon, who continued to support himself and his wife Neurlee as a musician in an orchestra in Jackson.

Bo returned to New Orleans in February 1936 to record for Bluebird Records. At the St. Charles Hotel in October 1936, he took part in an amazing session, the first part of which featured the Chatmon brothers, Lonnie and Sam, but not Bo, with assistance on guitar from Eugene Powell, of Greenville. Sam and Lonnie recorded twelve songs, of which Bluebird released ten. Each of the ten songs sounds like Lonnie Chatmon only slowed down a little, dragging. The next twenty-one sides feature a second guitarist named Willie Harris Jr. and the session workhorse Eugene Powell.

Henderson Chatmon (ca. 1851–1934), the Musical Patriarch of the Chatmon Family

The Chatmon family was a large group of talented instrumentalists, many of whom possessed the type of creativity and versatility from which a new form of music emerged in the Black communities at the turn of the twentieth-century South. Henderson Chatmon fathered twenty-four children in and out of wedlock and many of them developed into fine musicians.

The Hinds County plantation of Colonel M. L. Cook served as the antebellum setting for the Chatmon family story.[19] Nancy (b. 1831) and Polk Chapman (b. 1832) were enslaved and living on the Cook farm when they conceived Henderson Chatmon in 1849.[20] Several slave owners in Hinds County were named Chatmon, which makes it difficult to discern the identity of the genesis of the family's last name. After the birth of Henderson, Polk Chatmon was sold to another slave owner, and he ended up around Newton in Scott County after emancipation. Henderson's mother was named Nancy, and she married the much older John Perry after emancipation, but she did not live to an advanced age. John and Nancy lived in the household of Ben and Rose Hennington in Hinds County in 1870.[21] By 1880 John had passed and Nancy lived in Bolton with her two youngest children.[22]

Both Polk and Henderson Chatmon served in the Confederate Army in some capacity during the Civil War. In a 1978 interview for Worth Long and Alan Lomax in *The Land Where the Blues Began*, Sam recalled his father talking about the high number of casualties. The bodies of the dead were piled up in the creeks "until they could drive their wagons on across." This sobering recollection only made sense in the vicinity of a major battle. The Union army scored a decisive victory about four miles west of Bolton in mid-May 1863. The Battle of Champions Hill made it into the *Personal Memoirs* of General Ulysses S. Grant, who claimed to have seen "his enemy mowed down by the thousand, or the ten thousand."[23] Though the number of casualities at the battle did not reach as high as ten thousand, an estimated eight hundred men died and several thousand more were wounded or missing.[24]

Just as Grant tended to embellish in his memoirs, Sam Chatmon often stretched the truth in his later interviews. In several interviews, Sam claimed that his father "worked in the field [and] played music in slavery time," but his father was not yet a teenager when the war broke out. In the film *The Land Where the Blues Began*, Sam claims that his father "and old man Milton Bracey were the fiddle players."[25] Born around 1829, Milton Bracey had fled his owner's farm south of Jackson in Lawrence County to enlist in the United States Colored Troops at Vicksburg in early 1865.[26] By 1870 he had moved to Hinds County, gotten married, and had several children; he continued living in the area until at least 1910.[27] It is unlikely that Bracey had known Henderson Chatmon before he moved to Bolton. Sam likely knew the elder fiddler and may have even played music with him as a youth, but it's doubtful that his father, Henderson, played with Bracey during "slavery times."

Henderson appears in the household of Polk Chapman in Beat 5 of Scott County, located east of the state capital, in 1870.[28] This "Polk Chapman" ranks in and ranks out as a "musician" in Company C of the 46th Regiment of the Mississippi Infantry.[29] While many of the enslaved accompanied their masters as body servants during the conflict, none of them were included in the enlistment rolls. The desperation enrollment of slaves would not have included musicians. The fact that he served as a "musician" supports the idea that he was the musical genesis of the Chatmon family, but his enlistment on the side of the Confederacy suggests that he enjoyed a status above that of an enslaved body servant. Indeed, it suggests he was not Black at all, and therefore, not the man identified in the 1870 census that had named his two children, born in the wake of emancipation, after the most popular and brutally effective generals in the Union Army. Sherman and Grant Chapman were five and three years old, respectively.[30]

T. DeWayne Moore

Regardless of this most peculiar recording of his service, the Black heads of household in 1870 were part of a million enslaved Blacks sold into the flourishing domestic slave trade, which, according to historian Steven Deyle, not only contributed greatly to the emergence of the deep South, but also exacerbated tensions between the upper and lower South and helped push the country toward Civil War.[31] The speculators and traders who dominated the interregional slave traffic between the upper and lower South were practical and likely motivated overwhelmingly by economic concerns when sending him from his Virginia home to the cotton fields of Mississippi. The internal trade in human property led to the creation of the Cotton Kingdom and contributed to its eventual demise, as the enslaved had simply become too valuable to surrender for the South.[32]

Sam claimed to remember that his grandmother, Nancy Perry, had lived over one hundred years. Henderson's mother was indeed named Nancy, and she married the much older John Perry after emancipation, but she did not live for more than one hundred years. Both of them lived in the household of Ben and Rose Hennington in Hinds County in 1870.[33] By 1880 her husband had passed and she lived in Bolton with her two youngest children.[34] The 1880 census listed Henderson Chatmon as being twenty-nine years old and married to a twenty-five-year-old woman named Mary Simmons. The emancipated couple lived at Beat 2 in the Bolton precinct of Hinds County. His younger brother Grant also lived with them.[35] Henderson and Mary Chatmon had seven children in total, with three sons; Ferdinand, age five, Fleming, four, and Henderson Jr., two; and four daughters, Gina, seven, Molly three, Elise, one, and the infant Lena.

Sometime after 1881, Henderson's first wife Mary Simmons passed away. Henderson married his widow's niece, Eliza Jackson, on August 18, 1886. Eliza Jackson had been born around 1863 to Daniel and Creasy Jackson, with whom she lived in Bolton in 1870.[36] Eliza may have learned to play the guitar while growing up around Bolton, possibly developing her musical skills after Henderson and Mary moved there in the 1870s.[37] According to Josie Williams, Eliza Jackson was "the mother of nine boys and three girls, and every one of them was a musician."

Sam Chatmon referred to several deaths in the family between 1936 and 1938, but we have found no evidence to support this claim. Chatmon family researcher Ed Payne located Sam's death certificate in 2016. Henderson Chatmon passed on July 21, 1934.[38] His daughter Josie Moore is the informant listed on his death certificate. She told researcher Michael Beebie that her father died a pauper. Though Sam was not there at the end, he considered his father to have been a rich man. "He has always been well off, but the thing about it, he always did rent land; he never did buy. If he would have bought, he would have owned his own house."[39] According to Josie:

> Gaddis offered to sell him the place and he wouldn't buy it. And we could have paid for it in two years, because land wasn't but ten dollars an acre then. Papa–I begged him hard, after I got grown I begged him hard to buy that tract of land. Oh, it was a big place though. It had plenty of cows on it, big pasture. And he wouldn't buy nothing. We begged him. He wouldn't have died a pauper.[40]

Henderson had to move off the farm late in life. In 1930, when Henderson and Eliza lived in Jackson, the city directory listed his occupation as "musician." The remains of Henderson Chatmon were buried in Bolton Cemetery on July 24, 1934.

In 1930 several members of the Chatmon family played together in a hotel orchestra in Jackson. Both the city directory and the census recorded Lonnie and Clementine Chatmon living on Pascagoula Street at that time. In April, the census recorded Lonnie and his wife Clementine, their daughter Ruby Bell, and the children by her previous marriage, Alex, Lithania, and Queenie, as living in Jackson. Lonnie worked as a musician in a "hotel orchestra." Bert Chatmon tried his hand at playing professionally in Jackson in 1930. Henderson and Eliza Chatmon also lived in Jackson and worked as musicians. Ishmon Bracey lived in Jackson and worked as a musician in a "hotel orchestra." Bracey and the

Chatmons may have been playing in the Edwards Hotel Orchestra, which performed on the radio as well as live at the hotel. The leader of the orchestra, Mrs. H. H. Hutcherson, was the best violinist in the state, and, according to the *Clarion-Ledger*, "These musicians were always ready to give the audience any preferred number and make a feature of the very latest in all hits, and [they] are proving very popular and an invaluable acquisition."[41]

The fiddle remained the instrument at the center of various other conglomerations of the Chatman family band. Lamar (Bert), Larry, and Harry Chatmon performed with two guitars and a fiddle in Jackson during the 1940s. In Nitta Yuma, Larry played with Edgar (Med) Chatmon, and Bo got together with Harry and Edgar to perform for children in the town of Anguilla in the 1950s. In fact, this author discovered a few photographs from one such performance of Bo Carter. Edgar Chatmon is the fiddler performing with his brother.[42]

After Henderson's death, Eliza Chatmon had to move back to Jackson and live with her daughter, Josie.[43] In fact, as late as 1945 she is listed in the Jackson City Directory, living at 235 Fairbanks. While we have evidence of Harry Chatmon's existence in the 1940s, we lose track of all the Chatmons at that point. All their deaths would have been after 1945.

Henderson Chatmon and Charley Patton

The unproven and highly questionable claim that Henderson Chatmon was the father of Charley Patton—as opposed to Bill Patton—was disseminated in John Fahey's 1970 biography *Charley Patton*, the blues book that perhaps best reveals how ignorance about African American history and the Black experience in America is often a breeding ground for racial prejudice.[44] Based on the claims of Sam Chatmon, who he believed primarily due to his almost pale complexion, Fahey writes: "Charley Patton was the son of Henderson Chatmon . . . and Anney [sic] Patton . . . and was born . . . in the late 1880s. Since Henderson Chatmon was born of a mixed union, and had very little Black blood, Charley was evidently of primarily white and Indian

descent."[45] This was the first time that Sam Chatmon had claimed Patton as his brother, and it happened to be for Patton's naive and gushing biographer.

Sam never mentioned Patton in any of his earlier interviews. He also never revealed this information to a graduate student named Michael Beebie later in the 1970s. In his master's thesis, which contains his interview with Sam's oldest sister Josie (Chatmon) Williams, Beebie learned that Henderson Chatmon was the father of twenty-four children during his lifetime. He had seven children in his first marriage to Molly Simmons and twelve children in his second marriage to Eliza Jackson. "In addition to these children," Beebie writes, "Henderson was the father of *outside* children whose mothers were *outside* wives, i.e., wives outside of wedlock, a social arrangement which the informants said was not uncommon in their youth."[46] Sam had told Fahey the same thing—that "morals were much relaxed in those days" and his father had many "outside women and nobody seemed to mind"—in support of his claim that he was the brother of Patton. In the later interview with Michael Beebie, however, he never mentions Patton.

Though Sam and Josie both admit that their father sometimes had affairs with other women, he might not have been married at the time of Charley Patton's conception. His first wife died either during or after the birth of their last child Molly in 1885, and Henderson married Eliza Jackson at the courthouse in Raymond on August 18, 1886. He may not have needed an outside wife.

The most compelling evidence against Henderson Chatmon being the father of Charley Patton is the marriage of Bill and Annie Patton. The couple received their marriage license on December 5, 1882. While it might have been more acceptable for Henderson Chatmon to have affairs with other women and return to his wife, it is unlikely that the same was true of married women. Annie Patton would have had to have an affair around the same time that Henderson was between marriages, but since she remained married to Bill Patton, and the couple had children before and after their son Charlie, it's doubtful that Sam Chatmon told the truth to John Fahey about being his blood brother.

T. DeWayne Moore

Children of Molly Simmons	Instruments	Births/Deaths
Gina		b. 1873
Ferdinand (Bud)		b. 1875
Ezell (Fleming)	cornet	b. 1876
Henderson Jr. (Sonny)		b. 1878
Lena		b. 1879
Elise		b. 1881
Molly (Babe)		b. 1885
Children of Eliza Jackson	**Instruments**	**Births/Deaths**
Charlie	mandolin, guitar	
Josie	guitar, bass	1887–1975
Lonnie	violin	b. 1887
Edgar "Med"	mandolin, violin, tenor banjo, guitar, vocals	
Irene "Schul"		b. 1892
Armenter "Bo"	guitar, vocals, tenor banjo, clarinet, bass	b. 1894
Willie "Crook"	guitar, vocals	1895–1918 (died in farm accident)
Lamar "Bert"	guitar	b. 1897
Vivian "Sam"	bass, tenor banjo, guitar, vocals	b. 1899
Larry "Pootchie"	guitar, drums	b. 1902
Harry "Tie"	harp, piano, mandolin, violin	b. 1904
Susanna		died as an infant

Alonzo "Lonnie" Chatmon (1887–1950) and Walter Vinson (ca. 1901–1975)

"Lonnie" Chatmon was born to Henderson Chatmon and Eliza Jackson on February 21, 1887.[47] He was originally thought to have been born in the early 1890s, but a more complete and a more discerning look into his family history reveals that he was a little older. The 1900 Census lists "Launie" as born in June 1888. The 1920 Census claims he was born in 1886. The 1930 Census listed him as born in 1894. The 1940 Census claims that he was born in 1888. His World War I registration card suggests that he was born as early as February 21, 1884, and, considering that his older stepbrother Ferdinand was probably born around 1875, Lonnie was probably a bit older

than previously believed, making him about the same age as Charley Patton.

Lonnie was an engaging figure whose leadership ability earned him respect from the record companies. Blues writer Stephen Calt claimed that his blustering manner earned him the family nickname "Big Guff." His father Henderson provided his earliest musical lessons and it is likely that he learned from fiddler Milton Bracey. He learned to read sheet music sometime before World War I from his fiddling brother-in-law, Neil Winston.[48] His sister, Josie Williams, said, "I believe it was Lonnie" who "got the first fiddle and papa know a heap of old-time songs, you know. And that's what Lonnie learned by him. And then he began to take lessons from my brother-in-law."[49] According to Sam Chatmon, he soon surpassed Winston himself and became practically unequaled in country blues. The prestige his sight-reading of music earned him from his untrained brothers and other associates was indicative of his talent.

His ability to read music also gave the Chatmon brothers a competitive advantage over other groups. Lonnie Chatmon specialized in audience requests. His patrons would sometimes give him a copy of the sheet music to their favorite songs, and he bought copies of the current pop tunes at Jackson music stores so that he could always present the most recent music. Lonnie learned to play the blues, waltzes, fox trots, and old-time tunes indiscriminately in a string band made of his brothers and known simply as the "Chatmon Brothers."

In 1913 Lonnie met the love of his life. She was born Clementine Davis to Felix Davis and Dora Rollins Davis around 1882. Josie Williams later referred to her as "Sang." She married George McGee shortly after the turn of the century, and the couple had a son, Alex, in 1905. The 1910 Census places George and Clemy McGee in Beat 4 of Warren County. The couple had another two children, Queen (b. 1910) and Lithania (b. 1911), but Clementine lost her first husband unexpectedly about 1912.

It is not clear how Clementine met Lonnie Chatmon, but the couple received a marriage license at the courthouse in Raymond on August 22, 1913.[50] The newlyweds were not long in Hinds County. As early as 1916, according to Josie Williams, Lonnie and his three younger brothers Edgar, Bo, and Willie moved to William H. Stovall's farm in Coahoma County.[51] Corroborating her memory, the *Hinds County Gazette* listed all four of the brothers as delinquent in paying the poll tax on March 23, 1917.[52] The brothers moved up to Stovall to farm, but "they played music too. And whenever they get a call Mrs. Stovall would never stop them, the white lady of the place. Because they made their arrangement that whenever they get a call they'd have to step out of the field and go."[53]

While staying just outside of Clarksdale, Clementine gave birth to the couple's only child, Ruby Bell, in the spring of 1918.[54] According to his World War I registration card, Lonnie and Clementine lived at Stovall, Mississippi, on September 18, 1918, but the couple left town after the unexpected death of his brother, Willie. Willie was killed in a freak accident involving farm machinery at Stovall. His death provided the next oldest Chatmon brother a chance to fill in for his deceased sibling; Lamar "Bert" Chatmon started to play the guitar.[55]

The 1920 Census found Lonnie and Clementine living at 1606 Court Street in Vicksburg, Mississippi. It was during this time in his life that Lonnie developed his animus for farm labor. Beginning with his marriage to Clementine in 1913, Lonnie Chatmon had settled down to farming. His brother Sam claimed that his oldest brother simply could not stand working on the farm, and he possessed a disdain for the Christian life of an agrarian. Sam believed it was their mutual dislike of farm work that explained Lonnie's collaboration with Vinson: "Lonnie took up with Walter and used him 'cause Walter was just like he was. He didn't wanna work in no field." By Vinson's own recollection, Lonnie pursued music as a livelihood because he "got tired of smellin' mule farts."[56] So Lonnie moved his family back to Hinds County, where he and Walter Vinson set their minds to musical performance. Most of the rest of the Chatmon family never quit farming.

Even though Lonnie Chatmon devoted his energies to music making, he also started to devote more and more of his time inside, and sometimes operating, the rural barrelhouses or "jook" houses. The jook was the place that both provided the foundations on which he built his performance and recording career, and it offered him a chance to pursue his favorite hobbies: gambling and the opposite sex. As Lonnie drifted further and further away from his life as a farmer, he started to demand a larger percentage of the band's earnings. "Lonnie would always think he oughta get the most 'cause he was lead," Sam admitted. "Well, I never did figure that."[57] The rest of the band wanted to evenly split the band's income of four or five dollars per night. According to Walter Vinson, Lonnie's insistence that he get the largest share of the band's earnings resulted in the Chatmon family band's dissolution and the beginning of the Mississippi Sheiks. "Lonnie and them, they fight . . . He got 'em all to playing music,

T. DeWayne Moore

so they'd have to do what *he* said . . . He'd keep the biggest end of the money . . . go play (Georgia) Skin . . . Them fellas, they woke up to their selves, they found out that he was takin' all the money, gamblin' it off, givin' it to his women. . . ."[58] African American folklorist Zora Neale Hurston described a game of Georgia Skin on one of her recorded field trips into the barrelhouses of Florida in the 1940s.[59]

During the early 1920s, as Lonnie started to spend more money and time in the barrelhouse and on other women, his younger brothers started coming into their own as musicians. Sam, Larry, and Harry Chatmon were only a few of the musicians who made up the younger generation of talented instrumentalists who came up in the Pine Hills outside of Jackson. It was the African Americans who came of age at this time that became the dynamic, versatile, and highly skilled professional musicians who suffered the most due to the limited recording opportunities. On occasion, however, as we shall later see with the Mississippi Sheiks, Black musicians made records that the record companies marketed to white audiences.

Walter Vinson, who grew equally adept at the bass fiddle, mandolin, guitar, and violin, did not begin to play with the Chatmons until he was fifteen or sixteen. Born Walter Jacobs in Bolton, perhaps as early as 1901, he was the son of Walter Vinson, Sr. and of Mary Jacobs. He first played guitar at the age of six when his mother's boyfriend, P. G. Hodges, taught him "Shimmy-She-Wobble," a version of a song known to Caldwell Bracey and later recorded by Bo Chatmon as "Old Devil." He also recalled Eddie Johnson and Commodore Johnson, the latter born in 1888, playing around Bolton. Walter's uncles, Vance, Alec, Joe, and Bill Vinson, all played guitar or mandolin and gave him pointers. He also recalled an aunt, Nellie Vinson, who played mandolin. By the time Walter was eight he could net three or four dollars on weekends by serenading Bolton shoppers from a wagon. By around 1919 he had developed his basic blues theme: "Overtime Blues." Although his fingerpicking then rivaled that of Bo Carter, he did not work as a soloist or lead guitarist. Vinson saw his role as providing accompaniment for the unique blues sound of Lonnie's fiddle.

In spite of the recording sessions, performances at resorts, and large parties in the Delta, all of these talented musicians who came up around Bolton worked hard for most of their lives as farmers. "Walter [Vinson] could sing and that carried him," Sam told Michael Beebie, "and he and Lonnie could go everywhere, all through the Delta. And when they came back sometimes they'd have twenty or thirty dollars [but] ain't none of them who made their living by music," not even Lonnie Chatmon. "Lonnie always run the café," he explained, "He'd just play whenever he'd have a job to play. . . . He'd play a night and he'd hardly play until next week sometimes. Along about once maybe twice a week . . . so we was all farming except Lonnie. Lonnie would run a café or a jook house."[60]

Lonnie Chatmon's extramarital interests and gambling habits took their toll on his marriage to Clementine, and the couple split up at some point during his recording career. In the 1930s, he took up with another woman, a widow from Bolton named Phyllis Neely, with whom he moved to the Delta town of Glen Allan. He invested his money in a café. After selling his café, Lonnie left Glen Allan and returned to Bolton, where he continued to operate assorted enterprises (including the management of a fishing spot) until his death. The 1940 Census found a fifty-two-year-old Lonnie Chatmon living with his new wife in Beat 1 of Washington County. At that time, he worked as a "cashier" in a "café." He also received a homestead exemption of fifty dollars in 1942.[61] He suffered from heart trouble in the late 1940s. Having been born in 1887, he would have been in his early sixties at that time. According to his brother Sam, Lonnie blamed his ill health upon the blues: "When I'd go out to see him," Sam recalls, "he says: 'Whenever I get up, if I live to get up, me and you gonna put out nothin' but gospel music . . . I done joined the church and I don't wanna play no more blues.'" But Sam "wasn't lookin' for him to get up."

Lonnie Chatmon, the leader of the most popular African American string band of the pre–World War II era of recording, passed away sometime around 1950. Chatmon family researcher Ed Payne has never found the death certificate of Lonnie

Chatmon, which suggests that he died after 1945. After 1945, the public cannot view death certificates in Mississippi. Without his death certificate to confirm, we suspect that the remains of Lonnie Chatmon were buried in the Black section of Bolton Cemetery, near the remains of his father in the unmarked family plot. On a visit to the cemetery in the summer of 2018, Ed and I found the last trace of evidence that remains to identify the Chatmon family plot. On a long stone coffin marker, a few black plastic letters spell out the name of Ezell Chatmon, the son of Armenter (Bo Carter) Chatmon, or Bo Carter. Though several stone markers surround his long crypt, all the lettering, if it ever existed, has been washed away over the past eighty years. It is likely that the graves of Henderson, Lonnie, and Harry Chatmon are unmarked along the western entrance about a hundred feet on the left in what we believe is the Chatmon family plot.

Henry "Son" Simms

Even though he moved away from Stovall before 1920, Lonnie Chatmon made quite an impression on a couple of slightly younger musicians living in the Friar's Point area. Henry "Son" Simms had been strongly attracted to the "string bands" in his youth, and he learned to play the guitar very well while growing up near Anguilla in Sharkey County. He became well known later in Farrell for his performances of "Bill Bailey," "Spoonful," and "The Bully of This Town," and he taught a young McKinley Morganfield the rudiments of guitar playing. Simms never had thought much about playing the violin, however, until the arrival of two fiddlers, Lonnie Chatmon and Rand Smith, in Coahoma County during World War I. According to folklorist John W. Work III, Simms was so enthralled with the instrument "that he forsook the guitar for it."[62] Lonnie Chatmon "taught him to play the fiddle" at Stovall, and he made a deep impression on Simms, who remained dedicated to his new instrument.

With few playing models to follow, he developed an individual performance style that consisted largely of bowed tremolos, trills, and counterpoint to the melodies of accompanying instruments. Work maintained that the fiddle, in the hand of Simms, was not a solo instrument, nor did it carry the melody, its usual function in folk music. Regardless of his unusual style, Simms recorded with Charley Patton in 1930. He also accompanied McKinley "Muddy Waters" Morganfield in 1941 during the historic 1941–42 Library of Congress/Fisk University expedition.

Indeed, African American fiddlers such as Henry Simms offered a rich variety of technique and material on early phonograph records. While record label owner Marshall Wyatt claims that "many share stylistic traits that distinguish their music from that of white performers," he also asserts "it would be a mistake to pigeonhole Black and white fiddling styles, especially considering the long history of musical exchanges between the races."[63] The approach of African American fiddlers, in his opinion, is strongly rhythmic, with a penchant for improvisation and variation of the melody. The fiddle was often used to paraphrase their voices, echoing the nuances of the singer with flexible phrasing and shifting tones. African American fiddlers, he opined, eschew rote performance and engage spontaneously in repartee with colleagues and listeners during a performance. These tendencies can be heard on the early recordings of Delta blues accompanist Henry Simms and polished jazz fiddler Leroy Pickett. Wyatt emphasizes, however, that fiddlers such as Jim Booker, of Kentucky, recorded the same sort of hoedown music as his white contemporaries.

The early recording career of Charlie McCoy demonstrates the broad and dynamic repertoires of African American musicians in the pre–World War II period. The prodigious young guitar and mandolin player played in as many as fifty, possibly as many as a hundred, recording sessions between 1928 and 1944, making him one of the most prolific accompanists in the history of the recording industry. Transcriptions of all of his recordings with the Mississippi Mud Steppers, an offshoot of the Mississippi Sheiks, are included in this book.

Charlie's grandfather, Anderson McCoy, was born in slavery around 1840 in Alabama. In 1863

Charlie McCoy. Photo courtesy Frog Records, UK.

Anderson McCoy fled his master's home and enlisted in the Union Army, according to the 1890 Veterans Schedules.[64] He served for an estimated four years, and within a year of his discharge, he married Eliza Jordan at Bolton. In 1873 the couple gave birth to their third son, Pat McCoy, who, at the age of twenty-three, married a local girl named Alice McCoy, the mother of Charlie McCoy.

The 1900 Census entries for the 58th enumeration district contained the family of Charley Patton, Pat and Alice McCoy, the parents of Charlie and Joe McCoy, Henry Sloan, the mentor of Charley Patton, and the family of Henderson Chatmon. Though Pat and Alice McCoy moved to Jackson sometime before 1907, according to the city directory, they had left the city by the time Alice gave birth to their youngest son. Perhaps it was the death of his father Anderson McCoy, who had always lived near Raymond in Beat 4, that impelled the exodus from Jackson back out to the farm. Charlie McCoy had not yet been born at the time of the 1910 census.[65] At that time, Pat and Alice McCoy lived in Beat 4 of Hinds County near Raymond

with their other children, including six-year-old Wilbur (Joe) McCoy.

Born between 1910 and 1912, Charlie McCoy grew up near the small town of Raymond, not Jackson as previously thought. His father no longer lived with the family in 1920, but Charlie is listed in the household with his mother and siblings living in Beat 4, not far at all from that hotbed of musical activity in Bolton. Pat McCoy remained married to Alice, but he had taken a job working for the railroad as a section hand in Vicksburg.

Charlie found a certain kinship as well as his earliest and most salient influence as a musician in the persona of the youngest son of Henderson Chatmon, Harry, who Sam later claimed was the best musician of all his brothers on the fiddle. According to Michael Beebie's unpublished master's thesis, Harry trained Charlie McCoy to sing and play accompaniment on mandolin and guitar. "But he took him and trained him," exclaimed Sam, "Just like my brother Harry . . . took Charlie McCoy and trained him. He played the violin and Charlie played the guitar."[66]

Charlie McCoy grew into the role of a professional musician at a very young age, and he even started to perform with the Chatmon family band at local parties and other events. According to Sam's older sister, Josie (Williams) Chatmon: "I know you heard of this Wells, Cooper's Wells. A health resort near Bolton famed for its mineral waters. Well they played out there every season. Not all of them. It was four of them play out there regular. Lonnie, Bo, Lamar, Sam, and no, it was another boy who came in there. Charlie McCoy. Charlie McCoy played the guitar with them at Cooper's Wells." According to Stephen Calt in a letter to Michael Beebie, Charlie and Joe McCoy moved to Jackson and started playing with Harry Chatmon. Harry, who played violin when he fronted this group, introduced Charlie to the mandolin and showed Joe how to be an accompanist.[67]

Harry Chatmon taught McCoy the music that he had learned from his musician brothers and sisters. At the same time that he was learning to play mandolin in the string band of Harry Chatmon, blues musician Rubin Lacy maintained, Charlie followed me just like I was his daddy until he learned how to play. . . . I believe that Charlie got to be a better musician than I was. He was young, but he got to be about the best musician in our band, Charlie McCoy. He was wonderful. He could play anything pretty well you sing. He couldn't sing, but anything you sing he could play. He learned right under me, followed me from a little boy, me and I'd say Son Spand around Jackson. His mother and daddy wouldn't know where he was part of the time. He'd be with us. Every time I'd put my guitar down or Son would put the mandolin down, he'd grab it. And I mean he wasn't long learning. He was as good as I ever want to see.[68]

In Jackson, Charlie McCoy found a host of musical influences in the personas of Tommy Johnson, Rubin Lacy, Ishmon Bracey, Son Spand, and other players. According to David Evans, "the best musicians knew each other and apparently got along well together. Often they were hired in groups to play at dances, or they would go out on their own 'serenading' on the streets to win money from passersby. They played for white almost as often as for [Black] audiences."[69] McCoy, however, was at least ten years younger than Rubin Lacy, and he was fifteen years younger than Tommy Johnson. Yet he quickly earned the reputation of being Jackson's foremost string musician, equally adept on guitar, banjo, and mandolin.

Indeed, Lacy admitted that for "seconding," Charlie McCoy was the best around. And it was McCoy who, on Ishmon Bracey's recommendation, made the trip to Memphis in February 1928 to accompany Tommy Johnson, Bracey, and Rosie Mae Moore on the session for Victor that produced the magnificent "Big Road Blues," "Cool Drink of Water Blues," "Maggie Campbell Blues," and "Bye Bye Blues." McCoy played superb second guitar behind Johnson. Not only does he duplicate Johnson's guitar part, but as David Evans notes, McCoy "added something of his own playing to the performance. He is using a flat pick and often strums the strings like a mandolin on his bass part, occasionally doing the same on the treble strings as a beautiful contrast."[70] McCoy also played second guitar

behind Ishmon Bracey in a similar fashion on a couple of sides called "Saturday Blues" and "Left Alone Blues," and he provided excellent support of the guitar for the powerful, rough singing voice of Rosie Rae Moore. His debt to the self-proclaimed "Blues King" Rubin Lacy can be heard on her two sides, "School Girl Blues" and "Stranger Blues."

This session produced what Robert Palmer called "the deepest blues," which "had a slippery, danceable swing that derived from his superbly controlled mixing of duple and triple-meter strumming patterns."[71] These songs stand up, in Palmer's opinion, "as the most perfectly realized and most influential blues to have emerged . . . during this period."[72] Indeed, Victor invited Johnson, Bracey, and McCoy back to Memphis in August for another session. Charlie McCoy did not second behind Johnson on this trip for whatever reason, but he did play the mandolin on a couple of tunes with Ishmon Bracey. His subdued performance on the beautiful and somber "Trouble Hearted Blues" stands in bold contrast to the rippling mandolin heard so loud and clear on "Brown Mama Blues."

McCoy followed up on his initial two recording sessions with of a variety of sides between 1928–31. Most of them have him in a string band with Walter Vinson and Bo Carter, but Paul Oliver, in *Songsters and Saints*, contends that Charlie McCoy played with his brother Joe McCoy and Bo Carter on four of six sides at the recording session of an unknown pianist and singer named Alec Johnson in Atlanta on November 2, 1928. Alec Johnson's music invoked the sounds of an earlier era. According to Tony Russell, the backup band formed a "lively and expressive pit orchestra to accompany a set of antique minstrel songs and a couple of blues." While the performances of the band are superb on "Miss Meal Cramp Blues" and older sounding material like "Sister Maud Mule," record collector John Heneghan has recently challenged Oliver's claim that the band included the McCoys and Carter.[73] "The mandolin doesn't sound like Charlie [McCoy] even a little bit," Heneghan argued in a recent discussion of Alec Johnson's records on the Facebook group "The Rarest 78s," and "I'd say it's almost impossible that it's those guys. If you play

T. DeWayne Moore

an instrument you should be able to hear that the style, approach and execution are all completely opposite of any McCoy/Sheiks band."[74]

And now we know why it sounds different. The fiddle player and pianist in the band of Alec Johnson as well as the following year in Chatman's Mississippi Hot Footers was almost certainly Harry Chatmon, who we know played in a string band with Charlie and Joe McCoy at this time. In one early 1970s correspondence with Michael Beebie, Stephen Calt claimed that Charlie and Joe McCoy had moved to Jackson and started playing with Harry Chatmon. Harry, who played the fiddle when he fronted this group, had already introduced Charlie to the mandolin and then he showed Joe how to be an accompanist.[75] Even though Elijah Wald credits Bo Carter with the "very effective vaudeville violin on a record by an older singer named Alec Johnson called 'The Mysterious Coon,'" which contains crude, offensive minstrel-show lyrics, not a single member of the Chatmon family ever claimed the fiddle as one of Bo's many instruments. Michael Beebie does not include the fiddle as one of his many instruments in his thesis. The only fiddlers in the family were Alonzo, Edgar (Med), and Harry Chatmon. The fiddle playing on "The Mysterious Coon," therefore, is fascinating and most likely one of the only examples of the type of music that Harry Chatmon performed in the string band with Carter and the McCoys.

Another reason that I doubt the aural deductions of John Heneghan regarding the identity of Alec Johnson and his band is the type of songs recorded at the very next session, in New Orleans for Brunswick in November 1928. Bo Carter cut at least five tunes with Charlie McCoy on mandolin and his cousin Walter Vinson on guitar, the first of those songs being "The Yellow Coon Has No Race" and the second being "Good Old Turnip Greens." The record company never issued the first side for whatever reason, but it released the second old-time minstrel song, which concerned the stereotypical passions of poor African Americans for turnip top leaves. The minstrel songs recorded in these first two sessions by members of the Chatmon family are indicative of the older styles of music performed by African Americans during the early recording era, particularly the repertoire of Harry Chatmon's string band in 1928–29.

Carter, Vinson, and McCoy also performed the instrumentation on four songs for singer Mary Butler, who may, in fact, have been Rosie Mae Moore. McCoy had backed her earlier in February. McCoy plays mandolin on three of the four tracks including the tough-minded "Electrocuted Blues (Electric Chair Blues)," "Bungalow Blues," and "Mary Blues." At the initial session for Brunswick, Carter, and McCoy also produced the blues ballad "Corrine Corrina."[76]

In a previous article, I wrote that Bo Carter had to be the fiddler on the records cut in Memphis by Charlie McCoy and Walter Vinson for Brunswick in September 1929, but the fiddle heard on the recordings of Chatman's Mississippi Hot Footers is not Bo Carter. I now contend that the fiddler must be Harry Chatmon, who remained employed as a musician in a hotel orchestra in Jackson throughout the Great Depression. Harry Chatmon worked as a musician in the state capital as early as 1929. In fact, Harry Chatmon appears in all the city directories working as a musician until 1940, when the census listed him as the "manager" of an "orchestra." The last sessions of Harry Chatmon on the fiddle produced "Your Friend's Gonna Use It Too" Part 1 and 2 under the name of Charlie McCoy, and "It Ain't No Good" Part 1 and 2 under the name of Walter Vinson.

Harry Chatmon had the option for steady employment in Jackson as a musician in a hotel orchestra, which allowed his older, good-timing brother Alonzo the opportunity to recruit Charlie McCoy and Walter Vinson away from his youngest brother's string band. This new arrangement set the stage for the recording of almost all of the Sheiks' old-time tunes examined in this volume.

In 1930 several members of the Chatmon family played together in a hotel orchestra in Jackson. Both the city directory and the census recorded Alonzo and Clementine Chatmon living on Pascagoula Street. In April one census enumerator recorded Alonzo and his wife Clementine, their daughter Ruby Bell, and the children by her previous marriage, Alex, Lithania, and Queenie living in Jackson. Alonzo worked as a musician in a "hotel orchestra." Bert Chatmon tried his hand at playing professionally in Jackson in 1930. Henderson and Eliza Chatmon also lived in Jackson and worked as musicians. Ishmon Bracey lived in Jackson and worked as a musician in a "hotel orchestra." Bracey and the Chatmons may have been playing in the Edwards Hotel Orchestra, which performed on the radio as well as live at the hotel. The leader of the orchestra, moreover, was the best violinist in the state.

Country music scholar Patrick Huber, in his section on the Mississippi Sheiks in *Hidden in the Mix*, states "a dozen of the band's sides ... were listed under racially ambiguous pseudonyms in OKeh's 'Old Time Tunes' series, which the label marketed to white record buyers." He points out that two of the band's eight selections from its initial Shreveport session, "The Sheik Waltz"/"The Jazz Fiddler," were released as a coupling for the hillbilly market under the billing Walter Jacobs and Lonnie Carter. OKeh marketed another four tunes from their second session in San Antonio four months later in its hillbilly series, and the label credited the Sheiks this time as Walter Jacobs and the Carter Brothers. He also notes that all the records of the Mississippi Mud Steppers appeared in OKeh's hillbilly catalogue, "but none of the accompanying promotional literature alluded to the race of the band members who had recorded them."[77]

By examining the artist billings associated with only the records released in the hillbilly series, Huber makes it seem as if OKeh intentionally created such billings to deceive white record buyers into purchasing and listening to the music of African Americans. Huber does not mention, however, that all the billings on the records associated with the Sheiks contained racially ambiguous names and pseudonyms. Alec Johnson, Charlie McCoy, Charlie McCoy with Rosie Mae Moore, Chatman's Mississippi Hot Footers, Jackson Blue Boys, Leroy Carter, Mary Butler, and Sam Hill From Louisville are all equally as racially ambiguous as the Walter Jacobs and the Carter Brothers and the Mississippi

Mud Steppers. The Mississippi Blacksnakes is the only billing of a race record that might conceivably betray the Sheiks' identity as much as the Mud Steppers. While most of us would not be surprised to learn that record companies concealed the racial identity of artists to sell more records during Jim Crow, the racial ambiguity of the different billings for the Sheiks' releases simply do not provide a suitable evidence base for analysis.

The characteristic sound of Lonnie's fiddle playing and Walter Vinson's vocals and guitar mark the Sheiks' recordings in the King Edward Hotel in December 1930. The duo recorded more than fifteen tunes on December 15 and 19. Bo is most likely playing guitar behind Charlie McCoy on December 15 and 16, and recorded his first sides under his nom de plume Bo Carter on December 15 as well. Walter Vinson was second vocalist for two sides, but Walter did not play guitar for the Bo Carter sides.

Hollandale is about ninety miles north of Vicksburg on Highway 61. Its name comes from one of the early planters who allowed the railroad to go through his land. On one side of the railroad tracks were white-owned businesses including a hardware store, two clothing stores, a drugstore, a bank, a post office, a large chain grocery store, and the office of a cotton broker. On the other side of the track was the "Blue Front," the name by which African Americans in Hollandale called the downtown area. The edge of the Blue Front boasted a row of entertainment venues. A man of Chinese descent operated an independent grocery store, and across the street was a liquor store and club called Little Harlem.[78]

Houston Stackhouse remembered hearing Robert Nighthawk and the Mississippi Sheiks playing in two drugstores in Hollandale around 1930: "The Black Cat Drugstore was down on the low end, that's kinda colored place, like where they hung out. They had a little old piano player there at that time. I can't think of his name, but anyhow, William Warren, he was a good guitar picker, and Robert was blowin' the harp. Then Bo and Lonnie [Chatmon] and them, they'd play at the next drugstore, on Saturday evenings and things like that. White people owned it, but they had colored people in there playin.'"

It was there that Powell first met the several musicians in the Chatmon family. Around this time, Powell started to work under the moniker of Sonny Boy Nelson, a name he took in recognition of his stepfather Sid Nelson. He would sometimes join the Sheiks on guitar at their performances over the following decade, and he also worked with piano tuner and amazing guitarist Richard "Hacksaw" Harney as well as vocalist "Mississippi Matilda," whom he later married. A proficient musician, Powell could play a number of different instruments, including the banjo, mandolin, fiddle, and harmonica. Powell added a seventh string on his guitar to ensure a unique sound, and he even placed an aluminum plate in the sound-hole of his Silvertone to mimic the tonal qualities of a resonator.[79] He was fully prepared for the marathon session.

Powell takes turns on vocals on the twenty-one sides with his girlfriend, Matilda Powell, and a harmonica player named Robert Hill. Bluebird released a few sides under the name "Mississippi Matilda," who produced the acceptable "Happy Home Blues" and "Hard Working Woman," the second of which answered Bumble Bee Slim's 1934 recording of "Cruel Hearted Woman Blues." Powell recorded a total of six sides with Harris as "Sonny Boy Nelson." Eugene Powell's guitar style demonstrates how someone from the same generation as Robert Johnson could develop his own style of Delta blues, adopting the inflections of Leroy Carr, hokum, and swing. Indeed, Bo probably wanted him on guitar for these sessions due to his versatility. Robert Hill recorded a total of ten sides on vocals and harmonica, backed on guitar by Powell and Harris. In fact, Powell played guitar on thirty-two straight songs during the session—an amazing display of stamina and endurance.

In many ways, it was a historic session. It is perhaps most historic for being the last session of Alonzo Chatmon. In 1936 he and Walter Vinson headed up to Chicago and joined the musicians' union. The Sheiks played at different clubs for three

to five dollars a night. They played the West Side for about a month, but they could not make it on the club circuit. According to Vinson, "It got so cold that I had to stop before I had another stroke. I stopped, Lonnie stopped. then we went back to Shreveport" to work for a man on the radio, but "he didn't have no recording for us to do at that time; [we just] played in his studio." This engagement ended soon enough for the Sheiks and brought them back to Bolton.

Although the Mississippi Sheiks' recording contract expired in 1935, several members of the band continued to make records until World War II. Leading the small band known as Papa Charlie's Boys, McCoy cut the last four sides under his own name in April 1936. Each cut demonstrated how much his vigorous mandolin playing, which the Victor engineer captured well, had developed since his time in the Hot Footers. From 1936 to 1939, he recorded as a member of the studio group The Harlem Hamfats, a tight little band that featured the very sinewy mandolin of McCoy on every track the group laid down. His rhythms were steadily hopping, but he tore into some chiming arpeggios on occasion, too. His solo mandolin work can be heard on "Southern Blues," "Hamfat Swing," and "Growling Dog." McCoy also went into the studio with Rosetta Howard and Frankie Jaxon, and recorded with his former sister-in-law Memphis Minnie for Vocalion in 1938. He even backed John Lee "Sonny Boy" Williamson for Bluebird in 1941. McCoy reentered the studio with his brother, Joe McCoy, from 1941 to 1944 for his last recorded sides, which were released on Bluebird.

In 1946 the two brothers worked at Martin's Corner at 1700 West Lake Street, Chicago. According to Roosevelt Scott in a 1972 interview, Charlie McCoy lived near the corner of 31st and South Rhodes Streets in the late 1940s. On July 26, 1950, however, while convalescing at Chicago's Psychopathic Hospital, Charlie McCoy's hopes of ever returning to the studio ended, when he died of a paralytic brain disease. His remains sat unmarked at Restvale Cemetery in Worth, Illinois, for the next sixty years.[80]

Charlie McCoy's achievements as a recording artist stand in comparison to the careers of Bo Carter and Memphis Minnie as far as number of recording sessions, and he developed an approach to playing guitar that stands up with the likes of Scrapper Blackwell as an element of the "small group sound." McCoy made a living from his recording career, which lasted much longer and began much earlier than most. Rosie Mae Moore hollered at him during that first session in 1928, "Play it, Mr. Charlie, a long time and a heap of it." He seems to have taken her words to heart, because that is exactly what he did.

As I explain in my article "The Genius of the Country Blues," Bo Carter enjoyed a distinguished career as a solo blues artist.[81] He recorded more than one hundred sides between 1928 and 1940, and he continued to perform locally and at home until his death in 1964. The last surviving member of the Mississippi Sheiks was Walter Vinson, who lived in Chicago when he appeared at the Chicago Folk Festival in January 1972. The same year Vinson reconnected with Sam Chatmon and collaborated on an album for Rounder Records under the name the New Mississippi Sheiks. He and Sam Chatmon also performed together at the Smithsonian Festival of American Folklife in Washington, DC. He died at the South Shore Nursing Center on April 22, 1975. He was buried in Alsip, Illinois.

If secondary source material and the research of previous scholars is all that we might consult in our quest to write more human biographies, he Huber would have a point about our abilities in regard to African American artists. However, we have tools at our disposal to solve problems, to fill the silences that exist in the place of stories and contextualize the lives of these musicians. In 2019 the growing number of digitally archived documents available online hold unbelievable amounts of information that have the power to end these silences, put names to recordings, and empower these forgotten figures from the American past and tell their stories. Indeed, most digital archives do not even require that we leave our desks to discover new evidence and insight.

According to Ralph Waldo Emerson, "Action is with the scholar subordinate." Yet, action certainly has its place in serious research. Though the physical process of digging through the archives to find new information in those few special collections is time-consuming and frustrating, the hard, wooden chairs in the reading rooms remain important elements of the historian's craft. This monograph also serves as a testament to the crucial nature of field research even "from this historical distance." In the fields of history and ethnomusicology, the imperatives of conducting field research and wiping away the myths of the past are as important now as they ever were. Whereas discographies provide only the names of the artists who made records and, therefore, offer an inadequate and uneven portrait of the landscape of American music before World War II, the examination of extant secondary source material, efforts at field research, and the mining of digital archives are crucial to finding leads about musicians who remain silent on record, yet enjoyed a measure of popularity in the rural communities and hamlets of Mississippi. The "historical distance" and lack of evidence serves as a call to action to the serious researcher, who requires an appropriate and comprehensive body of research before ever considering analysis.

Before the segregation of sound took hold of the reins and rigidly monitored the color line after the December 1930 sessions at the King Edward Hotel, the Mississippi Sheiks were some of the earliest musicians from Mississippi to record such a wide-ranging repertoire and to possess an almost chosen sense of determination to make records. Alonzo Chatmon, Charlie McCoy, Walter Vinson, Bo Carter, and Harry Chatmon were some of the most die-hard musicians from Mississippi ever to pick up an instrument. Their sheer passion and skill made a deep mark on American popular music. The commercial recording of race and hillbilly records certainly opened doors for a diverse range of talented musicians, but the decision of talking-machine companies to create separate race and hillbilly catalogues meant that an inestimable number of musicians whose

T. DeWayne Moore

music did not fit with the perceptions of racial difference held by A&R men were left out. That is the rationale behind our inclusion of short biographies about the unrecorded African American fiddlers from Mississippi.

—T. DeWayne Moore

NOTES

1. The presence of Alonzo's brother, Bo Carter, at the Sheiks' initial recording session suggests that Ralph Lembo played a crucial role in his unusually long recording career, and the discovery of more circumstantial evidence comes from ethnomusicologist David Evans, who also conducted an interview with Eura Gay Lembo, the widow of Ralph Lembo, before she remarried in the late 1960s. He admits that, much like the later experience of Wardlow, the interview proffered very little useful material. Yet she remembered a very important bit of information that suggests her husband worked with Bo Carter. The only musician with whom she remembered her husband working was one who sang about "Corinna." She likely referred to Bo Carter since he liked to introduce himself to folks as the composer of "Corrine Corrina." In a later article written by Elaine Hughes, the daughter of Farris Novelty Company proprietor J. D. Farris of Vicksburg, she recalls an intimate performance by the songwriter at her parents' house: "The first thing he said to me was, 'You know I wrote Corrine Corrina. I can sing it for you.'" He clearly left an impression on the jukebox salesman's daughter, who did not put her memories down on paper until over forty years later. In all likelihood, he left an impression on the wife of the talent scout from Itta Bena as well. See Eura Gay Lembo, interview with David Evans, August 24, 1967, Itta Bena, Mississippi; T. DeWayne Moore, "Bo Carter: The Genius of the Country Blues," *Blues & Rhythm* 330 (May 2018): 14–24; Elaine Hughes, "The Day Bo Carter Played on My Mother's Porch," *Living Blues* 173 (July/August 2004): 42–43; Walter Vinson, interview with Jim O'Neal and Karl Gert zur Heide, 1972, Chicago.

2. Frank Proschan and Bruce Kaplan, liner notes to *The New Mississippi Sheiks* (Rounder 2004, 1972).

3. Bernard MacMahon and Allison McGourty, *American Epic: The First Time America Heard Itself* (New York: Simon & Schuster, 2017), 120.

4. T. DeWayne Moore, "Revisiting Ralph Lembo: Complicating Charley Patton, the 1920s Race Record Industry, and the Italian American Experience in the Mississippi Delta," *Association for Recorded Sound Collections Journal* 49, no. 2 (December 2018): 153–84.

5. Walter Vinson, interview with Jim O'Neal and Karl Gert zur Heide, 1972, Chicago.

6. Proschan and Kaplan, liner notes to *The New Mississippi Sheiks*.

7. Stephen Calt and Gayle Wardlow, *King of the Delta Blues* (Rock Chapel Books, 1988), 214.

8. "The Sheik Waltz" (403803-A or -B), "The Jazz Fiddler" (403804A), "Stop and Listen Blues" (403806-A), "Driving That Thing" (403800-B), "Sitting on Top of the World" (403805-A or -B), "Lonely One in This Town" (403807-B), "Alberta Blues" (403801-B), "Winter Time Blues" (403802-B).

9. Stephen Calt, Michael Stewart, and Don Kent, liner notes to Mississippi Sheiks, *Stop and Listen* (LP, Mamlish S 3804, 1974).

10. The major problem with the research methodology of Patrick Huber is his decision to write the histories of African American musicians solely from the liner notes of record collectors and A&R men. Rather than conduct research into the extant primary sources that contain information about African Americans, he merely cites a curious series of record producers and music enthusiasts who have neither the training or awareness of resources that contain information about the African American experience. "Dr. Richard Cherry," for example, who wrote the liner notes for *Vintage Mandolin Music 1927–1946 (Rags, Breakdowns, Stomps and Blues)* in 2003 was a "head teacher" character in a book series about an overweight British youth named Billy Bunter. The actual author (who used a pseudonym) of the notes to Document DOCD-32–20–3 was Paul Swinton, owner and producer of older music on his Frog Records label out of London. Huber also cites the problematic liner notes of record collectors Stephen Calt, Don Kent, and Michael Stewart from the 2006 release of *Mississippi Sheiks: Stop and Listen*. While he failed to examine the original notes on the 1974 release of the same album, he avoided republishing a little of the dated information printed on the back of the LP cover. I'm not sure why he cites the liner notes of Grammy award–winning record producer Lawrence Cohn for *Honey Babe Let The Deal Go Down*, which contains no new evidence about the Chatmon family band. Huber also relies on the liner notes written by Marshall Wyatt for *Violin, Sing the Blues for Me: African American Fiddlers, 1926–1949* (Old Hat CD-1002) and *Folks, He Sure Do Pull Some Bow! Vintage Fiddle Music, 1927–1935* (Old Hat CD-1003). He refers to Wyatt as a "music scholar," but he is a Grammy-nominated producer and the founder of Old Hat Records of Raleigh, North Carolina, which released the compilations.

11. Samuel Charters, *The Bluesmen* (Oak Publications, 1967), 139.

12. On December 15, Walter Vinson and Alonzo Chatmon recorded "Sitting on Top of the World No. 2," "Times Done Got Hard," "Your Good Man Caught the Train and

Gone," "Still I'm Traveling On," and "Unhappy Blues." The duo also showed back up on December 19 at King Edward Hotel to record "Ramrod Blues," "Honey Babe Let the Deal Go Down," "She Ain't No Good," "Church Bell Blues," "Stop and Listen Blues No. 2" (404785-A or -B).

13. 1930; Census place: Memphis, Shelby, Tennessee; page: 22B; Enumeration District: 0036; FHL microfilm: 2342008.

14. Woody Mann, *Six Early Blues Roots Guitarists* (New York: Oak, 1973, repr. 2014).

15. "Young People of Edwards at Dance," *Clarion-Ledger*, Jackson, MS, July 31, 1932.

16. Jim O'Neal, Alex van der Tuuk, and Guido van Rijn, "Paramount Records: A Centennial Celebration," *Living Blues* 247:48:1 (February 2017): 27–38.

17. Sam Chatmon, interview by Fred Hoeptner and Bob Pinson, 1959, Hollandale, Mississippi.

18. "Sweet Maggie," "Sales Tax," "Hitting the Numbers," "It's Done Got Wet," "Pencil Won't Write No More," "I Am the Devil," "Good Morning Blues," "Blues On My Mind," "She's Got Something Crazy," "You'll Work Down to Me Someday," "Baby, Please Make a Change," "Somebody's Got to Help Me."

19. The Martin/Cook connection is a product of the research conducted about the Chatmon family by Ed Payne, formerly of Bolton, Mississippi, whose exhaustive searches turned up many marriage certificates and other information about the family. Indeed, his deep well of knowledge is reflected in many sections throughout this article.

20. In his earliest interview, Sam Chatmon told Fred Hoeptner and Bob Pinson that the overseer (not the owner) of the plantation where his father grew up was named Martin, and a survey of census records in Hinds County in 1860 reveals that twenty-four-year-old Thos. D. Martin worked as the overseer of the $115,000 farm of Col. Cook, who owned over eighty slaves, several of whom were in the age range of Henderson; see Sam Chatmon, interview by Fred Hoeptner and Bob Pinson, 1959, Hollandale, Mississippi; and 1860 US Census, Hinds, Mississippi; Roll: M653_582; 600; Family History Library Film: 803582.

21. Josie Williams recalled the names of several of the children living with the couple; see 1870 US Census, Township 6 Range 3, Hinds, Mississippi; roll: M593_730; 615A; Family History Library Film: 552229.

22. "Nancy Perry," 1880 US Census, Boltons Depot, Hinds, Mississippi; roll: 648; Family History Film: 1254648; page: 174A; Enumeration District: 007.

23. Ulysses Simpson Grant, *Personal Memoirs of U.S. Grant* (New York: Charles L. Webster & Company, 1885; repr. Dover, 1995), 205.

24. Michael B. Ballard, *Vicksburg: The Campaign that Opened the Mississippi* (Chapel Hill: University of North Carolina Press, 2004), 282–319.

25. Even though Alan Lomax believed that Sam Chatmon said "old man Miller Davis," the name is transcribed correctly in other interviews with Haxton Ayers in Hollandale 1977, Lou Curtiss in San Diego, and Hoeptner and Pinson in Hollandale 1959. See Sam Chatmon, interview with Alan Lomax, August 1978, Hollandale, Mississippi, https://youtu.be/L_MvcU-qIuY, accessed August 8, 2017.

26. US, Colored Troops Military Service Records, 1863–1865, Ancestry.com, 2007.

27. "Milton Bracey," 1870 US Census, Township 5, Hinds, Mississippi; roll: M593_730; page: 545B; Family History Library Film: 552229; 1910 US Census, Beat 5, Hinds, Mississippi; roll: T624_742; page: 39B; Enumeration District: 0016; FHL microfilm: 137475.

28. A Black woman named Manda Chapman is also listed above his name in the census, and a younger woman named Laura is listed directly below him, followed by Sherman, age five, Grant, three, and a twenty-one-year-old formerly enslaved farmer from Georgia named Henry Walls; see 1870 US Census, Beat 5, Scott, Mississippi; roll: M593_748, 249A.

29. U.S. Civil War Soldiers, 1861–1865, M232 roll 7, Ancestry.com, 2007.

30. In 1880 Sherman lived in Edwards, a small town about eight miles west of Bolton; he is listed as an "orphan," which suggests that Polk Chapman was dead. His brother, Grant, married one Mary Johnson in 1889, but no other records exist about him. Sherman moved back to Newton County in 1900, but he apparently died before the 1910 US Census, when one census enumerator listed his wife, "Alice Chapman," as a widow.

31. Steven Deyle, *Carry Me Back: The Domestic Slave Trade in American Life* (New York: Oxford University Press, 2005), 97.

32. The 1870 census lists his birthplace as Virginia; see also Michael Tadman, *Speculators and Slaves: Masters, Traders, and Slaves in the Old South* (Madison: University of Wisconsin Press, 1989).

33. Josie Williams recalled the names of several of the children living with the couple; see 1870 US Census, Township 6 Range 3, Hinds, Mississippi; roll: M593_730; page: 615A; Family History Library Film: 552229.

34. "Nancy Perry," 1880 US Census, Boltons Depot, Hinds, Mississippi; roll: 648; Family History Film: 1254648; page: 174A; Enumeration District: 007.

35. 1880 US Census, Boltons Depot, Hinds, Mississippi; roll: 648; Family History Film: 1254648; page: 175C; Enumeration District: 007.

36. Daniel and Creasy Jackson lived with several children in Bolton; see 1870 US Census, Township 6, Hinds, Mississippi; roll: M593_730; page: 624A; Image: 392598; Family History Library Film: 552229.

37. Raymond Courthouse marriage records (license 10–380), courtesy of Ed Payne.

38. "Henderson Chatmon," death certificate 11070, Mississippi State Board of Health, July 21, 1934.

39. Beebie, thesis, 17.

40. Beebie, thesis, 20.

41. *Clarion-Ledger*, Jackson, MS, March 24, 1930.

42. Harry Chatmon is also lost in the official record. He appears in the Jackson city directories until the late 1940s, when he is simply gone. Larry Chatmon died the same year as Sam, 1982, and was buried at Chapel Hill M.B. Church in Bolton. Edgar Chatmon is most likely buried in Nitta Yuma Cemetery with his brother Bo.

43. "Leza Chatmon," 1940 US Census, Place: Jackson, Hinds, Mississippi; roll: T627_2026; page: 5B; Enumeration District: 25–10A.

44. Fahey offers a fictional explanation of the sharecropping system: "blacks who worked on Delta plantations were always provided with housing (called 'quarters') and frequently with food. When the depression came and there was no work, the black workers were fed by the plantation owners, protected by the benevolent southern land-owner tradition." In addition to such bombastic historical context, Fahey did not think too much really of Patton or his family members. Even though "two of his sisters, Kattie [*sic*] and Viola [we]re still alive," Fahey does not explain his conclusion that both of them were "unreliable informants," nor does he identify the "numerous people who were acquainted with Patton at different stages during his life" other than erasing them as "people too numerous to mention." Since Sam Chatmon looked like a white man, however, Fahey concludes that he was "entirely honest." Fahey, *Charley Patton*, 25–32.

45. Fahey, *Charley Patton*, 18.

46. Beebie, thesis, 15.

47. The World War I registration card of Alonzo Chatmon located him married and working for Bill Stovall near Clarksdale.

48. Stephen Calt, Michael Stewart, and Don Kent, liner notes, *The Mississippi Sheiks: Stop and Listen* (1974).

49. Beebie thesis, 20.

50. Raymond Courthouse marriage records, courtesy of Ed Payne.

51. Beebie, thesis, 21.

52. *Hinds County Gazette*, Raymond, MS, March 17, 1917.

53. Beebie thesis, 21.

54. The 1920 census states that Ruby Bell Chatmon was one year and nine months old in January, when one enumerator visited their home at 1606 Court Street in Vicksburg, Mississippi. Thus the child was likely born at Stovall.

55. The Warner Brothers and First National Studios traveled from Burbank, California, to Stovall, Mississippi, in March 1932. For future use in a film rendition of the book *Cabin in the Cotton*, the film crews set up to shoot the Stovall Mansion, located six miles from Clarksdale. They filmed the mansion as it burned to the ground with all its contents, valued at $100,000; *Winona Times*, Winona MS, March 18, 1932.

56. Calt, Stewart, and Kent, liner notes.

57. Calt, Stewart, and Kent, liner notes.

58. Calt, Stewart, and Kent, liner notes.

59. Zora Neale Hurston, "Georgia Skin," https://www.youtube.com/watch?v=L4qJSSmmaoo, accessed February 8, 2019. On one tape, she explained, "The men are playing a game called Georgia Skin. That's the most favorite gambling game among the workers of the South. And they lose money on the drop of a card, the fall of a card. And there is a rhythm to the fall of the card."

60. Beebie, thesis, 26.

61. *Delta Democrat Times*, Greenville, MS, July 23, 1943.

62. John W. Work III, "Untitled Manuscript," in *Lost Delta Found: Rediscovering the Fisk University–Library of Congress Coahoma County Study, 1941–1942*, eds. Robert Gordon and Bruce Nemerov (Nashville: Vanderbilt University Press, 2005), 118.

63. Marshall Wyatt, *Violin, Sing the Blues for Me: African-American Fiddlers on Early Phonograph Records*, Old Hat Records, http://www.oldhatrecords.com/ResearchAAViolin.html, accessed December 27, 2018.

64. 1890 Veterans Schedules, Ancestry.com, 2005.

65. The fact that Charlie McCoy is not listed in the 1910 census contradicts the information on his Social Security application, which claimed he was born 1909. It also proves false the information recently engraved on a headstone and placed on his unmarked grave by the Killer Blues Headstone Project.

66. Beebie, thesis, 20.

67. Stephen Calt, personal correspondence to Michael Beebie, 1973.

68. David Evans, *Tommy Johnson* (London: November Books, 1971), 37.

69. David Evans, notes to *Jackson Blues, 1928–1938* (Yazoo L-1007).

70. Evans, *Tommy Johnson*, 47.

71. Robert Palmer, *Deep Blues* (New York: Viking Press, 1981), 59, 275, 59.

72. Palmer, *Deep Blues*, 59.

73. Paul Oliver, *Songsters and Saints: Vocal Traditions on Race Records* (Cambridge: Cambridge University Press, 1984), 97.

74. John Heneghan, comment on Alex van der Tuuk's post about Alec Johnson's "Miss Meal Cramp Blues" in the Facebook group "The Rarest 78s," July 26, 2017.

75. Stephen Calt, personal correspondence to Michael Beebie, 1973.

76. In Cliff Bruner's version for Decca 5350, master 61645, the composer credits are shown as shared by J. N. Williams and Bo Chatman [*sic*], which suggests Mayo Williams was involved somehow in the recording as well

as the publishing of the song. "Corrine Corrina" was first copyrighted in 1929, and then again in 1932, with Mitchell Parish also involved somehow.

77. Huber, 46.

78. Beebie, thesis, 2.

79. Simon J. Bronner, "Living Blues Interview: Eugene Powell: Sonny Boy Nelson," *Living Blues* 43 (Summer 1979): 14–25; Enzo Castella and Gianni Marcucci, *Eugene Powell: Police in Mississippi Blues* (Italy: Albatros VPA 8422, ca. 1984); Bob Eagle, "'Born in the Desert, Raised in the Sandy Field': The Story of Eugene Powell," *Blues Unlimited* 139 (Autumn 1980): 18–19.

80. His grave sits in Section 1-E, Row 13, Grave 125 at Restvale Cemetery in Worth, Illinois.

81. T. DeWayne Moore, "Bo Carter: The Genius of the Country Blues," *Blues and Rhythm* 330 (May 2018): 14–24.

T. DeWayne Moore

Alma Waltz

Guitar

Gtr.

Mando alt m 4-5

Author's note: This transcription is from the Mississippi Mud Steppers recording OKeh 45504, recorded Jackson, MS, 12/15/1930.

Comparable versions: None known

Farewell Waltz

Author's note: This transcription is from the Mississippi Mud Steppers recording OKeh 45532, recorded Jackson, MS, 12/15/1930.

Comparable versions:
In this book: "Honeymoon Waltz," Nations Brothers, 10/13/1935, Jackson, MS, ARC 7–15–78
"Farewell Waltz," Doc Roberts Trio, 03/05/1931, New York, Banner 32176

T. DeWayne Moore

Fingering with Your Fingers

Author's note: This transcription is from the Mississippi Sheiks recording Bluebird B5949, recorded New Orleans, 01/19/1935.
M1–6 and M11–14 have a droned D string.

Comparable versions: None known

Jackson Stomp

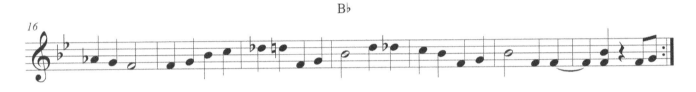

Author's note: This transcription is from the Mississippi Mud Steppers recording OKeh 45504, recorded Jackson, MS, 12/15/1930.
  This is basically a one-part tune, but the first eight measures have three variations. A1 is only played the first time, guitar
  doesn't come in until M7, A2 is played on passes 2, 3, 5, 6, and 8. A3 is played on passes 4 and 7.

Comparable versions:
"Cow Cow Blues," Cow Cow Davenport, 07/16/1928, Chicago, Vocalion 1198
"That Lonesome Train That Took My Baby Away," Charlie McCoy, 12/15/1930, Jackson, MS, OKeh 8863

T. DeWayne Moore

Mississippi Low Down

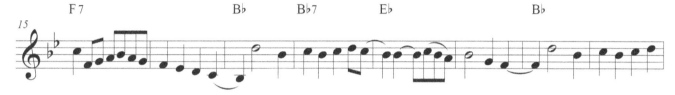

D.C. al Coda

Author's note: This transcription is from OKeh 45482 by "Walter Jacobs and the Carter Brothers," recorded San Antonio, TX, 06/10/1930.

Comparable versions: None known

Morning Glory Waltz

Author's note: This transcription is from the Mississippi Mud Steppers recording OKeh 45532, recorded Jackson, MS, 12/15/1930. The 4/4 version is played on the third of four passes through the tune.

Comparable versions: None known

Sheik's Special (Waltz)

Author's note: This transcription is from OKeh 45468, by "Walter Jacobs and the Carter Brothers," recorded San Antonio, TX, 06/10/1930.

Comparable versions: None known

The Sheik Waltz

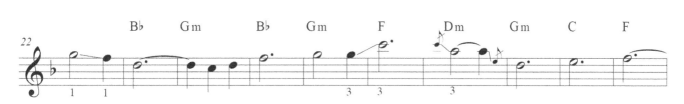

The Mississippi Sheiks

Author's note: This transcription is from the Mississippi Sheiks recording OKeh 45436, recorded Shreveport, LA, 02/17/1930.

Comparable versions: None known

T. DeWayne Moore

Sunset Waltz

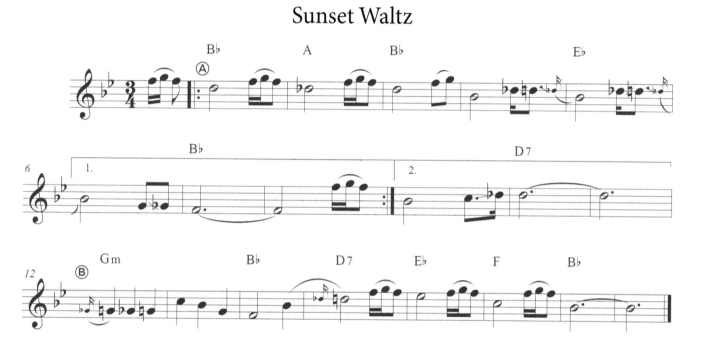

Author's note: This transcription is from the Mississippi Mud Steppers recording OKeh 45519, recorded Jackson, MS, 12/15/1930.

Comparable versions: None known

That's It

Author's note: This transcription is from OKeh 45482, by "Walter Jacobs and the Carter Brothers," recorded San Antonio, TX, 06/10/1930. The third time through M23, the high C is altered to a G. The second repeat is used with M25 following the repeat and the final "ending" is used.

Comparable versions: None known

Vicksburg Stomp

Author's note: This transcription is from the Mississippi Mud Steppers recording OKeh 45519, recorded Jackson, MS, 12/15/1930.

Comparable versions: None known

SYLVESTER S. MORAN (8/21/1893–8/17/1987)

What little we know of Mr. Moran comes from the notes on the 1980 LP *Mississippi Sawyers* and from his appearance at the 1974 Festival of American Folklife in Washington, DC. He was born near Gulfport, about thirty miles from New Orleans, in Kiln, MS. The youngest of nine children, he was a third-generation fiddler, starting on fiddle around age twelve with some tunes from his father. He also learned tunes by going to Saturday night socials and from fiddlers at local logging camps. "Catahoula Blues" is a tune that he first heard in a logging camp around 1917.[1]

—Harry Bolick 2019

Recordings

Mississippi Sawyers, A Collection of Old-Time Mississippi Fiddling (LP, Sawyer Productions, 1980): Catahoula Blues; Golden Slippers.

Sylvester Moran, from 1980 *Mississippi Sawyers* LP cover. Photo by Gil Ford.

Bayou Le Croix

Author's note: In M3, 8, 28, and 31, Moran slides into the A unison note on the string below.

Comparable versions: None known

Sylvester S. Moran

Catahoula Blues

Author's note: This is a version of "Sweet Sunny South" with an inconsistent number of beats, and it varies on each pass through the tune. It's very loose.

Comparable versions:
W. L. Bloomfield, 1853, and/or Raymond, ca. 1850s, lyric and music
Buckley's New Orleans Serenaders, *Song Book for the Parlour* (New York: J. Cozans, 1855)
In this book: "Miles Monroe Standish," Jabe Dillon
"Take Me Back to the Sweet Sunny South," Da Costa Woltz's Southern Broadcasters, 05/1927, Richmond, IN, Gennett 6176
"Sweet Sunny South," Charlie Poole & The North Carolina Ramblers, 09/1927, Chicago, Paramount 3136

Harry Bolick

Real Corn Tom and Jerry

Alt m1-8

Sylvester S. Moran

Comparable versions: None known

Sweet Nellie

Author's Note: This is from the 1974 Smithsonian festival stage performance. The second part is just the first part an octave lower. The alt M7 is played first time only.

Comparable versions: None known
   1. Mississippi Sawyers: A Collection of Old-Time Mississippi Fiddling (LP, Sawyer Productions, 1980).

WILLIE T. NARMOUR AND SHELLIE WALTON SMITH

Okeh recording directors Bob Stephens and Tommy Rockwell were canvassing for new recording artists in Mississippi when they came up with the idea to simplify their search for fiddlers by hosting a fiddle contest. They sponsored a contest in Winona where nine fiddlers from Montgomery, Carroll, and Coahoma counties competed in February 1928. Stephens, Rockwell, and the organist of the Methodist Church, Mrs. N. V. Hutchinson, judged the contest. Narmour (1889–1961) and Smith (1895–1968) placed first, winning cash, a recording contract, and expense money to travel to Memphis to record later that month, where they recorded six tunes.

In the chapter on Doc Bailey, Tony Russell writes that, in his interview, Bailey took credit for organizing fiddle contests at the courthouse in Winona and putting up posters advertising the possibility of recording opportunities. Bailey did not mention Ralph Lembo's participation in the event.

Bob Stephens had met with Ralph Lembo in Itta Bena. The *Greenwood Commonwealth* newspaper of January 19, 1928 quotes him as telling Lembo that, "he must have some Mississippi Delta negro talent for some of his records," and he expected "to bring a recording machine to the south soon."

Willie T. Narmour and Shell Smith. Collection of Tony Russell.

Doc Carpenter and
Willie T. Narmour.
Photo courtesy
Mack Allen Smith.

Lembo "had several records made from local talent" for Columbia.[1] Just weeks later Narmour, Rockwell, and Stephens drove late one night to Avalon to try out "Mississippi" John Hurt. Gayle Dean Wardlow interviewed Ralph Lembo's widow twice in the 1960s. After the second interview, Wardlow recorded an audio note to his collaborator Stephen Calt, wherein he states that she had remembered a "trip they made to the hills around Carrollton, Mississippi—some twenty miles to the east of Itta Bena—and listened to a hillbilly group."[2] Most of Lembo's artists were discovered in his music store, but he had scouted the Carroll County area before Bob Stephens's arrival in Itta Bena. Lembo had previously designed posters to promote his son Frank's dancing career. Bob Stephens had an idea to organize a fiddlers' contest with first prize to be an OKeh recording contract. Lembo "thought it

was a great idea and made signs and hung them up all over the county."[3]

Narmour and Smith's second recording session was on March 11 in Atlanta. "Carroll County Blues"/"Charleston #1" was "one of the biggest selling records of 1929," according to a recording industry trade paper, the *Talking Machine World*. The recording of the waltz "Someone I Love" was nearly as well received. Their popularity continued even as the recording industry began to suffer during the Depression. Along with the Ray Brothers, they were the last of the Mississippi fiddle bands to record in that period.

They recorded thirty-two tunes for OKeh, with the last recorded in 1931. But on July 30, 1934, they recut sixteen tunes for Bluebird, sounding virtually the same as the earlier session recordings. Many of the tunes only received titles at the recording

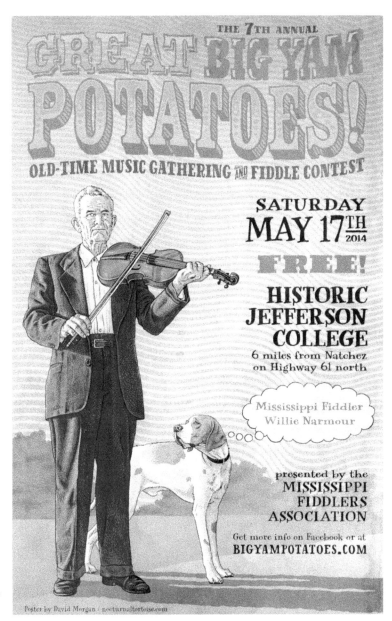

2014 festival poster by and courtesy David Morgan.

sessions. Narmour and Smith were popular enough to be included in one of the OKeh Medicine Show skit records, each featuring short bits from "hit" country artists along with short, stilted speeches.

Their travels to record in Memphis in 1928, Atlanta in 1929 and 1934, New York in 1929, and San Antonio in 1930 were the only times in their lives that they left the state. Their records were very popular in Texas, Mexico, and the West. During their recording trip to San Antonio in 1930, the

recording agent offered to give them farmland near San Antonio if they would move and settle there. They never toured, but played locally for dances, county fairs, fiddle contests, and picnics.

Their tune titles reflect their region of Mississippi. The titles "Charleston," "Avalon Quickstep," "Winona Echoes," "Carroll County Blues," "Mississippi Breakdown," and "Mississippi Wave Waltz" all document local towns, the county, or the state. "Where the Southern Crosses the Dog" celebrates

Miss Marian Michaelson, Miss Mar- a humorous painolog, "Johnnie's

Late Recordings
of
Old Time Music

45329	Midnight Waltz / Someone I Love	—Narmour and Smith
45397	Beaumont Rag / Billy on the Low Ground	—Oscar and Doc Harper
45344	Kiss Me Waltz / Gallop to Georgia-Breakdown	—Narmour and Smith
45420	Dallas Bound / Terrel' Texas Blues	—Oscar and Doc Harper
45390	Rose Waltz / Dry Gin Rag	—Narmour-Smith
45276	Heel and Toe—Polka / Little Star	—Narmour and Smith

THE TWO BLACK CROWS IN—

| 1929-D | Foolishments / Esau Buck | —Moran and Mack |

Also Harmony Records—3 for $1

PILOT BUTTE PHARMACY

Columbia Records advertisement, 1930.

the crossing of the Southern Railway and the Yazoo Delta (Yellow Dog) Railroad at Moorhead, about forty miles west of Carrollton.

◆ ◆ ◆

William Thomas Narmour (1889–1961) was one of Mississippi's most influential early fiddlers, widely known for "Carroll County Blues," his distinctive fiddle style, and a unique body of tunes. Narmour was born in Ackerman, Choctaw County,

Mississippi. Seven years later, his family moved to Carroll County, where he remained until he died at the age of seventy-two. His family included his wife, Uelena, his sons, Coleman and Charles, and his daughter, Hazel.

Willie first learned to play on a cigar-box fiddle that his father, John made for him. John Narmour played fiddle; John's brother, Henry, played fiddle, bass fiddle, beat straws, and clogged. Henry's wife, Jimmie, sang. Willie is best known as a fiddler but he also played guitar, as can be heard on the recording of "Rose Waltz," where he played in the same style as Shellie Smith. He did not read music and had little formal education. In an area where men tended to be taciturn, his personality was described as being as engaging as his music. He played fiddle, drove a school bus, farmed, ran an auto mechanic garage to support his family, and loved to hunt. Though not religious, Willie occasionally attended the Pisgah Church, which was very close to his home in Valley.

Local dances were rife with drinking and fighting. Willie was of small stature. According to Hoyt Ming, he was "between a midget and a medium-sized person." Charles Campbell, the deputy sheriff in the area when and where Willie played, responded to the question, "Did he ever get into fights at these dances?" with "No, he had friends," implying large muscular friends, who protected him.

Virginia Huffman Williamson was a childhood playmate of Willie's daughter, Hazel. She remembered that the Narmour, Smith, and Duke families would gather on Saturday nights around a piano at her house and sing gospel and bluegrass songs. Willie had played some Bill Monroe tunes. "He could hear a tune once and then play it. It was a miracle!"[4]

Narmour entered local fiddle contests, occasionally announcing beforehand what tunes he would play. In Greenwood in May 1934, he played "Whistling Coon" and "Midnight Waltz" and was accompanied by his neighbor W. E. Duke (1883–1958) on guitar. Duke also competed on fiddle, playing "Wednesday Night Waltz" and "Valley School Blues." In this contest, thirteen-year-old Ed Kittrell[5] won first, eleven-year-old Charles T. Smith came in third, and A. E. Clardy took second playing "Home Brew Rag."[6] Also competing on fiddle were Mr. F. Ezell (1870–1955) playing "Billy in the Lowground,"[7] Chief Two House, Walter White, Mazie Harper, M. E. Tindall backed up by A. E. Clardy, Robert Lewis, and L. L. Clark. There were contests in Winona at least in the years 1917, 1923, and 1928, according to the *Winona Times*, and likely many more. Narmour would also enter the fiddle contest in Kosciusko. According to his daughter, Hazel, "Daddy always won, till they wouldn't let him enter anymore."[8]

Narmour continued to play in public after his recording career ended in 1934, although not with

Shell Smith. One venue was the Alice Cafe in Greenwood, where he was known to play for admirers, possibly as late as the 1950s. Lonnie Ellis of the Mississippi Possum Hunters also recalls seeing Willie at the 1929 or 1930 fiddlers' contest in Kosciusko with another guitarist. The fiddler Charles T. Smith recalled playing socially with Narmour around 1946. According to Smith, after the death of his twelve-year-old son Narmour quit playing for several years.

Narmour is credited with composing "Carroll County Blues." Hazel Wiggins, his daughter, said that "when Daddy did 'Carroll County Blues,' he did it all in his head, like with my math problems, but he couldn't write it down on paper. He got to whistling what he could hear in his head and called me: 'Sis, listen to me, what I am playing,' and had me whistle while he worked it. I'd say, 'why, that's pretty; what is it?' He said, 'I don't know, Sis, but we're going to find out. Set here and whistle and fill in.'"[9] Narmour appears to have composed "Carroll County Blues 2" and "Carroll County Blues 3" in a failed attempt to cash in on the success of his previous effort. Many of the rest of his known tunes are individual creations only loosely or partly, if at all, related to widely known fiddle tunes.

◆ ◆ ◆

Shellie Walton Smith (1895–1968) was known for his powerful and very straightforward guitar backup on the Narmour and Smith records. However, for the "Rose Waltz," he recorded on fiddle. His wife Lillian, who he married on September 17, 1916, also played fiddle. They seem to have been less and less musically active after the birth of their children. Some time after their marriage, Lillian taught herself to play piano by ear. They did not own a piano, so she walked across the yard to the Pisgah Church piano, which was unused during the week. Late in Shellie's life when he was too rusty to play, their youngest child, Donald "Sonny" Smith, remembers bringing a fiddle home for Shellie. To his surprise, Lillian grabbed it and played a waltz, apparently playing well. His older brothers played a little mandolin and accordion.

The Duke Family

As close neighbors, the Narmour, Smith, and Duke families got together for music on Saturday nights. Mr. William E. Duke played fiddle and guitar. His son Grover was a good friend of Willie Narmour and later became a professional musician playing the pop music of his day with his own band. He was known to play "Carroll County Blues" on guitar. His brother Guy played washtub bass with him in a high school band.

"Mississippi" John Hurt (1893-1966)

Interviewed in 1963 by Tom Hoskins, Hurt said that he substituted for Shell Smith on many occasions between 1923 and 1930 when Smith was unavailable to play a dance. The three of them did not play together. When backing Narmour, Hurt used a flat-pick and did not sing. Keith Worrell of Greenwood recalls Narmour and Smith playing a dance at his twenty-first birthday and John Hurt "spelled" them. John Hurt got his chance to record in 1928 after being referred to the recording company by Narmour and Smith. There were two sessions, the first in Memphis and the second in New York City. He recorded again in the 1960s.

Guy Duke described a day when Grover Duke was at the general store in Valley when John Hurt came in. John kept eyeing Grover's new guitar, and finally asked to play it, which he did for hours. The owner of the store, according to his daughter, Dardanelle Hadley of Winona, played some ragtime piano and was friendly to musicians. In her 1994 cassette she describes the store: "The traveling Black musicians came through Avalon and always played on the porch of Daddy's country store. Daddy would hold me up on his shoulders and get such a kick out of my response to the music, some kind of Dixieland. The leader, I remember, was 'Big Boy' who played tuba. And they also had trombone."[10]

Their Music

Narmour and Smith were very popular for dancing. But they played many tunes of irregular length, which is unusual for southern square dancing. According to members of the Smith and Duke families and Anne Smith of Carroll County, there was no square dancing in the county during that period. The only dances were the waltz and a very simple two-step referred to as the "Carroll County Hop." However, Willie Narmour's uncle was known to clog or step dance. For these kinds of dances only a strong beat, not necessarily in regular phrases, would have been required. As is usual in Mississippi, Narmour and Smith's recorded repertoire has a high percentage of waltzes, about 25 percent. Some of the tunes, such as "Avalon Blues" and "Gallop to Georgia," are polkas and suggestive of Mexican influence. Narmour was a very confident, assertive fiddler sliding up for high C and E notes, beyond the usual limit of first position for folk fiddlers, but not always hitting the expected pitch. Smith's guitar work was powerful but simple. Except for waltzes, which he played in the usual downbeat-2-3 timing, he seemed to hear the meter as a sequence of downbeats, which is a very practical tactic for tunes of irregular length and phrasing. He did not alternate bass notes and only rarely played a bass run. He would play a downstroke on the tonic note on the downbeat, then brush the chord on the upbeat.

Playing so very firmly on the downbeat created space for Narmour to accent in interesting places on the upbeat. Homer Ellis recalled that Narmour "tuned the fiddle highest of anybody I ever seen."

While the Narmour and Smith recordings quote fragments of traditional fiddle tunes, they never play a tune unaltered. They added new bits of melody and left out parts that they perhaps forgot or found uninteresting. The resulting music is creatively woven into something unique and personal. Most of Narmour and Smith's records credit them at composers. However, there are no composer credits from the first recording session in 1928 or for "Texas Shuffle" or "Tequila Hop Blues" from the June 7 session in San Antonio. Many of the tune titles were made up at the recording sessions.

—Harry Bolick with updated information
based on additional research done
by T. DeWayne Moore

NOTES

1. "Seek Negro Talent for Phonograph Records," *Greenwood* (MS) *Commonwealth*, January 18, 1928.

2. In the middle of a recorded interview with Hayes McMullan, the tape stops around 27:41 and Wardlow begins reciting his notes from yet another disappointing interview with the former Mrs. Ralph Lembo on March 13, 1969, who had by then remarried to Itta Bena mayor Paul Stowers. She started to work in the music store around 1931, and therefore did not recall his trip to record in Chicago; see, Hayes McMullan, interview with Gayle Dean Wardlow, May 18, 1968, Greenwood, MS, tta0182mm, http://music-man.mtsu.edu/broadsides/Wardlow/pdfs/cpm_94048_tta182x_010101_pres_HayesMcMullan.pdf, accessed September 13, 2017, by T. DeWayne Moore.

3. MacMahon and McGourty, American Epic: The First Time America Heard Itself, 120.

4. Telephone interview with Virginia Huffman Williamson (daughter of Lillian Mae Narmour, a cousin of Willie Narmour), November 12, 2005.

5. Bolick and Austin, Mississippi Fiddle Tunes and Songs from the 1930s, 127, 128.

6. Greenwood Commonwealth, May 5, 1934.

7. Bolick and Austin, Mississippi Fiddle Tunes and Songs from the 1930s, 104.

8. Susie James, "Carroll Duo Left Stamp on Music," *Clarion-Ledger*, November 24, 1997, 3B.

9. Susie James, "Music to the Ears," *Greenwood Commonwealth*, March 25, 1999, 12C.

10. Dardanelle Hadley, *Dardanelle Down Home—The Way Things Used to Be* (cassette, Hadley Music 101, 1994).

Avalon Blues

Author's note: This transcription is from OKeh 45414, recorded New York, 09/23/1929.

Comparable versions: None known

Harry Bolick

Avalon Quickstep

Author's note: This transcription is from OKeh 45469, recorded San Antonio, TX, 06/07/1930. Avalon was a community in Leflore County in the Delta, not far from where Narmour lived. Notice that in M11 and M16, where there is a temptation to add an F chord, Smith does not. This tune is often played in the key of D, but close listening to the recordings suggests that the key was C. The guitar has a capo at the fifth fret and is fingered in the key of G.

Comparable versions: "A" parts are somewhat similar.
"Grasshopper Sitting on a Sweet Potato Vine," Luther Davis, *The Old Time Way: The Music and Times of Luther Davis, Roscoe Parrish* (, Galax, VA: Heritage Records 070, 1986).
Bolick and Austin, *Mississippi Fiddle Tunes and Songs from the 1930s*: W. E. Claunch, "Pass Around the Bottle," 268
"Pass Around the Bottle, and We'll All Take a Drink," Gid Tanner & His Skillet Lickers, 04/17/1926, Atlanta, Columbia 15074-D
"Pass Around the Bottle," Georgia Yellow Hammers, 02/08/1927, Atlanta, Victor 20550
"Pass Around the Bottle," Ernest V. Stoneman, 05/10/1927, New York, Banner 2157

Willie T. Narmour and Shellie Walton Smith

Bouquets of June Waltz

Author's note: This transcription is from OKeh 45480, recorded San Antonio, TX, 06/07/1930. Note how Smith delays by a measure the F chord in the B part, in M38 and M39.

Comparable versions:
In this book: "Flow Rain Waltz," Mumford Bean and His Itawambians, 02/17/1928, Memphis, TN, OKeh 45303 (loosely related)

Harry Bolick

Captain George Has Your Money Come

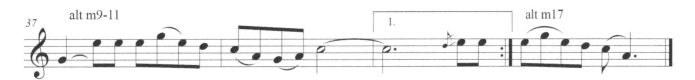

Author's note: This transcription is from OKeh 45242, recorded Memphis, TN, 02/15/1928. Narmour and Smith repeat roughly
in the pattern ABABC with the A part played once through or with the repeat as shown. Notice that in M7, where you might
expect to hear an F chord, Smith holds the G. The guitar has a capo at the fifth fret and is fingered in the key of G.

"Captain George Has Your Money Come?" The title is the first line from an African American levee work song, and is followed
by "what do you care, boy, I don't owe you none." The melody seems to be unrelated. The lament is about the levee work
camps where African American workers were often not paid.

Comparable versions: None known

Carroll County Blues

Author's note: This transcription is from OKeh 45317, recorded Atlanta, 03/11/1929. This recording was the source for this very
popular Mississippi fiddle tune. The guitar has a capo at the seventh fret and is fingered in the key of C.

Comparable versions:
In this book: "Carroll County Blues," John Gatwood
"Carroll County Blues," Doc Roberts Trio, 02/03/1933, New York Banner 32713
"Tennessee River Bottom Blues," Mike Shaw & His Alabama Entertainers, 12/10/1930, Atlanta, OKeh 45518

Harry Bolick

Carroll County Blues No. 2

Author's note: This transcription is from OKeh 45377, recorded New York, 09/23/1929. The first note is omitted in M1 to make the phrasing clear; Narmour plays it as shown in "Actual M1." The first note begins just a bit before the downbeat of M1. The tune repeats are: first pass as written, second pass add M14 between M22 and M23, passes three and four skip M20–26, last pass end on M9.

Comparable versions: None known

Carroll County Blues No. 3

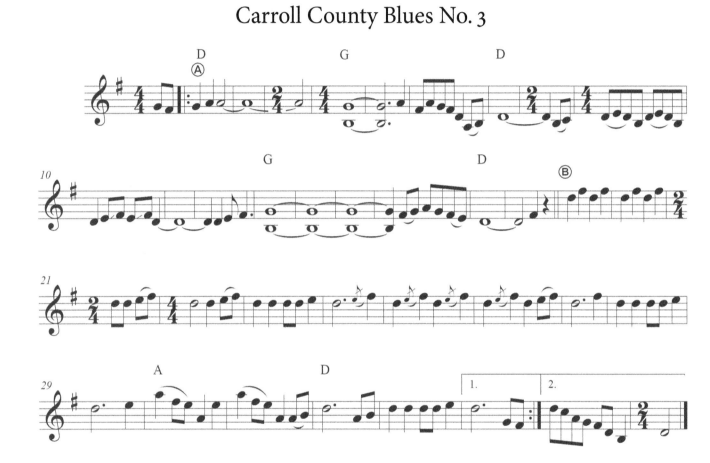

Author's note: This transcription is from OKeh 45459, recorded San Antonio, TX, 06/06/1930. The guitar has a capo at the second fret.

Comparable versions: None known

Harry Bolick

Charleston No. 1

Author's note: This transcription is from OKeh 45317, recorded Atlanta, 03/11/1929. Charleston is a town in Tallahatchie County, MS.

Comparable versions:
"Charleston #1," Doc Roberts Trio, 02/03/1933, New York, Banner 32713
"Done Gone," A. C. "Eck" Robertson, 07/01/1922, New York, Victor 19372
"Done Gone," Clayton McMichen and Riley Puckett, 04/21/1930, Atlanta, Columbia 15594-D

Willie T. Narmour and Shellie Walton Smith

Charleston No. 2

Author's note: This transcription is from OKeh 45377, recorded New York, 09/23/1929.

Comparable versions:
In this book: "Charleston #2," Hoyt Ming and His Pep Steppers, *New Hot Times* (Homestead LP 103, 1973)

Charleston No. 3

Author's note: This transcription is from OKeh 45459, recorded San Antonio, TX, 06/06/1930.

Comparable versions:

"College Hornpipe," *A New and Highly Improved Violin Preceptor* (Utica, NY: William Williams, 1817), 11.

"Medley College Hornpipe," Don Richardson, 05/19/1921, New York, Columbia A3527

"Sailor's Hornpipe," John Baltzell, 06/1927, New York, Banner 2159

Willie T. Narmour and Shellie Walton Smith

Dry Gin Rag

Author's note: This transcription is from OKeh 45390, recorded New York, 09/25/1929.

Comparable versions: None known

Harry Bolick

Gallop to Georgia

Author's note: This transcription is from OKeh 45344, recorded Atlanta, 03/11/1929. The gallop was a popular French society dance in the 1820s, usually the final dance of the evening.

Comparable versions: None known

Willie T. Narmour and Shellie Walton Smith

Heel and Toe Polka

Author's note: This transcription is from OKeh 45276, recorded Memphis, TN, 02/15/1928. Henry Ford's Old Time Dance Orchestra had previously recorded a medley of "Heel and Toe Polka/Jenny Lind." Perhaps Narmour confused the tune and title. "The Jenny Lind Polka" was composed in honor of the opera singer Jenny Lind, "the Swedish Nightingale," for her US tour in 1846.

The guitar has a capo at the seventh fret and is fingered in the key of C.

Comparable versions:

"Jenny Lind Polka and Waltz," Robert Kelley, William Hall and Son, New York, 1848

Bolick and Austin, *Mississippi Fiddle Tunes and Songs from the 1930s*: Charlie Edmundson, "The Jenny Lind Polka," 97

"Jenny Lind Polka," Henry Whitter's Virginia Breakdowners, 07/22/1924, New York, OKeh 40211

"Heel and Toe Polka," Henry Ford's Old Time Dance Orchestra, 12/02/1926, Dearborn, MI, Victor 19909

"Dance with a Girl with a Hole in Her Stocking," Doc Roberts & Asa Martin, 05/15/1928, Richmond, IN, Gennett 6495

Jake Leg Rag

Author's note: This transcription is from OKeh 45469, recorded San Antonio, TX, 06/06/1930. The title refers to an incident of patent medicine contamination, whereby unknown thousands of closet drinkers were maimed, paralyzed, or killed.

Comparable versions: None known

Willie T. Narmour and Shellie Walton Smith

Kiss Me Waltz

Author's note: This transcription is from OKeh 45344, recorded Atlanta, 03/11/1929.

Comparable versions: None known

Harry Bolick

Limber Neck Blues

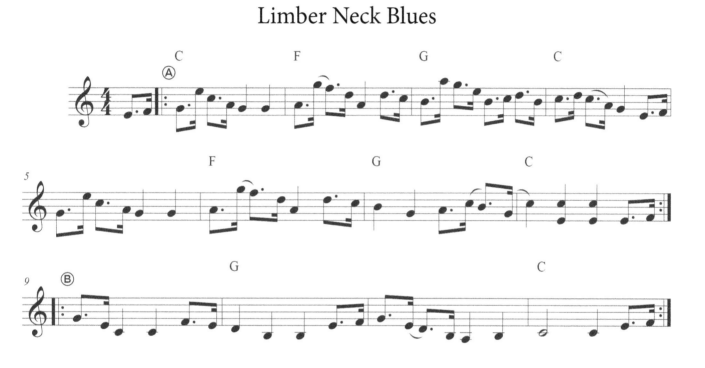

Author's note: This transcription is from OKeh 45548, recorded San Antonio, TX, 06/06/1930. The dotted eighth/sixteenth pattern in this transcription is a bit extreme, but the feel is swung and somewhere between what is noted and straight eighths.

Comparable versions:
See Andy Kuntz, *Fiddler Magazine* 21, Nos. 3 and 4 (Fall and Winter 2014/15); Fiddle Tune History: Rustic Dance Schottische
"Nightingale Clog," *Ryan's Mammoth Collection* NYC, Elias Howe, Boston, 1883
"Moonlight Clog," Gene Clardy and Stan Clements ("B" part only)

Willie T. Narmour and Shellie Walton Smith

Little Star

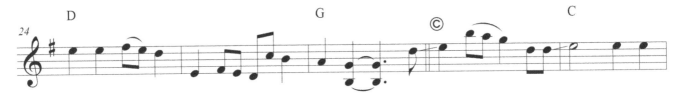

Author's note: This transcription is from OKeh 45276, recorded Memphis, TN, 02/15/1928. The chord in M24 once through the tune is a G, more often it is a D.

Comparable versions:
Fred MacEvit, words and music, 1879
Bolick and Austin, *Mississippi Fiddle Tunes and Songs from the 1930s*: W. E. Claunch, "Untitled (Twinkle, Twinkle, Little Star)," 276
"Twinkle, Twinkle, Little Star," Smith's Garage Fiddle Band, 12/1928, Dallas, Vocalion 5268
"Twinkle, Twinkle, Little Star," Bob Wills and His Texas Playboys, 11/28/1938, Dallas, Vocalion 05401

Midnight Waltz

Author's note: This transcription is from OKeh 45329, recorded Atlanta, 03/11/1929.

Comparable versions: None known

Willie T. Narmour and Shellie Walton Smith

Mississippi Breakdown

Author's note: This transcription is from OKeh 45492, recorded San Antonio, TX, 06/07/1930.

Comparable versions:

"Mississippi Breakdown," Leake County Revelers, 12/18/1930, Jackson, MS, Columbia 15668-D (Unrelated melody with the same title)

"Mississippi Breakdown," Mississippi Possum Hunters, 05/28/1930, San Antonio, TX, Victor 23595 (Unrelated melody with the same title)

　　　　　Harry Bolick

Mississippi Waves Waltz

Author's note: This transcription is from OKeh 45424, recorded New York, 09/25/1929. It demonstrates Smith's typical and rather minimalist approach to chords. For comparison, I have indicated chords in parentheses that are implied by the contour of the melody. Smith's chords generate a very different feel.

Comparable versions: None known

Willie T. Narmour and Shellie Walton Smith

The Rose Waltz

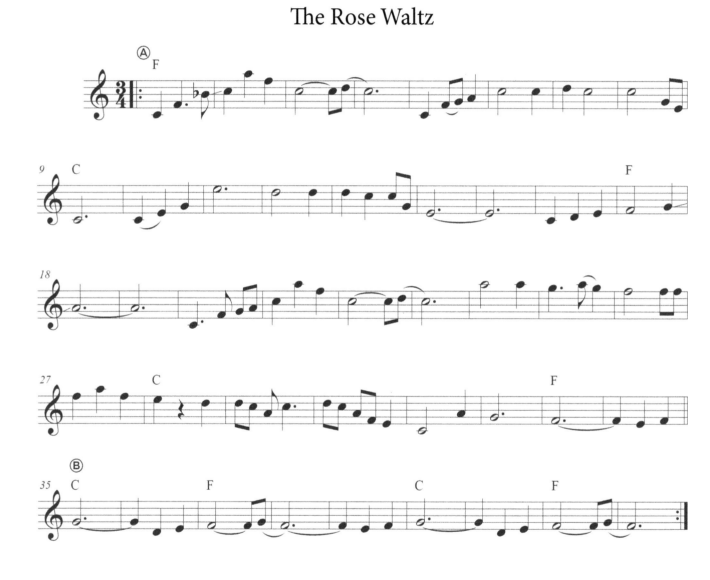

Author's note: This transcription is from OKeh 45390, recorded New York, 09/25/1929. On this recording, Narmour and Smith switch instruments, with Smith on fiddle.

Comparable versions: None known

Harry Bolick

Someone I Love

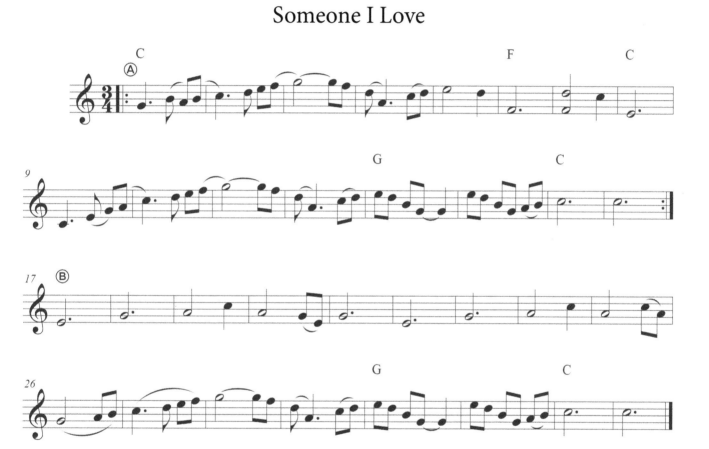

Author's note: This transcription is from OKeh 45329, recorded Atlanta, 03/11/1929.

Comparable versions: None known

Willie T. Narmour and Shellie Walton Smith

[449]

The Sunny Waltz

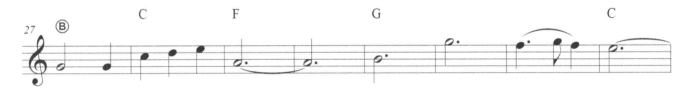

Author's note: This transcription is from OKeh 45242, recorded Memphis, TN, 02/15/1928.

Comparable versions: None known

Harry Bolick

Sweet Milk and Peaches

Author's note: This transcription is from OKeh 45424, recorded New York, 09/25/1929. On the recording, Narmour and Smith play this tune ten times. The transcription is the most complete setting. Alternate playing the B and C parts in the form of ABAC. The tune is made shorter on most passes by leaving out repeated phrases, which gives the recording an improvised feel. The guitar seems to have the capo at the second fret.

Comparable versions:

In this book: Compare M21–26 with M20–26 of "Sullivan's Hollow" by Freeny's Barn Dance Band. "Sullivan's Hollow," in the key of C, is often played in the key of D, which makes the similarity more apparent.

"Belle of Lexington," Emmett Lundy, Grayson County, VA, 1941, AFS 4938-B2 (somewhat similar)

"Wimbush Rag," Theodore & Gus Clark, 03/12/19/29, Atlanta, OKeh 45339 (somewhat similar)

Take Me As I Am

Author's note: This transcription is from OKeh 45548, recorded San Antonio, TX, 06/06/1930.

Comparable versions: None known

Harry Bolick

Tequila Hop Blues

Author's note: This transcription is from OKeh 45536, recorded San Antonio, TX, 06/07/1930. The tune is in D. Guitar is fingered in key of C with the capo at the second fret.

Comparable versions: None known

Willie T. Narmour and Shellie Walton Smith

Texas Breakdown

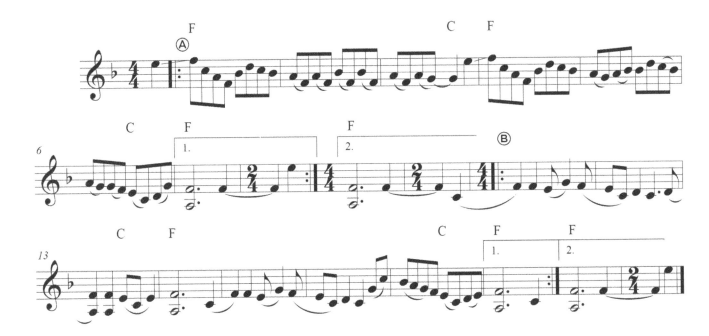

Author's note: This transcription is from OKeh 45492, recorded San Antonio, TX, 06/06/1930. In the B part of this tune, Smith plays the C bass note, suggesting the C chord in various places in M12–13 and M17, including as noted. The guitar has a capo at the fifth fret and is played in the key of C.

Comparable versions for the A part:

"Fisher's Hornpipe," J. Fishar (ca. 1780), *A New and Highly Improved Violin Preceptor*, 23.

Bolick and Austin, *Mississippi Fiddle Tunes and Songs from the 1930s*: All versions titled "Fisher's Hornpipe": Billie Mansfield and Chris Martin, 135; Mr. N. Odom, 157; Unknown, 188; Charles Long, 322; Stephen B. Tucker, 354; Alvis Massengale, 414

"Old Zip Coon and Medley Reels," Doc Roberts & Asa Martin, 05/15/1928, Richmond, IN, Gennett 6495

"Fisher's Hornpipe," The Hillbillies, 10/21/1926, New York, Vocalion 5017

"Fisher's Hornpipe," Clayton McMichen, Hoyt "Slim" Bryant & Jerry Wallace, 06/01/1939, New York, Decca 2649

Harry Bolick

Texas Shuffle

Author's note: This transcription is from OKeh 45536, recorded San Antonio, TX, 06/07/1930. On the first pass only, Narmour plays the first ending both times in the first part of the tune. "Texas Shuffle" was recorded in San Antonio along with "Texas Breakdown" and probably named in anticipation or celebration of the trip. However, there was also a "Little Texas" community within a few miles north of Avalon, which may have inspired the titles. It was a very rough county line spot known for fights and moonshine.

Comparable versions: None known

Where the Southern Crosses the Dog

Played after preceeding part. first time only

Author's note: This transcription is from OKeh 45480, recorded San Antonio, TX, 06/07/1930. M9–31 constitute the main body of this tune. M1–8 and M 32–41 are played on the first pass only.

Comparable versions: None known

Harry Bolick

Whistlin' Coon

Author's note: This transcription is from OKeh 45263, recorded Memphis, TN, 02/15/1928. The offensive title for this tune would not be acceptable today but at the time of this recording was unfortunately in common usage. The chords indicated are from one pass of the tune; each pass positions the chords a bit differently, within the range of a measure or so. The melody may be original to Narmour and Smith. The Nations Brothers recorded a tune by this title in 1935 but it was unissued and no copies are known. George W. Johnson's 1905 "Laughing Coon" perhaps influenced Narmour, but this is not an obvious cover of that performance. The guitar has a capo at the second fret and is fingering in the key of C.

Comparable versions:
In this book: "Cripple Coon," Hoyt Ming
"Whistlin Coon," George W. Johnson, 10/31/1895, Berliner 196 (some small similarity)
"Whistlin' Coon," Short Brothers, 02/24/1928, Memphis, TN, OKeh 45206 (some similarity)

Who's Been Giving You Corn

Author's note: This transcription is from OKeh 45263, recorded Memphis, TN, 02/15/1928.

Comparable versions: None known

Harry Bolick

Winona Echoes

Author's note: This transcription is from OKeh 45414, recorded New York, 09/23/1929.

Comparable versions:
Sobre las Olas" (or "Over the Waves"), Juventino Rosas, 1888
"Over the Waves Waltz," Kessinger Brothers, 06/24/1929, New York, Brunswick 344
"Over the Waves," Stripling Brothers, 09/10/1934, New York, Decca 5041
In this book: "Over the Waves," Collier Trio, 12/1928, New Orleans, Brunswick 288

Willie T. Narmour and Shellie Walton Smith

THE NATIONS BROTHERS

Sheldon and Marshall Nations were from the Fair Oak Springs community, near Brookhaven, the county seat of Lincoln County. John Sheldon Nations (1910–1985) played fiddle, and Marshall Dee Nations (1912–1995) guitar.

In letters written in 1972–73, Marshall Nations gave some of the family background to their music. Their father, Luther C. Nations (1884–1968), played fiddle,[1] and most of his children—six boys and two girls—played something. In occasional breaks from farming their land, the six-piece Nations family band "played at various entertainments throughout the State for several years."

In October 1935, H. C. Speir organized a location recording session in Jackson for Brunswick–ARC. On October 13, Sheldon and Marshall cut ten

Sheldon Nations, May 1960. Photo courtesy Mary Nations Smith.

Sheldon and Marshall Nations promotional photo. Courtesy Scott Nations.

sides, and over the next few months three releases appeared on Vocalion. (Sheldon was misspelled Shelton on the record labels.) The best seller was the coupling of "Bankhead Blues" and "Magnolia One Step," which was also issued on dime-store labels for which ARC supplied material, such as Melotone, Perfect, and Banner. "Bankhead Blues," "Lincoln County Blues," and "Railroad Blues" are not straight blues but rather collections of blues phrases, somewhat in the manner of Narmour and Smith, and this description can also be applied to "Magnolia One Step" and "Sales Tax Toddle," the latter an extraordinary performance seemingly made up of curt fragments. Sheldon moves back

and forth among his mini-themes—like a dancer toddling, in fact, side to side, swaying and swerving—and Marshall's guitar is with him all the way.

"A few of our tunes were our father's," Marshall wrote (one was "Magnolia One Step," which his father called "Get Up in the Cool"), "but the others were our own compositions. My brother would sometimes take several old tunes, change them and put them together, making new ones, such as 'Sales Tax Toddle.'"

The fourth and last of the brothers' records, released in May 1937, was the coupling "Negro Supper Time" and "Honeymoon Waltz." The former sounded like an old "shout" tune, but vivaciously

ELECT

SHELDON NATIONS

AS YOUR

LINCOLN COUNTY

TAX ASSESSOR &

TAX COLLECTOR

YOUR VOTE AND INFLUENCE IS APPRECIATED

Sheldon's business card, from collection of Tony Russell.

VOTE FOR

MARSHALL NATIONS

FOR

CHIEF OF POLICE

YOUR VOTE AND INFLUENCE WILL BE APPRECIATED

Marshall's business card, from collection of Tony Russell.

syncopated, and had something of the style of the Stripling Brothers, then well-known in northern Alabama and adjacent parts of Mississippi. The Nations Brothers recorded another waltz, "Sunny Waltz," which remained unissued, perhaps because it had been recorded earlier by Narmour and Smith, as had the other unissued title in the Nations discography, "Whistlin' Coon."

The recording session, of course, was just an incident; the Nations Brothers played a great deal more, including many fiddlers' conventions "all over South Mississippi," with Sheldon generally (Marshall claimed) winning first place. He certainly did so at a contest in McCall Creek, Franklin County, in 1931: "Sheldon Nations of Brookhaven was awarded first prize as best fiddler."[2] The family also reports that he won the state fiddlers' contest at Jackson in 1936, for which he was awarded a fiddle and case, and in the same year "beat the 'Fiddling Fool' of Dallas in a fiddle

contest at the courthouse in Athens, Texas. Sheldon and Marshall returned to Athens several times and were always well received.... On one occasion, they broadcast a half-hour program over radio station WFAA in Dallas."[3]

"We were invited to play at all the schools in several surrounding counties," Marshall remembered. "Of course in political years we enjoyed ourselves playing at picnics and gatherings.... After we married we gradually quit playing so often because of family and responsibilities. World War II came along and I was drafted from training. I was shipped to England, across the Channel to Omaha Beach. There I served with the Second Infantry Division throughout Europe."

Meanwhile Sheldon, says his grandson Scott Nations, "[worked as] a carpenter and traveled around the county building Army camps. As far as I know this period was the only time he lived

Tony Russell

1. Luther C. Nations "tied for first place in fiddling" with Carlos Stewart at an event in Brookhaven in July 1928 ("Hog Callers Parade Streets of Brookhaven," *Daily Clarion-Ledger*, Jackson, MS, July 17, 1928, 3). A brief account in the *Hattiesburg American*, October 12, 1931, reports that L. C. Nations placed third in a fiddlers' contest at the Sarphie Theater in Brookhaven some days earlier.

2. *Daily Clarion-Ledger*, Jackson, MS, March 24, 1931, 3.

3. *Daily Leader*, Brookhaven, MS, undated but ca. mid-1970s.

4. *Daily Leader*, Brookhaven, MS, undated but ca. mid-1970s.

anywhere else other than Brookhaven.... He was also a farmer, growing crops and raising cattle. My Uncle [Marshall] was a farmer in the second half of his life and my Grandfather helped him with that after retiring from carpentry."

According to an article published, probably in the late '70s, in the Brookhaven *Daily Leader*, "Sheldon Nations is probably better known to Lincoln Countians as the retired contractor turned farmer who built such edifices as the Fair River, Friendship, Central Baptist, and Enterprise churches. Marshall was on the Brookhaven Police Force, [and] worked for years at the Piggly Wiggly Food Store.... A younger brother, Kees Nations [1919–1973], played guitar and sang with them on occasion."[4]

In later years, as family members recall, the brothers very seldom played music. "The last time I asked [my grandfather] to play," says Scott Nations, "he declined, saying his fingers weren't limber enough now. I think he felt like he ... would rather not play than play poorly.... Most of my memories of him playing are from ... about the time I started second grade.... The thing that amazed me most ... [was that] he could imitate donkeys braying and old-time steam trains with his fiddle, which to me at that age seemed downright magical."

—Tony Russell

Bankhead Blues

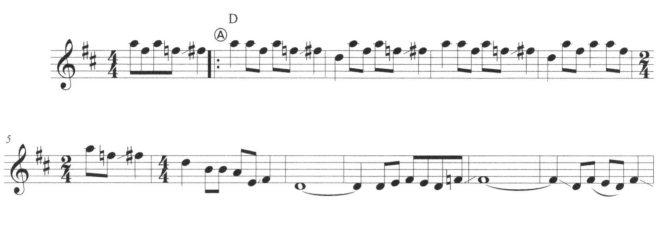

Tony Russell

Author's note: This transcription is from ARC 6–11–54, recorded Jackson, MS, 10/13/1935.

Comparable versions: None known

Honeymoon Waltz

Author's note: This transcription is from ARC 7–05–78, recorded Jackson, MS, 10/13/1935. The guitar line is quite nuanced in this waltz. In three sections there is a descending bass line on the downbeat of each measure that doesn't conform to the expected I, IV, or V chords. In M30–M32 it is F-E-D. In M49–M51 it is A-A#-G. In M61–M64 it is F-E-D-C. The chord strums in these measures are heard more as percussion, not pitch.

Comparable versions:
"Farewell Waltz," Doc Roberts Trio, 03/05/1931, New York, Banner 32176
"Farewell Waltz," Mississippi Mud Steppers, 12/15/1930, Jackson, MS, OKeh 45532

Lincoln County Blues

Author's note: This transcription is from Vocalion 03184, recorded Jackson, MS, 10/13/1935. In M18–19 and M26 the guitarist fingers a partial B chord but the rather jarring D# is lightly struck and barely heard.

Comparable versions: None known

The Little Black Mustache

Author's note: This transcription is from Vocalion 03152, recorded Jackson, MS, 10/13/1935. M14 has an Am chord indicated. Marshall Nations does not play a chord but begins a G-scale run at that point starting on an A note, which is a touch jarring but lovely.

Comparable versions:
In this book: "Black Mustache," Gene Clardy & Stan Clements, 02/18/1930, Memphis, TN, Vocalion 5418
There is a song, unrelated except by title, recorded by Vernon Dalhart, Henry Whitter, Ernest Stoneman, and others.

Tony Russell

Magnolia One Step

Author's note: This transcription is from ARC 6–11–54, recorded Jackson, MS, 10/13/1935. The guitarist is playing alternating
bass notes of G and D, either with the capo at third fret or playing out of the third fret partial bar chord with occasional
bass runs. The repeats: passes one and two as transcribed; third pass M1–M8 then M25 to end; fourth pass same as the first,
repeats B part; fifth and sixth passes are the same as pass three; seven and eighth passes are the same as three with alt M6–7.
Sheldon learned this tune from his father, Luther, who favored tunes in cross-key tuning but required Sheldon to use standard
tuning.

Comparable versions: None known

Negro Supper Time

Tony Russell

Author's note: This transcription is from ARC 7–05–78, recorded Jackson, MS, 10/13/1935. The B part is variously twelve, fourteen, sixteen, or eighteen measures and is accompanied by the tonic chord only.

Comparable versions:
"The Girl Slipped Down," Dr. D. D. Hollis, 04/1928, New York, Silvertone 3513

Railroad Blues

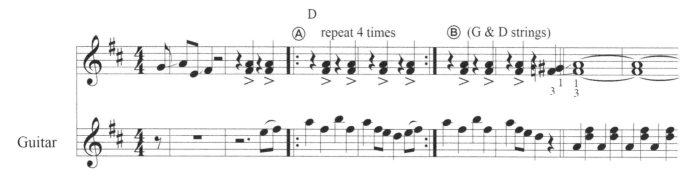

Tony Russell

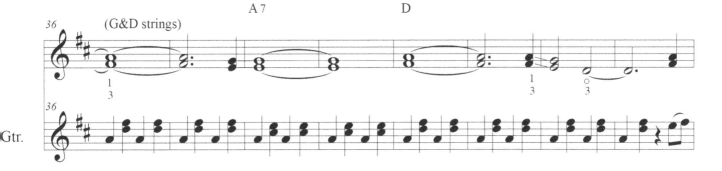

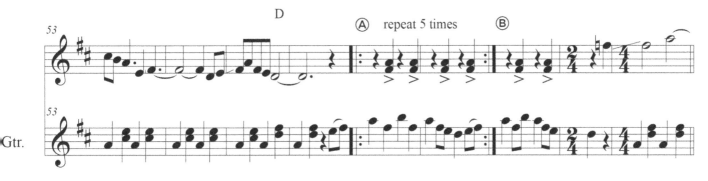

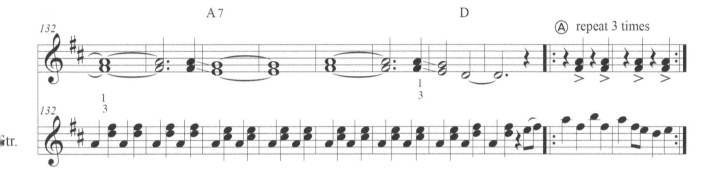

Author's note: This transcription is from Vocalion 03152, recorded Jackson, MS, 10/13/1935. I have notated the entire performance due to the variable part lengths. The guitar riff in M3–4 varies in repeats. Repeats are indicated in each case. The sliding fiddle position shifts are all using the index (1) and third (3) fingers, either on the G and D or A and E strings. The upbeat accent for the fiddle "chop" are indicated only the first time they appear but continue throughout. The guitar either has a capo at the fifth fret or is played in that position without a capo on the top four strings.

Comparable versions:

No melodic similarities, but see "Engineer Frank Hawk" by John Gatwood in this book for another tune featuring train sounds.

Sales Tax Toddle

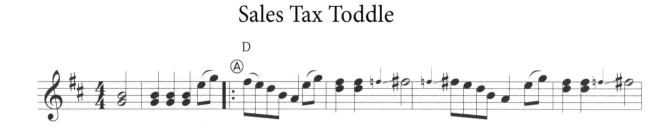

Ⓐ After first pass, play this version on each repeat.

Author's note: This transcription is from Vocalion 03184, recorded Jackson, MS, 10/13/1935. The repeats on the recording:

    1: As written. Note that the B part is a two-measure phrase repeated four times.
    2: Second A part; B, two-measure phrase repeated five times.
    3: Second A part M22–26 skips to M31–37; B, two-measure phrase repeated five times.
    4: Second A part M22–32, skips to M35; B, two-measure phrase repeated seven times.
    5: Second A part, M12–14 flubbed but there; B, two-measure phrase repeated seven times.
    6: Second A part; B, two-measure phrase repeated eight times.
    7: Second A part, M22–26 skips to M31–37; B, two-measure phrase repeated three times, then ends.

Guitar plays the F#-G changes in the later part of the tune as bar chords with the accent on the offbeat.

Comparable versions:
In this book: Jabe Dillon, "Unknown Instrumental"

THE NEWTON COUNTY
HILL BILLIES/ALVIS MASSENGALE

Alvis Massengale (1897–1993) recorded for OKeh Records with the Newton County Hill Billies in Jackson, Mississippi, on Tuesday, December 16, 1930. With Alvis on fiddle, Marcus Harrison on mandolin, and Andrew Harrison on guitar, they recorded six tunes: "Little Princess Footsteps," "Happy Hour Breakdown," "Nine O'clock Breakdown" (a cover of the Leake County Revelers' "Saturday Night Breakdown"), "Going to the Wedding to Get Some Cake," "Give Me a Bottle of I Don't Care What" (a cover of the Leake County Revelers' "Bring Me a Bottle"), and "Quaker Waltz."

Alvis started playing fiddle around the age of ten, learning from his father and grandfather, who were both fiddlers, and by listening to the radio and records. He claimed that at one point his repertoire reached one hundred and fifty tunes, seventy-five of which he still remembered in 1980 at the age of eighty-three. He was a highly skilled fiddler playing carefully phrased and ornamented tunes.

My granddaddy's favorite tune was "Arkansas Traveler." He'd just go to laughing when he played it or when he heard it played. Once I was with him in town when there was fellow called Blind Buddy Moore playing a fiddle on a street corner. It tickled

Alvis Massengale, from 1980 *Mississippi Sawyers* LP cover. Photo by Gil Ford.

granddaddy so much he jerked out a dollar and gave it to him.

My granddaddy came from southwest Texas. He came back here to get married and his wife was just never satisfied out there, so they eventually moved back, sometime in the 1800s. My daddy was born out there. My granddaddy could speak Spanish and play some Spanish tunes. He lived until 1927. I was a grown man and married before then. He'd come stay a week at a time with us. I learned more from him then than when I was a kid.[1]

He attributed one of his tunes, "Sebastapol," to learning it from his grandfather, who had learned it from a "Mexican musician."[2] Sebastapol is a town in Leake and Scott Counties in the area where Alvis lived. His uniquely titled "Bilbo Rag" resembles the "Doughboy Rag" as recorded by The Light Crust Doughboys in 1933. His "Fisher's Hornpipe" is an unusual and interesting variant of the usual tune, and was his contest-winning tune. Most of the rest of his known repertoire included well-known tunes, some apparently learned from 78 rpm recordings by other Mississippi fiddlers, such as the Leake County Revelers tunes "Crow Black Chicken," "Old Hat," "Goodnight Waltz," "Leake County Blues," "Magnolia Waltz," "Monkey in the Dogcart," and "Wednesday Night Waltz"; and Narmour and Smith's tunes "Carroll County Blues," "Charleston 1 and 2," "Gallop to Georgia," and "Someone I Love." As is usual in Mississippi, a significant portion of his repertoire was waltzes.

Playing the tune "Sebastapol," Alvis is a conduit of tradition. With the repertoire that he learned from radio and recordings, we get a picture of him as member of the first generation to come of age with the new communications technologies. The origins of "Happy Hour Breakdown," "Going to the Wedding to Get Some Cake," and "Quaker Waltz" are not known.

Alvis was the only child of Franklin and Emma Massengale of Newton County, Mississippi. He married Nellie Hillman Belk on May 5, 1918, and they went on to have seven children. Throughout his life, fiddling and drinking were Alvis's main interests. He infrequently worked, money was scarce, and

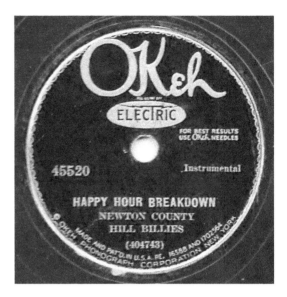

his large family struggled to get by. They lived in a three-room shack with no electricity or water until the 1970s. The 1940 census lists Alvis's occupation as a laborer in the wood industry, meaning that he hauled pulpwood. That may well have been the only time he was employed. In 1956, while riding in a pickup truck, drinking and arguing, Alvis shot and killed Willie D. Leach and was sent to prison.[3] He may have stopped drinking at that point.

His son, Cartis, learned guitar before he was twelve and backed up Alvis at local square dances and get-togethers. Cartis went on to learn to play fiddle and recorded on the 1980 LP *Mississippi Sawyers*, as did Alvis. From at least 1980[4] through 1982, Alvis played with the Leake County String Band.[5] Alvis's untitled tune transcribed in this book comes from cassettes recorded during this period of his life. Cartis also played with the Leake County String Band during and after those years.

Alvis gained his reputation playing at Saturday night socials around Union, MS, and in 1920s fiddling contests. He won the Mississippi state championship for fiddlers in the 1930s. He played on radio stations WMAG in Forrest for three years, WBKN in Newton, MS, for three years, and on WCOC in Meridian, MS. He also played dances at nightclubs and American Legion and VFW halls. Alvis, with the Newton County Hill Billies, furnished the music before Judge Paul B. Johnson addressed the voters assembled in Union, MS, at the school building on July 22, 1931.[6]

Jerome Sage of the WPA's Federal Music Project interviewed Alvis in 1939. Sage listed 110 tune titles in his repertoire. However, Herbert Halpert did not record him on his field-recording trip later that year, perhaps because he had recorded commercially or because so much of his repertoire had been learned from radio and recordings. Several of the tunes listed, such as "Shanty Town," were pop tunes and show Alvis adapting to changing local tastes. Another Mississippi fiddler, John Gatwood of the Gatwood Square Dance Band, also played "Shanty Town."

—Harry Bolick

Alvis recorded six tunes with the Newton County Hill Billies that are transcribed in this book.
Mississippi Sawyers: A Collection of Old-Time Mississippi Fiddling (LP, Sawyer Productions, 1980): "Leather Breeches"; "Golden Slippers"

Alvis Massengale, Mississippi Fiddle Music (Field Recorders Collective FRC 724, 2017), has thirty tunes from field tapes recorded by Gus Meade and Howard Marshall in the 1970s.

"Bilbo Rag," "Fisher's Hornpipe," "Goodnight Waltz," and "Sebastapol" are transcribed and included in Harry Bolick and Stephen T. Austin, *Mississippi Fiddle Tunes and Songs from the 1930s* (Jackson: University Press of Mississippi, 2015).

Cartis Massengale had several home-recorded cassettes of Alvis playing. The cassettes are in the possession of his widow, Irene Massengale. Except for his unknown tune included in this book, the tunes were all standards.

Special thanks to Frank Ricketts, Judi Reynolds, Pat Conte, Gus Meade, Howard Marshall, Jeff Place, and Gregg Adams.

NOTES

1. Mary Anne Wells, "Union's Alvis Massengale, Still Fiddlin' Around," *Union Appeal*, Union, MS, July 14, 1982, 5.

2. Gus Meade, field recording interview, 1970s.

3. "Charge Alvis Massengale with Murder," *Union Appeal*, Union, MS, March 29, 1956, 1.

4. "Fourth Annual Country Day Saturday," *Union Appeal*, Union, MS, August 20, 1980, 1.

5. Wells, "Union's Alvis Massengale, Still Fiddlin' Around," 5.

6. *Union Appeal*, July 23, 1931.

Give Me a Bottle of I Don't Care What

Author's note: This transcription is from OKeh 45544, recorded Jackson, MS, 12/16/1930.

Comparable versions:
In this book: "Bring Me a Bottle," Leake County Revelers, 12/12/1928, New Orleans, Columbia 15380-D

Similar A parts:
"Dance All Night with a Bottle in Your Hand," Gid Tanner & His Skillet Lickers, 11/02/1926, Atlanta, Columbia 150108-D
"Dance All Night with a Bottle in My Hand," Stripling Brothers, 08/19/1929, Chicago, Vocalion 5395

Similar B parts:
"Jenny Lind Polka and Waltz," Robert Kelley, William Hall and Son, New York, 1848
Bolick and Austin, *Mississippi Fiddle Tunes and Songs from the 1930s*: Charlie Edmundson, "Jenny Lind Polka," 97
"Jenny Lind Polka," Henry Whitter's Virginia Breakdowners, 07/22/1924, New York, OKeh 40211
"Heel and Toe Polka," Henry Ford's Old Time Dance Orchestra, 12/02/1926, Dearborn, MI, Victor 19909
"Dance with a Girl with a Hole in Her Stocking," Doc Roberts & Asa Martin, 05/15/1928, Richmond, IN, Gennett 6495
In this book: "Heel and Toe Polka," W. T. Narmour & S. W. Smith, 02/14/1929, Memphis, TN, OKeh 45276

Harry Bolick

Going to the Wedding, to Get Some Cake

Author's note: This transcription is from OKeh 45549, recorded Jackson, MS, 12/16/1930. The guitarist did not play the implied D chord in M10.

Comparable versions:
"Hop Light Lady," Fiddlin' John Carson & His Virginia Reelers, 06/30/1925, Atlanta, OKeh 45011
"Did You Ever See the Devil, Uncle Joe?" Paul Miles and the Red Fox Chasers, 04/15/1928, Richmond, IN, Gennett 6461
"McCloud's Reel," Kessinger Brothers, 06/25/1929, New York, Brunswick 580

Happy Hour Breakdown

Author's note: This transcription is from OKeh 45520, recorded Jackson, MS, 12/16/1930. Only the first time through the first part, the guitar plays a D chord in M4.

Comparable versions: This tune has some similarity to the A part of "Billy in the Lowground."

Harry Bolick

Little Princess's Footsteps

Author's note: This transcription is from OKeh 45549, recorded Jackson, MS, 12/16/1930.

Comparable versions: None known

Nine O'Clock Breakdown

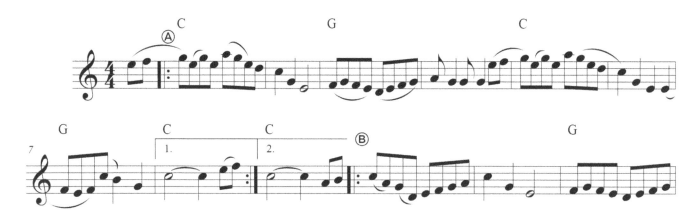

Author's note: This transcription is from OKeh 45544, recorded Jackson, MS, 12/16/1930.

Comparable versions:
In this book: "Saturday Night Breakdown," Leake County Revelers, 04/16/1929, Atlanta, Columbia 15470-D
In this book: "Mississippi Breakdown," Mississippi Possum Hunters, 05/28/1930, Memphis, TN, Victor 23595

Harry Bolick

Quaker Waltz

Author's note: This transcription is from OKeh 45520, recorded Jackson, MS, 12/16/1930. M7, M15, and M24 are used interchangeably.

Comparable versions:
"Beautiful Valley Waltz," Theron Hale & His Daughters, 10/03/1928, Nashville, TN, Victor V40019
"St. Jobe's Waltz," Red Headed Fiddlers, 10/29/1929, Dallas, Brunswick 460
"Dawn Waltz," Jack Cawley's Oklahoma Ridge Runners, 11/24/1930, Memphis, TN, Victor 23521

GROVER CLATER O'BRIANT

O'Briant (1912–1995) played fiddle, guitar, banjo, harmonica, piano, and mandolin and sang very well. Although he never recorded commercially, family recordings show that he was quite accomplished on guitar and fiddle. Grover acquired a reel-to-reel recorder in the 1960s and his son Jerry kept the recordings.

Grover started out in the Providence Community of Attala County and remained in the county for the rest of his life. He and his close friend Earl "Buster" Reynolds learned to play by ear when they were young. While they were still young, both families moved about twenty-five miles from Providence to Kilmichael.

Grover earned his first fiddle as a prize for selling two boxes of Beech-Nut chewing gum. "Later on I traded a milk cow for one."[1] "I used to hear the late Earl Reynolds and his brother play down the road from me and I used to listen to Gid Tanner and Clayton McMichen's records. I always liked the fiddle music."[2]

After he finished his schooling and before he joined the Army in 1945, Grover played with several country bands including an often low-paying one with Buck Turner: "One boy that used to play with us was Buck Turner, and we were starvation box beaters...."[3] "Still, "He said that he made way more money playing music than working

Grover O'Briant. Photo courtesy of Jerry O'Briant.

on the farm or in the sawmill."[4] Jackson, Tennessee, newspapers list radio appearances of Buck Turner between 1933 and 1966. The band appearances followed a familiar pattern for string bands of that era. They would play a short spot on the radio in the morning to advertise a schoolhouse

Grover and Evelyn O'Briant, J. H. and Mae Ellis. Photo courtesy Jerry O'Briant.

Homer Grice, Billy Cook, Grover O'Briant, Mr. Womble, Mr. Ward. Photo courtesy Jerry O'Briant.

Grover practiced calligraphy and could draw, as well as play music. Photo courtesy of Jerry O'Briant.

Grover O'Briant and Clayton Tyler at fiddle contest in French Camp, MS, 1975. Photo by Carl Fleischhauer.

appearance that night. Some nights their shows were so well attended that they would clear out the schoolhouse and play a second show, to accommodate the overflow crowd. Grover played fiddle on radio stations in Kosciusko, Jackson, and Birmingham, Alabama. Buck Turner and O'Briant appeared at the Municipal Auditorium in Birmingham for a broadcast of the WSM Grand Old Opry as guests of one of the official bands. On one occasion Grover was part of the warm-up band for an appearance by Tex Ritter.

One of Grover's favorite fiddle tunes was "Carroll County Blues." Sometime in the 1930s, he and some friends rode a flatbed truck over roughly fifty miles of rutted dirt roads to Carroll County to meet and play with Willie T. Narmour. It would have been an arduous trip.

Grover remembered attending the Kosciusko fiddle contest in 1920, as a child of nine or ten years old. He somewhat unsuccessfully tried to revive it in the 1970s and then succeeded in getting it going again in 1984. He emceed and played in the contest. The Grand Champion Trophy for the Natchez Trace Festival was named for him. Homer Grice was a friend and lived nearby. From the 1940s through the 1970s, Grover and Homer visited and played often. Grice also competed in Kosciusko contests and was quite intent on winning.

In the late 1930s, Grover was plowing a field near the community of Tabernacle near Ethel, about eighteen miles from his home. His friend, Buster, found him and convinced him to come and back up Buster's fiddling at a nearby gospel singing school. Grover unhitched his mule, picked up his guitar, and rode the mule to Tabernacle, where he met his wife-to-be, Evelyn. World War II interrupted their romance when Grover was drafted in 1940. When he was released from service in 1945, they married and eventually had two children, Jerry and Martha.[5]

Evelyn Ellis O'Briant was also a fine musician, able to play guitar, piano, mandolin, banjo, fiddle, and accordion. She only had the accordion for a short while. It was purchased in installments and stolen, before the payments were completed, while she and Grover were playing a performance. Early in Evelyn's life, her brother, Leo, insisted that she learn to read music and play gospel music. Evelyn and her sister, Melba, her brother, Leo, and her father, Homer, had a gospel singing group. Homer and Leo Ellis recorded with Milner and Curtis. Her Uncle Lonnie Ellis recorded with the Mississippi Possum Hunters.

Grover worked as a farmer. Of the over eighty acres he purchased from his father-in-law, Homer Ellis, in 1946, only about ten were usable for farming. That was enough to feed the family, but not much more than that. Perhaps a couple acres of cotton could be worked with horses. During the Depression years, when Homer owned the farm, there was little cash in circulation and there was little to purchase, since most folks were in a similar situation. Substance farmers in Mississippi took little notice of the Great Depression, since times were hard before, during, and after the crash. Homer's farm was paid for over thirty years in forty-five-dollar installments, with taxes of about twenty dollars, and still he came close to losing it several times.

Grover far preferred police work and music to farming. He served as an Attala County constable from 1956 to 1964, a deputy sheriff from 1972 to 1973, marshal of Ethel and French Camp from 1972 to 1983, and fire control aid and assistant park ranger on the Natchez Trace Parkway from 1961 to 1971.

—Harry Bolick

NOTES

1. Barbara Shoemake, "Fiddling Convention Revived," *Star-Herald*, Kosciusko, MS, March 29, 1984, 2.

2. Pam Garner, "Gum prize starts fiddling career," *Star-Herald*, Kosciusko, MS, March 19, 1987, 2.

3. Garner, "Gum prize starts fiddling career," 2.

4. Lela Garlington, "O'Briant began as musician, later was law officer," *Commercial Appeal*, Memphis, TN, May 9, 1995.

5. Author's interview with Jerry O'Briant, Kilmichael, MS, February 6, 2019.

Recordings

Jerry O'Briant shared his father's collection of five circa mid-1960s reel-to-reel tapes, six cassettes, and three borrowed cassettes from Grover's friend Tommy Sanders. The tunes transcribed and the recordings posted at mississippifiddle.com come from those unlabeled tapes of mostly untitled tunes.

On one of Tommy Sanders's cassettes, Sanders announces the fiddler as Grover O'Briant. On one of O'Briant's reel-to-reel tapes, Grover announces that his friend Buster Reynolds is playing fiddle. Based on the fiddle styles, I have attributed the transcribed tunes to Grover or Buster; however, the fiddlers on those recordings may have been someone else in Grover's circle of musician friends, which included Homer Grice and Billy Cook.

O'Briant's known fiddle repertoire, in addition to the transcribed tunes:

Bile Them Cabbage Down
Carroll County Blues
Charleston No. 1
Chicken Reel
Devil's Dream
Dixie
Faded Love
Goodnight Waltz
Maiden's Prayer
Old Joe Clark
Over the Waves
Rubber Dolly
Rye Whiskey
Saturday Night Breakdown
Tennessee Waltz
Under the Double Eagle

Reynolds Waltz

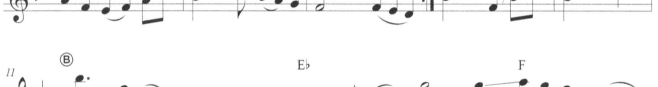

Author's note: Fiddler Buster Reynolds made up this tune as his variation on another waltz. Grover O'Briant played guitar on the circa mid-1960s home recording.

Comparable versions: None known

Harry Bolick

Untitled No. 1

Author's note: Grover O'Briant on fiddle.

Comparable versions: None known

Untitled No. 2

Author's note: On the home recording, the tune is played as written above and then repeats the B part twice before ending. The guitar ends the C part with a D chord on the half note G, which sounds like a mistake. The fiddler was Grover O'Briant.

Comparable versions: None known

Harry Bolick

Untitled No. 3 (Walk Right In)

Author's note: The fiddler on this home recording was Buster Reynolds, with Grover O'Briant on guitar.

Comparable versions:
"Walk Right In," (Gus) Cannon's Jug Stompers, 10/01/1929, Memphis, TN, Victor V38611

Untitled No. 4

Author's note: In the home recording, the repeats seem to be ABABC but vary, with the A part sometimes doubled. Grover O'Briant is on fiddle, Tommy and Mervin Sander on guitars.

Harry Bolick

Untitled No. 5

Author's note: The fiddler on this home cassette recording is Grover O'Briant.
Only on the first pass through the tune, M4 has an extra beat as shown in alt M4 (and 5).

Untitled No. 6

Author's note: The fiddler on this home cassette recording is Grover O'Briant.

Harry Bolick

Untitled No. 7 (Devil's Dream)

Author's note: This transcription is from a family reel-to-reel recording in the collection of Jerry O'Briant. Listen to it at mississippifiddle.com.

Comparable versions:

Elias Howe, *Howe's School for the Violin* (Boston: Oliver Ditson, 1851), 29

Bolick and Austin, *Mississippi Fiddle Tunes and Songs from the 1930s*: T. W. Cooper, "Untitled," 86; W. E. Claunch, "Devil's Dream," 256; Stephen B. Tucker, "Devil's Dream," 352

In this book: "(Devil's Dream)," Claude Kennedy

"Devil's Dream," Kessinger Bros, 02/10/1928, Ashland, KY, Brunswick 256

"Devil's Dream," Clayton McMichen, 06/01/1931, New York, Decca 2649

Untitled No. 8 (Wolves A Howling)

Author's note: The fiddler on this home cassette recording is Grover O'Briant.

Comparable versions:
Marion Thede, *The Fiddle Book* (New York: Oak Publication, 1970), 133
"Wolves Howling" (C 4135-), Stripling Brothers, 08/19/1929 Chicago, Vocalion 5412
Bolick and Austin, *Mississippi Fiddle Tunes and Songs from the 1930s*: John Brown, "Wolves A Howling," 235; W. E. Claunch, "Wolves A Howling," 279

Harry Bolick

Untitled No. 9 (Waltz)

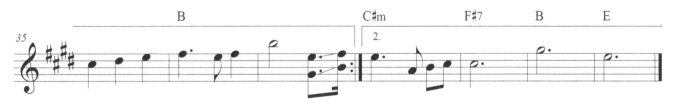

Author's note: On this home recording Grover O'Briant is on guitar and Buster Reynolds on fiddle.

Comparable versions: None known

JIMMIE PORTER

Jimmie Porter (1906–1996), from Steens, MS, played with such a rich tone that folks who heard him believed he had a better violin and a longer bow than other fiddlers. "Everywhere I've ever been someone wanted to come measure my bow," remembered Porter in 1984. "They said it looked like it was six foot long. But theirs was as long as mine."[1]

Jimmie Vasco Porter was born in 1906 in Ashcraft Corner, literally in the corner of Fayette County touching upon Lamar and Pickens Counties, Alabama. This small community abounded in good fiddlers. Among them was Uncle Plez Carroll (1850–1930), one of eight fiddling brothers who added tunes like "The Lost Child" and "Wolves Howling" to local repertoires. There was Charlie Stripling, ten years older than Jimmie, who became a recording artist and champion fiddler, and there was E. D. "Monkey" Brown, nine years older, whose trick fiddling antics helped him win numerous contests and a place in Carl Carmer's *Stars Fell on Alabama*.[2]

When Jimmie was about six years old, his uncle, Jim Porter, came back from Arkansas to visit the homeplace after being gone for thirty years. He asked his brother if there was a fiddle in the house and Jimmie was surprised when his father opened a chifforobe and pulled out a fiddle. It had no strings, but a store nearby stocked them, so neighbors were able to hear Uncle Jim play on Saturday night. During the following week he showed Jimmie how to play. "I just happened to be the right age to grab it and go to playing. . . . Sounds strange to say, but I didn't have to hunt for a thing. I probably didn't make too good a music, but I was playing it. And the people was coming in a'visiting to hear him play the first week and me the next."

It wasn't long before his father came home from Fayette with a fiddle for Jimmie. "He never did tell me where he got it, how much it cost, or nothing." The label inside read Rudolph Wurlitzer, USA. In 1963 Charlie Stripling told interviewer Bob Pinson about one of his chief competitors at fiddlers' conventions: "And another fellow that I dreaded was a fellow by the name of Porter—Jimmie Porter. And he had the best fiddle . . . I declare that was the best sounding fiddle I ever heard in my life."[3]

Fiddlers' conventions in the area were frequent and the competition was fierce. Local fiddlers had their choice of numerous contests in high school auditoriums and county courthouses in West Alabama and Eastern Mississippi. The largest and most important area conventions, sponsored by the United Daughters of the Confederacy, were held in the Fayette County Courthouse twice a year. They were well promoted, offered impressive cash

Jimmy Porter, 1927.
Photo courtesy
Virginia Porter Estes.

prizes to the finalists, and gave consolation prizes to all others who entered. Between 1929 and 1933 Porter regularly competed with Charlie Stripling, beating him once and more often coming in second. Several times the contests ended in three- or four-way ties with Porter, Stripling, and one or both of the Brown brothers, Monkey and Charlie.[4] Stripling told Bob Pinson that Porter "didn't play this ragtime breakdown music hardly a'tall. He played slow waltzes and he'd really sound good. They had judges that liked that kind. That's the only time he ever got a prize over me."[5] Though Porter excelled in playing waltzes, he did play breakdowns such as

"Horseshoe Bend," "Leather Breeches," and "Lost John." Trick fiddling was common at the conventions, mainly "Pop Goes the Weasel," played from various contorted positions. Porter's trick number was "Johnson's Old Gray Mule," in which he made his fiddle bray like a mule. The courthouse would be fully packed, and Porter recalled that the audience would "nearly tear the floor down, if you played a good piece that they liked. They'd about wreck the place. Just like a speech, they'd give the feller a good [clapping motion] if he made a good speech. Well they'll let you know. If you play a good tune, they'll let you know."

Jimmy Porter, 1990. Photo courtesy Virginia Porter Estes.

Porter married Arline Shepherd on November 27, 1927. Though both grew up in Ashcraft Corner, they married in Lowndes County and settled in Tabernacle Community, Mississippi.[6] In the spring of 1928, he traveled to Birmingham to enter a big contest that featured popular recording artists such as Gid Tanner, Bert Lane, Clayton McMichen, and Lowe Stokes. Such contests were held in larger cities and the big names drew big audiences though often those artists didn't make an appearance. If they showed up at all they performed, but few competed. Porter said, "There was only eleven of us got to stay [for the finals]. Some of them good fiddlers that had out records all over the country—the Georgia Skillet Lickers, they didn't even make it to the top." When the points were tallied Clayton McMichen had eighty and Porter seventy-six. He took home twenty-five dollars.

Perhaps more exciting than the prize was the fact Porter came home with an invitation from the Victor Recording Company to record in New Orleans.[7] It is likely that his mastery of waltzes impressed a record company scout in the audience. There was a market for fiddle waltzes at the time. The Leake County Revelers' record "Wednesday Night Waltz"/"Goodnight Waltz" for Columbia Records in 1927 had been a huge hit that sold more than 195,000 copies over the next five years.[8]

Porter invited his twenty-year old nephew to accompany him. "He could really pick a guitar and it tickled him to death to know we was going to make some records. We woke up the next morning ready to go and it was just coming one big storm cloud after another and he wouldn't go with me. I wrote him off right then and never have used him no more." According to Porter's daughter, Virginia Estes, the nephew wasn't to blame. His mother wouldn't let him go.[9] Storms in that part of the country frequently turn into tornados with no warning. Porter, however, was so disgusted that

Joyce Cauthen

Jimmy Porter's barber shop. Photo by Joyce Cauthen.

he didn't try to arrange another recording session. "I just come on home and went to work and forgot about it," said Porter in his 1984 interview, though it is clear that it was a major disappointment and he did not forget about it.

In January 1930, the Porters opened a grocery store and barbershop in Steens. He barbered while Arline ran the store while raising their first child "under the counter."[10] He became the Steens community fiddler, providing music for school plays, concerts, high school graduations, and dances. He never had a regular band, just a "haphazard bunch" that included some teenage boys who practiced in the barbershop. He said he taught them to play mandolin, tenor banjo, and guitar in three weeks and joked that he "had to kick them to get them to change chords." Even without a tight band he was in demand as a fiddler who could play breakdowns for square dances as well as waltzes and popular music for "round" dances.

Recalling his early days of dance fiddling, Porter said, "I was raised on a farm, and I'd plow until dark and carry my fiddle, walk through the woods over yonder to play for a party. I've walked as high as four miles. Wouldn't let me ride the mule 'cause the mule was tired. It didn't matter how tired *I* was." After opening his barbershop in Steens, things didn't get easier, especially on Saturday nights. That's when farmers got their hair cut. "They'll plow the mule till dark and then come get their hair cut. I've cut hair out there from early morning till flat midnight Saturday night without ever stopping for a bite or anything. Never sat down, either. The dances wouldn't get started until way in the night." People would pick him up after he closed his shop and drive him to play for a dance.

Square dances were particularly arduous for the fiddler because each couple danced a figure or two with every other couple in the set, one after another. "I played for those things until I was just worn out. The last one was right after World War II. I didn't want to play. It's too long. When you wait until all them gets around, you're going to be just about holding out a stub!"

Like many fiddlers of his era, he put away his fiddle for a number of years. He gave up fiddlers' conventions in the early 1930s and dances in the early '40s. "After I stopped going to conventions, I just quit playing. To tell you the truth, I didn't care about it anymore. I was running a store, barbering back at the end of it. And I started fixing watches and clocks—all together—and when I failed to make those records, I just went to cutting hair and fixing watches and stayed at home."

However, when the folk revival of the 1960s and '70s came along, bringing bluegrass festivals, community jams, and fiddlers' conventions with it, Porter took up his fiddle and continued to play it until his death at age ninety. He helped his neighbor Jack May learn to play the fiddle and encouraged May's two young sons as they entered fiddlers' contests across the country. One of them, Tim May, is now a Nashville sideman, session player, band member, and multi-instrumentalist performer.[11]

When interviewed at age eighty-six, Porter admitted that he had forgotten more fiddle tunes than he could remember: "'Leather Breeches.' That's done got away from me. 'Lost John.' That's done got away from me. I just play a few easy ones now." It is a shame that we did not get to hear him in his prime on a 1928 Victor recording. However, he remained a master of waltzes and hymns and songs like "Sweet Bunch of Daisies" and "When You and I were Young, Maggie." When he played at public gatherings like the Saturday Night Gardener Boulevard Jamboree in Columbus, jaws would drop whenever the oldest man in the room would come to the stage and draw tunes played with a rich tone and on-the-mark intonation out of his admirable fiddle. His last performance took place there on January 17, 1996, one week before his death.[12]

—Joyce Cauthen

NOTES

1. J. V. Porter, interview with author, Steens, MS, December 13, 1984. Unless otherwise noted, all quotations and anecdotes from Jimmie Porter were drawn from this interview.

2. Carl Carmer, *Stars Fell on Alabama* (1934; reprint, Birmingham: University of Alabama Press, 1985), 44.

3. Charlie and Ira Stripling, interview by Bob Pinson, Kennedy, AL, September 2, 1963.

4. Porter interview and articles in the *Fayette Banner*, 1929–33.

5. Charlie and Ira Stripling interview. "Ragtime breakdown" was Charlie Stripling's term for quick, bluesy tunes, such as Stripling's own "Kennedy Rag," that were popular for modern couple dances.

6. Virginia Porter Estes, *Fayette County Heritage* (Clanton, MS: Heritage Publishing Consultants, 1999), 386.

7. Porter interview. Porter recalled that this contest was held in the spring "during crop time." Porter may have been invited to the Victor recording sessions In New Orleans, April 24–28, 1928, according to the Discography of American Historical Recordings, https://adp.library.ucsb.edu/index.php/resources/detail/212.

8. Eugene Chadbourne, "The Leake County Revelers," https://www.allmusic.com/artist/the-leake-county-revelers-mn0000788337; Wikipedia, https://en.wikipedia.org/wiki/The_Leake_County_Revelers.

9. Virginia Porter Estes, interview with author, Steens, MS, May 22, 2019.

10. Virginia Porter Estes interview.

11. Dr. Jack R. May Sr., interview with author, Steens, MS, May 22, 2019.

12. Virginia Porter Estes interview.

Catfish Medley

Author's note: This transcription is from a Jim and Joyce Cauthen field recording made in Alabama 1984.

Comparable versions:
"Catfish Medley March," Jimmie Wilson's Catfish String Band, 10/17/1929, Dallas, Victor V-40216

Porter's Tune

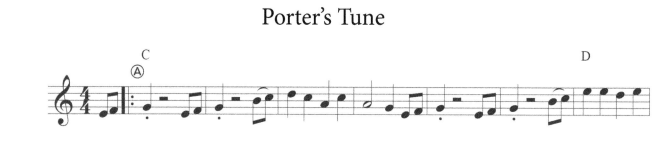

Author's note: This transcription is from a Jim and Joyce Cauthen field recording made in Alabama 1984.

Comparable versions: None known

Joyce Cauthen

BOB PRATCHER

Bob Pratcher (1893–1968) was born near Glenville in Panola County. Alan Lomax recorded Bob with his brother Miles on guitar in Como, MS, on September 21, 1959. Their recordings can be heard at www.culturalequity.org. There appears to have been no interview recorded by Lomax, and thus little is known about the Pratchers.

Bob Pratcher, 1959. From the Alan Lomax Collection at the American Folklife Center, Library of Congress. Courtesy of the Association for Cultural Equity.

Miles and Bob Pratcher, 1959. From the Alan Lomax Collection at the American Folklife Center, Library of Congress. Courtesy of the Association for Cultural Equity.

Bill Bailey

Author's note: The fiddle is nearly inaudible behind the vocal and guitar on this recording. The "fiddle m6, 7" notated at the end is all that is clearly heard, suggesting that elsewhere the fiddle approximates the vocal line.

Comparable versions:
Hughie Cannon, words and music, 1902
"Bill Bailey Won't You Please Come Home," Young Brothers Tennessee Band, 11/08/1927, Atlanta, Columbia 15219-D
"Bill Bailey Won't You Please Come Home," John McGhee, 04/1927, Richmond, IN, Gennett 6479
"Won't You Please Come Home," Homer Briarhopper, 12/15/1937, Charlotte, NC, Bluebird B6903

Buttermilk

Long time, so glad Long time, so glad Long time, so glad Long time, so glad Long Take me back, take me back Now that's all right Gal, I had you, you wouldn' do Got me a-nother 'un, don't want you

---

Author's note: The feel and repeats, particularly of the B part, are very loose. The A part is only played as an introduction.

Comparable versions: None known

Lyrics:

Long time, so glad
Long time, so glad
Long time, so glad
Long time, so glad

Take me back, take me back
Now that's all right
Gal, I had you, you wouldn' do
Got me a-nother 'un, don't want you
Well then, take me
So bad, long time, [etc., ad lib]

Take me back, take me back
Now that's all right
Gal, I had you, you wouldn' do
Got me another 'un, don't want you
Then ta-me
Run today
So bad, long time
O Lord ...

I'm Gonna Live Anyway Till I Die

Author's note: Alan Lomax wrote the title for this piece as "I'm Gonna Live Anyhow Till I Die," but on close listening to the recording I hear the word "anyhow" as "highwoods." "I'm gonna live in the high woods till I die" is the usual lyric for this song.

Comparable versions:
"I'm Gonna Live Anyhow Till I Die," Shepherd N. Edmonds, words and music, 1901
"Old Time Tunes," Gid Tanner & His Georgia Boys, 10/03/1925, Atlanta, Columbia 15059-D
"Coon from Tennessee," Charlie Poole & the North Carolina Ramblers, 07/25/1927, New York, OKeh 45098
"Tennessee Coon," Georgia Yellow Hammers, 08/19/1927, Charlotte, NC, Victor 21073

Lyrics:

I'm gonna shake it well for my lord
I'm gonna shake it well for you, gal
Well sticks and stones gonna break my bones
Talk about me when I'm dead and gone
I'm gonna live [in the highwoods] till I die

I'm gonna live anyhow till I die
Well, sticks and stones gonna break my bones
Talk about me when I'm dead and gone
I'm gonna live [in the highwoods] till I die

Goodbye Lord
Goodbye Lord

Goodbye, lord, honey, what you do
Goodbye, lord, honey, what you do

Well, sticks and stones gonna break my bones
Talk about me when I'm dead and gone
I'm gonna live [in the highwoods] till I die

I'm gonna live anyhow till I die
Well, I'm gonna live [in the highwoods] till I die

I'm gonna shake it well for my lord
I'm gonna shake it well for my lord
Well, sticks and stones gonna break my bones
Talk about me when I'm dead and gone
I'm gonna live [in the highwoods]

I'm gonna live well for my lord
I'm gonna live well for my lord
Well, sticks and stones gonna break my bones
Talk about me when I'm dead and gone
I'm gonna live [in the highwoods]

Harry Bolick

Joe Turner

Author's note: Bob Pratcher plays melody throughout with Miles interjecting partial lyrics. Bob stays close to the two melody variations as shown.

Comparable versions:
"Joe Turner Blues," W. C. Handy ca. 1919
"Joe Turner Blues," Lester McFarland, 05/06/1927, New York, Brunswick 168
"Joe Turner Blues," Milton Brown & His Musical Brownies, 04/04/1935, San Antonio, TX, Bluebird B5775
"Joe Turner Blues," The Hi-Flyers, 06/13/1937, Dallas, ARC 7–10–55

Lyrics:

Tell me Joe Turner he's done gone, Lord, Lord, well they tell me
Well they tell me Joe Turner he's done gone

JERRY PRESCOTT

Jerry Prescott (1931–2017) expertly played mandolin, guitar, and composed a lovely handful of tunes. Although he described himself as a bluegrass musician, his playing harkened back to old-time music, in that he favored an elegant melody over improvisation. His repertoire was split between bluegrass and old-time tunes.

Jerry had five brothers who played some music and a sister who didn't. Jerry learned his first tune, "Whistlin' Rufus," from his uncle, Rufus Prescott

Jerry Prescott, May 2016. Photo by Harry Bolick.

Jerry Prescott and Lee Fulcher used this photo for the covers of all of Jerry's home-produced CDs.

L to R: Jerry and his son Steve Prescott, May 2016. Photo courtesy Tonie Prescott.

Jerry Prescott, Lee Fulcher, Paul Phillips, Senator George C. McLeod. Photo courtesy James Fulcher.

of Waynesboro, MS. While a teenager, on his first gig, he performed "Turkey in the Straw" for a high school dance. Much later he performed a few bluegrass gospel songs with his son, Steve, for the American National Baptist Convention in Biloxi. He played on stage at a few local bluegrass festivals, but was never a professional or even a semi-professional musician. A modest and quiet man, he loved to play but not perform.

To document his long friendship and collaboration with guitarist Lee Fulcher, they recorded four self-produced CDs, copying them one at a time for friends. Fulcher had recorded with Senator George C. McLeod on his 1979 LP record *The*

Collins, MS, for the rest of his life. His son-in-law, Bill Rogers, is a well-known and respected Mississippi bluegrass fiddler.[1]

—Harry Bolick 2019

NOTES

1. Telephone interview with Steve Prescott, August 21, 2017

Recordings

Jack Youngblood, *Mississippi Fiddler*, 2001 CD self-published by Jerry Prescott, who plays on it.

Fiddling Senator. Senator McLeod visited and played with Jerry at his home.

Surprisingly, in 2001 he produced, played on, and composed the title tune for a bluegrass fiddle CD featuring Jack Youngblood, a well regarded bluegrass fiddler who had retired to Mississippi. The tunes are common, traditional tunes such as "Fire on the Mountain," "Lost Indian," and "Bully of the Town," along with one Bill Monroe tune, one Bob Wills tune, Youngblood's "Hitchhiker Blues," and Jerry's "Mississippi Fiddler." The CD, *Mississippi Fiddler*, is well played and recorded but Jerry did little to market it and gave away most of the copies.

Born in Petal, MS, near Hattiesburg in Forrest County, Jerry earned a degree from Louisiana State University, served in the US Army, and worked in the forestry industry as a timber assessor. He married Sarah Ann Bond in the early 1950s and had five children, all of whom learned at least a small amount of guitar, although none became serious musicians. At family gatherings he would often play a few songs with his son, Steve. There was time for music when he was a teenager, while in the Army, and then again after his children were grown. There was little time to play while raising a family. He married for the second time in 2003 on Valentine's Day to Tonie Rogers and lived in

Known compositions

Guitar Serenade
Grandmother Reel
Honey Bee Hornpipe
Mac Prescott Jig
Mississippi Fiddler
Mississippi Turnpike
Mississippi Traveler
Prescott's Hornpipe

Missing compositions

Virginia Turnpike
Colorado Turnpike

Known repertoire

Abba Dabba Honeymoon
Angelina Baker
Arab Bounce
Arkansas Traveler
Back Up and Push
Beautiful Dreamer
Billy in the Lowground
Blackberry Blossom
Bully of the Town
Camptown Races

Carolina Wren Rag

Cheyenne

Down Yonder

Dragging the Bow

Fire on the Mountain

Fifty Year Ago Waltz

Florida Rag

Forkee Deer

Grey Eagle

Hitchhiker Blues

Huckleberry Hornpipe

In the Garden

Irish Spring

Jerusalem Ridge

Just Because

Kentucky Mandolin

Lead Out

Liberty

Limerock

Listen to the Mockingbird

Lost Indian

Maiden's Prayer

Mississippi Sawyer

Paddy on the Turnpike

Ragtime Annie

Rebecca

Red Haired Boy

Red Wing

Rickett's Hornpipe

Rose of Sharon Waltz

Santa Claus

Silver Bells

Sleepy Eyed Joe (from Norman Blake)

Soldier's Joy

St. Ann's Reel

Staten Island Hornpipe

Stoney Creek

Sweet Potato Reel

Swainson's Reel

Tammy's Waltz (Theme from the 1957 movie *Tammy and the Bachelor* with Debbie Reynolds)

The Waltz You Saved for Me

Twinkle Little Star

Waltz of the Whippoorwill

Wabash Cannonball

Wheel Hoss

When They Ring Those Golden Bells

Whiskey Before Breakfast

Grandmother Reel

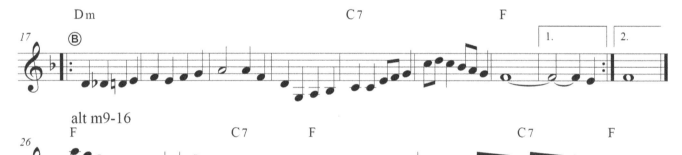

alt m9-16

Author's note: Transcribed from Prescott's home recording; listen to it at mississippifiddle.com. The composition is from 2002.

Comparable versions:
The first strain is similar to the 1963 pop tune "Yakety Sax" by Homer Louis ("Boots") Randolph III.

Harry Bolick

Honeybee Hornpipe

Author's note: Transcribed from Prescott's home recording; listen to it at mississippifiddle.com. The composition is from 2004.

Comparable versions: None known

Jerry Prescott

Mac Prescott Jig

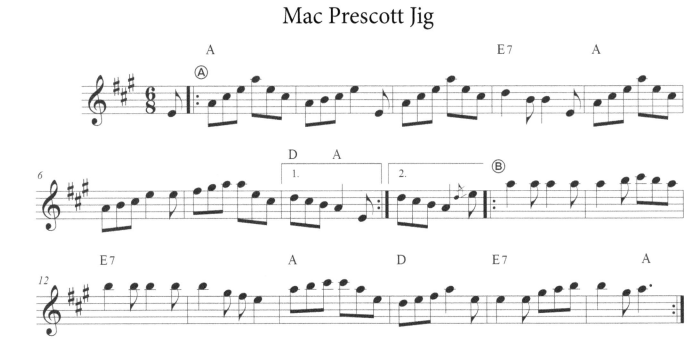

Author's note: Transcribed from Prescott's home recording; listen to it at mississippifiddle.com. The composition is from 2008.

Comparable versions: None known

Harry Bolick

Mississippi Fiddler

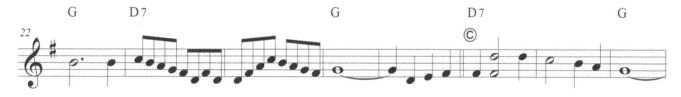

Author's note: Transcribed from Prescott's home recording; listen to it at mississippifiddle.com. The composition is from 1994. Jerry has a solo on the Jack Youngblood, *Mississippi Fiddler* CD that Jerry produced.

Comparable versions: None known

Mississippi Traveler

Author's note: Transcribed from Prescott's home recording; listen to it at mississippifiddle.com. The composition is from 1991.
The second part, second ending is for the last time only.

Comparable versions: None known

Harry Bolick

Mississippi Turnpike

Author's note: Transcribed from Prescott's home recording; listen to it at mississippifiddle.com.

Comparable versions: None known

Prescott Hornpipe

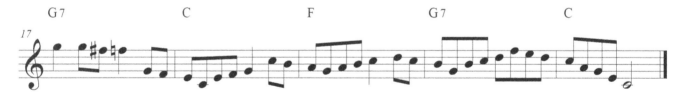

Author's note: Transcribed from Prescott's home recording; listen to it at mississippifiddle.com. The composition is from 1996.

Comparable versions: None known

Harry Bolick

Silver Bells

Author's note: Transcribed from Prescott's home recording; listen to it at mississippifiddle.com. A2 and B2 are just small variations of the melody in the lower octave.

Comparable versions:
"Silver Bell," Edward Madden, lyric, Percy Wenrich, music, 1910
"Silver Bell," Clayton McMichen's Home Town Band, 07/07/1925, Atlanta, OKeh 40445
"Silver Bell," Ernest V. Stoneman & Joseph Samuels, 08/1926, New York, OKeh 45060
"Silver Bell," Scottsdale String Band, 08/10/1928, Atlanta, OKeh 40445.

HERB QUINN

In my fieldwork with African American musicians from Mississippi in the 1960s and 1970s, I only encountered four who played fiddle or mandolin. These included Mott Willis and Willis Taylor from Copiah County, both of them fiddlers but better known as guitarists.[1] The others were Herb Quinn (violin, mandolin, and guitar) and his protégé, Dink Brister (mandolin), from Walthall County but by this time settled in Louisiana. My main interest in these musicians was in their roles as blues performers, either as featured artists with guitar or as accompanists on violin or mandolin. I did not question them about their knowledge of fiddle tunes and other instrumental pieces and recorded very little of this music from them. I also did not obtain extensive autobiographical information about them.

I recorded Herb Quinn several times between 1966 and 1970, variously with Marc Ryan and Marina Bokelman or on my own. Most of my visits to him were at his home out in the country just east of Clifton, Louisiana, where he lived with his longtime wife Luella and their two children, Betty and Charles. On some of these visits other blues guitarists were present, such as Babe Stovall

or Roosevelt Holts, both also originally from the Tylertown area in Walthall County. Marina and I also took Quinn to Tylertown to visit and record with fellow musician Isaac Youngblood. In those years, Herb Quinn owned his own small farm and appeared to be making a reasonably good living. He was no longer active as a musician and did not own an instrument but was widely regarded by the younger Tylertown musicians as more or less the dean among them. The fact is, however, that he was quite rusty, having played little for the past ten or fifteen years. He was best on guitar, which perhaps he had kept up with a bit, since guitar blues still had some currency in his community. He also fairly quickly recovered some of his skills on mandolin, his favorite instrument.

Walthall County was formed in 1910 from parts of neighboring Pike and Marion Counties. Quinn is a common surname there, both among Blacks and whites, and it is likely that Herb's ancestors were slaves in the area. The best known person from the area with the surname is Herb's niece Aylene Quin (1920–2001), whose house in nearby McComb was bombed in 1964 during the Civil Rights struggle after she had allowed the café she operated to be

Herb Quinn, 1970. Photo courtesy David Evans.

used as a meeting place for the Student Non-Violent Coordinating Committee (SNCC) and the Council of Federated Organizations (COFO).[2] Herb himself expressed no political opinions to me, but he did take the opportunity to vote as soon as it became available in the 1960s.

Herb Quinn told me he was born in 1896, although the year was actually supplied by a family member. In the US Census taken on April 26, 1910, his age is listed as twelve, and in the 1920 Census he is said to be twenty-two. He registered for the military draft in both 1917 and 1918 and gave his date of birth first as September 13, 1894, and later as August 21, 1897. When he applied for Social Security, he listed his birthdate as November 15, 1894. In the 1930 census his age is listed as thirty, but in 1940 he is listed as forty-two. Either 1897 or 1898 seems most likely to be his birth year.

In the 1910 census, Herbert is listed as the son of Lila Quinn, with older brothers Mack (twenty-four), Lucius (twenty-two), and Cleveland (eighteen). His brothers held railroad and sawmill jobs, but Herbert was described as a servant for a private family, while his mother was a cook for a private family, probably the same one Herb worked for. No father is listed, and I could not trace him or his family in earlier records. Whoever his father was, Herb seems to have stayed in contact with him, because he stated that he learned some of his fiddling from his father. Herbert was described as not attending school and unable to read and write. In the 1940 census, however, it is recorded that he had achieved a fourth grade education. In later life he and his wife bought an encyclopedia set for their children, and their daughter was starting college when I last had contact with the family.

In 1917 Herbert Quinn stated that he was born in Mesa, Mississippi, a settlement about two miles northwest of Tylertown, and that he was a married farmer working for W. A. Boyd of Tylertown. In 1918, however, he stated that he worked for the Fernwood Lumber Company of Kokomo, a small town east of Tylertown, and that his nearest relative was his mother Lila Quinn of Mesa. On both occasions he signed his name with an X, indicating that he was illiterate. In the 1920 census he is listed as married and employed as a servant in the household of white merchant Seth Ginn on Magnolia Road in Tylertown. His wife is not listed with him. Nevertheless, a white Hurbert [sic] Quinn, twenty-four, is also listed in Tylertown in the 1920 census as a farmer on his own account, unable to read and write, and married to Louella Quinn, twenty-one. They lived next door to W. A. Boyd and his wife. It seems very likely that these Quinns' racial designation was recorded incorrectly and that this couple is Herb Quinn, the African American musician, and his wife Luella. In the 1930 census Herbert (thirty) and Lou E. (twenty-six) Quinn are listed as farmers in Pike County, to the west of Walthall County; but in the 1940 census Hub [sic] (forty-two) and Lula [sic] (forty-one) are once again farmers in Walthall County. Sometime after 1940 they moved to Louisiana and at some point purchased their farm in Clifton. Herb Quinn died there in September 1972. Luella moved back to Mississippi and died in Columbia on April 5, 2000, at the age of 101.

Given his meager formal education, Herb Quinn's connections to wealthy whites in Walthall County probably benefited him in life. The Boyds were prominent landowners, and merchant and plantation owner Seth Ginn (1885–1947) was a powerful political figure, serving for a time as mayor of Tylertown and four terms as chancery clerk at the county courthouse. The nature of the relationship between Herb Quinn and Seth Ginn might even extend backward through the generations. Quinn, Guin, Ginn, and similar spellings, are all prominent surnames among both whites and Blacks in the area and appear to be variants of a single surname, suggesting connections dating back to antebellum times and waves of migration and settlement in the

area from some specific slavery site further to the east. Whatever the case, Herb Quinn's white patrons would have offered him some sense of assurance that he might have protection if he were ever in dire need or in trouble with the law. This could be especially useful for a musician, who might find himself in a situation where violence occurred, or even be involved in violence himself, not to mention illegal activities such as gambling and drinking alcohol that often occurred at places where music was played. (Mississippi's long era of prohibition was just ending when I first met Quinn.) His white patronage would also have provided increased opportunities for musical employment at white dances and parties and offered protection there, especially given the fact that Tylertown and Walthall County had a particularly strained and tense racial climate that persists to the present day. Although he seemed to express solidarity with the less secure members of his community in song, Herb Quinn was certainly not the character he evoked in a line heard in many of his blues: "Ain't got nobody to speak in my behalf."

I was able to observe his interactions with whites both in the case of myself and with a white couple in Tylertown he had known for many years. The Quinns always treated me and my white research associates formally as guests in their home. We sat in their living room parlor, and Mrs. Quinn delighted in preparing delicious meals for us from products of their farm and gave jars of preserves as gifts, mentioning that she had cooked for white folks for many years and was considered the biscuit-baking champion. Here we were in her home, not as her boss but as her guests. The Quinns sent Marina Bokelman and me an announcement of their daughter's high school graduation. When we visited, if Herb was out at work, we simply waited for him to return home. No one felt a need to summon him, and no attempt was ever made. We made plans for future visits around his work schedule. I felt a considerable sense of social equality despite differences of age, race, educational status, and role. In encouraging Quinn to take up the mandolin again, we drove with him up to Tylertown to see a white couple, the Magees, who had two instruments for sale. Herb had been their neighbor for years, worked for them and played music at dances they attended. Mrs. Magee was home, and she and Herb had a long, relaxed, and pleasant conversation about old times and other Black and white musicians in the area before she showed Herb the two mandolins. He liked one of them but didn't like her husband's asking price of fifteen dollars, pointing out a split in the body that needed repair and stating that it was worth no more than six. Mrs. Magee didn't want to negotiate with him but had enough confidence in Herb to allow him to take the mandolin into town to Mr. Magee and see if he could "Jew him down." Her husband ran the commodities distribution center in Tylertown, and in giving directions Mrs. Magee asked Herb if he received commodities in a way that seemed to assume that he did. Herb proudly assured her that he didn't! In the car on the way to town he stated that Mr. Magee was stingy and had plenty of money. In the store the two men compromised at ten dollars, and the mandolin was sold.

Herb Quinn was a difficult man to interview. Specific questions about his life or music tended to elicit a chuckle and some generalized comment about the good old days of playing music ("I used to could make the hair rise on your head"), or the fact that he had given up music after "everyone got scattered" and had given all his instruments away, or that a throat operation a few years ago had made his voice weak and hoarse ("I used to could sing up a storm"), or that he would be able to get his skills back if only he had someone to play with, someone to encourage him, or the time to devote to it. Specific facts were more likely to come out as spontaneous remarks rather than as answers to questions.

Herb did state that in addition to farm work and other local types of manual labor, such as in the lumber industry, he had at one time driven a truck to haul migrant farm workers to and from Florida, also hauling agricultural products from there to sell elsewhere. He even said that he had been to the Bahamas. He also said that he had traveled to the Mississippi Delta in the northern part of the state. Probably this was mainly for agricultural work in the fall harvest season, when many Black workers from other parts of the state descended on the region, some also being musicians who could make additional money from their skills. Herb recalled an especially good blues guitarist in the 1920s around Moorhead named Willie Wilson, who might have been the man of that name recalled by Delta bluesman Son House in nearby Mattson as one of his early influences.[3] Herb had earlier known Wilson when they worked together in Columbia and said Wilson's home was in Monticello.

Herb Quinn's string band, which was active around the end of World War I, traveled as far as Jackson and New Orleans. However, most of their engagements were closer to home in Walthall County, which was situated between the two cities and about eighty miles distant from either one. This area around Tylertown was one of the earliest parts of Mississippi to be settled by whites and the slaves they brought with them or acquired after their arrival. The process began in the second decade of the nineteenth century, allowing for two generations of Black men and women to come to physical maturity under slavery, with many of their descendants remaining in the area to the present day. Older musical traditions could and did survive in such an environment, not only old-time string band and fiddle music but other styles more closely related to African music. In Bogalusa, Louisiana, between 1970 and 1973 I recorded Eli Owens, a former resident of Sandy Hook in Walthall County. Owens had learned to play a set of tuned whistles and a mouth bow, both of partial African derivation, from his great grandfather, whose parents had been some of the original slaves brought to the area from Virginia.[4] Herb Quinn himself remembered seeing a man in Darbun, near where he was raised, play a string attached to a gourd that had been fastened in some manner to the floor. The man would tighten or slacken the string with one hand and strike it with the other. This seems to have been some sort of African-derived one-string bass, here played as a solo instrument in the African manner and with a traditional resonator rather than the substitution of a metal tub or bucket. Herb's "knife" style of guitar playing also had African antecedents.[5]

Much more prominent in the area's African American music in the first half of the twentieth century were the sounds of string bands, the blues, and spiritual and gospel songs, all of them hybrid forms in which the African elements were less overt.[6] By the mid-1960s Herb Quinn was the elder statesman among the musicians who had performed these types of music and was spoken of with universal respect by those who were some ten to twenty years younger. The latter included Babe Stovall, Dink Brister, O. D. Jones, Herb's second cousin Frank Butler, Roosevelt Holts, and Isaac Youngblood. Some of them were related to one another, and they were part of a larger group that also included Babe's brother Tom, Dink's brother Tom and cousin Babe, and O. D.'s father. Most of them had grown up northeast of Tylertown in the area where Herb was raised and had played with and been influenced by him. They played in various combinations, often solo or in duos when the audience was Black and the music was mainly blues, or in string bands of violin, mandolin, guitar, and bass violin for white and sometimes Black audiences. Herb had a repertoire of guitar blues in standard and open tunings, including some pieces in "knife" style. He also used the guitar to complement the lead instruments in a string band (i.e., play rhythm and chords) or would switch to mandolin or violin. He also said he could play a bit of piano and harmonica. Around the end of World War I, when he was about twenty years old, Herb formed or joined a string band consisting variously of himself and his contemporaries Sing Wallis, Cleve Sibley, Alex Conerly, Jeff Smith, and Lucius Magee (fiddle). They considered themselves to be a "jazz" band and remained active for a number of years. ("Jazz" was a new musical term that had become popularized in 1917 through recordings by the Original Dixieland Jazz Band from New Orleans.) For a time the band played "everywhere," six nights a week, mostly performing for the white folks. They were paid twelve dollars apiece for playing from 8:00 p.m. until midnight, the money coming from the "door fee" of a dollar per couple. Herb said he also worked during the days. Perhaps the day work was to keep from being viewed as a vagrant, for twelve dollars was a good week's pay for a farm worker at this time!

Herb seems to have kept his musical activity up into the 1950s, gradually playing more with the younger musicians in his area, until musical tastes began to change, he had his throat operation, he and his playing partners scattered to various towns in Louisiana, and he had to devote more attention to his farm and growing family. During his musically active years Herb also played violin and mandolin in a band with a couple of white boys around Columbia for about a month, playing both blues and fox trots, and he taught guitar to the white Beardon brothers, who were "raised up" with Herb, working with them every night until they learned. Their band was still active in Tylertown in the 1960s.

There were two famous Mississippi musicians who passed through the area near Tylertown and crossed paths with Herb Quinn. One was blues singer and guitarist Tommy Johnson, from Crystal Springs in Copiah County.[7] Johnson had married Rosa Youngblood, who grew up not too far from Herb, and the couple lived in or frequently visited the area in the late 1920s and into the 1930s. Herb said Johnson would mostly play blues for Black audiences, with Herb "rapping" second guitar behind him or switching to mandolin and playing lead figures. Sometimes they would play "fox trots" and "ragtime" for the white folks. Herb learned Johnson's famous "Big Road Blues" from him as well as a song called "T.B. Blues," probably adapted by Johnson from Victoria Spivey's 1927 hit record of that title.

The other famous musician Herb met was America's blue yodeler, Jimmie Rodgers. This was around 1923, when Herb's band had split up for a time and he was working and playing music in the area around Lumberton. Rodgers was "just a country-raised boy" living and farming between Talowah and Purvis. At the time he was just starting out in music, though he was already yodeling. Rodgers learned from white and colored, "all mixed up together," Herb stated, though he said the two of them never played together. These two towns are just north of Lumberton and are stops on the Southern railroad line running between New Orleans and Rodgers's home in Meridian. Rodgers worked off and on as a brakeman for the railroad before devoting his full attention to music. Later, after he became famous through his recordings, Rodgers passed through Tylertown for a special appearance and received $200 for singing one song!

Herb Quinn was one of the many fine African American rural musicians of his era who never got the chance to record his music in his prime. Musicians like him could be locally or regionally famous, but that did little good. Tylertown was far from the locations where music was even occasionally recorded in the 1920s and 1930s (New Orleans, Jackson, Hattiesburg), and there were no entrepreneurs there promoting local musicians to the record companies. No folklorist did fieldwork with local Black musicians until the 1960s. And even if there had been an opportunity to make records, Herb's music would probably have been rejected as either not fitting the expectations for "race records" (i.e., being too "white") or, if he featured his guitar blues, being a bit too old-fashioned in sound. From him and his fellow musicians we have only fragmentary reflections of what once must have been an impressive body of music.

—David Evans

NOTES

1. David Evans, *Tommy Johnson* (London: Studio Vista, 1971), 31–33; David Evans, *Big Road Blues: Tradition and Creativity in the Folk Blues* (Berkeley: University of California Press, 1982), *passim*.

2. "Aylene Quin," SNCC Digital Gateway, https://snccdigital.org/people/aylene-quinn/.

3. David Evans, "An Early Interview with Son House," *Frog Blues and Jazz Annual* 5 (2017): 29–44, 176–94.

4. David Evans, "The Music of Eli Owens: African Music in Transition in Southern Mississippi," in *For Gerhard Kubik*, ed. August Schmidhofer and Dietrich Schuller (Frankfurt: Peter Lang, 1994), 329–59.

5. David Evans, "Afro-American One-Stringed Instruments," *Western Folklore* 29 (1970), 229–45.

6. See Various Artists, *South Mississippi Blues* (LP, Rounder 2009, 1973), and various albums by Babe Stovall and Roosevelt Holts.

7. Evans, *Tommy Johnson*, 74–80.

Ragtime Joe

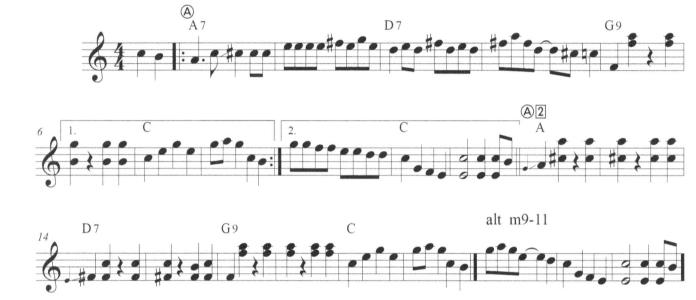

Author's note: Transcribed from a 1966 David Evans field recording of Herb Quinn on mandolin with Babe Stovall on guitar. A2 is Quinn's chordal backup.

Comparable versions: None known

Sweet Bunch of Daisies

Author's note: Quinn was from Tylertown, MS, as was Fiddlin' Jabe Dillon. The recording was made by David Evans in 1967.

Comparable versions:
Anita Owen, words and music, 1894
"Sweet Bunch of Daisies," (Clayton) McMichen's Home Town Band, 07/07/1925, Atlanta, OKeh 40445
"Sweet Bunch of Daisies," Al Hopkins & His Buckle Busters, 05/13/1927, New York, Brunswick 174
"Sweet Bunch of Daisies," Stripling Brothers, 09/10/1934, New York, Decca unissued

Untitled No. 1

Author's note: Transcribed from a 1966 David Evans field recording of Herb Quinn on mandolin with Babe Stovall on guitar. The alt M11 is played on the lass pass through the tune. The guitar is faintly doubling the melody and implying, not stating the chords.

Comparable versions:
"Just Because," Nelstone's Hawaiians, 11/30/1929, Atlanta, Victor V-40273
"Just Because," The Shelton Brothers, 02/23/1935, Chicago, Decca 5100
"Just Because," The Prairie Ramblers, 08/15/1935, New York, ARC 5–11–51

David Evans

Untitled No. 2

Author's note: Transcribed from a 1966 David Evans field recording of Herb Quinn on solo fiddle. B2 is played after the first pass through the tune. It's a short recording; perhaps Quinn alternated the B parts. On the second pass, Quinn plays the A part twice, then the C part.

Comparable versions: None known

Herb Quinn

THE RAY BROTHERS

Columbus and Nancy Ray of Choctaw County had six sons, Lester, Sam, Will, Wesley, Sandy Vardaman, and Alvin, all of whom could play music. But when a group called the Ray Brothers made records, it was only a two-piece.

William E. Ray (1896–1971) was a very notable fiddler of his day and place. He won the Kosciusko fiddlers' contest on at least one occasion (believed to be in the early 1930s), and was recalled by Hoyt Ming and Lonnie Ellis, among others. Ellis remembered the reserve of the Ray Brothers at the May 1930 recording session in Memphis that they all attended: unlike the other old-time players present, the Rays would not join casual picking sessions but kept to their room. Dr. A. M. Bailey also spoke about the Rays' guarded reception of overtures of interest in their music.

Will Ray's fiddling is of a quality to make one pardon any eccentricities. While his tunes are less surprising than, say, Willie Narmour's, his playing is uncommonly graceful, the frequent slides beautifully executed, the high parts rendered with sweetness. The fluid bowing occasionally recalls Gene Clardy, who lived for some years in Choctaw County and may have been known to him.

Sandy Vardaman Ray (1903–1977), guitarist on the records and singer of the two vocal numbers,

taught in local public schools. He could also play banjo. Will Ray farmed, but in 1940 he was enumerated as a public-school teacher of music. In later years, both men lived in Kilmichael.

◆ ◆ ◆

The Ray Brothers' first recordings, at the May 1930 session referred to above, were two waltzes, "Honeysuckle" and "Friday Night," the "Choctaw County Rag," a very smoothly played fast breakdown partly drawn from "At a Georgia Camp Meeting," and the odd, impressionistic piece "Jake Leg Wobble." "Jake Leg Wobble"/"Friday Night Waltz" sold 3,632 copies; "Choctaw County Rag"/"Honeysuckle Waltz" sold 2,178.

These sales were evidently sufficient to encourage Victor to summon the Rays back to another session in Memphis that November. Again they played a couple of waltzes, "Tuscaloosa" and "Hometown," and two breakdowns, "Mississippi Echoes" and "Winona Rag." In addition, Vardaman Ray sang two songs, "Got the Jake Leg Too" and "The Folks Back Home." Virtually all these numbers are unique to the Ray Brothers.

"Got the Jake Leg Too," bought by Doc Bailey from the local songwriter Clayton Tyler, referred—like the earlier (but purely instrumental) "Jake Leg

Ray Brothers promotional photo. Guitarist on left is Vardaman Ray; fiddler in rear is William E. Ray. The other brothers are unidentified. Newspaper articles of the period list other Ray brothers and their instruments: Lester L. Ray, tenor banjo; J. A. Ray, fiddle; Sam E. Ray, cello; Webb Ray, harmonica. Vardaman also played banjo.

Wobble"—to the epidemic of "jake leg" paralysis, caused by drinking adulterated Jamaica Ginger extract, that swept through the USA in early 1930.[1] The song remains in copyright and a transcription is not included here. A transcription for "The Folks Back Home" is also omitted for the same reason. Its copyright is credited to W. E. Ray; however, the record label lists Mrs. W. E. Ray, his wife Bessie, as the composer. "Got the Jake Leg Too"/"The Folks Back Home" sold 2,229; "Tuscaloosa Waltz"/"Mississippi Echoes," 1,365. No sales figures survive for "Home Town Waltz"/"Winona Rag," but the record is unlikely to have sold more than a few hundred. Rather oddly, this was the one coupling by the Rays that was selected for reissue on Bluebird in the mid-1930s (though that record is almost as rare).

◆ ◆ ◆

Will and Vardaman's recordings were only one aspect of the family's music-making. A larger group consisting of Will, Vardaman, Lester (tenor banjo), and Sam Ray ('cello) played on WCOC in Meridian in December 1931 and twice more in January 1932.[2] An unspecified number of Ray brothers also

played on WHEF in Kosciusko in December 1934.[3] Members of the Ray clan were active in the Winston County Singing Convention,[4] and a Ray Brothers Quartet frequently contributed to local musical programs in the early 1930s. Vardaman also sang in the Choctaw Jubilee Quartet along with James and Doyle Blackwood, founder members soon afterward of the famous Blackwood Brothers Quartet.[5]

—Tony Russell

NOTES

1. See, e.g., John Morgan and Thomas C. Tulloss, "The Jake Walk Blues: A Toxicological Tragedy Mirrored in Popular Music," *JEMF Quarterly* (1977): 122–26; and "The Jake Walk Blues," *Old Time Music* 28 (Spring 1978): 17–24.

2. "Ray Brothers Broadcast," *Choctaw Plaindealer*, Ackerman, MS, January 1, 15, and 29, 1932.

3. *Choctaw Plaindealer*, Ackerman, MS, December 7, 1934.

4. *Choctaw Plaindealer*, Ackerman, MS, May 22 and 29, 1931.

5. *Choctaw Plaindealer*, Ackerman, MS, August 11, 1933.

Choctaw County Rag

Author's note: This transcription is from Victor V-40313, recorded Atlanta, 5/28/1929. The C part is only played once; after that the A and B parts alternate.

Comparable versions:
"At a Georgia Camp Meeting," Kerry Mills words and music, 1897
"Peaches Down in Georgia," Georgia Yellow Hammers, 11/27/1929, Atlanta, Victor 23683

Friday Night Waltz

Author's note: This transcription is from Victor V-40291 recorded Memphis, TN, 05/28/1930.

Comparable versions:
"Katy-Did Waltz," Frank Wilson & His Blue Ridge Mountain Trio, 02/20/1929, New York, Columbia 15372-D
"Mary Jane Waltz," Kessinger Brothers, 09/16/1930, New York, Brunswick 484
"Walter Family Waltz," Walter Family, 03/29/1933, Richmond, IN, Champion 16622

Tony Russell

Home Town Waltz

Author's note: This transcription is from Victor 23713, recorded Memphis, TN, 11/21/1930.

Comparable versions: None known

Honeysuckle Waltz

Author's note: This transcription is from Victor V-40313, recorded Memphis, TN, 05/28/1930.

Comparable versions: None known

Tony Russell

Jake Leg Wobble

Author's note: This transcription is from Victor V-40291, recorded Memphis, TN, 05/28/1930.

Comparable versions: None known

Mississippi Echoes

Author's note: This transcription is from Victor 23552, recorded Memphis, TN, 11/21/1930.

Comparable versions: None known

Tony Russell

Tuscaloosa Waltz

Author's note: This transcription is from Victor 23552, recorded Memphis, TN, 11/21/1930. In M32 the F/A indicates an A bass note. M24 and M42 have a slight quick E string downward slide from the F♭, and immediately a slide on the A string into the E as almost one motion.

Comparable versions:
"Tuscaloosa Waltz," "Ted" Sharp, Hinman & Sharp, 11/08/1933, Richmond, IN, Champion 16739

Winona Rag

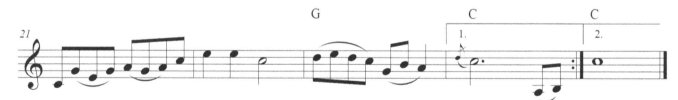

Author's note: This transcription is from Victor 23713, recorded Memphis, TN, 11/21/1930.

Comparable versions: None known

Tony Russell

AFTERWORD

Tracking Down the Echoes of the Music

Searching for Grover O'Briant

I'm about a thousand miles from home, driving up a lonely Mississippi two-lane road in the dark. It's been about ten miles since I've seen a mailbox or a house light. All I have is an address. Conflicting visions alternate through my mind as I drive: When I get there the son will be home and delight me with stories about his fiddling father. He will have photos and recordings and I'll be able to add another chapter to the story. Or, I'll arrive and the house is abandoned. Or, the current occupants have no idea who I am looking for. Or, the son will turn out to be deranged and is waiting, shotgun in hand.

When I finally see a dimly lit home, I park carefully and thoughtfully, I emerge with my hands clearly visible, even though it is too dark to see them. Loudly and quickly I announce the purpose of my visit. "I'm looking for Jerry O'Briant, the son of the fiddler Grover O'Briant. I'm writing a book on Mississippi fiddlers!" And I wait for a long heartbeat. The backlit figure by the screen door says, "Well, come on in and sit on the porch, you found him."

We talked for hours. Jerry had good and fond memories of his father, Grover. In addition to being a good conversationalist, for a non-musician, he remembered a great deal that was of interest about Grover and his music. I asked the obvious questions about recordings and photographs of Grover with instruments, but alas, Jerry did not have any. He kept looking at me, kinda sideways and puzzled, finally saying, "I've seen you somewhere before." That was a little surprising. My mother was from about thirty miles away in Carroll County; however, I never lived there, only visited. I'd never been in Attala County near Jerry's place. Together we pondered a bit and came across a few tenuous possible connections before we realized that Jerry had seen me on Mississippi Public TV, promoting my first book. Now that I was placed within a web of Mississippi connections, and with hours of conversation where I would occasionally interject with information on dates, places, or fiddlers that surprised Jerry, he seemed to make a decision.

Jerry abruptly said, "Let me get a flashlight," and then, "Come on." Momentarily, I revisited my sinister thoughts about a shotgun and discarded them. We walked about sixty feet or so to an adjacent house, Grover's house. It was untouched since his father had died. Jerry pointed out some family photos on the walls in the orderly home. As we entered another room, Jerry mentioned that he had not been in that room, Grover's bedroom, since Grover passed. I stared at the cracked Milner and Curtis fiddle 78 rpm record screwed into the wall above the chest of drawers. Jerry began to look through drawers in the two chests of drawers. The first drawer contained pieces of cloth and mouse nests, as did the second drawer. The third drawer had Grover's modest 78 rpm record collection, a Jimmie Rodgers disc and a few gospel recordings. But there was an envelope of photographs! In subsequent drawers, we found four reel-to-reel tapes and six cassettes. It was just what I had hoped for but not expected to find; stories, photographs, and recordings of a previously unknown Mississippi fiddler. We chatted while I scanned the photos and Jerry generously agreed to let me borrow these precious recordings. I mentioned the Milner and Curtis disc, and Jerry pointed out that Luther Curtis's homestead was literally across the road. When we were finished, I was a touch reluctant to leave, as I had grown fond of my new friend Jerry. As I drove away I smiled, recalling that I'll need to go back to return the recordings, and thus get to visit again.

The Leake County String Band

It had been a long, great afternoon, being introduced around Leake County by Pastor Tim Freeny of the Freeny Baptist Church on Freeny Road in Freeny, Mississippi. We had visited Shelby Sanders, the last living member of the band who had shared a bucket of audio and video cassettes with us; Beth Alford, Carlton Freeny's daughter; and Irene Massengale, Cartis Massengale's widow, both of whom had treasures to share. After warm visits and then goodbyes, I prepared to drive my loaded car back to Jackson. It was around 5 p.m., and I had a sudden thought: how far was Walnut Grove? Morgan Gilmer, the founder of the band, had printed his address on the label of their sole published recording and I suspected that I might find his grave in Walnut Grove. It's a small town; how many cemeteries can there be?

I arrived in Walnut Grove at 5:30. The town hall, police station, and library were closed. No one at the gas station, which was all that was open, knew

anything. However, I spotted a police car in the library parking lot, parked next to a young fellow repairing a car. The policeman didn't know about the cemetery, nor did the repairman, but a fellow standing there watching them, Carl Ware, offered to call his sister to ask about the cemetery. He said that she was "into that genealogy stuff." He couldn't get her on the phone, so he drove me by two of the three Walnut Grove cemeteries himself. He took my phone number and left me to search the cemetery on my own. I had no luck finding the tombstone, but at least I had tried.

That night his sister called me and told me how to find the gravestones online and gave me Morgan's birth and death dates. Surprisingly, she even knew Morgan and his second wife, Virginia, and gave me Virginia's phone number. The next day I called Virginia to arrange a visit in the afternoon. She seemed very happy for the visit. She is ninety-five and very sharp. She told me what she could remember about Morgan and his music, and her photos were just perfect. As she remembered her days with Morgan she recalled, "They were great times."

Jabe Dillon

When I walked into the dark and quiet office at Mac's Used Cars, on this 93° afternoon in Tylertown, Mississippi, and announced, "I'm looking for Dee McCullough," the woman in the office looked at me like I might be from the FBI. I said, "Peggy at the Tax Assessor's office sent me over." She was still very quiet, just staring at me. Slowly realizing how odd my sudden appearance was, I quickly explained that I wanted to know about Jabe Dillon, the fiddler. She sighed, looked down at her shoes, looked up at the ceiling, relaxed, and said, "We need to go out on the porch." When we were settled there, she collected her thoughts, lit a cigarette, and then for more than an hour she concisely told me everything she could remember about her grandfather. Overwhelmed with my success and at the warm reception in having met another fiddler's family, and having gotten an earful of stories, I said my goodbyes and drove away humming. That night, back in Jackson, I received her text message with snapshots of the framed photos on her wall at home and they were amazing! I texted back and arranged to return with a scanner a few days later.

Outside of Waltham County, I doubt that more than five people have ever heard of the fiddler Jabe Dillon. His two recordings are rare, and stunning. My friend Pat Conte had shared digital copies of Jabe's 45 rpm and 78 rpm recordings with me. For years we knew next to nothing about Jabe Dillon. Then Pat came across a newspaper photo with a caption indicating that Jabe was from Walthall County. With no more information than the name of the county, I drove to Tylertown, the county seat of Walthall County, to look for fiddler Jabe Dillon's descendants. Walking into the courthouse, I picked out an office and asked the clerk about Jabe. She replied, "You need to talk to Peggy Dillon Hillburn, the tax assessor, she's two doors down the hall." Peggy was very friendly and helpful once I explained my mission. She remembered seeing Jabe play in front of the courthouse for local events. She gave me a local map and marked it up to show me how to get to the cemetery to find Jabe's gravestone for his birth and death dates. Verbally, she sketched out a basic Dillon family tree and then she marked the spot on her map where Dee McCullough, his granddaughter, worked with her husband at Mac's Used Cars.

On my second visit with Dee, we again sat out under the carport at the dealership and talked while I scanned her photos and posters. She also brought the "records" I was expecting to be the records I had already heard. I was stunned when she unwrapped four home-recorded single-copy 78 recordings. I had known nothing about Jabe Dillon; now we had eight more unknown Jabe Dillon tunes, great photos, and many stories! On that day, however, I had no way of digitizing the 78s and would not even consider asking to borrow them. Dee had not even heard them. We both very much wanted to digitize and hear the records. I promised her that I would find a way to get that done.

As I was preparing to leave, Dee mentioned that her cousin, Pat Sumrall, was back in town and might be willing to see me. Pat has lived all of her life in Tylertown and had been around Jabe Dillon even more than Dee. Pat welcomed me into her home, where I heard even more stories and scanned photos and some newspaper clippings. After a great visit, as I was preparing to leave I mentioned the 45 rpm record that Jabe had made. Pat went into another room and came out with a small box full of the 45s. Minutes before, I had only known of two existing copies of that 45 rpm record. Now, I was holding a very precious gift of several copies. I was overjoyed, grinning all the way back to Jackson.

I've continued to keep in touch with Dee and Pat. Later Pat mentioned that her brother, Frank Dillon, had recorded Jabe on cassette in the 1980s and had been keeping the cassettes in his safe-deposit box for the last nearly forty years. Of course I followed up on that and called Frank, who was very friendly and welcomed my offer to visit him, as he had no way to play the cassette and wanted to hear it again. On my next trip, I visited him in Birmingham and digitized the cassette, gathering in another bounty of Jabe Dillon's music.

The Time Flew By

I was unprepared for this nearly ten-year dive into fiddle research and writing, when I realized that my first book was insisting that I write it. English was never my favorite subject. I never suspected that I'd become an author.

For my first field trip, I planned to drive to Mississippi from my home in New York State. After more than twenty years sitting behind a desk at corporate graphic-design jobs, I started with a plan to travel efficiently so I could get back to work.

Then I thought, "Oh, what job?"

My second thought was to take my time, take the first real chance to enjoy the trip itself. On that long drive I made eleven different stops to visit friends and play music.

On subsequent trips, I got better at conducting interviews. I became something of a detective, learning how to locate the children or grandchildren of the fiddlers that I researched, and pored over old newspaper accounts for more stories. There was a large amount of actual work, writing, getting permissions, reading, and the transcribing of the tunes. Much of it could have been tedious, but the obsession of discovering all that could be known about this music pulled me through.

The stories in this book are from eventful and exciting days. But the most surprising turn of events in this new life of mine has been the warm, helpful, and genuinely delightful acquaintances, connections, and new friends I have met and made in the state where I was born.

—Harry Bolick

APPENDIX A

Recommended Reading and Listening

Bolick, Harry and Austin, Stephen T. *Mississippi Fiddle Tunes and Songs from the 1930s.* Jackson: University Press of Mississippi, 2015.

Cauthen, Joyce. *With Fiddle and Well-Rosined Bow: Old-Time Fiddling in Alabama.* Tuscaloosa: University of Alabama Press, 1989.

Ferris, William. *Blues from the Delta.* Boston: Da Capo Press, 1978.

Ginn, Dan William. *Slim.* Light Switch Press, 2017.

Goertzen, Chris. *George Cecil McLeod, Mississippi's Fiddling Senator, and the Modern History of American Fiddling.* American Music Series. Urbana: University of Illinois Press, 2004.

Goertzen, Chris. "Old, New, and Real: The Case of Mississippi's Senator George Cecil McLeod." In *Southern Fiddlers and Fiddle Contests.* Jackson: University Press of Mississippi, 2008, 14.

Goertzen, Chris. "Bill Rogers, Contemporary Traditional Mississippi Fiddler." *American Music* (Winter 2015, University of Illinois).

Goertzen, Chris. *George Knauff's Virginia Reels and the History of American Fiddling.* Jackson: University Press of Mississippi, 2017.

Hudson, Arnold Palmer. *Folksongs of Mississippi.* Chapel Hill: University of North Carolina Press, 1936.

Lomax, Alan. *The Land Where the Blues Began.* New York: Pantheon Books, 1993.

Meade, Guthrie T., Dick Spottswood, and Douglas Meade. *Country Music Sources; A Biblio-Discography of Commercially Recorded Traditional Music.* Chapel Hill: Southern Folklife Collection, 2002.

Milner, Clare, and Walt Koken. *The Milner-Koken Collection of American Fiddle Tunes.* Kennett Square, PA: Mudthumper Music, 2011.

Moore, T. DeWayne. "Uncovering Henry 'Son' Simms." *Living Blues* (June 2014): 74–77.

Moore, T. DeWayne. "Bo Carter: The Genius of the Country Blues." *Blues and Rhythm* 330 (May 2018): 14–24.

Moore, T. DeWayne. "Revisiting Ralph Lembo: Complicating Charley Patton, the 1920s Race Record Industry, and the Italian American Experience in the Mississippi Delta." *Association for Recorded Sound Collections Journal* 49, no. 2 (December 2018): 153–84.

Russell, Tony. *Country Music Originals.* Oxford: Oxford University Press, 2004.

Russell, Tony. *Country Music Records: A Discography, 1921–1942.* Oxford: Oxford University Press, 2007.

Websites

Traditional Tune Archive, editor Andy Kuntz, http://www.tunearch.org/wiki/TTA, for tune history and comparison

Slippery Hill, www.slippery-hill.com, a fine resource for learning fiddle tunes

Youtube.com, a resource for learning fiddle tunes

www.mississippifiddle.com (or www.harrybolick.com/mississippi-music/field-recordings): recordings of Tim Avalon, Enos Canoy, "Jabe" Dillon, John Gatwood, Homer Grice, Grover O'Briant, Jerry Prescott, and Claude Kennedy, supplied by the fiddlers or their families, are posted here.

Recordings

Classic Old-Time Fiddle. Smithsonian Folkways 40193, 2017. One track by Hoyt Ming.

The Completely Lost Mississippi Fiddle Tunes, New Timey, 2019; *Mississippi Travelers*, New Timey, 2018; *Tunes from* the Book, New Timey, 2015; *Carroll County, Mississippi,* New Timey, 2005. Harry Bolick, Hopewell, Junction, NY, www.mississippifiddle.com.

Mike Compton: www.mikecompton.net.

Mike Compton and Norman Blake. *Gallop to Georgia.* Taterbug Records, 2018. Contains sixteen tracks of Narmour and Smith tunes.

Mike Compton. *Rotten Taters.* Taterbug Music, 2011. Contains "Yankee Gal," transcribed in this book.

Document Records (UK) has most of the Mississippi string band 78 rpm recordings in print:

Leake County Revelers, Vol. 1 DOCD-8029, Vol. 2 DOCD-8030. Document Records, 1998.

Mississippi String Bands, Vol. 1 DOCD-8009, Vol. 2 DOCD-8028. Document Records, 1997.

Narmour and Smith, Complete Recordings. Vol. 1 DOCD-8065, Vol. 2 DOCD-8066. Document Records, 2013.

Fiddle Tunes and Songs from the 1930s: 1939 Library of Congress Recordings Collected in Mississippi by Herbert Halpert. 3-CD set, Document Records DOCD-8071, 2015.

Tom Dumas:

Voices of Mississippi: Artists and Musicians Documented by William Ferris. Dust-to-Digital, 2018. Contains the Dumas recording of "Cotton-Eyed Joe."

Other field recordings of Tom Dumas are located in the William R. Ferris Collection at the Southern Folklife Collection, Wilson Special Collections Library, University Libraries, University of North Carolina at Chapel Hill, NC.

Sid Hemphill:

The Devil's Dream: Alan Lomax's 1942 Library of Congress Recordings. Global Jukebox, 2013.

Rock Me Shake Me: Field Recordings Vol. 15 1941–1942. Document Records DOCD-5672.

Afro-American Folk Music from Tate and Panola Counties, Mississippi. Rounder, 2000.

The Leake County String Band. Field Recorders Collective FRC 730.

Alvis Massengale. Field Recorders Collective FRC 724, 2017.

Charlie McCoy:

Charlie McCoy: Complete 1928-1932 Recordings. Document Records, BDCD-6018.

The McCoy Brothers, Vol. 2: 1936-1944. Document Records, BDCD-6020.

Mississippi String Bands and Associates 1928-1931. Document Records, DOCD-6013.

Jackson Stomp: The Charlie McCoy Story. Frog Records, UK, NEH02.

Jack MaGee. *Give the Fiddler a Dram.* Soundwagon, self-published, ca. 2010.

Mississippi String Bands. Vol. 1 CO-3513, Vol. 2 CO-3514. County Records, 1998.

Out-of-Print Recordings

Ode To Billy Joe (original soundtrack recording). Warner Brothers, 1976. Includes tracks from Hoyt Ming and Morgan Gilmer.

Great Big Yam Potatoes: Anglo-American Fiddle Music from Mississippi. Mississippi Department of Archives and History AH-002, 1985.

Mississippi Sawyers. LP, Sawyer Productions, 1980.

Tim Avalon. *Rural.* Self-released CD, ca. 2005.

Homer Grice and the Box Family Band. NR14197, Kilmichael, MS, 1982.

Leake County String Band (Morgan and George Gilmer). Small-quantity self-produced LP, Walnut Grove, MS, 1971.

Senator George C. McLeod. *The Fiddling Senator.* Self-released LP, 1979.

Hoyt Ming and his Pep-Steppers. *New Hot Times!* Homestead 103, 1975.

Clayton Tyler. *Down Home.* Self-released LP, ca. 1970s, Tupelo, MS.

Jack Youngblood. *Mississippi Fiddler.* Self-released by Jerry Prescott, 2001.

APPENDIX B

Tunes by Title

Folks Back Home, The (no transcription) (Ray)
Friday Night Waltz, 538 (Ray)
Gallop to Georgia, 439 (Narmour)
Georgia Camp Meeting, 267 (Leake Co. Revelers)
Girl I Left Behind Me, The, 130 (Dillon)
Give Me a Bottle of I Don't Care What, 480 (Newton)
Give Me a Chaw Tobacco, 80 (Carter)
Give the Fiddler a Dram, 81 (Carter)
Going to the Wedding, to Get Some Cake, 481(Newton)
Untitled No. 5 (Golden Slippers), 236 (Kennedy)
Good Fellow, 268 (Leake Co. Revelers)
Goodnight Waltz, 269 (Leake Co. Revelers)
Got the Jake Leg Too (no transcription) (Ray)
Grandmother Reel, 516 (Prescott)
Grub Springs, 42 (Anderson)
Happy Home Waltz, 105 (Collier)
Happy Hour Breakdown, 482 (Newton)
Harvest Home Waltz, 94 (Clardy)
Heel and Toe Polka, 440 (Narmour)
Home Town Waltz, 539 (Ray)
Honeybee Hornpipe, 517 (Prescott)
Honeymoon Waltz, 466 (Nations)
Honeysuckle Waltz, 540 (Ray)
Howling Hounds, 132 (Dillon)
I'm Gwine Back to Dixie, 274 (Leake Co. Revelers)
I'm Gonna Live Anyway Till I Die, 510 (Pratcher)
Ida Red, 200 (Grice)
In the Good Old Summertime, 270 (Leake Co. Revelers)
Indian War Whoop, 362 (Ming)
Irene Waltz, 106 (Collier)
Jackson Stomp, 406 (MS Sheiks)
Jake Leg Rag, 441 (Narmour)
Jake Leg Wobble, 541 (Ray)
Jenny on the Railroad, 82 (Carter)
Joe Turner, 511 (Pratcher)
John Henry, 156 (Dumas), 216 (Hemphill)
Untitled (Johnnie Boy Blues), 191 (Gatwood)
Johnson Gal, 276 (Leake Co. Revelers)
Julia Waltz, 277 (Leake Co. Revelers)
Jungle Waltz, 278 (Leake Co. Revelers)
Keep My Skillet Good and Greasy, 218 (Hemphill)
Kennie Wagner, 201 (Grice)
Kiss Me Waltz (442 Narmour)
Last Shot Got Him, The, 374 (MS Possum Hunters)
Lazy Cat, 58 (Avalon)
Lazy Kate, 279 (Leake Co. Revelers)
Leake County Blues, 280 (Leake Co. Revelers)
Leake County Two Step, 171 (Freeny)
Leather Breeches/Britches, 83 (Carter), 220 (Hemphill), 281
    (Leake Co. Revelers)
Limber Neck Blues, 443 (Narmour)
Lincoln County Blues, 467 (Nations)
Listen to the Mocking Bird, 282 (Leake Co. Revelers)
Little Black Mustache, 95 (Clardy), 468 (Nations)

Little Princess's Footsteps, 483 (Newton)
Little Star, 444 (Narmour)
Liza Jane, 84 (Carter)
Lonesome Blues, 284 (Leake Co. Revelers)
Mac Prescott Jig, 518 (Prescott)
Magnolia One Step, 469 (Nations)
Magnolia Waltz, 44 (Anderson), 285 (Leake Co. Revelers)
Make Me a Bed on the Floor, 286 (Leake Co. Revelers)
Memories, 287 (Leake Co. Revelers)
Memphis Mail, 136 (Dillon)
Merry Widow Waltz, 288 (Leake Co. Revelers)
Midnight Waltz, 445 (Narmour)
Miles Monroe Standish, 138 (Dillon)
Miss Brown, 85 (Carter)
Mississippi Breakdown, 446 (Narmour), 375 (MS Possum
    Hunters), 289 (Leake Co. Revelers)
Mississippi Echoes, 542 (Ray)
Mississippi Fiddler, 519 (Prescott)
Mississippi Low Down, 407 (MS Sheiks)
Mississippi Moon Waltz, 290 (Leake Co. Revelers)
Mississippi Sawyer, 363 (Ming)
Mississippi Shuffle, 330 (Leake Co. St Bd)
Mississippi Square Dance, 1, 172 (Freeny)
Mississippi Square Dance 2, 173 (Sally Ann) (Freeny)
Mississippi Traveler, 520 (Prescott)
Mississippi Turnpike, 521 (Prescott)
Mississippi Waves Waltz, 447 (Narmour)
Molly Put the Kettle On, 291 (Leake Co. Revelers)
Monkey in the Dog Cart, 292 (Leake Co. Revelers)
Moonlight Clog, 96 (Clardy)
Morning Crow, 59 (Avalon)
Morning Glory Waltz, 409 (MS Sheiks)
My Bonnie Lives Over the Ocean (Leake Co. Revelers)
My Honey By the Fire, 60 (Avalon)
My Waltz, 331 (Leake Co. St Bd)
My Wild Irish Rose, 294 (Leake Co. Revelers)
Nancy Rowland, 45 (Anderson), 86 (Carter)
Napoleon March, 108 (Collier)
Negro Supper Time, 470 (Nations)
New Hot Times, 364 (Ming)
Nine O'clock Breakdown, 484 (Newton)
Northeast Texas, 346 (Milner)
Noxapater Stomp, 46 (Anderson)
Old Bill, 139 (Dillon)
Old Dan Tucker, 140 (Dillon)
Old Hat, The, 296 (Leake Co. Revelers)
Old Hen Cackled, 157 (Dumas)
Old Joe Bone, 87 (Carter)
Old Red, 365 (Ming)
Orange Peeling, 142 (Dillon)
Over the Waves, 109 (Collier)
Untitled No. 6 (Paddy on the Turnpike), 237 (Kennedy)
Parting Waltz, 47 (Anderson)
Pep Steppers Waltz, 366 (Ming)

Picture No Artist Can Paint, 298 (Leake Co. Revelers)
Pink Lady's Slipper, 61 (Avalon)
Podunk Toddle, 174 (Freeny)
Porter's Tune, 506 (Porter)
'Possum on the Rail, 376 (MS Possum Hunters)
Possum Up a Gum Stump, 48 (Anderson)
Precious Memories, 332 (Leake Co. St Bd)
Prescott Hornpipe, 522 (Prescott)
Pretty Little Girl, 159 (Dumas)
Put Me in My Little Bed, 300 (Leake Co. Revelers)
Quaker Waltz, 485 (Newton)
Queen City Square Dance, 341 (Meridian Hustlers)
Untitled No. 7 (Rachael), 238 (Kennedy)
Ragtime Joe, 530 (Quinn)
Railroad Blues, 472 (Nations)
Rattlesnake Daddy, 367 (Ming)
Real Corn Tom and Jerry, 419 (Moran)
Reynolds Waltz, 490 (O'Briant)
Rocking Yodel, 302 (Leake Co. Revelers)
Rose Waltz, 448 (Narmour)
Rufus Rastus, 377 (MS Possum Hunters)
Rye Straw, 221 (Hemphill)
Saddle Up the Grey, 88 (Carter)
Sales Tax Toddle, 476 (Nations)
Sally Ann. See Mississippi Square Dance—Part Two
Sally Goodin, 160 (Dumas), 240 (Kennedy)
Saturday Night Breakdown, 304 (Leake Co. Revelers)
Shear the Sheep Bobbie, 187 (Gatwood)
Sheik's Special Waltz, 410 (MS Sheiks)
Sheik Waltz, 411 (MS Sheiks)
Silver Bells, 523 (Prescott)
Sitting on Top of the World, 188 (Gatwood), (MS Sheiks)
Sleeping Time Waltz, 97 (Clardy)
Slow Time Waltz, 65 (Bean)
So Soon I'll Be at Home, 222 (Hemphill)
Soggy Bottom, 244 (Kennedy)
Someone I Love, 449 (Narmour)
Stop-Time, 69 (Brister)
Sullivan's Hollow, 176 (Freeny)
Sunset Waltz, 413 (MS Sheiks)
Sunny Waltz, The, 450 (Narmour)
Sweet Bunch of Daisies, 531 (Quinn)
Sweet Milk and Peaches, 451 (Narmour)
Sweet Nellie, 420 (Moran)
Sweet Rose of Heaven, 305 (Leake Co. Revelers)
Take Me As I Am, 452 (Narmour)
Tequila Hop Blues, 453 (Narmour)
Texas Breakdown, 454 (Narmour)
Texas Fair, 306 (Leake Co. Revelers)
Texas Shuffle, 455 (Narmour)
That's It, 414 (MS Sheiks)
They Go Simply Wild Over Me, 307 (Leake Co. Revelers)
Third Party, 190 (Gatwood)
Thirty-First Street Blues, 309 (Leake Co. Revelers)

Untitled No. 8 (Tom and Jerry), 245 (Kennedy)
Tombigbee Waltz, 49 (Anderson)
Traveling Blues, 177 (Freeny)
Tupelo Blues, 368 (Ming)
Turkey in the Straw, 369 (Ming)
Tuscaloosa Waltz, 543 (Ray)
Uncle Ned, 311 (Leake Co. Revelers)
Unknown Tune, 143 (Dillon)
Untitled /Johnnie Boy Blues, 191 (Gatwood)
Untitled No. 1 (Bill Cheatham), 230 (Kennedy)
Untitled No. 1, 491 (O'Briant)
Untitled No. 1, 532 (Quinn)
Untitled No. 2 (Casey Jones), 231 (Kennedy)
Untitled No. 2, 492 (O'Briant)
Untitled No. 2, 533 (Quinn)
Untitled No. 3 (Clarinet Polka), 232 (Kennedy)
Untitled No. 3 (Walk Right In), 493 (O'Briant)
Untitled No. 4 (Devil's Dream), 234 (Kennedy)
Untitled No. 4, 494 (O'Briant)
Untitled No. 5 (Golden Slippers), 236 (Kennedy)
Untitled No. 5, 495 (O'Briant)
Untitled No. 6 (Paddy on the Turnpike), 237 (Kennedy)
Untitled No. 6, 496 (O'Briant)
Untitled No. 7 (Rachael), 238 (Kennedy)
Untitled No. 7 (Devil's Dream), 497 (O'Briant)
Untitled No. 8 (Tom and Jerry), 245 (Kennedy)
Untitled No. 8 (Wolves A Howling), 498 (O'Briant)
Untitled No. 9 (Waltz), 499 (O'Briant)
Untitled No. 9 Waltz, 246 (Kennedy)
Vicksburg Stomp, 415 (MS Sheiks)
Wednesday Night Waltz, 312 (Leake Co. Revelers)
When You and I Were Young, Maggie, 110 (Collier)
Where the Silv'ry Colorado Wends Its Way, 313 (Leake Co.
    Revelers)
Where the Southern Crosses the Dog, 456 (Narmour)
Whistlin' Coon, 457 (Narmour)
White Mule, 370 (Ming)
Who's Been Giving You Corn, 458 (Narmour)
Wild Irish (Leake Co. Revelers)
Winona Echoes, 459 (Narmour)
Winona Rag, 544 (Ray)
Wolves a Howling, 50 (Anderson), 498 (O'Briant)
Yankee Gal, 114 (Compton)

Tunes by Key

A

Untitled No. 1 (Bill Cheatham), 230 (Kennedy)
Brown Skinned Girl, 126 (Dillon)
Burden Down, 153 (Dumas)
Untitled No. 2 (Casey Jones), 231 (Kennedy)
Cindy, 154 (Dumas)

Cotton-Eyed Joe, 155 (Dumas)
Untitled No. 4 (Devil's Dream), 234 (Kennedy)
Give the Fiddler a Dram, 81 (Carter)
Grub Springs, 42 (Anderson)
Ida Red, 200 (Grice)
Jenny on the Railroad, 82 (Carter)
John Henry, 156 (Dumas)
Keep My Skillet Good and Greasy, 218 (Hemphill)
Liza Jane, 84 (Carter)
Mac Prescott Jig, 518 (Prescott)
Mississippi Square Dance Part 1, 172 (Freeny)
Mississippi Square Dance Part 2, 173 (Sally Ann) (Freeny)
Mississippi Turnpike, 521 (Prescott)
Old Bill, 139 (Dillon)
Old Joe Bone, 87 (Carter)
Untitled No. 6 (Paddy on the Turnpike), 237 (Kennedy)
Pink Lady's Slipper, 61 (Avalon)
Put Me in My Little Bed, 300 (Leake Co. Revelers)
Sally Goodin, 160 (Dumas), 240 (Kennedy)
Sweet Nellie, 420 (Moran)
They Go Simply Wild Over Me, 307 (Leake Co. Revelers)
Untitled No. 2 (Casey Jones), 231 (Kennedy)
Untitled No. 4 (Devil's Dream), 234 (Kennedy)
Untitled No. 6 (Paddy on the Turnpike), 237 (Kennedy)
Untitled No. 6, 496 (O'Briant)
Untitled No. 7 (Devil's Dream), 497 (O'Briant)
Untitled No. 8 (Tom and Jerry), 245 (Kennedy)
Wolves a Howling, 50 (Anderson)

B♭

Farewell Waltz, 404 (MS Sheiks)
Fingering with your Fingers, 405 (MS Sheiks)
Jackson Stomp, 406 (MS Sheiks)
Mississipi Mississippi Low Down, 407 (MS Sheiks)
Morning Glory Waltz, 409 (MS Sheiks)
Reynolds Waltz, 490 (O'Briant)
Sunset Waltz, 413 (MS Sheiks)
Untitled No. 3 (Walk Right In), 493 (O'Briant)

C

After the Ball, 68 (Brister), 102 (Collier)
Avalon Quickstep, 429 (Narmour)
Beautiful Bells, 260 (Leake Co. Revelers)
Beautiful Texas, 355 (Ming)
Ben Hur March, 103 (Collier)
Birds in the Brook, 262 (Leake Co. Revelers)
Little Black Mustache, 95 (Clardy), 468 (Nations)
Boll Weevil, 210 (Hemphill)
Bouquets of June Waltz, 430 (Narmour)
Captain George Has Your Money Come, 431 (Narmour)
Catfish Medley, 505 (Porter)
Charleston No. 1, 435 (Narmour)

Charleston No. 2, 358 (Ming), 436 (Narmour)
Charleston No. 3, 437 (Narmour)
Chicken Reel, 359 (Ming)
Choctaw County Rag, 537 (Ray)
Crawford March, 185 (Gatwood)
Croquet Habits, 169 (Freeny)
Drafting Blues, 361 (Ming)
Dry Gin Rag, 438 (Narmour)
Engineer Frank Hawk, 186 (Gatwood)
Fatback and Dumplings, 40 (Anderson)
Flow Rain Waltz, 64 (Bean)
Friday Night Waltz, 538 (Ray)
Gallop to Georgia, 439 (Narmour)
Georgia Camp Meeting, 267 (Leake Co. Revelers)
Goodnight Waltz, 269 (Leake Co. Revelers)
Happy Hour Breakdown, 482 (Newton)
Honeymoon Waltz, 466 (Nations)
Honeysuckle Waltz, 540 (Ray)
Jake Leg Rag, 441 (Narmour)
Untitled/Johnnie Boy Blues, 191 (Gatwood)
Kiss Me Waltz, 442 (Narmour)
Last Shot Got Him, The, 374 (MS Possum Hunters)
Leake County Blues, 280 (Leake Co. Revelers)
Limber Neck Blues, 443 (Narmour)
Little Black Mustache, 95 (Clardy), 468 (Nations)
Little Princess's Footsteps, 483 (Newton)
Lonesome Blues, 284 (Leake Co. Revelers)
Magnolia Waltz, 285 (Leake Co. Revelers)
Make Me a Bed on the Floor, 286 (Leake Co. Revelers)
Midnight Waltz, 445 (Narmour)
Mississippi Breakdown, 375 (MS Possum Hunters), 289
    (Leake Co. Revelers)
Mississippi Echoes, 542 (Ray)
Mississippi Waves Waltz, 447 (Narmour)
Monkey in the Dog Cart, 292 (Leake Co. Revelers)
Morning Crow, 59 (Avalon)
My Waltz, 331 (Leake Co. St Bd)
New Hot Times, 364 (Ming)
Nine O'clock Breakdown, 484 (Newton)
Northeast Texas, 346 (Milner)
Noxapater Stomp, 46 (Anderson)
Porter's Tune, 506 (Porter)
Precious Memories, 332 (Leake Co. St Bd)
Prescott Hornpipe, 522 (Prescott)
Quaker Waltz, 485 (Newton)
Untitled No. 7 (Rachael), 238 (Kennedy)
Ragtime Joe, 530 (Quinn)
Rose Waltz, 448 (Narmour)
Rufus Rastus, 377 (MS Possum Hunters)
Saturday Night Breakdown, 304 (Leake Co. Revelers)
Sheik's Special Waltz, 410 (MS Sheiks)
Silver Bells, 523 (Prescott)
Sleeping Time Waltz, 97 (Clardy)
Someone I Love, 449 (Narmour)

Stop-Time, 69 (Brister)
Sullivan's Hollow, 176 (Freeny)
Sunny Waltz, The, 450 (Narmour)
Sweet Bunch of Daisies, 531 (Quinn)
Sweet Rose of Heaven, 305 (Leake Co. Revelers)
Take Me As I Am, 452 (Narmour)
Texas Fair, 306 (Leake Co. Revelers)
Texas Shuffle, 455 (Narmour)
Tupelo Blues, 368 (Ming)
Tuscaloosa Waltz, 543 (Ray)
Untitled /Johnnie Boy Blues, 191 (Gatwood)
Untitled No. 1, 532 (Quinn)
Untitled No. 5, 495 (O'Briant)
Untitled No. 7 (Rachael), 238 (Kennedy)
Wednesday Night Waltz, 312 (Leake Co. Revelers)
Where the Southern Crosses the Dog, 456 (Narmour)
Winona Rag, 544 (Ray)

C, F, B♭

Podunk Toddle, 174 (Freeny)

D

Arkansas Traveler, 74 (Canoy), 209 (Hemphill)
Bankhead Blues, 464 (Nations)
Bill Tyler, 55 (Avalon)
Billy Cochran, 56 (Avalon)
Captain Waldo's Old Hat, 57 (Avalon)
Carrier Line, 212 (Hemphill)
Catahoula Blues, 418 (Moran)
Civil War March, 339 (McLeod)
Courtin' Days Waltz, 264 (Leake Co. Revelers)
Dead Cat on the Line, 198 (Grice)
Dunkirk (Eighth of January), 235 (Kennedy)
Got the Jake Leg Too (no transcription) (Ray)
Home Town Waltz, 539 (Ray)
Honeybee Hornpipe, 517 (Prescott)
I'm Gonna Live Anyway Till I Die, 510 (Pratcher)
Irene Waltz, 106 (Collier)
John Henry, 216 (Hemphill)
Lazy Cat, 58 (Avalon)
Lazy Kate, 279 (Leake Co. Revelers)
Memphis Mail, 136 (Dillon)
Merry Widow Waltz, 288 (Leake Co. Revelers)
Mississippi Sawyer, 363 (Ming)
Molly Put the Kettle On, 291 (Leake Co. Revelers)
My Honey By the Fire, 60 (Avalon)
Possum Up a Gum Stump, 48 (Anderson)
Railroad Blues, 472 (Nations)
Real Corn Tom and Jerry, 419 (Moran)
Sales Tax Toddle, 476 (Nations)
So Soon I'll Be at Home, 222 (Hemphill)
Soggy Bottom, 244 (Kennedy)

Sweet Milk and Peaches, 451 (Narmour)
Tequila Hop Blues, 453 (Narmour)
Untitled No. 9 Waltz, 246 (Kennedy)
Untitled No. 4, 494 (O'Briant)
Whistlin' Coon, 457 (Narmour)

E

Untitled No. 9 (Waltz), 499 (O'Briant)

E♭

Vicksburg Stomp, 415 (MS Sheiks)

F

Alma Waltz, 403 (MS Sheiks)
Cripple Coon, 360 (Ming)
Dry Town Blues, 266 (Leake Co. Revelers)
Grandmother Reel, 516 (Prescott)
Julia Waltz, 277 (Leake Co. Revelers)
Jungle Waltz, 278 (Leake Co. Revelers)
Mississippi Moon Waltz, 290 (Leake Co. Revelers)
Napoleon March, 108 (Collier)
Sheik Waltz, 411 (MS Sheiks)
Texas Breakdown, 454 (Narmour)
That's It, 414 (MS Sheiks)
Traveling Blues, 177 (Freeny)
Yankee Gal, 114 (Compton)

G

Avalon Blues, 428 (Narmour)
Bayou Le Croix, 417 (Moran)
Been to the East, Been to the West, 261 (Leake Co. Revelers)
Big Eyed Rabbit, 54 (Avalon)
Bill Bailey, 508 (Pratcher)
Bluebird Waltz, 104 (Collier)
Bonny Blue Flag, 356 (Ming)
Bring Me a Bottle, 263 (Leake Co. Revelers)
Buggy and a Hoss, 129 (Dillon)
Buttermilk, 509 (Pratcher)
Bye, Bye, My Honey I'm Gone, 197 (Grice)
Cackling Hen, 357 (Ming)
Carroll County Blues, 184 (Gatwood), 432 (Narmour)
Carroll County Blues #2, 433 (Narmour)
Carroll County Blues #3, 434 (Narmour)
Untitled No. 3 (Clarinet Polka), 232 (Kennedy)
Claude's Dream, 233 (Kennedy)
Cotton Eyed Joe, 79 (Carter)
Crow Black Chicken, 265 (Leake Co. Revelers)
Don't You Remember the Time, 170 (Freeny)
Eighth of January, 214 (Hemphill)
El Rancho Grande, 329 (Leake Co. St Bd)

Tunes in non-standard tunings

AEAE or GDGD

GDAD

All other tunes in GDAE

Jig

Mac Prescott Jig, 518 (Prescott)

Waltzes

After the Ball, 68 (Brister), 102 (Collier)
Alma Waltz, 403 (MS Sheiks)
Bayou Le Croix, 417 (Moran)
Beautiful Bells, 260 (Leake Co. Revelers)
Bluebird Waltz, 104 (Collier)
Bouquets of June Waltz, 430 (Narmour)
Claude's Dream, 233 (Kennedy)
Courtin' Days Waltz, 264 (Leake Co. Revelers)
Don't You Remember the Time, 170 (Freeny)
Farewell Waltz, 404 (MS Sheiks)
Flow Rain Waltz, 64 (Bean)
Friday Night Waltz, 538 (Ray)
Goodnight Waltz, 269 (Leake Co. Revelers)
Happy Home Waltz, 105 (Collier)
Harvest Home Waltz, 94 (Clardy)
Home Town Waltz, 539 (Ray)
Honeymoon Waltz, 466 (Nations)
Honeysuckle Waltz, 540 (Ray)
In the Good Old Summertime, 270 (Leake Co. Revelers)
Irene Waltz, 106 (Collier)
Julia Waltz, 277 (Leake Co. Revelers)
Jungle Waltz, 278 (Leake Co. Revelers)
Kiss Me Waltz, 442 (Narmour)
Magnolia Waltz, 44 (Anderson), 285 (Leake Co. Revelers)
Memories, 287 (Leake Co. Revelers)
Merry Widow Waltz, 288 (Leake Co. Revelers)
Midnight Waltz, 445 (Narmour)
Mississippi Moon Waltz, 290 (Leake Co. Revelers)
Mississippi Waves Waltz, 447 (Narmour)
Morning Glory Waltz, 409 (MS Sheiks)
My Bonnie Lies Over the Ocean, 293 (Leake Co. Revelers)
My Waltz, 331 (Leake Co. St Bd)
My Wild Irish Rose, 294 (Leake Co. Revelers)
Over the Waves, 109 (Collier)
Parting Waltz, 47 (Anderson)
Pep Steppers Waltz, 366 (Ming)
Picture No Artist Can Paint, 298 (Leake Co. Revelers)
Pink Lady's Slipper, 61 (Avalon)
Quaker Waltz, 485 (Newton)
Reynolds Waltz, 490 (O'Briant)
Rocking Yodel, 302 (Leake Co. Revelers)
Rose Waltz, 448 (Narmour)
Sheik Waltz, 411 (MS Sheiks)
Sheik's Special Waltz, 410 (MS Sheiks)
Sleeping Time Waltz, 97 (Clardy)
Slow Time Waltz, 65 (Bean)

Stop-Time, 69 (Brister)
Sunny Waltz, The, 450 (Narmour)
Sunset Waltz, 413 (MS Sheiks)
Sweet Bunch of Daisies, 531 (Quinn)
Sweet Rose of Heaven, 305 (Leake Co. Revelers)
Tombigbee Waltz, 49 (Anderson)
Tuscaloosa Waltz, 543 (Ray)
Untitled No. 9 Waltz, 246 (Kennedy)
Untitled No. 9 (Waltz), 499 (O'Briant)
Wednesday Night Waltz, 312 (Leake Co. Revelers)
When You and I Were Young, Maggie, 110 (Collier)

INDEX